The American Record

Images of the Nation's Past
Volume One: To 1877

The American Record

Images of the Nation's Past
Volume One: To 1877

THIRD EDITION

EDITED BY

William Graebner
State University of New York,
College at Fredonia

Leonard Richards
University of Massachusetts,
Amherst

McGraw-Hill, Inc.

New York   St. Louis   San Francisco   Auckland   Bogotá   Caracas
Lisbon   London   Madrid   Mexico City   Milan   Montreal   New Delhi
San Juan   Singapore   Sydney   Tokyo   Toronto

This book was set in Palatino by Ruttle, Shaw & Wetherill, Inc.
The editor was Peter Labella;
the production supervisor was Friederich W. Schulte.
The cover was designed by John Hite.
Project supervision was done by Ruttle, Shaw & Wetherill, Inc.
R. R. Donnelley & Sons Company was printer and binder.

Cover Art
Winslow Homer, "Bell-Time," Culver Picture, Inc.

THE AMERICAN RECORD
Images of the Nation's Past
Volume One: To 1877

This book is printed on acid-free paper.

4 5 6 7 8 9 0 DOC DOC 9 0 9

ISBN 0-07-023987-8

Library of Congress Cataloging-in-Publication Data

The American record: images of the nation's past / edited by William
    Graebner, Leonard Richards.—3rd ed.
        p.   cm.
    Includes bibliographical references (p.   )
    Contents: v. 1 To 1877
    ISBN 0-07-023987-8
    1. United States—History.   2. United States—History—Sources.
I. Graebner, William.   II. Richards, Leonard L.
E178.6.A4145   1995
973—dc20   94-26793

About the Editors

WILLIAM GRAEBNER is Professor of History at the State University of New York at Fredonia. He received the Frederick Jackson Turner Award from the Organization of American Historians for *Coal-Mining Safety in the Progressive Period: The Political Economy of Reform*. Another book, *A History of Retirement: The Meaning and Function of an American Institution, 1885-1978,* was published in 1980. He is also the author of *The Engineering of Consent: Democracy and Authority in Twentienth-Century America* (1987); *Coming of Age in Buffalo: Youth and Authority in the Postwar Era* (1990); and *The Age of Doubt: American Thought and Culture in the 1940s* (1991). In 1993, he was Fulbright Professor of American Studies at the University of Rome. He currently serves on the editorial boards of *American Studies* and *The Historian.*

LEONARD RICHARDS is Professor of History at the University of Massachusetts at Amherst. He was awarded the 1970 Beveridge Prize by the American Historical Association for his book *"Gentlemen of Property and Standing": Anti-Abolition Mobs in Jacksonian America.* Professor Richards is also the author of *The Advent of American Democracy* and *The Life and Times of Congressman John Quincy Adams.* He is planning another book on the "Slave Power" thesis.

Contents

Preface

During the past two or three decades, the study of history in the United States has become in many ways more sophisticated and, we think, more interesting. Until the mid-1960s the dominant tradition among American historians was to regard the historian's domain as one centered on politics, economics, diplomacy, and war. Now, in the mid-1990s, historians are eager to address new kinds of subjects and to include whole sections of the population that were neglected in the traditional preoccupation with presidential administrations, legislation, and treaties. Women and children, the poor and economically marginal, gays and native Americans, have moved nearer the center of the historians' stage. We have become almost as eager to know how our ancestors dressed, ate, reared their children, made love, and buried their dead as we are to know how they voted in a particular presidential election. In addition, ordinary Americans now appear on the stage of history as active players who possess the power to shape their lives, rather than as passive victims of forces beyond their control. The result is a collective version of our national past that is more inclusive, more complicated, and less settled.

The third edition of *The American Record* continues the effort begun in the first and second editions. We have attempted to bridge the gap between the old history and the new, to graft the excitement and variety of modern approaches to history on an existing chronological and topical framework with which most of us feel comfortable. Most of the familiar topics are here. We have included essays on the early colonial settlements, the Revolutionary War, the Founding Fathers, immigration, Progressivism, and the Great Depression. But by joining these essays to primary sources, we have tried to make it possible for teachers and students to see links between the Puritan social order and the lessons children learned from their primers; between the Revolutionary War and the colonial class structure; between the Founding Fathers and the physical layout of the nation's capital; between immigration and the prairie houses of Frank Lloyd Wright; between Progressivism and the proclamation of Mother's Day; and between the Great Depression and the murals that were painted on post office walls across the nation in the mid-1930s. The third edition also takes up issues and themes that are not so universally familiar, but which are beginning to reshape our understanding of the American past, among them the rise of a consumer society, the history of the environment, and the late–20th century conflict over "culture." This is a book that teaches the skill of making sense out of one's whole world.

Throughout, we have attempted to incorporate materials with *texture:* documents that are not only striking but can be given more than one interpretation; photographs that invite real examination and discussion; tables and maps that have something new and interesting to contribute; and essays, such as James H. Merrill's account of the "new world" as it appeared to the Catawba Indians, and Lizabeth Cohen's study of how Chicago workers experienced mass culture, that are at once superb examples of recent historical scholarship and accessible to undergraduates.

From the beginning, we realized that our approach to American history would require some adjustment for many students and teachers. It was one thing to expect a student to place an address by Teddy Roosevelt in the context of turn-of-the-century imperialism, yet quite another to expect students to do the same with Edgar Rice Burrough's *Tarzan of the Apes.* For this reason, we have offered a good deal of guidance. Introductions to primary and secondary materials are designed not just to provide basic background information, but also to suggest productive avenues of interpretation. Interpretive essays and questions are intended to create a kind of mental chemistry in which students will have enough information to experience the excitement of putting things together, and yet not so much guidance that conclusions become obvious.

We remain indebted to R. Jackson Wilson, who inspired the first edition of this book. We also wish to thank our editors at Alfred A. Knopf and McGraw-Hill—first David Follmer and Chris Rogers, later Niels Aaboe and Peter Labella—for their patient supervision of a difficult project. And we are especially grateful to the teachers and students who used the first and second editions of *The American Record* and showed us how to make the book better. Finally, thanks go to the following reviewers for their many helpful comments and suggestions: Jeffrey Adler, University of Florida; Bruce Cohen, Worcester State College; Peter Filene, University of North Carolina; Benjamin McArthur, Southern College of Seventh Day Adventists; Sonya Michel, University of Illinois at Urbana-Champaign; and David Sloan, University of Arkansas.

William Graebner

Leonard Richards

The American Record

Images of the Nation's Past
Volume One: To 1877

CHAPTER 1

The European
Conquest of America

The idea that Europeans discovered America in 1492 is of course absurd. And so are the maps of the Mediterranean area that describe it as the "known" world. The Western Hemisphere, and other areas that Europeans thought of as "terra incognita," were discovered and known to those who lived in them many centuries before white Europeans set sail on their momentous voyages. The importance of 1492 is not that Columbus stumbled on the New World—new, that is, to Europeans—in that year. What made his voyage, and those of other European explorers, important is what they set in motion: the conquest of vast areas of the world by a newly energized Europe. What the Europeans discovered was not new continents only, but new continents they could subject to their power. The expansion of Europe was an event in *world* history.

Innovations in navigational technology, combined with the economic and political development of Europe, created a vast new arena for domination. "Native" societies in Africa and Asia proved to be more resistant than Europeans hoped. But in the Americas, Indian cultures fell with relative ease before the European onslaught. Some of the native American societies were weak and disunited, and were technologically little advanced beyond the levels achieved in the Stone Age. But there were mighty and sophisticated empires in the Americas, too, particularly those of the Aztecs in Mexico and the Incas in Peru. One of the major mysteries of world history is the explanation for the speed and the completeness of their defeat, the rapid and total European conquest that has made North and South America modern extensions of European culture.

How have historians accounted for this astonishing fact? On the surface, differences in technology seem to provide an easy answer. The horse, gunpowder, and other devices certainly made a difference—even the most advanced American cultures do not seem to have grasped the principle of the wheel. But technology cannot fully explain how a tiny handful of European adventurers managed to defeat Indian populations with hundreds of thousands of skillful and resourceful warriors. Disunity among the Indians, all over both North and South America, has also been invoked as a part of the explanation. But the native civilizations were hardly more disunited and contentious than their European conquerors.

More recently, historians have begun to pay attention to a silent factor that few of the participants in the European conquest were fully aware of—and that few used intentionally. For countless generations, Europe had been ravaged by diseases like tuberculosis and smallpox. In the process, Europeans had developed natural immunities to the worst effects of their illnesses. The isolated Americans, on the other hand, had not been exposed to these diseases and had no immunities. They could be slain by the hundreds of thousands by sicknesses as harmless to whites as the measles. Such diseases literally wiped out entire tribes and their cultures and made it possible for Europeans to simply walk in and take over.

The conquest of the Americas was a complex process, and there are no clear-cut answers to our questions about it. What we know for certain is this: very few events in the history of the human race have had more far-reaching consequences, for the conquerors and their victims alike.

INTERPRETIVE ESSAY

James H. Merrell

The Indians' New World

The following essay, by the noted historian of native Americans James H. Merrell, turns the familiar story of European conquest on its head. Traditionally, the story has been told from the perspective of the European invaders. Merrell tells it from the perspective of the Catawbas, a collection of small tribes that had to cope with the strange "new world" of the European invaders. As you read this essay, you may want to think carefully about the various "new" factors that Europeans introduced. What order of importance does Merrell give them? How do you think these factors should be ranked? Also, you will notice that Merrell says that the Catawbas were able to "play the hand dealt them well enough to survive." How did they do this? And what did it cost them?

In August 1608 John Smith and his band of explorers captured an Indian named Amoroleck during a skirmish along the Rappahannock River. Asked why his men—a hunting party from towns upstream—had attacked the English, Amoroleck replied that they had heard the strangers "were a people come from under the world, to take their world from them." Smith's prisoner grasped a simple yet important truth that students of colonial America have overlooked: after 1492 native Americans lived in a world every bit as new as that confronting transplanted Africans or Europeans.

The failure to explore the Indians' new world helps explain why, despite many excellent studies of the native American past, colonial history often remains "a history of those men and women—English, European, and African— who transformed America from a geographical expression into a new nation." One reason Indians generally are left out may be the apparent inability to fit them into the new world theme, a theme that exerts a powerful hold on our historical imagination and runs throughout our efforts to interpret American development. From Frederick Jackson Turner to David Grayson Allen, from Melville J. Herskovits to Daniel C. Littlefield, scholars have analyzed encounters between peoples from the old world and conditions in the new, studying the complex interplay between Europeans or African cultural patterns and the American environment. Indians crossed no ocean, peopled no faraway land. It might seem logical to exclude them.

The natives' segregation persists, in no small degree, because historians still tend to think only of the new world as the New World, a geographic entity bounded by the Atlantic Ocean on the one side and the Pacific on the other. Re-

From James H. Merrell, "The Indians' New World: The Catawba Experience," *William and Mary Quarterly,* ser. 3, vol. 41, October 1984, pp. 537–565. Reprinted by permission of the author.

cent research suggests that process was as important as place. Many settlers in New England recreated familiar forms with such success that they did not really face an alien environment until long after their arrival. Africans, on the other hand, were struck by the shock of the new at the moment of their enslavement, well before they stepped on board ship or set foot on American soil. If the Atlantic was not a barrier between one world and another, if what happened to people was more a matter of subtle cultural processes than mere physical displacements, perhaps we should set aside the maps and think instead of a "world" as the physical and cultural milieu within which people live and a "new world" as a dramatically different milieu demanding basic changes in ways of life. Considered in these terms, the experience of natives was more closely akin to that of immigrants and slaves, and the idea of an encounter between worlds can—indeed, must—include the aboriginal inhabitants of America.

For American Indians a new order arrived in three distinct yet overlapping stages. First, alien microbes killed vast numbers of natives, sometimes before the victims had seen a white or black face. Next came traders who exchanged European technology for Indian products and brought natives into the developing world market. In time traders gave way to settlers eager to develop the land according to their own lights. These three intrusions combined to transform native existence, disrupting established cultural habits and requiring creative responses to drastically altered conditions. Like their new neighbors, then, Indians were forced to blend old and new in ways that would permit them to survive in the present without forsaking their past. By the close of the colonial era, native Americans as well as whites and blacks had created new societies, each similar to, yet very different from, its parent culture.

The range of native societies produced by this mingling of ingredients probably exceeded the variety of social forms Europeans and Africans developed. Rather than survey the broad spectrum of Indian adaptations, this article considers in some depth the response of natives in one area, the southern piedmont (see map). Avoiding extinction and eschewing retreat, the Indians of the piedmont have been in continuous contact with the invaders from across the sea almost since the beginning of the colonial period, thus permitting a thorough analysis of cultural intercourse. Moreover, a regional approach embracing groups from South Carolina to Virginia can transcend narrow (and still poorly understood) ethnic or "tribal" boundaries without sacrificing the richness of detail a focused study provides.

Indeed, piedmont people had so much in common that a regional perspective is almost imperative. No formal political ties bound them at the onset of European contact, but a similar environment shaped their lives, and their adjustment to this environment fostered cultural uniformity. Perhaps even more important, these groups shared a single history once Europeans and Africans arrived on the scene. Drawn together by their cultural affinities and their common plight, after 1700 they migrated to the Catawba Nation, a cluster of villages along the border between the Carolinas that became the focus of native life in the region. Tracing the experience of these upland communities both before and

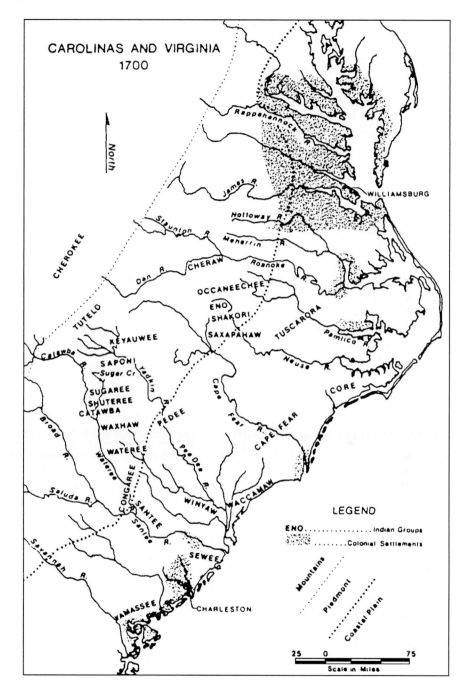

CAROLINAS AND VIRGINIA
1700

North

CHEROKEE

Rappahannock R.

James R.

Staunton R.

Nottoway R.

Meherrin R.

Dan R.   CHERAW   Roanoke R.

OCCANEECHEE

ENO

SHAKORI

TUTELO

SAXAPAHAW

TUSCARORA

Pamlico R.

KEYAUWEE

Catawba R.

SAPONI

Neuse R.

CORE

Sugar Cr.

Yadkin R.

SUGAREE

SHUTEREE

CATAWBA

WAXHAW

PEDEE

Cape Fear R.

CAPE FEAR

WATEREE

Broad R.

Wateree R.

Pee Dee R.

CONGAREE

Saluda R.

SANTEE

WINYAW

WACCAMAW

Santee R.

Savannah R.

SEWEE

YAMASSEE

CHARLESTON

WILLIAMSBURG

LEGEND

ENO .... Indian Groups

.... Colonial Settlements

Mountains

Piedmont

Coastal Plain

25   0   75

Scale in Miles

after they joined the Catawbas can illustrate the consequences of contact and illuminate the process by which natives learned to survive in their own new world.

For centuries, ancestors of the Catawbas had lived astride important aboriginal trade routes and straddled the boundary between two cultural traditions, a position that involved them in a far-flung network of contacts and affected everything from potting techniques to burial practices. Nonetheless, Africans and Europeans were utterly unlike any earlier foreign visitors to the piedmont. Their arrival meant more than merely another encounter with outsiders; it marked an important turning point in Indian history. Once these newcomers disembarked and began to feel their way across the continent, they forever altered the course and pace of native development.

Bacteria brought the most profound disturbances to upcountry villages. When Hernando de Soto led the first Europeans into the area in 1540, he found large towns already "grown up in grass" because "there had been a pest in the land" two years before, a malady probably brought inland by natives who had visited distant Spanish posts. The sources are silent about other "pests" over the next century, but soon after the English began colonizing Carolina in 1670 the disease pattern became all too clear. Major epidemics struck the region at least once every generation—in 1698, 1718, 1738, and 1759—and a variety of less virulent illnesses almost never left native settlements.

Indians were not the only inhabitants of colonial America living—and dying—in a new disease environment. The swamps and lowlands of the Chesapeake were a deathtrap for Europeans, and sickness obliged colonists to discard or rearrange many of the social forms brought from England. Among native peoples long isolated from the rest of the world and therefore lacking immunity to pathogens introduced by the intruders, the devastation was even more severe. John Lawson, who visited the Carolina upcountry in 1701, when perhaps ten thousand Indians were still there, estimated that "there is not the sixth Savage living within two hundred Miles of all our Settlements, as there were fifty Years ago." The recent smallpox epidemic "destroy'd whole Towns," he remarked, "without leaving one *Indian* alive in the Village." Resistance to disease developed with painful slowness; colonists reported that the outbreak of smallpox in 1759 wiped out 60 percent of the natives, and, according to one source, "the woods were offensive with the dead bodies of the Indians; and dogs, wolves, and vultures were . . . busy for months in banqueting on them."

Survivors of these horrors were thrust into a situation no less alien than what European immigrants and African slaves found. The collected wisdom of generations could vanish in a matter of days if sickness struck older members of a community who kept sacred traditions and taught special skills. When many of the elders succumbed at once, the deep pools of collective memory grew shallow, and some dried up altogether. In 1710, Indians near Charleston told a settler that "they have forgot most of their traditions since the Establishment of this Colony, they keep their Festivals and can tell but little of the reasons: their Old Men are dead." Impoverishment of a rich cultural heritage followed the spread of disease. Nearly a century later, a South Carolinian exaggerated but captured the general trend when he noted that Catawbas "have forgotten their antient rites, ceremonies, and manufactures."

The same diseases that robbed a piedmont town of some of its most precious resources also stripped it of the population necessary to maintain an independent existence. In order to survive, groups were compelled to construct new societies from the splintered remnants of the old. The result was a kaleidoscopic array of migrations from ancient territories and mergers with nearby peoples. While such behavior was not unheard of in aboriginal times, population levels fell so precipitously after contact that survivors endured disruptions unlike anything previously known.

The dislocations of the Saponi Indians illustrate the common course of events. In 1670 they lived on the Staunton River in Virginia and were closely affiliated with a group called Nahyssans. A decade later Saponis moved toward the coast and built a town near the Occaneechees. When John Lawson came upon them along the Yadkin River in 1701, they were on the verge of banding together in a single village with Tutelos and Keyauwees. Soon thereafter Saponis applied to Virginia officials for permission to move to the Meherrin River, where Occaneechees, Tutelos, and others joined them. In 1714, at the urging of Virginia's Lt. Gov. Alexander Spotswood, these groups settled at Fort Christanna farther up the Meherrin. Their friendship with Virginia soured during the 1720s, and most of the "Christanna Indians" moved to the Catawba Nation. For some reason this arrangement did not satisfy them, and many returned to Virginia in 1732, remaining there for a decade before choosing to migrate north and accept the protection of the Iroquois.

Saponis were unusual only in their decision to leave the Catawbas. Enos, Occaneechees, Waterees, Keyauwees, Cheraws, and others have their own stories to tell, similar in outline if not in detail. With the exception of the towns near the confluence of Sugar Creek and the Catawba River that composed the heart of the Catawba Nation, piedmont communities decimated by disease lived through a common round of catastrophes, shifting from place to place and group to group in search of a safe haven. Most eventually ended up in the Nation, and during the opening decades of the eighteenth century the villages scattered across the southern upcountry were abandoned as people drifted into the Catawba orbit.

No mere catalog of migrations and mergers can begin to convey how profoundly unsettling this experience was for those swept up in it. While upcountry Indians did not sail away to some distant land, they, too, were among the uprooted, leaving their ancestral homes to try to make a new life elsewhere. The peripatetic existence of Saponis and others proved deeply disruptive. A village and its surrounding territory were important elements of personal and collective identity, physical links in a chain binding a group to its past and making a locality sacred. Colonists, convinced that Indians were by nature "a shifting, wandring People," were oblivious to this, but Lawson offered a glimpse of the reasons for native attachment to a particular locale. "In our way," he wrote on leaving an Eno-Shakori town in 1701, "there stood a great Stone about the Size of a large Oven, and hollow; this the *Indians* took great Notice of, putting some Tobacco into the Concavity, and spitting after it. I ask'd them the Reason for their so doing, but they made me no Answer." Natives throughout the interior honored similar places—graves of ancestors, monuments of stones commemorating important events—that could not be left behind without some cost.

The toll could be physical as well as spiritual, for even the most uneventful of moves interrupted the established cycle of subsistence. Belongings had to be packed and unpacked, dwellings constructed, palisades raised. Once migrants had completed the business of settling in, the still more arduous task of exploiting new terrain awaited them. Living in one place year after year endowed a people with intimate knowledge of the area. The richest soils, the best hunting grounds, the choicest sites for gathering nuts or berries—none could be learned without years of experience, tested by time and passed down from one generation to the next. Small wonder that Carolina Indians worried about being "driven to some unknown Country, to live, hunt, and get our Bread in."

Some displaced groups tried to leave "unknown Country" behind and make their way back home. In 1716 Enos asked Virginia's permission to settle at "Enoe Town" on the North Carolina frontier, their location in Lawson's day. Seventeen years later William Byrd II came upon an abandoned Cheraw village on a tributary of the upper Roanoke River and remarked how "it must have been a great misfortune to them to be obliged to abandon so beautiful a dwelling." The Indians apparently agreed: in 1717 the Virginia Council received "Divers applications" from the Cheraws (now living along the Pee Dee River) "for Liberty to Seat themselves on the head of Roanoke River." Few natives managed to return permanently to their homelands. But their efforts to retrace their steps hint at a profound sense of loss and testify to the powerful hold of ancient sites.

Compounding the trauma of leaving familiar territories was the necessity of abandoning customary relationships. Casting their lot with others traditionally considered foreign compelled Indians to rearrange basic ways of ordering their existence. Despite frequent contacts among peoples, native life had always centered in kin and town. The consequences of this deep-seated localism were evident even to a newcomer like John Lawson, who in 1701 found striking differences in language, dress, and physical appearance among Carolina Indians living only a few miles apart. Rules governing behavior also drew sharp distinctions between outsiders and one's own "Country-Folks." Indians were "very kind, and charitable to one another," Lawson reported, "but more especially to those of their own Nation." A visitor desiring a liaison with a local woman was required to approach her relatives and the village headman. On the other hand, "if it be an *Indian* of their own Town or Neighbourhood, that wants a Mistress, he comes to none but the Girl." Lawson seemed unperturbed by this barrier until he discovered that a "Thief [is] held in Disgrace, that steals from any of his Country-Folks," "but to steal from the *English* [or any other foreigners] they reckon no Harm."

Communities unable to continue on their own had to revise these rules and reweave the social fabric into new designs. What language would be spoken?

How would fields be laid out, hunting territories divided, houses built? How would decisions be reached, offenders punished, ceremonies performed? When Lawson remarked that "now adays" the Indians must seek mates "amongst Strangers," he unwittingly characterized life in native Carolina. Those who managed to withstand the ravages of disease had to redefine the meaning of the term *stranger* and transform outsiders into insiders.

The need to harmonize discordant peoples, an unpleasant fact of life for all native Americans, was no less common among black and white inhabitants of America during these years. Africans from a host of different groups were thrown into slavery together and forced to seek some common cultural ground, to blend or set aside clashing habits and beliefs. Europeans who came to America also met unexpected and unwelcome ethnic, religious, and linguistic diversity. The roots of the problem were quite different; the problem itself was much the same. In each case people from different backgrounds had to forge a common culture and a common future.

Indians in the southern uplands customarily combined with others like themselves in an attempt to solve the dilemma. Following the "principle of least effort," shattered communities cushioned the blows inflicted by disease and depopulation by joining a kindred society known through generations of trade and alliances. Thus Saponis coalesced with Occaneechees and Tutelos—nearby groups "speaking much the same language"—and Catawbas became a sanctuary for culturally related refugees from throughout the region. Even after moving in with friends and neighbors, however, natives tended to cling to ethnic boundaries in order to ease the transition. In 1715 Spotswood noticed that the Saponis and others gathered at Fort Christanna were "confederated together, tho' still preserving their different Rules." Indians entering the Catawba Nation were equally conservative. As late as 1743 a visitor could hear more than twenty different dialects spoken by peoples living there, and some bands continued to reside in separate towns under their own leaders.

Time inevitably sapped the strength of ethnic feeling, allowing a more unified Nation to emerge from the collection of Indian communities that occupied the valleys of the Catawba River and its tributaries. By the mid-eighteenth century, the authority of village headmen was waning and leaders from the host population had begun to take responsibility for the actions of constituent groups. The babel of different tongues fell silent as "*Kàtahba*," the Nation's "standard, or court-dialect," slowly drowned out all others. Eventually, entire peoples followed their languages and their leaders into oblivion, leaving only personal names like Santee Jemmy, Cheraw George, Congaree Jamie, Saponey Johnny, and Eno Jemmy as reminders of the Nation's diverse heritage.

No European observer recorded the means by which nations became mere names and a congeries of groups forged itself into one people. No doubt the colonists' habit of ignoring ethnic distinctions and lumping confederated entities together under the Catawba rubric encouraged amalgamation. But Anglo-American efforts to create a society by proclamation were invariably unsuccessful; consolidation had to come from within. In the absence of evidence, it seems reasonable to conclude that years of contacts paved the way for a closer relationship. Once a group moved to the Nation, intermarriages blurred ancient kinship networks, joint war parties or hunting expeditions brought young men together, and elders met in a council that gave everyone some say by including "all the Indian Chiefs or Head Men of that [Catawba] Nation and the several Tribes amongst them together." The concentration of settlements within a day's walk of one another facilitated contact and communication. From their close proximity, common experience, and shared concerns, people developed ceremonies and myths that compensated for those lost to disease and gave the Nation a stronger collective consciousness. Associations evolved that balanced traditional narrow ethnic allegiance with a new, broader, "national" identity, a balance that tilted steadily toward the latter. Ethnic differences died hard, but the peoples of the Catawba Nation learned to speak with a single voice.

Muskets and kettles came to the piedmont more slowly than did smallpox and measles. Spanish explorers distributed a few gifts to local headmen, but inhabitants of the interior did not enjoy their first real taste of the fruits of European technology until Englishmen began venturing inland after 1650. Indians these traders met in upcountry towns were glad to barter for the more efficient tools, more lethal weapons, and more durable clothing that colonists offered. Spurred on by eager natives, men from Virginia and Carolina quickly flooded the region with the material trappings of European culture. In 1701 John Lawson considered the Wateree Chickanees "very poor in *English* Effects" because a few of them lacked muskets.

Slower to arrive, trade goods were also less obvious agents of change. The Indians' ability to absorb foreign artifacts into established modes of existence hid the revolutionary consequences of trade for some time. Natives leaped the technological gulf with ease in part because they were discriminating shoppers. If hoes were too small, beads too large, or cloth the wrong color, Indian traders refused them. Items they did select fit smoothly into existing ways. Waxhaws tied horse bells around their ankles at ceremonial dances, and some of the traditional stone pipes passed among the spectators at these dancers had been shaped by metal files. Those who could not afford a European weapon fashioned arrows from broken glass. Those who could went to great lengths to "set [a new musket] streight, sometimes shooting away above 100 Loads of Ammunition, before they bring the Gun to shoot according to their Mind."

Not every piece of merchandise hauled into the upcountry on a trader's packhorse could be "set streight" so easily. Liquor, for example, proved both impossible to resist and extraordinarily destructive. Indians "have no Power to refrain this Enemy," Lawson observed, "though sensible how many of them (are by it) hurry'd into the other World before their Time." And yet even here, natives aware of the risks sought to control alcohol by incorporating it into their ceremonial life as a device for achieving a different level of consciousness. Consumption was usually restricted to men, who "go as solemnly about it, as if it were part of their Religion," preferring to drink only at night and only in quantities sufficient to stupefy them. When ritual could not confine liquor to safe channels, Indians went still further and excused the excesses of overindulgence by refusing to hold an intoxicated person responsible for his actions. "They never call any Man to account for what he did, when he was drunk," wrote Lawson, "but say, it was the Drink that caused his Misbehaviour, therefore he ought to be forgiven."

Working to absorb even the most dangerous commodities acquired from their new neighbors, aboriginal inhabitants of the uplands, like African slaves in the lowlands, made themselves at home in a different technological environment. Indians became convinced that "Guns, and Ammunition, besides a great many other Necessaries, . . . are helpful to Man" and eagerly searched for the key that would unlock the secret of their production. At first many were confident that the "*Quera*," or good Spirit, would teach them to make these commodities "when that good Spirit sees fit." Later they decided to help their deity along by approaching the colonists. In 1757, Catawbas asked Gov. Arthur Dobbs of North Carolina "to send us Smiths and other Tradesmen to teach our Children."

It was not the new products themselves but the Indians' failure to learn the mysteries of manufacture from either Dobbs or the *Quera* that marked the real revolution wrought by trade. During the seventeenth and eighteenth centuries, everyone in eastern North America—masters and slaves, farmers near the coast and Indians near the mountains—became producers of raw materials for foreign markets and found themselves caught up in an international economic network. Piedmont natives were part of this larger process, but their adjustment was more difficult because the contrast with previous ways was so pronounced. Before European contact, the localism characteristic of life in the uplands had been sustained by a remarkable degree of self-sufficiency. Trade among peoples, while common, was conducted primarily in commodities such as copper, mica, and shells, items that, exchanged with the appropriate ceremony, initiated or confirmed friendships among groups. Few, if any, villages relied on outsiders for goods essential to daily life.

Intercultural exchange eroded this traditional independence and entangled natives in a web of commercial relations few of them understood and none controlled. In 1670 the explorer John Lederer observed a striking disparity in the trading habits of Indians living near Virginia and those deep in the interior. The "remoter Indians," still operating within a precontact framework, were content with ornamental items such as mirrors, beads, "and all manner of gaudy toys and knacks for children." "Neighbour-Indians," on the other hand habitually traded with colonists for cloth, metal tools, and weapons. Before long, towns near and far were demanding the entire range of European wares and were growing accustomed—even addicted—to them. "They say we English are fools for . . . not always going with a gun," one Virginia colonist familiar with piedmont Indians wrote in the early 1690s, "for they think themselves undrest and not fit to walk abroad, unless they have their gun on their shoulder, and their shot-bag by their side." Such an enthusiastic conversion to the new technology eroded ancient craft skills and hastened complete dependence on substitutes only colonists could supply.

By forcing Indians to look beyond their own territories for certain indispensable products, Anglo-American traders inserted new variables into the aboriginal equation of exchange. Colonists sought two commodities from Indians—human beings and deerskins—and both undermined established relationships among native groups. While the demand for slaves encouraged piedmont peoples to expand their traditional warfare, the demand for peltry may have fostered conflicts over hunting territories. Those who did not fight each other for slaves or deerskins fought each other for the European products these could bring. As firearms, cloth, and other items became increasingly important to native existence, competition replaced comity at the foundation of trade encounters as villages scrambled for the cargoes of merchandise. Some were in a better position to profit than others. In the early 1670s Occaneechees living on an island in the Roanoke River enjoyed power out of all proportion to their numbers because they controlled an important ford on the trading path from Virginia to the interior, and they resorted to threats, and even to force, to retain their advantage. In Lawson's day Tuscaroras did the same, "hating that any of these Westward *Indians* should have any Commerce with the *English,* which would prove a Hinderance to their Gains."

Competition among native groups was only the beginning of the transformation brought about by new forms of exchange. Inhabitants of the piedmont might bypass the native middleman, but they could not break free from a perilous dependence on colonial sources of supply. The danger may not have been immediately apparent to Indians caught up in the excitement of acquiring new and wonderful things. For years they managed to dictate the terms of trade, compelling visitors from Carolina and Virginia to abide by aboriginal codes of conduct and playing one colony's traders against the other to ensure an abundance of goods at favorable rates. But the natives' influence over the protocol of exchange combined with their skill at incorporating alien products to mask a loss of control over their own destiny. The mask came off when, in 1715, the traders—and the trade goods—suddenly disappeared during the Yamassee War.

The conflict's origins lay in a growing colonial awareness of the Indians' need for regular supplies of European merchandise. In 1701 Lawson pronounced the Santees "very tractable" because of their close connections with South Carolina. Eight years later he was convinced that the colonial officials in Charleston "are absolute Masters over the *Indians* . . . within the Circle of their Trade." Carolina traders who shared this conviction quite naturally felt less and less constrained to obey native rules governing proper behavior. Abuses against Indians mounted until some men were literally getting away with murder. When repeated appeals to colonial officials failed, natives throughout Carolina began to consider war. Persuaded by Yamassee ambassadors that the conspiracy was widespread and convinced by years of ruthless commercial competition between Virginia and Carolina that an attack on one colony would not affect relations with the other, in the spring of 1715 Catawbas and their neighbors joined the invasion of South Carolina.

The decision to fight was disastrous. Colonists everywhere shut off the flow of goods to the interior, and after some initial successes Carolina's native enemies soon plumbed the depths of their dependence. In a matter of months, refugees holed up in Charleston noticed that "the Indians want ammunition and are not able to mend their Arms." The peace negotiations that ensued revealed a desperate thirst for fresh supplies of European wares. Ambassadors from piedmont towns invariably spoke in a single breath of restoring "a Peace and a free Trade," and one delegation even admitted that its people "cannot live without the assistance of the English."

Natives unable to live without the English henceforth tried to live with them. No upcountry group mounted a direct challenge to Anglo-America after 1715. Trade quickly resumed, and the piedmont Indians, now concentrated almost exclusively in the Catawba valley, briefly enjoyed a regular supply of necessary products sold by men willing once again to deal according to the old rules. By mid-century, however, deer were scarce and fresh sources of slaves almost impossible to find. Anglo-American traders took their business elsewhere, leaving inhabitants of the Nation with another material crisis of different but equally dangerous dimensions.

Indians casting about for an alternative means of procuring the commodities they craved looked to imperial officials. During the 1740s and 1750s native dependence shifted from colonial traders to colonial authorities as Catawba leaders repeatedly visited provincial capitals to request goods. These delegations came not to beg but to bargain. Catawbas were still of enormous value to the English as allies and frontier guards, especially at a time when Anglo-America felt threatened by the French and their Indian auxiliaries. The Nation's position within reach of Virginia and both Carolinas enhanced its value by enabling headmen to approach all three colonies and offer their people's services to the highest bidder.

The strategy yielded Indians an arsenal of ammunition and a variety of other merchandise that helped offset the declining trade. Crown officials were especially generous when the Nation managed to play one colony off against another. In 1746 a rumor that the Catawbas were about to move to Virginia was enough to garner them a large shipment of powder and lead from officials in Charleston concerned about losing this "valuable people." A decade later, while the two Carolinas fought for the honor of constructing a fort in the Nation, the Indians encouraged (and received) gifts symbolizing good will from both colonies without reaching an agreement with either. Surveying the tangled thicket of promises and presents, the crown's superintendent of Indian affairs, Edmond Atkin, ruefully admitted that "the People of both Provinces . . . have I believe [sic] tampered too much on both sides with those Indians, who seem to understand well how to make their Advantage of it."

By the end of the colonial period delicate negotiations across cultural boundaries were as familiar to Catawbas as the strouds they wore and the muskets they carried. But no matter how shrewdly the headmen loosened provincial purse strings to extract vital merchandise, they could not escape the simple fact that they no longer held the purse containing everything needed for their daily existence. In the space of a century the Indians had become thoroughly embedded in an alien economy, denizens of a new material world. The ancient self-sufficiency was only a dim memory in the minds of the Nation's elders.

The Catawba peoples were veterans of countless campaigns against disease and masters of the arts of trade long before the third major element of their new world, white planters, became an integral part of their life. Settlement of the Carolina uplands did not begin until the 1730s, but once under way it spread with frightening speed. In November 1752, concerned Catawbas reminded South Carolina Governor James Glen how they had "complained already . . . that the white People were settled too near us." Two years later five hundred families lived within thirty miles of the Nation and surveyors were running their lines into the middle of native towns. "[T]hose Indians are now in a fair way to be surrounded by White People," one observer concluded.

Settlers' attitudes were as alarming as their numbers. Unlike traders who profited from them or colonial officials who deployed them as allies, ordinary colonists had little use for Indians. Natives made poor servants and worse slaves; they obstructed settlement; they attracted enemy warriors to the area. Even men who respected Indians and earned a living by trading with them admitted that they made unpleasant neighbors. "We may observe of them as of the fire," wrote the South Carolina trader James Adair after considering the Catawbas' situation on the eve of the American Revolution, "'it is safe and useful, cherished at proper distance; but if too near us, it becomes dangerous, and will scorch if not consume us.'"

A common fondness for alcohol increased the likelihood of intercultural hostilities. Catawba leaders acknowledged that the Indians "get very Drunk with [liquor] this is the Very Cause that they oftentimes Commit those Crimes that is offencive to You and us." Colonists were equally prone to bouts of drunkenness. In the 1760s the itinerant Anglican minister, Charles Woodmason, was shocked to find the citizens of one South Carolina upcountry community "continually drunk." More appalling still, after attending church services "one half of them got drunk before they went home." Indians sometimes suffered at the hands of intoxicated farmers. In 1760 a Catawba woman was murdered when she happened by a tavern shortly after four of its patrons "swore they would kill the first Indian they should meet with."

Even when sober, natives and newcomers found many reasons to quarrel. Catawbas were outraged if colonists built farms on the Indians' doorstep or tramped across ancient burial grounds. Planters, ignorant of (or indifferent to) native rules of hospitality, considered Indians who requested food nothing more than beggars and angrily drove them away. Other disputes arose when the Nation's young men went looking for trouble. As hunting, warfare, and other traditional avenues for achieving status narrowed, Catawba youths transferred older patterns of behavior into a new arena by raiding nearby farms and hunting cattle or horses.

Contrasting images of the piedmont landscape quite unintentionally generated still more friction. Colonists determined to tame what they considered a wilderness were in fact erasing a native signature on the land and scrawling their own. Bridges, buildings, fences, roads, crops, and other "improvements" made the area comfortable and familiar to colonists but uncomfortable and unfamiliar to Indians. "The Country side wear[s] a New face," proclaimed Woodmason proudly; to the original inhabitants, it was a grim face indeed. "His Land was spoiled," one Catawba headman told British officials in 1763. "They have spoiled him 100 Miles every way." Under these circumstances, even a settler with no wish to fight Indians met opposition to his fences, his outbuildings, his very presence. Similarly, a Catawba on a routine foray into traditional hunting territories had his weapon destroyed, his goods confiscated, his life threatened by men with different notions of the proper use of the land.

To make matters worse, the importance both cultures attached to personal independence hampered efforts by authorities on either side to resolve conflicts. Piedmont settlers along the border between the Carolinas were "people of desperate fortune," a frightened North Carolina official reported after visiting the area. "[N]o officer of Justice from either Province dare meddle with them." Woodmason, who spent even more time in the region, came to the same conclusion. "We are without any Law, or Order," he complained; the inhabitants' "Impudence is so very high, as to be past bearing." Catawba leaders could have sympathized. Headmen informed colonists that the Nation's people "are oftentimes Cautioned from . . . ill Doings altho' to no purpose for we Cannot be present at all times to Look after them." "What they have done I could not prevent," one chief explained.

Unruly, angry, intoxicated—Catawbas and Carolinians were constantly at odds during the middle decades of the eighteenth century. Planters who considered Indians "proud and deveilish" were themselves accused by natives of being "very bad and quarrelsome." Warriors made a habit of "going into the Settlements, robbing and stealing where ever they get an Oppertunity." Complaints generally brought no satisfaction—"they laugh and makes their Game of it, and says it is what they will"—leading some settlers to "whip [Indians] about the head, beat and abuse them." "The white People . . . and the Cuttahbaws, are Continually at varience," a visitor to the Nation fretted in June 1759, "and Dayly New Animositys Doth a rise Between them which In my Humble oppion will be of Bad Consequence In a Short time, Both Partys Being obstinate."

The litany of intercultural crimes committed by each side disguised a fundamental shift in the balance of physical and cultural power. In the early years of colonization of the interior the least disturbance by Indians sent scattered planters into a panic. Soon, however, Catawbas were few, colonists many, and it was the natives who now lived in fear. "[T]he white men [who] Lives Near the Neation is Contenuely asembleing and goes In the [Indian] towns In Bodys . . . ," worried another observer during the tense summer of 1759. "[T]he[y] tretton the[y] will Kill all the Cattabues."

The Indians would have to find some way to get along with these unpleasant neighbors if the Nation was to survive. As Catawba population fell below five hundred after the smallpox epidemic of 1759 and the number of colonists continued to climb, natives gradually came to recognize the futility of violent resistance. During the last decades of the eighteenth century they drew on years of experience in dealing with Europeans at a distance and sought to overturn the common conviction that Indian neighbors were frightening and useless.

This process was not the result of some clever plan; Catawbas had no strategy for survival. A headman could warn them that "the White people were now seated all round them and by that means had them entirely in their power." He could not command them to submit peacefully to the invasion of their homeland. The Nation's continued existence required countless individual decisions, made in a host of diverse circumstances, to complain rather than retaliate, to accept a subordinate place in a land that once was theirs. Few of the choices made survive in the record. But it is clear that, like the response to disease and to technology, the adaptation to white settlement was both painful and prolonged.

Catawbas took one of the first steps along the road to accommodation in the early 1760s, when they used their influence with colonial officials to acquire a reservation encompassing the heart of their ancient territories. This grant gave the Indians a land base, grounded in Anglo-American law, that prevented farmers from shouldering them aside. Equally important, Catawbas now had a commodity to exchange with nearby settlers. These men wanted land, the natives had plenty, and shortly before the Revolution the Nation was renting tracts to planters for cash, livestock, and manufactured goods.

Important as it was, land was not the only item Catawbas began trading to their neighbors. Some Indians put their skills as hunters and woodsmen to a different use, picking up stray horses and escaped slaves for a reward. Others bartered their pottery, baskets, and table mats. Still others traveled through the upcountry, demonstrating their prowess with the bow and arrow before appreciative audiences. The exchange of these goods and services for European merchandise marked an important adjustment to the settlers' arrival. In the past, natives had acquired essential items by trading peltry and slaves or requesting gifts from representatives of the crown. But piedmont planters frowned on hunting and warfare, while provincial authorities—finding Catawbas less useful as the Nation's population declined and the French threat disappeared—discouraged formal visits and handed out fewer presents. Hence the Indians had to develop new avenues of exchange that would enable them to obtain goods in ways less objectionable to their neighbors. Pots, baskets, and acres proved harmless substitutes for earlier methods of earning an income.

Quite apart from its economic benefits, trade had a profound impact on the character of Catawba-settler relations. Through countless repetitions of the same simple procedure at homesteads scattered across the Carolinas, a new form of intercourse arose, based not on suspicion and an expectation of conflict but on trust and a measure of friendship. When a farmer looked out his window and saw Indians approaching, his reaction more commonly became to pick up money or a jug of whiskey rather than a musket or an axe. The natives now appeared, the settler knew, not to plunder or kill but to peddle their wares or collect their rents.

The development of new trade forms could not bury all the differences between Catawba and colonist overnight. But in the latter half of the eighteenth century the beleaguered Indians learned to rely on peaceful means of resolving intercultural conflicts that did arise. Drawing a sharp distinction between "the good men that have rented Lands from us" and "the bad People [who] has frequently imposed upon us," Catawbas called on the former to protect the Nation from the latter. In 1771 they met with a prominent Camden storekeeper, Joseph Kershaw, to request that he "represent us when [we are] a grieved." After the revolution the position became more formal. Catawbas informed the South Carolina government that, being "destitute of a man to take care of, and assist us in our affairs," they had chosen one Robert Patten "to take charge of our affairs, and to act and do for us."

Neither Patten nor any other intermediary could have protected the Nation had it not joined the patriot side during the Revolutionary War. Though one scholar has termed the Indians' contribution to the cause "rather negligible," they fought in battles throughout the southeast and supplied rebel forces with food from time to time. These actions made the Catawbas heroes and laid a foundation for their popular renown as staunch patriots. In 1781 their old friend Kershaw told Catawba leaders how he welcomed the end of "this Long and Bloody War, in which You have taken so Noble a part and have fought and Bled with your white Brothers of America." Grateful Carolinians would not soon forget the Nation's service. Shortly after the Civil War an elderly settler whose father had served with the Indians in the revolution echoed Kershaw's sentiments, recalling that "his father never communicated much to him [about the Catawbas], except that all the tribe . . . served the entire war . . . and fought most heroically."

Catawbas rose even higher in their neighbors' esteem when they began calling their chiefs "general" instead of "king" and stressed that these men were elected by the people. The change reflected little if any real shift in the Nation's political forms, but it delighted the victorious revolutionaries. In 1794 the Charleston *City Gazette* reported that during the war "King" Frow had abdicated and the Indians chose "General" New River in his stead. "What a pity," the paper concluded, "certain people on a certain island have not as good optics as the Catawbas!" In the same year the citizens of Camden celebrated the anniversary of the fall of the Bastille by raising their glasses to toast "King Prow [*sic*]—may all kings who will not follow his example follow that of Louis XVI." Like tales of Indian patriots, the story proved durable. Nearly a century after the revolution one nearby planter wrote that "the Catawbas, emulating the examples of their white brethren, threw off regal government."

The Indians' new image as republicans and patriots, added to their trade with whites and their willingness to resolve conflicts peacefully, brought settlers to view Catawbas in a different light. By 1800 the natives were no longer violent and dangerous strangers but what one visitor termed an "inoffensive" people and one group of planters called "harmless and friendly" neighbors. They had become traders of pottery but not deerskins, experts with a bow and arrow but not hunters, ferocious warriors against runaway slaves or Tories but not against settlers. In these ways Catawbas could be distinctively Indian yet reassuringly harmless at the same time.

The Nation's separate identity rested on such obvious aboriginal traits. But its survival ultimately depended on a more general conformity with the surrounding society. During the nineteenth century both settlers and Indians owned or rented land. Both spoke proudly of their revolutionary heritage and their republican forms of government. Both drank to excess. Even the fact that Catawbas were not Christians failed to differentiate them sharply from nearby white settlements, where, one visitor noted in 1822, "little attention is paid to the sabbath, or religeon."

In retrospect it is clear that these similarities were as superficial as they were essential. For all the changes generated by contacts with vital Euro-American and Afro-American cultures, the Nation was never torn loose from its cultural moorings. Well after the revolution, Indians maintained a distinctive way of life rich in tradition and meaningful to those it embraced. Ceremonies conducted by headmen and folk tales told by relatives continued to transmit traditional values and skills from one generation to the next. Catawba children grew up speaking the native language, making bows and arrows or pottery, and otherwise following patterns of belief and behavior derived from the past. The Indians' physical appearance and the meandering paths that set Catawba settlements off from neighboring communities served to reinforce this cultural isolation.

The natives' utter indifference to missionary efforts after 1800 testified to the enduring power of established ways. Several clergymen stopped at the reservation in the first years of the nineteenth century; some stayed a year or two; none enjoyed any success. As one white South Carolinian noted in 1826, Catawbas were "Indians still." Outward conformity made it easier for them to blend into the changed landscape. Beneath the surface lay a more complex story.

Those few outsiders who tried to piece together that story generally found it difficult to learn much from the Indians. A people shrewd enough to discard the title of "king" was shrewd enough to understand that some things were better left unsaid and unseen. Catawbas kept their Indian names, and sometimes their language, a secret from prying visitors. They echoed the racist attitudes of their white neighbors and even owned a few slaves, all the time trading with blacks and hiring them to work in the Nation, where the laborers "enjoyed considerable freedom" among the natives. Like Afro-Americans on the plantation who adopted a happy, childlike demeanor to placate suspicious whites, Indians on the reservation learned that a "harmless and friendly" posture revealing little of life in the Nation was best suited to conditions in post-revolutionary South Carolina.

Success in clinging to their cultural identity and at least a fraction of their ancient lands cannot obscure the cost Catawba peoples paid. From the time the first European arrived, the deck was stacked against them. They played the hand dealt them well enough to survive, but they could never win. An incident that took place at the end of the eighteenth century helps shed light on the consequences of compromise. When the Catawba headman General New River accidentally injured the horse he had borrowed from a nearby planter named Thomas Spratt, Spratt responded by "banging old New River with a pole all over the yard." This episode provided the settler with a colorful tale for his grandchildren; its effect on New River and his descendants can only be imagined. Catawbas did succeed in the sense that they adjusted to a hostile and different world, becoming trusted friends instead of feared enemies. Had they been any less successful they would not have survived the eighteenth century. But poverty and oppression have plagued the Nation from New River's day to our own. For a people who had once been proprietors of the piedmont, the pain of learning new rules was very great, the price of success very high.

On that August day in 1608 when Amoroleck feared the loss of his world, John Smith assured him that the English "came to them in peace, and to seeke their loves." Events soon proved Amoroleck right and his captor wrong. Over the course of the next three centuries not only Amoroleck and other piedmont Indians but natives throughout North America had their world stolen and another put in its place. Though this occurred at different times and in different ways, no Indians escaped the explosive mixture of deadly bacteria, material riches, and alien peoples that was the invasion of America. Those in the southern piedmont who survived the onslaught were ensconced in their new world by the end of the eighteenth century. Population levels stabilized as the Catawba peoples developed immunities to once-lethal diseases. Rents, sales of pottery, and other economic activities proved adequate to support the Nation at a stable (if low) level of material life. Finally, the Indians' image as "inoffensive" neighbors gave them a place in South Carolina society and continues to sustain them today.

Vast differences separated Catawbas and other natives from their colonial contemporaries. Europeans were the colonizers, Africans the enslaved, Indians the dispossessed: from these distinct positions came distinct histories. Yet once we acknowledge the differences, instructive similarities remain that help to integrate natives more thoroughly into the story of early America. By carving a niche for themselves in response to drastically different conditions, the peoples who composed the Catawba Nation shared in the most fundamental of American experiences. Like Afro-Americans, these Indians were compelled to accept a subordinate position in American life yet did not altogether lose their cultural integrity. Like settlers of the Chesapeake, aboriginal inhabitants of the uplands adjusted to appalling mortality rates and wrestled with the difficult task of "living with death." Like inhabitants of the Middle Colonies, piedmont groups learned to cope with unprecedented ethnic diversity by balancing the pull of traditional loyalties with the demands of a new social order. Like Puritans in New England, Catawbas found that a new world did not arrive all at once and that localism, self-sufficiency, and the power of old ways were only gradually eroded by conditions in colonial America. More hints of a comparable heritage could be added to this list, but by now it should be clear that Indians belong on the colonial stage as important actors in the unfolding American drama rather than bit players, props, or spectators. For they, too, lived in a new world.

SOURCES

The Indians as Seen by European Artists

Europeans formed a fantastic variety of mental pictures of the lives and behavior of the natives of the Americas. On one hand, they might portray the Indians as vicious cannibals, with almost no social organization. On the other hand, Europeans often pictured Indian society as being rather orderly, advanced, and "civilized." Here are three very famous sixteenth-century representations. Pictures, we like to believe, tell us more than words. Suppose you were to try to translate these pictures into a few words, however. What would they be? Can you imagine other ways of depicting the Indians that Europeans might have used?

John White's Engraving of Indians Making a Canoe near Roanoke, 1588.
Rare Book Division, New York Public Library.

A Settlement of Virginia Indians.
From Part I, Plate XX, in Theodore DeBry's America. *Arents Collection/New York Public Library.*

Florida Battle Scene, 1564.
American Antiquarian Society.

Broken Spears: The Aztec Account
of the Conquest of Mexico

*What about the violent side of the story? The Europeans, as the above picture
suggests, made much of the brutality of the "savages." By the same token, native groups had plenty of horror stories to tell about European atrocities. From
various accounts, some written as early as 1528, the Mexican anthropologist
Miguel Leon Portilla has pieced together the Aztec memory of Cortes's invasion in 1521. At the time, almost a century before the Catawbas first encountered Europeans, the Aztecs ruled a mighty empire, thousands of times the size
of the Catawba Nation, rich and spectacular by both new and old world standards. As you read this story of the way Montezuma and his people experienced
the shock of invasion and the bitterness of their defeat, keep these questions in
mind: What do the Aztecs give as the cause of Spanish victory? Technology?
Divine intervention? Disease? Was the Aztec experience the same as that of the
Catawbas? In what respect was it different? Why?*

From *The Broken Spears,* edited and with an introduction by Miguel Leon-Portilla, Beacon Press,
Boston, 1962, pp. 29–149. Copyright © 1962 by Beacon Press. Originally published in Spanish under
the title *Vision de los Vencidos,* copyright © 1959 by Universidad Nacional Autonoma de Mexico.
Reprinted by permission of Beacon Press.

MOTECUHZOMA GOES OUT TO MEET CORTES

The Spaniards arrived in Xoloco, near the entrance to Tenochtitlan. That was the end of the march, for they had reached their goal.

Motecuhzoma now arrayed himself in his finery, preparing to go out to meet them. The other great princes also adorned their persons, as did the nobles and their chieftains and knights. They all went out together to meet the strangers.

They brought trays heaped with the finest flowers—the flower that resembles a shield; the flower shaped like a heart; in the center, the flower with the sweetest aroma; and the fragrant yellow flower, the most precious of all. They also brought garlands of flowers, and ornaments for the breast, and necklaces of gold, necklaces hung with rich stones, necklaces fashioned in the petatillo style.

Thus Motecuhzoma went out to meet them, there in Huitzillan. He presented many gifts to the Captain and his commanders, those who had come to make war. He showered gifts upon them and hung flowers around their necks; he gave them necklaces of flowers and bands of flowers to adorn their breasts; he set garlands of flowers upon their heads. Then he hung the gold necklaces around their necks and gave them presents of every sort as gifts of welcome. . . .

MOTECUHZOMA AWAITS WORD FROM THE MESSENGERS

While the messengers were away, Motecuhzoma could neither sleep nor eat, and no one could speak with him. He thought that everything he did was in vain, and he sighed almost every moment. He was lost in despair, in the deepest gloom and sorrow. Nothing could comfort him, nothing could calm him, nothing could give him any pleasure.

He said: "What will happen to us? Who will outlive it? Ah, in other times I was contented, but now I have death in my heart! My heart burns and suffers, as if it were drowned in spices . . . ! But will our lord come here?"

Then he gave orders to the watchmen, to the men who guarded the palace: "Tell me, even if I am sleeping: 'The messengers have come back from the sea.'" But when they went to tell him, he immediately said: "They are not to report to me here. I will receive them in the House of the Serpent. Tell them to go there." And he gave this order: Two captives are to be painted with chalk."

The messengers went to the House of the Serpent, and Motecuhzoma arrived. The two captives were then sacrificed before his eyes: their breasts were torn open, and the messengers were sprinkled with their blood. This was done because the messengers had completed a difficult mission: they had seen the gods, their eyes had looked on their faces. They had even conversed with the gods!

THE MESSENGERS' REPORT

When the sacrifice was finished, the messengers reported to the king. They told him how they had made the journey, and what they had seen, and what food the strangers ate. Motecuhzoma was astonished and terrified by their report, and the description of the strangers' food astonished them above all else.

He was also terrified to learn how the cannon roared, how its noise resounded, how it caused one to faint and grow deaf. The messengers told him: "A thing like a ball of fire comes out its entrails: it comes out shooting sparks and raining fire. The smoke that comes out with it has a pestilent odor, like that of rotten mud. This odor penetrates even to the brain and causes the greatest discomfort. If the cannon is aimed against a mountain, the mountain splits and cracks open. If it is aimed against a tree, it shatters the tree into splinters. This is a most unnatural sight as if the tree had exploded from within."

The messengers also said: "Their trappings and arms are all made of iron. They dress in iron and wear iron casques on their heads. Their swords are iron; their bows are iron; their shields are iron; their spears are iron. Their deer carry them on their backs wherever they wish to go. These deer, our lord, are as tall as the roof of a house."

The strangers' bodies are completely covered, so that only their faces can be seen. Their skin is white, as if it were made of lime. They have yellow hair, though some of them have black. Their beards are long and yellow, and their mustaches are also yellow. Their hair is curly, with very fine strands.

"As for their food, it is like human food. It is large and white, and not heavy. It is something like straw, but with the taste of a cornstalk, of the pith of a cornstalk. It is a little sweet, as if it were flavored with honey; it tastes of honey, it is sweet-tasting food.

"Their dogs are enormous, with flat ears and long, dangling tongues. The color of their eyes is a burning yellow; their eyes flash fire and shoot off sparks. Their bellies are hollow, their flanks long and narrow. They are tireless and very powerful. They bound here and there, panting, with their tongues hanging out. And they are spotted like an ocelot."

When Motecuhzoma heard this report, he was filled with terror. It was as if his heart had fainted, as if it had shriveled. It was as if he were conquered by despair. . . .

THE SPANIARDS TAKE POSSESSION OF THE CITY

When the Spaniards entered the Royal House, they placed Motecuhzoma under guard and kept him under their vigilance. They also placed a guard over Itzcuauhtzin, but the other lords were permitted to depart.

Then the Spaniards fired one of their cannons, and this caused great confusion in the city. The people scattered in every direction; they fled without rhyme or reason; they ran off as if they were being pursued. It was as if they had eaten the mushrooms that confuse the mind, or had seen some dreadful apparition. They were all overcome by terror, as if their hearts had fainted. And when night fell, the panic spread through the city and their fears would not let them sleep.

In the morning the Spaniards told Motecuhzoma what they needed in the way of supplies: tortillas, fried chickens, hens' eggs, pure water, firewood and charcoal. Also: large, clean cooking pots, water jars, pitchers, dishes and other pottery. Motecuhzoma ordered that it be sent to them. The chiefs who received this order were angry with the king and no longer revered or respected him. But they furnished the Spaniards with all the provisions they needed—food, beverages, and water, and fodder for the horses.

THE SPANIARDS REVEAL THEIR GREED

When the Spaniards were installed in the palace, they asked Motecuhzoma about the city's resources and reserves and about the warriors' ensigns and shields. They questioned him closely and then demanded gold.

Motecuhzoma guided them to it. They surrounded him and crowded close with their weapons. He walked in the center, while they formed a circle around him.

When they arrived at the treasure house called Teucalco, the riches of gold and feathers were brought out to them: ornaments made of quetzal feathers, richly worked shields, disks of gold, the necklaces of the idols, gold nose plugs, gold greaves and bracelets and crowns.

The Spaniards immediately stripped the feathers from the gold shields and ensigns. They gathered all the gold into a great mound and set fire to everything else, regardless of its value. Then they melted down the gold into ingots. As for the precious green stones, they took only the best of them; the rest were snatched up by the Tlaxcaltecas. The Spaniards searched through the whole treasure house, questioning and quarreling, and seized every object they thought was beautiful.

THE SEIZURE OF MOTECUHZOMA'S TREASURES

Next they went to Motecuhzoma's storehouse, in the place called Totocalec [Place of the Palace of the Birds], where his personal treasures were kept. The Spaniards grinned like little beasts and patted each other with delight.

When they entered the hall of treasures, it was as if they had arrived in Paradise. They searched everywhere and coveted everything; they were slaves to their own greed. All of Motecuhzoma's possessions were brought out: fine bracelets, necklaces with large stones, ankle rings with little gold bells, the royal crowns, and all the royal finery—everything that belonged to the king and was reserved to him only. They seized these treasures as if they were their own, as if this plunder were merely a stroke of good luck. And when they had taken all the gold, they heaped up everything else in the middle of the patio.

La Malinche called the nobles together. She climbed up to the palace roof and cried, "Mexicanos, come forward! The Spaniards need your help! Bring them food and pure water. They are tired and hungry; they are almost fainting from exhaustion! Why do you not come forward? Are you angry with them?"

The Mexicans were too frightened to approach. They were crushed by terror and would not risk coming forward. They shied away as if the Spaniards were wild beasts, as if the hour were midnight on the blackest night of the year. Yet they did not abandon the Spaniards to hunger and thirst. They brought them whatever they needed, but shook with fear as they did so. They delivered the supplies to the Spaniards with trembling hands, then turned and hurried away. . . .

THE MASSACRE IN THE MAIN TEMPLE DURING THE FIESTA OF TOXCATL

At this moment in the fiesta, when the dance was loveliest and when song was linked to song, the Spaniards were seized with an urge to kill the celebrants. They all ran forward, armed as if for battle. They closed the entrances and passageways, all the gates of the patio: the Eagle Gate in the lesser palace, the Gate of the Canestalk and the Gate of the Serpent of Mirrors. They posted guards so that no one could escape, and then rushed into the Sacred Patio to slaughter the celebrants. They came on foot, carrying their swords and their wooden or metal shields.

They ran in among the dancers, forcing their way to the place where the drums were played. They attacked the man who was drumming and cut off his arms. Then they cut off his head, and it rolled across the floor.

They attacked all the celebrants, stabbing them, spearing them, striking them with their swords. They attacked some of them from behind, and these fell instantly to the ground with their entrails hanging out. Others they beheaded: they cut off their heads, or split their heads to pieces.

They struck others in the shoulders, and their arms were torn from their bodies. They wounded some in the thigh and some in the calf. They slashed others in the abdomen, and their entrails all spilled to the ground. Some attempted to run away, but their intestines dragged as they ran; they seemed to tangle their feet in their own entrails. No matter how they tried to save themselves, they could find no escape.

Some attempted to force their way out, but the Spaniards murdered them at the gates. Others climbed the walls, but they could not save themselves. Those who ran into the communal houses were safe there for a while; so were those who lay down among the victims and pretended to be dead. But if they stood up again, the Spaniards saw them and killed them.

The blood of the warriors flowed like water and gathered into pools. The pools widened, and the stench of blood and entrails filled the air. The Spaniards ran into the communal houses to kill those who were hiding. They ran everywhere and searched everywhere; they invaded every room, hunting and killing.

THE SIEGE OF TENOCHTITLAN

Now the Spaniards began to wage war against us. They attacked us by land for ten days, and then their ships appeared. Twenty days later, they gathered all their ships together near Nonohualco, off the place called Mazatzintamalco. The allies from Tlaxcala and Huexotzinco set up camp on either side of the road.

Our warriors from Tlatelolco immediately leaped into their canoes and set out for Mazatzintamalco and the Nonohualco road. But no one set out from Tenochtitlan to assist us: only the Tlatelolcas were ready when the Spaniards arrived in their ships. On the following day, the ships sailed to Xoloco.

The fighting at Xoloco and Huitzillan lasted for two days. While the battle was under way, the warriors from Tenochtitlan began to mutiny. They said: "Where are our chiefs? They have fired scarcely a single arrow! Do they think they have fought like men?" Then they seized four of their own leaders and put them to death. The victims were two captains, Cuauhnochtli and Cuapan, and the priests of Amantlan and Tlalocan. This was the second time that the people of Tenochtitlan killed their own leaders. . . .

THE FIGHTING IS RENEWED

The Spaniards made ready to attack us, and the war broke out again. They assembled their forces in Cuepopan and Cozcacuahco. A vast number of our warriors were killed by their metal darts. Their ships sailed to Texopan, and the battle there lasted three days. When they had forced us to retreat, they entered the Sacred Patio, where there was a four-day battle. Then they reached Yacacolco.

The Tlatelolcas set up three racks of heads in three different places. The first rack was in the Sacred Patio of Tlilancalco [Black House], where we strung up the heads of our lords the Spaniards. The second was in Acacolco, where we strung up Spanish heads and the heads of two of their horses. The third was in Zacatla, in front of the temple of the earth-goddess Cihuacoatl, where we strung up the heads of Tlaxcaltecas.

The women of Tlatelolco joined in the fighting. They struck at the enemy and shot arrows at them; they tucked up their skirts and dressed in the regalia of war.

The Spaniards forced us to retreat. Then they occupied the market place. The Tlatelolcas—the Jaguar Knights, the Eagle Knights, the great warriors—were defeated, and this was the end of the battle. It had lasted five days, and two thousand Tlatelolcas were killed in action. During the battle, the Spaniards set up a canopy for the Captain in the market place. They also mounted a catapult on the temple platform.

EPIC DESCRIPTION OF THE BESIEGED CITY

And all these misfortunes befell us. We saw them and wondered at them; we suffered this unhappy fate.

> Broken spears lie in the roads;
> we have torn our hair in our grief.
> The houses are roofless now, and their walls
> are red with blood.
>
> Worms are swarming in the streets and plazas,
> and the walls are splattered with gore.
> The water has turned red, as if it were dyed,
> and when we drink it,
> it has the taste of brine.
>
> We have pounded our hands in despair
> against the adobe walls,
> for our inheritance, our city, is lost and dead.
> The shields of our warriors were its defense,
> but they could not save it.
>
> We have chewed dry twigs and salt grasses;
> we have filled our mouths with dust and bits of adobe;
> we have eaten lizards, rats and worms. . . .

When we had meat, we ate it almost raw. It was scarcely on the fire before we snatched it and gobbled it down.

They set a price on all of us: on the young men, the priests, the boys and girls. The price of a poor man was only two handfuls of corn, or ten cakes made from mosses or twenty cakes of salty couch-grass. Gold, jade, rich cloths, quetzal feathers—everything that once was precious was now considered worthless.

The captains delivered several prisoners of war to Cuauhtemoc to be sacrificed. He performed the sacrifices in person, cutting them open with a stone knife. . . .

Race War:
The New England Experience

As the Aztecs' memory of their defeat indicates, the European conquest of America involved a good deal of brutality and terrorism. And brutality was not confined to Central or South America, either. Wherever Indians were able to mount a significant resistance, the European retaliation was likely to be swift and very harsh. The following selections attempt to justify the beheading and quartering—the cutting into four pieces—of an Indian leader, King Philip. He was the leader of Indian resistance in New England that culminated in what the English settlers called King Philip's War (1675–1676). The second selection was written by the most highly educated man in New England, Increase Mather, and thus represents the most "enlightened" view of the Indian in New England. Do you believe the two descriptions of the Indians' behavior? How does Mather explain the causes of the Indians' attacks on whites? How does he explain the white victory?

King Philip's War:
A Contemporary Account

A True but Brief Account of our Losses sustained since this Cruel and Mischievous War began, take as follows:

In *Narraganset* not one House left standing.
At *Warwick*, but one.
At *Providence*, not above three.
At *Potuxit*, none left.
Very few at *Seaconicke*.
At *Swansey*, two, at most.
Marlborough, wholy laid in Ashes, except two or three Houses.
Grantham and *Nashaway*, all ruined but one House or two.
Many Houses burnt at *Springfield, Scituate, Lancaster, Brookfield,* and *Northampton.*
The greatest Part of *Rehoboth* and *Taunton* destroyed.
Great Spoil made at *Hadley, Hatfield,* and *Chelmsford.*
Deerfield wholy, and *Westfield* much ruined.
At *Sudbury*, many Houses burnt, and some at *Hingham, Weymouth,* and *Braintree.*

From "A New and Farther Narrative of the State of New-England, July 22, 1676" by N. S., from *The Old Indian Chronicle,* Samuel G. Drake, ed, Boston, 1867, pp. 244–246.

Besides particular Farms and Plantations, a great Number not be reckoned up, wholly laid waste, or very much damnified.

And as to Persons, it is generally thought, that of the English there hath been lost, in all, Men Women and Children, above Eight Hundred, since the War began. Of whom many have been destroyed with exquisite Torments, and most inhumane Barbarities; the Heathen rarely giving Quarter to those that they take, but if they were Women, they first forced them to satisfie their filthy Lusts and then murdered them; either cutting off the Head, ripping open the Belly, or skulping the Head of Skin and Hair, and hanging them up as Trophies; wearing Men's Fingers as Bracelets about their Necks, and Stripes of their Skins which they dress for Belts. They knockt one Youth of the Head, and laying him for dead, they flead (or skulp'd) his Head of Skin and Hair. After which the Boy wonderfully revived, and is now recovered, only he hath Nothing but the dry Skull, neither Skin nor Hair on his Head. Nor have our Cattle escaped the Cruelty of these worse than Brute and Savage Beasts: For what Cattle they took they seldom killed outright: or if they did, would eat but little of the Flesh, but rather cut their Bellies, and letting them go several Days, trailing their Guts after them, putting out their Eyes, or cutting off one Leg, &c.

Defeat of King Philip: Increase Mather's Account

August 6. An *Indian* that deserted his Fellows, informed the inhabitants of *Taunton* that a party of *Indians* who might be easily surprised, were not very far off, and promised to conduct any that had a mind to apprehend those *Indians* in the right way towards them, whereupon about twenty Souldiers marched out of *Taunton*, and they took all those *Indians*, being in number thirty and six, only the *Squaw-Sachem of Pocasset*, who was next unto *Philip* in respect to the mischief that hath been done, and the blood that hath been shed in this Warr, escaped alone; but not long after some of *Taunton* finding an *Indian Squaw* in *Metapoiset* newly dead, cut off her head, and it happened to be *Weetamoo*, i.e. *Squaw-Sachem her head.* When it was set upon a pole in *Taunton*, the *Indians* who were prisoners there knew it presently, and made a most horrid and diabolical Lamentation, crying out that it was their Queens head. Now here it is to be observed, that God himself by his own hand brought his enemy to destruction. For in that place, where the last year, she furnished *Philip* with Canooes for his men, she her self could not meet with a Canoo, but venturing over the River upon a Raft, that brake under her, so that she was drowned, just before the *English* found her. Surely *Philips* turn will be next.

August 10. Whereas *Potock* a chief Counsellor to the old Squaw-Sachem of *Narraganset*, was by some of Road-Island brought into *Boston*, and found guilty

From Increase Mather, *A History of King Philip's War*, Albany, 1862, pp. 191–195.

of promoting the War against the *English,* he was this day shot to death in the Common at *Boston.* As he was going to his execution, some told him that now he must dy, he had as good speak the truth, and say how many *Indians* were killed at the Fort-Fight last winter. He replyed, that the *English* did that day kill above seven hundred fighting men, and that three hundred who were wounded, dyed quickly after, and that as to old men, women and Children, they had lost no body could tell how many; and that there were above three thousand *Indians* in the Fort, when our Forces assaulted them, and made that notable slaughter amongst them.

August 12. This is the memorable day wherein *Philip,* the perfidious and bloudy Author of the War and wofull miseryes that have thence ensued, was taken and slain. And God brought it to pass, chiefly by *Indians* themselves. For one of *Philips* men (being disgusted at him, for killing an *Indian* who had propounded an expedient for peace with the *English*) ran away from him, and coming to Road-Island, informed that *Philip* was now returned again to *Mount-Hope,* and undertook to bring them to the swamp where he hid himself. Divine Providence so disposed, as that Capt. *Church* of *Plymouth* was then in Road-Island, in order to recruiting his Souldiers, who had been wearied with a tedious march that week. But immediately upon this Intelligence, he set forth again, with a small company of *English* and *Indians.* It seemeth that night *Philip* (like the man, in the Host of *Midian*) dreamed that he was fallen into the hands of the *English,* and just as he was saying to those that were with him, that they must fly for their lives that day, lest the *Indian* that was gone from him should recover where he was. Our Souldiers came upon him and surrounded the *Swamp* (where he with seven of his men absconded). Thereupon he betook himself to flight; but as he was coming out of the Swamp, an *English-man* and an *Indian* endeavoured to fire at him, the *English-man* missed of his aime, but the *Indian* shot him through the heart, so as that he fell down dead. The *Indian* who thus killed *Philip* did formerly belong to Squaw-Sachim of *Pocasset,* being known by the name of *Alderman.* In the beginning of the war, he came to the Governour of *Plymouth,* manifesting his desire to be at peace with the *English,* and immediately withdrew to an Island not having engaged against the *English* nor for them, before this time. Thus when *Philip* had made an end to deal treacherously, his own Subjects dealt treacherously with him. This Wo was brought upon him that spoyled when he was not spoyled. And in that very place where he first contrived and began his mischief, was he taken and destroyed, and there was he (like as Agag was hewed in pieces before the Lord) cut into four quarters, and is now hanged up as a monument of revenging Justice, his head being cut off and carried away to *Plymouth,* his Hands were brought to *Boston. So let all thine Enemies perish, O Lord!*

CHAPTER 2

Jamestown

We all know the story of Jamestown—or think we do. There was Captain John Smith, who put lazy gentlemen to work. There was Pocahontas, who made peace possible between whites and Indians. And there was John Rolfe, who figured out how to grow the "noxious weed," tobacco, successfully, and so ensured the struggling colony's eventual triumph.

But this familiar story had no meaning whatever to the original settlers of the colony of Virginia. For them, Virginia was not a setting for personal dramas. Life there was ugly, brutal, and very likely to be short. In fact, death was the most prominent feature of life. It came often and quickly—through illness, accident, and Indian resistance—but mainly through starvation.

The toll was awesome. The Virginia Company of London sent 144 colonists to Virginia late in 1606. Of these, thirty-nine died at sea. Forty-six more died within a few months of landing. Only thirty-eight were still alive when the next ship arrived in 1608. New settlers from England brought the population up to about five hundred. All but sixty of these died during the "starving time" of the winter of 1609–1610.

The figures for the longer run are almost as appalling. Between 1607 and 1624, four out of every five colonists who came over to Jamestown died.

Those who had been sent out to lose their lives in this deathtrap were the advance guard of a commercial concern, the Virginia Company. It had been chartered in 1606 by the English crown for the purpose of colonizing an area that was about half the size of the present United States. The investors in the company expected it to pay quick profits, perhaps from the discovery of gold or silver, or of an easy water passage through the continent (whose size no one yet knew) to the fabled markets of Asia.

The enterprise was, in short, a capital venture by a group of stockholders to whom the new world was an opportunity for investment. The investment failed. The stockholders eventually sank about 100,000 pounds (worth about 16 million of today's dollars) in their speculation. In return, they got nothing. The company paid no dividends, and its stock became worthless paper within a dozen years.

Why did the settlers and the investors alike fare so poorly? In the early years, the company did send over large numbers of "gentlemen," who wouldn't work. The original settlers also spent a lot of their time quarreling with each other and searching for gold. But surely such explanations do not account for the fact that Englishmen with the advantages of Iron Age technology had such difficulties, why they starved to death in an area where Indians had lived successfully for years.

INTERPRETIVE ESSAY

Edmund S. Morgan

The Labor Problem at Jamestown, 1607–1618

The following selection is by the most distinguished historian of the colonial period at work in the United States today. In it, he confronts the vexed problem of Jamestown. More precisely, he addresses a simple but puzzling question: why seventeenth-century Englishmen had so much difficulty coping with the wilderness, why they starved to death rather than put in a hard day's work getting food. Morgan traces the problem back to English attitudes toward work and comes to the unhappy conclusion that the only way Virginians could solve their labor problem was to introduce black slavery. As you read, you should pay particular attention to the logic of the essay, which governs the introduction of its factual detail. Does that logic seem plausible? Or could other kinds of connections explain the facts that Morgan introduces?

The story of Jamestown, the first permanent English settlement in America, has a familiar place in the history of the United States. We all know of the tribulations that kept the colony on the point of expiring: the shortage of supplies, the hostility of the Indians, the quarrels among the leaders, the reckless search for gold, the pathetic search for a passage to the Pacific, and the neglect of the crucial business of growing food to stay alive. Through the scene moves the figure of Captain John Smith, a little larger than life, trading for corn among the Indians and driving the feckless crew to work. His departure in October 1609 results in near disaster. The settlers fritter away their time and energy, squander their provisions, and starve. Sir Thomas Gates, arriving after the settlement's third winter, finds only sixty men out of six hundred still alive and those sixty scarcely able to walk.

In the summer of 1610 Gates and Lord La Warr get things moving again with a new supply of men and provisions, a new absolute form of government, and a new set of laws designed to keep everybody at work. But when Gates and La Warr leave for a time, the settlers fall to their old ways. Sir Thomas Dale, upon his arrival in May 1611, finds them at "their daily and usuall workes, bowling in the streetes." But Dale brings order out of chaos. By enlarging and enforcing the colony's new law code (the famous *Lawes Divine, Morall and Martiall*) he starts the settlers working again and rescues them from starvation by making them plant corn. By 1618 the colony is getting on its feet and ready to carry on without the stern regimen of a Smith or a Dale. There are still evil days ahead, as the

From Edmund S. Morgan, "The Labor Problem at Jamestown, 1607–18," *American Historical Review*, vol. 76, 1971, pp. 595–610. Copyright by Edmund S. Morgan.

Virginia Company sends over men more rapidly than the infant colony can absorb them. But the settlers, having found in tobacco a valuable crop for export,
have at least gone to work with a will, and Virginia's future is assured.

The story probably fits the facts insofar as they can be known. But it does
not quite explain them. The colony's long period of starvation and failure may
well be attributed to the idleness of the first settlers, but idleness is more an accusation than an explanation. Why did men spend their time bowling in the
streets when their lives depended on work? Were they lunatics, preferring to
play games rather than clear and plow and plant the crops that could have kept
them alive?

The mystery only deepens if we look more closely at the efforts of Smith,
Gates, La Warr, and Dale to set things right. In 1612 John Smith described his
work program of 1608: "the company [being] divided into tennes, fifteenes, or
as the businesse required, 4 hours each day was spent in worke, the rest in pas-
times and merry exercise." Twelve years later Smith rewrote this passage and
changed the figure of four hours to six hours. But even so, what are we to make
of a six-hour day in a colony teetering on the verge of extinction?

The program of Gates and La Warr in the summer of 1610 was no more
strenuous. William Strachey described it:

> it is to be understood that such as labor are not yet so taxed but that easily they
> perform the same and ever by ten of the clock have done their morning's work:
> at what time they have their allowances [of food] set out ready for them, and
> until it be three of the clock again they take their own pleasure, and afterward,
> with the sunset, their day's labor is finished.

The Virginia Company offered much the same account of this period. According to a tract issued late in 1610, "the setled times of working (to effect all themselves, or the Adventurers neede desire) [requires] no more pains than from six
of clocke in the morning untill ten, and from two of the clocke in the afternoone
till foure." The long lunch period described for 1610 was also a feature of the
Lawes Divine, Morall and Martiall as enforced by Dale. The total working hours
prescribed in the *Lawes* amounted to roughly five to eight hours a day in summer and three to six hours in winter.

It is difficult, then, to escape the conclusion that there was a great deal of unemployment or underemployment at Jamestown, whether it was the idleness of
the undisciplined in the absence of strong government or the idleness of the disciplined in the presence of strong government. How are we to account for this
fact? By our standards the situation at Jamestown demanded hard and continuous work. Why was the response so feeble?

One answer, given by the leaders of the colony, is that the settlers included
too many ne'er-do-wells and too many gentlemen who "never did know what
a dayes work was." Hard work had to wait until harder men were sent. Another
answer may be that the Jamestown settlers were debilitated by hunger and disease. The victims of scurvy, malaria, typhoid, and diphtheria may have been left
without the will or the energy to work. Still another answer, which was echoed
through the pages of our history books, attributed the difficulty to the fact that

the settlement was conducted on a communal basis: everybody worked for the Virginia Company and everybody was fed (while supplies lasted) by the company, regardless of how much he worked or failed to work. Once land was distributed to individuals and men were allowed to work for themselves, they gained the familiar incentives of private enterprise and bent their shoulders to the wheel. These explanations are surely all valid—they are all supported by the testimony of contemporaries—and they go far toward explaining the lazy pioneers of Jamestown. But they do not reach a dimension of the problem that contemporaries would have overlooked because they would have taken it for granted. They do not tell us what ideas and attitudes about work, carried from England, would have led the first English settlers to expect so little of themselves in a situation that demanded so much. The Jamestown settlers did not leave us the kind of private papers that would enable us to examine directly their ideas and attitudes, as we can those of the Puritans who settled New England a few years later. But in the absence of direct evidence we may discover among the ideas current in late sixteenth- and early seventeenth-century England some clues to the probable state of mind of the first Virginians, clues to the way they felt about work, whether in the old world or the new, clues to habits of thinking that may have conditioned their perceptions of what confronted them at Jamestown, clues even to the tangled web of motives that made later Virginians masters of slaves.

Englishmen's ideas about the new world at the opening of the seventeenth century were based on a century of European exploration and settlement. The Spanish, whose exploits surpassed all others, had not attempted to keep their success a secret, and by the middle of the sixteenth century Englishmen interested in America had begun translating Spanish histories and memoirs in an effort to rouse their countrymen to emulation. The land that emerged from these writings was, except in the Arctic regions, an Eden, teeming with gentle and generous people who, before the Spanish conquest, had lived without labor, or with very little, from the fruits of a bountiful nature. There were admittedly some unfriendly exceptions who made a habit of eating their more attractive neighbors; but they were a minority, confined to a few localities, and in spite of their ferocity were scarcely a match for Europeans armed with guns. Englishmen who visited the new world confirmed the reports of natural abundance. Arthur Barlowe, for example, reconnoitering the North Carolina coast for Walter Raleigh, observed that "the earth bringeth foorth all things in aboundance, as in the first creation, without toile or labour," while the people were "most gentle, loving and faithfull, void of all guile, and treason, and such as lived after the manner of the golden age."

English and European readers may have discounted the more extravagant reports of American abundance, for the same authors who praised the land often gave contradictory accounts of the hardships they had suffered in it. But anyone who doubted that riches were waiting to be plucked from Virginia's trees had reason to expect that a good deal might be plucked from the people of the land. Spanish experience had shown that Europeans could thrive in the new world without undue effort by exploiting the natives. With a mere handful of men the Spanish had conquered an enormous population of Indians in the Caribbean, Mexico, and Peru and had put them to work. In the chronicles of Peter Martyr Englishmen learned how it was done. Apart from the fact that the Indians were naturally gentle, their division into a multitude of kingdoms, frequently at odds with one another, made it easy to play off one against another. By aiding one group against its enemies the Spaniards had made themselves masters of both.

The story of English plans to imitate and improve on the Spanish strategy is a long one. It begins at least as early as Francis Drake's foray in Panama in 1572–73, when he allied with a band of runaway slaves to rob a Spanish mule train carrying treasure from Peru across the isthmus to Nombre de Dios on the Caribbean. The idea of joining with dissident natives or slaves either against their Spanish masters or against their wicked cannibalistic neighbors became an important ingredient in English plans for colonizing the new world. Martin Frobisher's experiences with the Eskimos in Baffin Land and Ralph Lane's with the Indians at Roanoke should perhaps have disabused the English of their expectations; but they found it difficult to believe that any group of natives, and especially the noble savages of North America, would fail to welcome what they called with honest pride (and some myopia) the "gentle government" of the English. If the savages first encountered by a colonizing expedition proved unfriendly, the thing to do was to make contact with their milder neighbors and rescue them from the tyranny of the unfriendly tribe, who must be their enemies and were probably cannibals to boot.

The settlers at Jamestown tried to follow the strategy, locating their settlement as the plan called for, near the mouth of a navigable river, so that they would have access to the interior tribes if the coastal ones were hostile. But as luck would have it, they picked an area with a more powerful, more extensive, and more effective Indian government than existed anywhere else on the Atlantic Coast. King Powhatan had his enemies, the Monacans of the interior, but he felt no great need of English assistance against them, and he rightly suspected that the English constituted a larger threat to his hegemony than the Monacans did. He submitted with ill grace and no evident comprehension to the coronation ceremony that the Virginia Company arranged for him, and he kept his distance from Jamestown. Those of his warriors who visited the settlement showed no disposition to work for the English. The Monacans, on the other hand, lived too far inland (beyond the falls) to serve as substitute allies, and the English were thus deprived of their anticipated native labor.

They did not, however, give up their expectations of getting it eventually. In 1615 Ralph Hamor still thought the Indians would come around "as they are easily taught and may be lenitie and faire usage . . . be brought, being naturally though ingenious, yet idlely given, to be no lesse industrious, nay to exceede our English." Even after the massacre of 1622 Virginians continued to dream of an Indian labor supply, though there was no longer to be any gentleness in obtaining it. Captain John Martin thought it better to exploit than exterminate the Indians, if only because they could be made to work in the heat of the day, when

Englishmen would not. And William Claiborne in 1626 invented a device (whether mechanical or political is not clear) that he claimed would make it possible to keep Indians safely in the settlements and put them to work. The governor and council gave him what looks like the first American patent or copyright, namely a three-year monopoly, to "have holde and enjoy all the benefitt use and profitt of this his project or inventione," and they also assigned him a recently captured Indian, "for his better experience and tryall of his inventione."

English expectations of the new world and its inhabitants died hard. America was supposed to be a land of abundance, peopled by natives who would not only share that abundance with the English but increase it under English direction. Englishmen simply did not envisage a need to work for the mere purpose of staying alive. The problem of survival as they saw it was at best political and at worst military.

Although Englishmen long remained under the illusion that the Indians would eventually become useful English subjects, it became apparent fairly early that Indian labor was not going to sustain the founders of Jamestown. The company in England was convinced by 1609 that the settlers would have to grow at least part of their own food. Yet the settlers themselves had to be driven to that life-saving task. To understand their ineffectiveness in coping with a situation that their pioneering descendants would take in stride, it may be helpful next to inquire into some of the attitudes toward work that these first English pioneers took for granted. How much work and what kind of work did Englishmen at the opening of the seventeenth century consider normal?

The laboring population of England, by law at least, was required to work much harder than the regimen at Jamestown might lead us to expect. The famous Statute of Artificers of 1563 (re-enacting similar provisions from the Statute of Laborers of 1495) required all laborers to work from five in the morning to seven or eight at night from mid-March to mid-September, and during the remaining months of the year from day break to night. Time out for eating, drinking, and rest was not to exceed two and a half hours a day. But these were injunctions not descriptions. The Statute of Laborers of 1495 is preceded by the complaint that laborers "waste much part of the day . . . in late coming unto their work, early departing therefrom, long sitting at their breakfast, at their dinner and noon-meat, and long time of sleeping after noon." Whether this statute or that of 1563 (still in effect when Jamestown was founded) corrected the situation is doubtful. The records of local courts show varying efforts to enforce other provisions of the statute of 1563, but they are almost wholly silent about this provision, in spite of the often-expressed despair of masters over their lazy and negligent laborers.

It may be said that complaints of the laziness and irresponsibility of workmen can be met with in any century. Were such complaints in fact justified in sixteenth- and early seventeenth-century England? There is some reason to believe that they were, that life during those years was characterized by a large amount of idleness and underemployment. The outstanding economic fact of the sixteenth and early seventeeth century in England was a rapid and more or less steady rise in prices, followed at some distance by a much smaller rise in wages, both in industry and in agriculture. The price of provisions used by a laborer's family rose faster than wages during the whole period from 1500 to 1640. The government made an effort to narrow the gap by requiring the justices in each county to readjust maximum wages at regular intervals. But the wages established by the justices reflected their own nostalgic notions of what a day's work ought to be worth in money, rather than a realistic estimate of what a man could buy with his wages. In those counties, at least, where records survive, the level of wages set by the justices crept upward very slowly before 1630.

Wages became so inadequate that productivity was probably impaired by malnutrition. From a quarter to a half of the population lived below the level recognized at the time to constitute poverty. Few of the poor could count on regular meals at home, and in years when the wheat crop failed, they were close to starvation. It is not surprising that men living under these conditions showed no great energy for work and that much of the population was, by modern standards, idle much of the time. The health manuals of the day recognized that people normally slept after eating, and the laws even prescribed a siesta for laborers in the summer time. If they slept longer and more often than the laws allowed or the physicians recommended, if they loafed on the job and took unauthorized holidays, if they worked slowly and ineffectively when they did work, it may have been due at least in part to undernourishment and to the variety of chronic diseases that undernourishment brings in its train.

Thus low wages may have begot low productivity that in turn justified low wages. The reaction of employers was to blame the trouble on deficiencies, not of diet or wages, but of character. A prosperous yeoman like Robert Loder, who kept close track of his expenses and profits, was always bemoaning the indolence of his servants. Men who had large amounts of land that they could either rent or work with hired labor generally preferred to rent because labor was so inefficient and irresponsible.

Even the division of labor, which economists have customarily regarded as a means of increased productivity, could be a source of idleness. Plowing, for example, seems to have been a special skill—a plowman was paid at a higher rate than ordinary farm workers. But the ordinary laborer's work might have to be synchronized with the plowman's, and a whole crew of men might be kept idle by a plowman's failure to get his job done at the appropriate time. It is difficult to say whether this type of idleness, resulting from failure to synchronize the performance of related tasks, was rising or declining; but cheap, inefficient, irresponsible labor would be unlikely to generate pressures for the careful planning of time.

The government, while seeking to discourage idleness through laws requiring long hours of work, also passed laws that inadvertently discouraged industry. A policy that might be characterized as the conservation of employment frustrated those who wanted to do more work than others. English economic policy seems to have rested on the assumption that the total amount of work for which society could pay was strictly limited and must be rationed so that everyone could have a little, and those with family responsibilities could have a little more. It was against the law for a man to practice more than one trade or one craft. And although large numbers of farmers took up some handicraft on the side, this was to be discouraged, because "for one man to be both an husbandman and an Artificer is a gatheringe of divers mens livinges into one mans hand." So as not to take work away from his elders, a man could not independently practice most trades until he had become a master through seven years of apprenticeship. Even then, until he was thirty years old or married, he was supposed to serve some other master of the trade. A typical example is the case of John Pikeman of Barking, Essex, a tailor who was presented by the grand jury because he "being a singleman and not above 25 years of age, does take in work of tailoring and works by himself to the hindrance of other poor occupiers, contrary to the law."

These measures doubtless helped to maintain social stability in the face of a rapid population increase, from under three million in 1500 to a probable four and a half million in 1640 (an increase reflected in the gap between wages and prices). But in its efforts to spread employment so that every able-bodied person would have a means of support, the government in effect discouraged energetic labor and nurtured the workingman's low expectations of himself. By requiring masters to engage apprentices for seven-year terms and servants (in agriculture and in most trades) for the whole year rather than the day, it prevented employers from hiring labor only when there was work to be done and prevented the diligent and effective worker from replacing the ineffective. The intention to spread work is apparent in the observation of the Essex justices that labor by the day caused "the great depauperization of other labourers." But labor by the year meant that work could be strung out to occupy an unnecessary amount of time, because whether or not a master had enough work to occupy his servants they had to stay and he had to keep them. The records show many instances of masters attempting to turn away a servant or apprentice before the stipulated term was up, only to have him sent back by the courts with orders that the master "entertain" him for the full period. We even have the extraordinary spectacle of the runaway master, the man who illegally fled from his servants and thus evaded his responsibility to employ and support them.

In pursuit of its policy of full employment in the face of an expanding population, the government often had to create jobs in cases where society offered none. Sometimes men were obliged to take on a poor boy as a servant whether they needed him or not. The parish might lighten the burden by paying a fee, but it might also fine a man who refused to take a boy assigned to him. To provide for men and women who could not be foisted off on unwilling employers, the government established houses of correction in every county, where the inmates toiled at turning wool, flax, and hemp into thread or yarn, receiving nothing but their food and lodging for their efforts. By all these means the government probably did succeed in spreading employment. But in the long run its policy, insofar as it was effective, tended to depress wages and to diminish the amount of work expected from any one man.

Above and beyond the idleness and underemployment that we may blame

on the lethargy and irresponsibility of underpaid labor, on the failure to synchronize the performance of related tasks, and on the policy of spreading work
as thinly as possible, the very nature of the jobs to be done prevented the systematic use of time that characterizes modern industrialized economies. Men
could seldom work steadily, because they could work only at the tasks that
could be done at the moment; and in sixteenth- and seventeenth-century England the tasks to be done often depended on forces beyond human control: on
the weather and the seasons, on the winds, on the tides, on the maturing of
crops. In the countryside work from dawn to dusk with scarcely an intermission
might be normal at harvest time, but there were bound to be times when there
was very little to do. When it rained or snowed, most farming operations had to
be stopped altogether (and so did some of the stages of cloth manufacture). As
late as 1705 John Law, imagining a typical economy established on a newly discovered island, assumed that the persons engaged in agriculture would necessarily be idle, for one reason or another, half the time.

To be sure, side by side with idleness and inefficiency, England exhibited the
first signs of a rationalized economy. Professor J. U. Nef has described the many
large-scale industrial enterprises that were inaugurated in England in the late
sixteenth and early seventeenth centuries. And if the development of systematic
agricultural production was advancing less rapidly than historians once supposed, the very existence of men like Robert Loder, the very complaints of the
idleness and irresponsibility of laborers, the very laws prescribing hours of
work all testify to the beginnings of a rationalized economy. But these were beginnings only and not widely felt. The laborer who seemed idle or irresponsible
to a Robert Loder probably did not seem so to himself or to his peers. His England was not a machine for producing wool or corn. His England included activities and pleasures and relationships that systematic-minded employers
would resent and that modern economists would classify as uneconomic. At the
opening of the seventeenth century, England was giving him fewer economic
benefits than she had given his grandfathers so that he was often ready to pull
up stakes and look for a better life in another county or another country. But a
life devoted to more and harder work than he had known at home might not
have been his idea of a better life.

Perhaps we may now view Jamestown with somewhat less surprise at the idle
and hungry people occupying the place: idleness and hunger were the rule in
much of England of the time; they were facts of life to be taken for granted. And
if we next ask what the settlers thought they had come to America to do, what
they thought they were up to in Virginia, we can find several English enterprises
comparable to their own that may have served as models and that would not
have led them to think of hard, continuous disciplined work as a necessary ingredient in their undertaking.

If they thought of themselves as settling a wilderness, they could look for
guidance to what was going on in the northern and western parts of England
and in the high parts of the south and east. Here were the regions, mostly
wooded, where wastelands still abounded, the goal of many in the large mi-

grant population of England. Those who had settled down were scattered widely over the countryside in isolated hovels and hamlets and lived by pasture farming, that is, they cultivated only small plots of ground and ran a few sheep or cattle on the common land. Since the gardens required little attention and the cattle hardly any, they had most of their time to themselves. Some spent their spare hours on handicrafts. In fact, they supplied the labor for most of England's minor industries, which tended to locate in pasture-farming regions, where agriculture made fewer demands on the inhabitants, than in regions devoted to market crops. But the pasture farmers seem to have offered their labor sporadically and reluctantly. They had the reputation of being both idle and independent. They might travel to the richer arable farming regions to pick up a few shillings in field work at harvest time, but their own harvests were small. They did not even grow the wheat or rye for their own bread and made shift to live in hard times from the nuts and berries and herbs that they gathered in the woods.

Jamestown was mostly wooded, like the pasture-farming areas of England and Wales; and since Englishmen used the greater part of their own country for pasture farming, that was the obvious way to use the wasteland of the new world. If this was the Virginians' idea of what they were about, we should expect them to be idle much of the time and to get grain for bread by trading rather than planting (in this case not wheat or rye but maize from the Indians); we should even expect them to get a good deal of their food, as they did, by scouring the woods for nuts and berries.

As the colony developed, a pasture-farming population would have been quite in keeping with the company's expectation of profit from a variety of products. The Spaniards' phenomenal success with raising cattle in the West Indies was well known. And the proposed employment of the settlers of Virginia in a variety of industrial pursuits (iron works, silk works, glass works, shipbuilding) was entirely fitting for a pasture-farming community. The small gardens assigned for cultivation by Governor Dale in 1614 will also make sense: three acres would have been far too small a plot of land to occupy a farmer in the arable regions of England, where a single man could handle thirty acres without assistance. But it would be not at all inappropriate as the garden of a pasture farmer. In Virginia three acres would produce more than enough corn to sustain a man for a year and still leave him with time to make a profit for the company or himself at some other job—if he could be persuaded to work.

Apart from the movement of migrant workers into wastelands, the most obvious English analogy to the Jamestown settlement was that of a military expedition. The settlers may have had in mind not only the expeditions that subdued the Irish but also those dispatched to the European continent in England's wars. The Virginia Company itself seems at first to have envisaged the enterprise as partly military, and the *Lawes, Divine, Morall and Martiall* were mostly martial. But the conception carried unfortunate implications for the company's expectations of profit. Military expeditions were staffed from top to bottom with men unlikely to work. The nucleus of sixteenth-century English armies was the nobility and the gangs of genteel ruffians they kept in their service, in wartime to accompany them into the field (or to go in their stead), in peacetime to follow them about as living insignia of their rank. Work was not for the nobility nor for those who wore their livery. According to the keenest student of the aristocracy in this period, "the rich and well-born were idle almost by definition." Moreover they kept "a huge labor force . . . absorbed in slothful and parasitic personal service." Aside from the gentlemen retainers of the nobility and their slothful servants the military expeditions that England sent abroad were filled out by misfits and thieves whom the local constables wished to be rid of. It was, in fact, government policy to keep the able-bodied and upright at home and to send the lame, the halt, the blind, and the criminal abroad.

The combination of gentlemen and ne'er-do-wells of which the leaders at Jamestown complained may well have been the result of the company's using a military model for guidance. The Virginia Company was loaded with noblemen (32 present or future earls, 4 countesses, 3 viscounts, and 19 barons). Is it possible that the large number of Jamestown settlers listed as gentlemen and captains came from among the retainers of these lordly stockholders and that the rest of the settlers included some of the gentlemen's personal servants as well as a group of hapless vagabonds or migratory farm laborers who had been either impressed or lured into the enterprise by tales of the new world's abundance? We are told, at least, that persons designated in the colony's roster as "laborers" were "for most part footmen, and such as they that were Adventurers brought to attend them, or such as they could perswade to goe with them, that never did know what a dayes work was."

If these men thought they were engaged in a military expedition, military precedent pointed to idleness, hunger, and death, not to the effective organization of labor. Soldiers on campaign were not expected to grow their own food. On the other hand they *were* expected to go hungry often and to die like flies even if they never saw an enemy. The casualty rates on European expeditions resembled those at Jamestown and probably from the same causes: disease and undernourishment.

But the highest conception of the enterprise, often expressed by the leaders, was that of a new commonwealth on the model of England itself. Yet this, too, while it touched the heart, was not likely to turn men toward hard, effective, and continuous work. The England that Englishmen were saddled with as a model for new commonwealths abroad was a highly complex society in which the governing consideration in accomplishing a particular piece of work was not how to do it efficiently but who had the right or the duty to do it, by custom, law, or privilege. We know that the labor shortage in the new world quickly diminished considerations of custom, privilege, and specialization in the organization of labor. But the English model the settlers carried with them made them think initially of a society like the one at home, in which each of them would perform his own special task and not encroach on the rights of other men to do other tasks. We may grasp some of the assumptions about labor that went into the most intelligent planning of a new commonwealth by considering Richard Hakluyt's recommendation that settlers include both carpenters and joiners, tallow chandlers and wax chandlers, bowyers and fletchers, men to rough-hew pike staffs and other men to finish them.

If Jamestown was not actually troubled by this great an excess of specialization, it was not the Virginia Company's fault. The company wanted to establish at once an economy more complex than England's, an economy that would include not only all the trades that catered to ordinary domestic needs of Englishmen but also industries that were unknown or uncommon in England: a list of artisans the company wanted for the colony in 1611 included such specialists as hemp planters and hemp dressers, gun makers and gunstock makers, spinners of pack thread and upholsterers of feathers. Whatever idleness arose from the specialization of labor in English society was multiplied in the new world by the presence of unneeded skills and the absence or shortage of essential skills. Jamestown had an oversupply of glassmakers and not enough carpenters or blacksmiths, an oversupply of gentlemen and not enough plowmen. These were Englishmen temporarily baffled by missing links in the economic structure of their primitive community. The later jack-of-all-trades American frontiersman was as yet unthought of. As late as 1618 Governor Argall complained that they lacked the men "to set their Ploughs on worke." Although they had the oxen to pull them, "they wanted men to bring them to labour, and Irons for the Ploughs, and harnesse for the Cattell." And the next year John Rolfe noted that they still needed "Carpenters to build and make Carts and Ploughs, and skilfull men that know how to use them, and traine up our cattell to draw them; which though we indeavour to effect, yet our want of experience brings but little to perfection but planting Tobacco."

Tobacco, as we know, was what they kept on planting. The first shipload of it, sent to England in 1617, brought such high prices that the Virginians stopped bowling in the streets and planted tobacco in them. They did it without benefit of plows, and somehow at the same time they managed to grow corn, probably also without plows. Seventeenth-century Englishmen, it turned out, could adapt themselves to hard and varied work if there was sufficient incentive.

But we may well ask whether the habits and attitudes we have been examining had suddenly expired altogether. Did tobacco really solve the labor problem in Virginia? Did the economy that developed after 1618 represent a totally new set of social and economic attitudes? Did greater opportunities for profit completely erase the old attitudes and furnish the incentives to labor that were needed to make Virginia a success? The study of labor in modern underdeveloped countries should make us pause before we say yes. The mere opportunity to earn high wages has not always proved adequate to recruit labor in underdeveloped countries. Something more in the way of expanded needs or political authority or national consciousness or ethical imperatives has been required. Surely Virginia, in some sense, became a success. But how did it succeed? What kind of success did it have? Without attempting to answer, I should like very diffidently to offer a suggestion, a way of looking ahead at what happened in the years after the settlement of Jamestown.

The founders of Virginia, having discovered in tobacco a substitute for the sugar of the West Indies and the silver of Peru, still felt the lack of a native labor force with which to exploit the new crop. At first they turned to their own overpopulated country for labor, but English indentured servants brought with them the same haphazard habits of work as their masters. Also like their masters, they were apt to be unruly if pressed. And when their terms of servitude expired—if they themselves had not expired in the "seasoning" that carried away most immigrants to Virginia—they could be persuaded to continue working for their betters only at exorbitant rates. Instead they struck out for themselves and joined the ranks of those demanding rather than supplying labor. But there was a way out. The Spanish and Portuguese had already demonstrated what could be done in the new world when a local labor force became inadequate: they brought in the natives of Africa.

SOURCES

Jamestown: The Physical Setting

These pictures are modern—and probably very accurate—representations of Jamestown as it looked in its early years. If these were the only sources of information you had about Jamestown, how would you describe the relationship between the town center and the outlying land? Why would you think the settlers chose this particular site of their point of beginning? Look back at the picture of the Indian village in Chapter 1 (p. 21). What similarities can you see between it and these representations of Jamestown? What details would signal you that Jamestown was more technologically advanced?

Painting by Sidney King/Photo by Thomas L. Williams.

Jamestown-Yorktown Foundation.

Life and Death in Virginia: Richard Frethorne's Account, 1623

Today it is virtually impossible for us to fully understand those who lived and died in Virginia. Our world is much different, and most of us have never experienced the anxiety, suffering, and isolation that were so much a part of everyday life in early Virginia. Fortunately, a few personal documents have survived those miserable years, and they help us to understand the predicament of the first settlers. Most of these documents were written by leaders. But the one that follows was written by an indentured servant, Richard Frethorne, in 1623, to his parents in England. All we know of Frethorne is contained in this letter.

Loving and kind father and mother:

My most humble duty remembered to you, hoping in God of your good health, as I myself am at the making hereof. This is to let you understand that I your child am in a most heavy case by reason of the nature of the country, [which] is such that it causeth much sickness, [such] as the scurvy and the bloody flux and diverse other diseases, which maketh the body very poor and weak. And when we are sick there is nothing to comfort us; for since I came out of the ship I never ate anything but peas, and loblollie (that is, water gruel). As for deer or venison I never saw any since I came into this land. There is indeed

Richard Frethorne, Letter to his father and mother, March 20, April 2 and 3, 1623, in Susan M. Kingsbury, ed., *The Records of the Virginia Company of London,* IV, Government Printing Office, Washington, DC, 1935, pp. 58–62. Reprinted from Report of the Royal Commission on Historical Manuscripts, *Report on the Mss. of His Grace the Duke of Manchester,* London, 1881, VIII Report, Appendix II, pp. 40–41.

some fowl, but we are not allowed to go and get it, but must work hard both early and late for a mess of water gruel and a mouthful of bread and beef. A mouthful of bread for a penny loaf must serve for four men which is most piti- ful. [You would be grieved] if you did know as much as I [do], when people cry out day and night—Oh! that they were in England without their limbs—and would not care to lose any limb to be in England again, yea, though they beg from door to door. For we live in fear of the enemy every hour, yet we have had a combat with them on the Sunday before Shrovetide, and we took two alive and made slaves of them. But it was by policy, for we are in great danger; for our plantation is very weak by reason of the death and sickness of our company. For we came but twenty for the merchants, and they are half dead just; and we look every hour when two more should go. Yet there came some four other men yet to live with us, of which there is but one alive; and our Lieutenant is dead, and [also] his father and his brother. And there was some five or six of the late year's twenty, of which there is but three left, so that we are fain to get other men to plant with us; and yet we are but 32 to fight against 3000 if they should come. And the nighest help that we have is ten miles of us, and when the rogues over- came this place [the] last [time] they slew 80 persons. How then shall we do, for we lie even in their teeth? They may easily take us, but [for the fact] that God is merciful and can save with few as well as with many, as he showed to Gilead. And like Gilead's soldiers, if they lapped water, we drink water which is but weak.

And I have nothing to comfort me, nor is there nothing to be gotten here but sickness and death, except [in the event] that one had money to lay out in some things for profit. But I have nothing at all—no, not a shirt to my back but two rags (2), nor no clothes but one poor suit, nor but one pair of shoes, but one pair of stockings, but one cap, [and] but two bands. My cloak is stolen by one of my own fellows, and to his dying hour [he] would not tell me what he did with it; but some of my fellows saw him have butter and beef out of a ship, which my cloak, I doubt [not], paid for. So that I have not a penny, nor a penny worth, to help me to either spice or sugar or strong waters, without the which one cannot live here. For as strong beer in England doth fatten and strengthen them, so water here doth wash and weaken these here [and] only keeps [their] life and soul together. But I am not half [of] a quarter so strong as I was in England, and all is for want of victuals; for I do protest unto you that I have eaten more in [one] day at home than I have allowed me here for a week. You have given more than my day's allowance to a beggar at the door; and if Mr. Jackson had not re- lieved me, I should be in a poor case. But he like a father and she like a loving mother doth still help me.

For when we go to Jamestown (that is 10 miles of us) there lie all the ships that come to land, and there they must deliver their goods. And when we went up to town [we would go], as it may be, on Monday at noon, and come there by night, [and] then load the next day by noon, and go home in the afternoon, and unload, and then away again in the night, and [we would] be up about mid- night. Then if it rained or blowed never so hard, we must lie in the boat on the water and have nothing but a little bread. For when we go into the boat we [would] have a loaf allowed to two men, and it is all [we would get] if we stayed there two days, which is hard; and [we] must lie all that while in the boat. But that Goodman Jackson pitied me and made me a cabin to lie in always when I [would] come up, and he would give me some poor jacks [to take] home with me, which comforted me more than peas or water gruel. Oh, they be very godly folks, and love me very well, and will do anything for me. And he much marvelled that you would send me a servant to the Company; he saith I had been better knocked on the head. And indeed so I find it now, to my great grief and misery; and [I] saith that if you love me you will redeem me suddenly, for which I do entreat and beg. And if you cannot get the merchants to redeem me for some little money, then for God's sake get a gathering or entreat some good folks to lay out some little sum of money in meal and cheese and butter and beef. Any eating meat will yield great profit. Oil and vinegar is very good; but, father, there is great loss in leaking. But for God's sake send beef and cheese and butter, or the more of one sort and none of another. But if you send cheese, it must be very old cheese; and at the cheesemonger's you may buy very good cheese for twopence farthing or halfpenny, that will be liked very well. But if you send cheese, you must have a care how you pack it in barrels; and you must put cooper's chips between every cheese, or else the heat of the hold will rot them. And look whatsoever you send me—be it never so much—look, what[ever] I make of it, I will deal truly with you. I will send it over and beg the profit to redeem me; and if I die before it come, I have entreated Goodman Jackson to send you the worth of it, who hath promised he will. If you send, you must direct your letters to Goodman Jackson, at Jamestown, a gunsmith. (You must set down his freight, because there be more of his name there.) Good father, do not forget me, but have mercy and pity my miserable case. I know if you did but see me, you would weep to see me; for I have but one suit. (But [though] it is a strange one, it is very well guarded.) Wherefore, for God's sake, pity me. I pray you to remember my love to all my friends and kindred. I hope all my brothers and sisters are in good health, and as for my part I have set down my resolution that certainly will be; that is, that the answer of this letter will be life or death to me. Therefore, good father, send as soon as you can; and if you send me any thing let this be the mark.

ROT

Richard Frethorne,
Martin's Hundred

The names of them that be dead of the company [that] came over with us to serve under our Lieutenants:

John Flower	George Goulding
John Thomas	Jos. Johnson
Thos. Howes	our lieutenant, his father and brother
John Butcher	Thos. Giblin
John Sanderford	George Banum
Rich. Smith	a little Dutchman
John Olive	one woman
Thos. Peirsman	one maid
William Cerrell	one child

All these died out of my master's house, since I came; and we came in but at Christmas, and this is the 20th day of March. And the sailors say that there is two-thirds of the 150 dead already. And thus I end, praying to God to send me good success that I may be redeemed out of Egypt. So *vale in Christo.*

Loving father, I pray you to use this man very exceeding kindly, for he hath done much for me, both on my journey and since. I entreat you not to forget me, but by any means redeem me; for this day we hear that there is 26 of [the] Englishmen slain by the Indians. And they have taken a pinnace of Mr. Pountis, and have gotten pieces, armor, [and] swords, all things fit for war; so that they may now steal upon us and we cannot know them from [the] English till it is too late—[till the time] that they be upon us—and then there is no mercy. Therefore if you love or respect me as your child, release me from this bondage and save my life. Now you may save me, or let me be slain with infidels. Ask this man— he knoweth that all is true and just that I say here. If you do redeem me, the Company must send for me to my Mr. Harrod; for so is this Master's name. April, the second day.

Your loving son,
Richard Frethorne

Moreover, on the third day of April we heard that after these rogues had gotten the pinnace and had taken all furnitures [such] as pieces, swords, armor, coats of mail, powder, shot and all the things that they had to trade withal, they killed the Captain and cut off his head. And rowing with the tail of the boat foremost, they set up a pole and put the Captain's head upon it, and so rowed home. Then the Devil set them on again, so that they furnished about 200 canoes with above 1000 Indians, and came, and thought to have taken the ship; but she was too quick for them—which thing was very much talked of, for they always feared a ship. But now the rogues grow very bold and can use pieces, some of them, as well or better than an Englishman; for an Indian did shoot with Mr. Charles, my master's kinsman, at a mark of white paper, and he hit it at the first, but Mr. Charles could not hit it. But see the envy of these slaves, for when they could not take the ship, then our men saw them threaten Accomack, that is the next plantation. And now there is no way but starving; for the Governor told us and Sir George that except the *Seaflower* [should] come in or that we can fall foul of these rogues and get some corn from them, above half the land will surely be starved. For they had no crop last year by reason of these rogues, so that we have no corn but as ships do relieve us, nor we shall hardly have any crop this year; and we are as like to perish first as any plantation. For we have but two hogshead of meal left to serve us this two months, if the *Seaflower* do stay so long before she come in; and that meal is but three weeks bread for us, at a loaf for four [men] about the bigness of a penny loaf in England—that is but a halfpenny a day for a man. Is it not strange to me, think you? But what will it be when we shall go a month or two and never see a bit of bread, as my master doth say we must do? And he said he is not able to keep us all. Then we shall be turned up to the land

and eat barks of trees or molds of the ground; therefore with weeping tears I beg of you to help me. Oh, that you did see my daily and hourly sighs, groans, and tears, and [the] thumps that I afford mine own breast, and [the way I] rue and curse the time of my birth, with holy Job. I thought no head had been able to hold so much water as hath and doth daily flow from mine eyes.

But this is certain: I never felt the want of father and mother till now; but now, dear friends, full well I know and rue it, although it were too late before I knew it.

I pray you talk with this honest man. He will tell you more than now in my haste I can set down.

Your loving son,
Richard Frethorne

Virginia, 3rd April, 1623

CHAPTER 3

Puritan Order

The settling of Jamestown was proclaimed to be God's work, in which spreading the Gospel took precedence over everything else. But few Englishmen set off for Virginia to establish a holy community. The first to embark on such a venture were the Pilgrims, a small group of Puritan extremists who had separated from the Church of England on the grounds that the king's church was hopelessly corrupt. After a brief spell in Holland, they came to Plymouth in 1620 hoping to establish a Zion in the wilderness. Ten years later, a much larger and more affluent group of Puritans settled just north of the Pilgrims, in and around Boston. They too hoped to establish a holy commonwealth. In both the Pilgrim colony at Plymouth and the Puritan settlement in Massachusetts Bay order was a primary goal and value. The Puritans and Pilgrims both felt that they had escaped an England that was in decline. There, they believed, the poor, servants, children—the powerless in general—no longer felt bound to submit to authority. And those with power—the court and the nobility—had become hopelessly corrupt. New England was more than a new beginning, then. It was an attempt to recover something that had been lost in the old world. And recovery meant discipline, the sacrifice of individual interests to the community's paramount interest in order. To the leaders, discipline also meant the rounding off of individual beliefs to fit an agreed-upon consensus. At both Plymouth and Massachusetts Bay, there was a heavy preoccupation with compacts and covenants—agreements signed by the adult males who were heads of households, efforts to ward off dissent and disruption.

Despite their compacts and covenants, both groups had trouble with internal dissension. One of the ironies of Puritanism—with Protestantism generally—was its tendency to split into warring factions. Puritans never abandoned the ideal of establishing a single universal church. But the Bible—their sole source of authority—was subject to various interpretations. Truths that seemed self-evident to one Puritan did not seem so to others who were equally eager to find the true path to salvation. Ministers denounced one another for teaching false doctrine. Congregations split into bickering cliques. And community leaders constantly had to worry about firebrands such as Roger Williams and Anne Hutchinson who challenged established norms.

To overcome disunity, and to establish a godly community in an ungodly world, Puritans relied not only on deep religious faith but also on such basic social institutions as the family. Early Virginia was settled mainly by bachelors. New England Puritans would not even permit single persons to live as bachelors. Puritan New England was settled by families, and all single persons had to live within a family. Outside the family, so Puritans believed, ungodliness and anarchism were sure to gain the upper hand. In turn, all families had to live within a specified distance of the church, which was seen as the larger family to which all individual families were subordinate.

INTERPRETIVE ESSAY

Laurel Thatcher Ulrich

Deputy Husbands

In the following selection, Professor Laurel Thatcher Ulrich, a historian at the University of New Hampshire, examines the role of women in Puritan New England. Puritan society was male-dominated and father-oriented. But Ulrich finds that in everyday life women were regarded as fully capable of handling male duties, and were expected to do so if it furthered the good of their families and was acceptable to their husbands. As you read, think about the way Puritans dealt with questions of sex differentiation. Were they basically rigid or flexible? Do you see any contradictions? Think also about how the Puritan family may have been a model of the problem of the larger society: how to keep order and still allow a measure of "Christian liberty" to all participants.

Many historians have assumed, with Page Smith, that "it was not until the end of the colonial era that the idea of a 'suitable' or 'proper' sphere of feminine activities began to emerge." For fifty years historians have relied upon the work of Elizabeth A. Dexter, who claimed that there were more "women of affairs" proportionally in eighteenth-century America than in 1900. Colonial newspapers yield evidence of female blacksmiths, silversmiths, tinworkers, shoemakers, shipwrights, tanners, gunsmiths, barbers, printers, and butchers, as well as a great many teachers and shopkeepers. Partly on the basis of such evidence, Richard Morris concluded in his pioneering study of female legal rights that American women in the colonial period attained "a measure of individuality and independence in excess of that of their English sisters."

Recently, however, a few historians have begun to question these assumptions. Mary Beth Norton has carefully studied the claims of 468 loyalist women who were refugees in Great Britain after the American Revolution. Only forty-three of these women mentioned earning money on their own or even assisting directly in their husbands' business. As a group, the loyalist women were unable to describe their family assets, other than household possessions, and they repeatedly described themselves as "helpless" to manage the business thrust upon them. She has concluded that these women were "almost wholly domestic, in the sense that that word would be used in the nineteenth-century United States." In a study of widowhood in eighteenth-century Massachusetts, Alexander Keyssar came to similar conclusions. Economic dependency, first upon husbands, then upon grown sons, characterized the lives of women in the agricultural village of Woburn.

From Laurel Thatcher Ulrich, *Good Wives: Images and Reality in the Lives of Women in Northern New England, 1650–1750*, Alfred A. Knopf, Inc., New York, 1982, pp. 35–50. Copyright © 1980, 1982 by Laurel Thatcher Ulrich. Reprinted by permission of Alfred A. Knopf, Inc.

Both groups of historians are right. The premodern world did allow for greater fluidity of role behavior than in nineteenth-century America, but colonial women were by definition basically domestic. We can account for these apparently contradictory conclusions by focusing more closely upon the economic relationship of husband and wife. There is a revealing little anecdote in a deposition recorded in Essex County in 1672. Jacob Barney of Salem had gone to Phillip Cromwell's house to negotiate a marriage. Although both Cromwell and his wife were present, Barney had turned to the husband, expecting, as he said, "to have their minds from him." But because Cromwell had a severe cold, which had impaired his hearing, he simply pointed to his wife and said that whatever she agreed upon, "he would make it good." This incident dramatizes three assumptions basic to family government in the traditional world:

1. The husband was supreme in the external affairs of the family. As its titular head, he had both the right and the responsibility to represent it in its dealings with the outside world.
2. A husband's decisions would, however, incorporate his wife's opinions and interest. (Barney expected to hear *their* minds from *him*.)
3. Should fate or circumstance prevent the husband from fulfilling his role, the wife could appropriately stand in his place. As one seventeenth-century Englishman explained it, a woman "in her husband's absence, is wife and deputy-husband, which makes her double the files of her diligence. At his return he finds all things so well he wonders to see himself at home when he was abroad."

To put it simply, Dexter's evidence points to what was permissible in colonial society, Norton's to what was probable. As deputy husbands a few women, like Mistress Cromwell, might emerge from anonymity; most women did not. Yet both sets of evidence must be analyzed apart from modern assumptions about the importance of access to jobs in expanding female opportunity. The significance of the role of deputy husband cannot be determined by counting the number of women who used it to achieve independence. To talk about the independence of colonial wives is not only an anachronism but a contradiction in logic. A woman became a wife by virtue of her dependence, her solemnly vowed commitment to her husband. No matter how colorful the exceptions, land and livelihood in this society were normally transmitted from father to son, as studies like Keyssar's have shown.

One can be dependent, however, without being either servile or helpless. To use an imperfect but nonetheless suggestive analogy, colonial wives were dependent upon patriarchal families in somewhat the same way seventeenth-century ministers were dependent upon their congregations or twentieth-century engineers are dependent upon their companies. That is, they owned neither their place of employment nor even the tools of their trade. No matter how diligently they worked, they did not expect to inherit the land upon which they lived any more than a minister expected to inherit his meetinghouse or an engineer his factory. Skilled service was their major contribution, secure support their primary compensation. Unlike professionals in either century, they could not resign their position, but then neither could they be fired. Upon the death of a husband they were entitled to maintenance for life—or until they transferred their allegiance (symbolized by their name) from one domestic establishment to another.

The skilled service of a wife included the specialized housekeeping skills described in the last chapter, but it also embraced the responsibilities of a deputy husband. Since most productive work was based within the family, there were many opportunities for a wife to "double the files of her diligence." A weaver's wife, like Beatrice Plummer, might wind quills. A merchant's wife, like Hannah Grafton, might keep shop. A farmer's wife, like Magdalen Wear, might plant corn.

Looking backward to the colonial period from the nineteenth century, when "true womanhood" precluded either business enterprise or hard physical labor, historians may miss the significance of such work, which tells us less about economic opportunity (which for most women was limited) than about female responsibility (which was often very broad). Most occupations were indeed gender-linked, yet colonial Englishmen were far less concerned with abstract notions like "femininity" than with concrete roles like "wife" or "neighbor." Almost any task was suitable for a woman as long as it furthered the good of her family and was acceptable to her husband. This approach was both fluid and fixed. It allowed for varied behavior without really challenging the patriarchal order of society. There was no proscription against female farming, for example, but there were strong prescriptions toward dutiful wifehood and motherhood. Context was everything.

In discussing the ability of colonial women to take on male duties, most historians have assumed a restrictive ideology in Anglo-American society, an essentially negative valuation of female capacity. Some historians have argued that this negative ideology was offset by the realities of colonial life; others have concluded it was not. This chapter reverses the base of the argument, suggesting that even in America ideology was more permissive than reality. Under the right conditions any wife not only *could* double as a husband, she had the responsibility to do so. In the probate courts, for example, widows who did not have grown sons were routinely granted administration of their husbands' estates. Gender restrictions were structural rather than psychological. Although there was no female line of inheritance, wives were presumed capable of husbanding property which male heirs would eventually inherit.

To explain fully the contradictions in such a system, we must return to the day-to-day behavior of individual husbands and wives, first examining the factors that enhanced the role of deputy husband and then exploring conditions that muted its significance for colonial women.

Historians can read wills, account books, and tax records, documents in which males clearly predominate, but they cannot so easily explore the complex decision-making behind these records. Scattered glimpses of daily interaction suggest that there was as much variation in seventeenth- and eighteenth-century families as there is today. Some wives were servile, some were shrews, others were respected companions who shared the authority of their spouses in the management of family affairs. Important conditions, however, separated the colonial world from our own. The most basic of these was spatial. Earlier we described an imaginary boundary stretching from house to yard, separating the domain of the housewife from the world of her husband. It is important to recognize that in reality no such barrier existed. Male and female space intersected and overlapped. Nor was there the sharp division between home and work that later generations experienced. Because servants and apprentices lived within the household, a family occasion—mealtime or nightly prayer—could become a business occasion as well.

In June 1661 a young maid named Naomi Hull described a discussion that took place in the parlor of the Samuel Symonds's home in Ipswich, Massachusetts, early in that year. The case concerned the length of indenture of two Irish servants. According to the maid, all of the family had gathered for prayer when one of the Irishmen asked if a neighbor's son was coming the next day to plow. *Mistress* Symonds said she thought so. One of the men asked who would plow with him. *Mistress* Symonds said, "One of you." When the two men announced that their indenture was up and that they would work no longer, both the master and the mistress questioned the servants. At one point Mistress Symonds interrupted her husband. "Let them alone," she said. "Now they are speaking let them speak their own minds." Because the involvement of Mistress Symonds was not at issue, this casual description of her participation is all the more impressive. Such an anecdote shows the way in which boundaries between male and female domains might blur in a common household setting.

Ambitious men in early America were often involved in many things at once—farming and running a gristmill, for example, or cutting timber and fishing. Because wives remained close to the house, they were often at the communications center of these diverse operations, given responsibility for conveying directions, pacifying creditors, and perhaps even making some decisions about the disposition of labor. On a day-to-day basis this might be a rather simple matter: remembering to send a servant to repair a breach in the dam after he finished in the field, for example, or knowing when to relinquish an ox to a neighbor. But during a prolonged absence of her husband a woman might become involved in more weighty matters.

Sometime in the 1670s Moses Gilman of Exeter, New Hampshire, wrote to his wife from Boston:

> Loving wife Elisabeth Gillman these are to desire you to speake to John Gillman & James Perkins and so order the matter thatt Mr. Tho. Woodbridge may have Twelve thousand fott of merchantable boards Rafted by thirsday night or sooner is poseble they Can for I have Absolutly sould them to him & if John Clough sen or any other doe deliver bords to make up the sum Give Receits of whatt you Receive of him or any other man and lett no bote bee prest or other ways disposed of untill I Returne being from Him who is yos till death
>
> Moses Gilman

If Gilman had doubted his wife's ability to "order the matter," he could have written a number of separate letters—to John Gilman, James Perkins, John Clough, and perhaps others. But securing a shipment of twelve thousand feet of merchantable boards entirely by letter would have been complicated and time-consuming. Instead, Gilman relied on the good sense of his wife, who would be respected as his surrogate, and who probably had acquired some expertise in making out receipts for forest products and in conveying instructions to lumbering and shipping crews. A "loving wife" who considered herself his "till Death" was more trustworthy than a hired servant or business associate. As a true consort, she would know that by furthering her husband's interest she furthered her own.

Thus, a wife with talent for business might become a kind of double for her husband, greatly extending his ability to handle affairs. This is beautifully illustrated in a document filed with the New Hampshire court papers. In February 1674 Peter Lidget of Boston signed a paper giving Henry Dering of Piscataqua full power of attorney "to collect all debts due to him in that place and thereabout." On the reverse side of the document Dering wrote: "I Henry Dering have, and do hereby Constitute, ordaine, and appoint my loveing wife, Anne Dering my Lawful Attourney" to collect and sue for Peter Lidget's debts "by virtue of the Letter of Attourney on the other side." (Anne Dering was the widow of Ralph Benning of Boston. She left her married name—and perhaps some of her business accumen—to her great-grandson, Governor Benning Wentworth of New Hampshire.)

Court cases involving fishermen give some glimpses of the kinds of responsibility assumed by their wives, who often appear in the foreground as well as the background of the documents. Depositions in an action of 1660 reveal Anne Devorix working alongside her husband, "taking account" as a servant culled fish from a spring voyage. She herself delivered a receipt from the master of the ship to the shop where the final "reckoning" was made. When her husband was at sea, she supervised spring planting on the family corn land as well as protecting the hogsheads, barrels, and flakes at the shore from the incursions of a quarrelsome neighbor. Even more visible in the records is Edith Creford of Salem, who frequently acted as an attorney for her husband, at one point signing a promissory note for £33 in "merchantable cod fish at price current." Like the fishwives of Nantucket whom Crèvecoeur described a hundred years later, these women were "necessarily obliged to transact business, to settle accounts, and in short, to rule and provide for their families."

At a different social level the wives of merchant sea captains played a similar role. Sometime in the year 1710 Elizabeth Holmes of Boston sat down with Patience Marston of Salem and settled accounts accumulated during a voyage to Newfoundland. Neither woman had been on the ship. They were simply acting as attorneys for their husbands, Captain Robert Holmes, who had commanded the brigantine, and Mr. Benjamin Marston, who owned it. Family letters give a more detailed picture of Mistress Marston's involvement in her husband's business.

In the summer of 1719 Benjamin Marston took command of one of his own

ships, taking his twenty-two-year-old son Benjamin with him. Young Benjamin
wrote his mother complete details of the first stage of the journey, which ended
at Casco Bay in Maine. He included the length of the journey, the state of the
family enterprises in Maine, and the price of lumber and staves, adding that he
was "Sorry you should sett so long in ye house for no Adv[ance] but perhaps to
ye prejudice of your health." Patience was obviously "keeping shop." A week
later Benjamin wrote again, assuring his mother that he was looking after the
business in Maine. "My father w[oul]d have been imposed upon by m———c
had I not interposed and stood stiffly to him," he explained. Was the son acting
out some Oedipal fantasy here, or was he perhaps performing as his *mother's*
surrogate, strengthening the resolve of the presumably more easygoing father?
The next day he wrote still another letter, asking for chocolate, complaining boy-
ishly that "ye Musketo's bitt me so prodigiously as I was writing that I can
hardly tell what it was I wrote," and conveying what must by then have been a
common request from the absent husband. Mrs. Marston was to get a witnessed
statement regarding a piece of family business and send it by "the first Oppertunity."

Because the business activities of wives were under the "wing, protection,
and cover" of a husband (to repeat Blackstone's phrase), they are difficult to
measure by standard methods. Patience Marston was a custodian of messages,
guardian of errands, preserver of property, and keeper of accounts. Yet without
the accidental survival of a few family papers there would be no way of knowing about her involvement in her husband's business. In Benjamin's will she received the standard "thirds." She may have become impatient with her chores
or anxious about her husband's business acumen, but there is no indication of
this in the only writings preserved in her hand. She served as "deputy husband"
as circumstances demanded, and when her husband perished from smallpox
soon after arriving in Ireland, she declared herself grateful for the dear son who
returned "as one from the dead" to take over his father's business.

The role of deputy husband deserves more careful and systematic study.
But two cautions are in order. First, the biases of the twentieth century may
tempt historians to give undue significance to what were really rather periph-
eral enterprises. Acting as attorney to one's husband is not equivalent to practicing law. To colonial women, it may even have been less desirable than keeping house. This leads to the second point. The value of any activity is
determined by its meaning to the participant, not to the observer. In early America position was always more important than task. Colonial women might appear to be independent, even aggressive, by modern standards, yet still have derived their status primarily from their relationship to their husbands.

This is well illustrated in a New Hampshire court record of 1671. A carpenter named John Barsham testified about an argument he had heard between
Henry Sherburne and his second wife, Sarah, who was the widow of Walter Abbott. Barsham had come to the house to get some nails he needed for repairing
a dwelling he had rented from them. According to Barsham, Sarah became so
angry at her husband's opposition that she "rose off from the seat where she was
setting & came up to him with her arms akimbo saying we should have nayles

& he had nothing to [do] in it." As if to add the final authority to her demand, she asked him "why he trode upon Walter Abbotts floor & bid him get out of doors, & said that he had nothing to do there." Sarah Sherburne was an experienced and assertive woman. She had kept tavern "with two husbands and none." The house in which she and Sherburne lived had been part of her inheritance from her first husband. But in the heat of the argument she did not say, "Get out of *my* house" or "Get out of the house *I* provided." She said, "Get out of Walter Abbott's house." Her identity was not as property owner, but as wife. To assert her authority over her husband, she invoked the memory of his predecessor.

For some women, the realities of daily life in coastal New England enhanced the role of deputy husband. For others, discrepancies in education as well as the on-again-off-again nature of the role made involvement in the family business just another chore. A woman who worked effectively as an assistant, especially with the authority of a living husband behind her, could still be insecure in handling complex business arrangements. Finally (and perhaps the most important point of all), most women had other things to do. A closer examination of female economic life suggests not only separate education and separate duties but separate lines of trade.

Selectman's indentures from mid-eighteenth-century Newbury show the contrasting training offered boys and girls at the lowest end of the social spectrum in a commercial town. Between 1743 and 1760 the selectman indentured sixty children of the town poor. Forty-nine of these were boys, who were apprenticed to blacksmiths, shipwrights, cordwainers, coopers, weavers, tanners, tailors, joiners, blockmakers, riggers, mastmakers, and even a perriwig-maker in the town. The eleven girls, on the other hand, were promised instruction in the generalized skills of "housewifery" or "women's work," though occasionally spinning, carding, sewing, and knitting were also specified. Often the phrase "Art, Trade, or Mystery" on these printed forms was crossed out in the girls' indentures. All of the children were assured instruction in reading, but only the boys were to learn "to write a Ledgable hand & cypher as far as the Gouldin Rule" or "to write & Cypher as far as ye Rule of three or so far as to keep a Tradesmans Book."

That more than four times as many boys as girls were apprenticed suggests that the support of poor girls was usually handled in some other way. Either they remained with their families or were placed as day workers or maids on a less formal basis among the housewives of the town. The crossed-out passages in the indentures highlight the anomalous position of these female apprentices. Clearly, the training of artisans and the training of their wives were two separate processes belonging to two separate systems. A female might learn the mysteries of blacksmithing or tanning—but only informally, by working as a helper to the men in her family. Predictably, in the region as a whole, women lagged far behind men in their ability to write, a discrepancy that actually increased over the eighteenth century.

What this meant in the daily lives of ordinary women is suggested by extant account books from the period. Although many such books survive, in the entire century between 1650 and 1750 there is not a single one known to have been kept by a woman. Purchasing an account book was a significant step for a farmer or village craftsman. A Topsfield weaver recognized this when he wrote in the inside of his new book, "John Gould his Book of accounts I say my Book my owne book and I gave one shillin and four pence for it so much and no more." Books like Gould's fall somewhere between the systematic, literate, merchant-oriented economy that came to dominate the external trade of New England and the local, personal, largely oral trade networks that were central to village life. As deputy husbands a few women might participate in the former, but for most wives economic life was centered in the latter.

Something of the range of bookkeeping methods employed in colonial America is preserved in an anonymous account book from Portsmouth, New Hampshire. One segment of this record was kept in the unformed scrawl typical of ordinary craftsmen and farmers; another was neatly posted in the hand of a professional clerk. But evidence of a third and quite different method is preserved in entries for a laborer named Richard Trip, who traded work in the "gundalow" (a Piscataqua sailing vessel) for "75 meals of victualls" and "75 nights of lodging brot from the acco[un]t kept in chaulk on the wall." The wife of the unknown shopkeeper may have been responsible for the chalk account as well as for providing the "diet," "washing," and "mittins" recorded in Trip's debits. For this sort of bookkeeping she had no need for "cyphering."

Judging only from the account books, one might conclude that most married women were seldom involved in trade even on the village level. Yet account books represent but one strand of the village economy. Other sources point to an extensive, less systematic, and largely oral trade network in which women predominated. A court case of 1682 provides an interesting example. When a woman named Grace Stout appeared to answer several charges of theft, the witnesses against her included thirty-four persons, among them twenty-one housewives who were able to give precise accounts of the value of work performed or goods received. These were petty transactions—kneading bread for one woman, purchasing stockings knitted by another—not the sort of thing to turn up in a colonial trade balance but nevertheless an essential part of the fabric of economic life.

The account books themselves give negative evidence of a separate female network. Although most ledgers include a few female names, the great majority of written accounts are with men, with credits reflecting the dominant commodities in each community. Ipswich farmers traded grain, farm labor, and animal products for shoes, weaving, rum, tobacco, skillets, and cotton wool. Householders from Marblehead paid for the same items in cash and fish, while those from Exeter usually offered pine, oak, and hemlock boards as well as labor. Entries for the products of female craft are infrequent; most sustained accounts for butter, cheese, sewing, or spinning are listed under the names of widows. This pattern is especially striking in the few accounts that shift from the name of a husband to the name of his widow. Thomas Bartlett, a Newbury shoemaker, listed twenty-one entries under the name of Ephraim Blesdel from

March 13, 1725, until October 16, 1730. Until the middle of July 1728 the credits included hides, cider, onions, codfish, veal, and cash. But on that date Bartlett reckoned with "the widow Debrath Blesdel." Nine of the twelve credits that follow are for spinning. There is pathos in a second series recorded in Bartlett's book. From November 1729 until September 1733 he listed twenty-seven debits under John Wood's name, all for making and mending shoes. The credits already included some spinning as well as cash and skins when, on June 8, 1732, he noted in a taciturn entry: "husbands shoes sent back." From that point on, the account was with "Widow Anne Wood," who now attempted to pay for her shoes in dried sage from her garden and in additional spinning.

Anne Wood was probably trading small amounts of sage long before her husband's death. The accumulation of minor transactions that composed female trade could become substantial without ever appearing in written accounts. Suggestive evidence of this appears in the account book of Thomas Chute, a tailor from Marblehead, Massachusetts, who became one of the first settlers of New Marblehead in frontier Maine. In May 1737 Chute reckoned with Joseph Griffin of Marblehead, matching his own charges for tailoring against £8 debited in Griffin's book, finally balancing the whole with £4 pending, "By you[r] wives accoumpt with mine." A similar entry appears forty years later, in 1766, when he added to a £25 total accumulated by John Farrow of New Marblehead the sum of £3 "by yr wifes & mine acoumpts." For the most part, the trade of Thomas Chute and the trade of his wife were harmoniously separate.

Informal, oral, local, petty—female enterprise appears as the merest flicker on the surface of male documents. That it existed seems clear enough. The problem is in determining its value to the participants.

Potentially at least, managing a female specialty might be even more attractive than simply helping in a husband's work. An Ipswich woman known in the records only as Mistress Hewlett became so successful in the poultry business that she was able to loan money to her husband. When a friend expressed surprise at this arrangement, arguing that the wife's income really belonged to him if he needed it, Ensign Hewlett replied, "I meddle not with the geese nor the turkeys for they are hers for she has been and is a good wife to me." To the neighbor, loaning money to one's spouse was contradictory, an assertion of individual rather than communal values. But to Hewlett, no such threat was implied. His wife had "been a good wife." As long as independent female trade remained a minor theme within a larger communal ethic, it did not threaten either male supremacy or the economic unity of the family.

Yet consider the case of Mary Hunt of Portsmouth. Her encounter with Samuel Clark suggests both the opportunities and the limitations of female trade. When she found a cheese missing from her house after the fast day in October 1675, she suspected Clark, who was a near neighbor. Storming into his house, she opened a drawer. There between two pieces of biscuit was the evidence she needed, an uneaten morsel notched, as she later testified, "with the very same marke which I put upon my best cheeses." Mary Hunt's accusation was brash, for Clark had once served on a jury that convicted her of stealing from the prominent Cutt family when she lived with them as a maidservant.

Her new status as a housewife and as a cheese dealer had obviously given her a sense of power as well as an opportunity for revenge.

The story does not end there, however. A marked cheese does not have the durability of a marked tankard or clock. Unfortunately, Mary Hunt's cheese did not make it to court in November, much less into the stream of physical artifacts from which we derive our understanding of a culture. Clark's servant apparently swallowed the evidence. Though Hunt won her case in the fall, Clark successfully appealed in June, standing on his dignity as a man never before suspected of "any crime much less so base a crime as theft and for so sorry a matter as cheese." Part of his long—and professionally inscribed—defense was a counter-accusation: it was well known in the neighborhood, he said, that Goody Hunt sold her products to "one and another" and was apt to do so without her husband's knowledge, crying theft if called to reckon.

Clearly, the informal nature of female trade might work to the advantage of a woman who wanted a little extra income independent of her husband, yet ultimately the economic power of any woman was inseparable from her larger responsibility as wife. The role of housewife and the role of deputy husband were two sides of the same coin. Whether trading cheese or shipping barrel staves, a good wife sustained and supported the family economy and demonstrated her loyalty to her husband.

In the absence of a husband, the same skills might prove inadequate to independence. An anonymous document in the Essex Institute at Salem, Massachusetts, reveals the chasm which might develop between "female trade" and "male business." The unknown author of this little treatise had been accused of fraudulently securing a deed from an aged widow. In his defense he methodically itemized the charges against him, then answered each in turn. Two are of particular interest here—first, that the woman knew but little of the "common commerce of life," and, second, that she was unable to form a "just idea" of what belonged to her or its value. The man answered the first charge with a flat denial: "I nor no other Person In this Neaborrhood I donte believe Ever heard of her not knowing how for to Trade."

But he at least partly acknowledged the second:

> How could she or any other Person forme any just Idia of what they are worth when it is Eveadent that Part of it was In Another Persons hands . . . and She Not Knowing how for to Right so as for to keep my Acc[ount] nor she could not Read Righting nor she could not Chipher so as for to Cast up my Acc[ount].

These two statements summarize much of what we have said here. A talent for trade was one thing; the ability to handle complex business affairs was another. Although northern New England produced many Elizabeth Gilmans and Edith Crefords, women who successfully handled business in the absence of their husbands, it probably produced even more women like this anonymous widow of Salem. In her years as a housewife she had acquired considerable skill in the "common commerce of life" but little that would prepare her to deal with a sophisticated and aggressive assault on her property, especially when legal documents were involved. No longer able to rely upon a spouse or a son, she had truly become a "relict."

In February 1757 Mary Russell of Concord, Massachusetts, wrote a letter to her brother-in-law Samuel Curwen of Salem in which she joked, "I should have answered Your letter long before this had I known when we were to come to Boston but you know I am a Femme Covert and cannot act for my self." Her wit betrays a deeper feeling—if not yet a *feminist* sense of injustice, certainly a quite consciously *feminine* annoyance at the officious pedantry of the law, at least as it was discussed in her own parlor. Mary Russell knew that the restrictions of the common law had little relationship to the ordinary decisions of her daily life. Within her own domain she acted confidently and independently.

Yet the predicament that she described in jest became a reality for at least some women in the course of the eighteenth century as both business and law became increasingly sophisticated. The loyalist widows whom Mary Beth Norton described were in this position. Without their husbands or the familiar surroundings of home, they were forced to deal with the complexities of an English court. Little wonder that they declared themselves "helpless."

Norton's more recent work has shown, however, that the American Revolution affected many patriot women in a strikingly different way. At first reluctantly and then with increasing confidence and skill, these wives took up the management of farms and businesses while their husbands were away at war. Norton believes that the war had dissolved traditional boundaries, altering a "line between male and female behavior, once apparently so impenetrable." Our evidence from early New England suggests a quite different conclusion. If there was an "impenetrable" gender barrier in mid-eighteenth-century America, it was a new one. The avowed helplessness of the loyalist women may be a measure of increasing specialization in economic life just before the revolution. The competence of the patriot women is even clearer evidence of the persistence of the old role of deputy husband. That patriot women failed to establish permanent changes in female roles is hardly surprising, since they acted within rather than against traditional gender definitions.

The economic roles of married women were based upon two potentially conflicting values—gender specialization and identity of interest. A wife was expected to become expert in the management of a household and the care of children, but she was also asked to assist in the economic affairs of her husband, becoming his representative and even his surrogate if circumstances demanded it. These two roles were compatible in the premodern world because the home was the communication center of family enterprise if not always the actual place of work. As long as business transactions remained personal and a woman had the support of a familiar environment, she could move rather easily from the role of housewife to the role of deputy husband, though few women were prepared either by education or by experience to become "independent women of affairs."

The role of deputy husband reinforced a certain elasticity in premodern notions of gender. No mystique of feminine behavior prevented a woman from driving a hard bargain or chasing a pig from the field, and under ideal conditions day-to-day experience in assisting with a husband's work might prepare her to function competently in a male world—should she lose her husband, should she find herself without a grown son, should she choose not to remarry or find it impossible to do so. But in the immediate world such activities could have a far different meaning. The chores assigned might be menial, even onerous, and, whatever their nature, they competed for attention with the specialized housekeeping responsibilities that every woman shared.

SOURCES

New England Primer, 1690

Puritan New England may have been the most literate community in the world. The ability to read was essential to these Protestant reformers. Even more than other Protestants, they were committed to the idea of the "priesthood of all believers"—the notion that the individual church member had to understand God's truth as well as any priest. The ability to read the Bible was the most important key to this possibility. Therefore, the Puritans tried to make sure that their children learned to read by requiring each town to maintain a public school, long before any European country had such an educational system. One of the first books published in the English-speaking colonies was a reading book for children, the New England Primer *(1690). In format it was an alphabet book. But it was also a way of teaching morality and religion. How do the ideas presented in this alphabet book resemble those discussed in Ulrich's essay? Can you detect any differences between these ideas and the attitudes of the Virginia settlers discussed by Morgan in the preceding chapter?*

American Antiquarian Society.

(14)
N.
NOAH did view
The old World and new.

O.
Young OBADIAS,
David, Josias,
All were pious.

P.
PETER deny'd
His Lord, and cry'd.

Q.
Queen ESTHER sues,
And saves the Jews.

R.
Young pious RUTH
Left all for Truth.

S.
Young SAMUEL dear,
The Lord did fear.

(15)
T.
Young TIMOTHY
Learnt Sin to fly,

V.
VASHTI for Pride,
Was set aside.

W.
WHALES in the Sea,
God's Voice obey.

X.
XERXES did die,
And so must I.

Y.
While YOUTH do cheer
Death may be near.

Z.
ZACCHEUS he
Did climb the Tree,
Our Lord to see.

Harvard, 1636–1642

The New England colonists not only wanted to make certain that all the members of their society could read. They also wanted a supply of learned ministers. And they knew they could not count on the English universities to give them the preachers they needed. In 1636, very shortly after the first large migration to Massachusetts Bay, the colony founded a college, Harvard, to train its ministers. The following documents will give you considerable insight into the reasons why the college was created, its rules, and its program of study. How do the ideas that guided the college match up with the kinds of attitudes discussed in Ulrich's essay? Or do they coincide at all? How would you compare this educational system to the one you have experienced? Many differences are obvious, but are there any continuities and similarities? What does the administration of the college tell you about the relationship of church and state in Massachusetts?

After God had carried us safe to New England, and we had builded our houses, provided necessaries for our livelihood, reared convenient places for God's worship, and settled the civil government, one of the next things we longed for, and looked after, was to advance learning and perpetuate it to posterity, dreading to leave an illiterate ministry to the churches when our present ministers shall lie in the dust. And as we were thinking and consulting how to effect this great work, it pleased God to stir up the heart of one Mr. Harvard (a godly gen-

From "New England's First Fruits," London, 1643, in *Sabin's Reprints*, New York, 1865, Quarto Series, no. vii.

tleman and a lover of learning, there living amongst us) to give the one half of his estate (it being in all about 1700 £) towards the erecting of a College, and all his library. After him another gave 300 £, others after them cast in more, and the public hand of the state added the rest. The College was, by common consent, appointed to be at Cambridge (a place very pleasant and accommodate), and is called (according to the name of the first founder) Harvard College.

The edifice is very fair and comely within and without, having in it a spacious hall (where they daily meet at commons, lectures, [and] exercises), and a large library with some books to it, the gifts of divers of our friends, their chambers and studies also fitted for and possessed by the students, and all other rooms of office necessary and convenient, with all needful offices thereto belonging. And by the side of the College a fair grammar school, for the training up of young scholars, and fitting of them for academical learning, that still, as they are judged ripe, they may be received into the College of this school; Master Corlet is the master, who hath very well approved himself for his abilities, dexterity, and painfulness in teaching and education of the youth under him.

Over the College is Master Dunster placed, as President, a learned, conscionable, and industrious man, who hath so trained up his pupils in the tongues and arts, and so seasoned them with the principles of Divinity and Christianity, that we have to our great comfort, (and in truth) beyond our hopes, beheld their progress in learning and godliness also.* The former of these hath appeared in their public declamations in Latin and Greek, and disputations logical and philosophical which they have been wonted (besides their ordinary exercises in the college hall) in the audience of the magistrates, ministers, and other scholars, for the probation of their growth in learning, upon set days, constantly once every month to make and uphold. The latter hath been manifested in sundry of them by the savory breathings of their spirits in their godly conversation. Insomuch that we are confident, if these early blossoms may be cherished and warmed with the influence of the friends of learning and lovers of this pious work, they will by the help of God come to happy maturity in a short time.

Over the College are twelve Overseers chosen by the General Court. Six of them are of the magistrates, the other six of the ministers, who are to promote the best good of it and (having a power of influence into all persons in it) are to see that every one be diligent and proficient in his proper place.

Rules and Precepts that are observed in the College

1. When any scholar is able to understand Tully, or such like classical Latin author *extempore*, and make and speak true Latin in verse and prose . . . and decline perfectly the paradigms of nouns and verbs in the Greek tongue, let him then and not before be capable of admission into the College.

*Henry Dunster (1609–1658/59), the first president of Harvard, was forced to resign in 1654 because of his heretical beliefs regarding the efficacy of infant baptism although he was a satisfactory president in all other respects.

2. Let every student be plainly instructed and earnestly pressed to consider well [that] the main end of his life and studies is *to know God and Jesus Christ which is eternal life,* John 17:3, and therefore to lay Christ in the bottom, as the only foundation of all sound knowledge and learning. And seeing the Lord only giveth wisdom, let everyone seriously set himself by prayer in secret to seek it of him . . .

3. Everyone shall so exercise himself in reading the Scriptures twice a day that he shall be ready to give such an account of his proficiency therein, both in theoretical observations of the language and logic, and in practical and spiritual truths, as his tutor shall require, according to his ability . . .

4. That they, eschewing all profanation of God's name, attributes, word, ordinances, and times of worship, do study with good conscience carefully to retain God and the love of His truth in their minds, else let them know that (notwithstanding their learning) God may give them up to strong delusions, and in the end to a reprobate mind . . .

5. That they studiously redeem the time: observe the general hours appointed for all the students, and the special hours for their own classes, and then diligently attend the lectures without any disturbance by word or gesture. And if in anything they doubt, they shall inquire, as of their fellows, so (in case of *non satisfaction*), modestly of their tutors.

6. None shall, under any pretence whatsoever, frequent the company and society of such men as lead an unfit and dissolute life. Nor shall any without his tutors leave, or (in his absence) the call or parents of guardians, go abroad to other towns.

7. Every scholar shall be present in his tutor's chamber at the seventh hour in the morning, immediately after the sound of the bell, at his opening the Scripture and prayer; so also at the fifth hour at night, and then give account of his own private reading, as aforesaid in particular the third, and constantly attend lectures in the hall at the hours appointed. But if any (without necessary impediment) shall absent himself from prayer or lectures, he shall be liable to admonition, if he offend above once a week.

8. If any scholar shall be found to transgress any of the laws of God, or the school, after twice admonition, he shall be liable, if not *adultus*, to correction; if *adultus*, his name shall be given up to the Overseers of the College, that he be admonished at the public monthly act.

The times and order of their studies, unless experience shall show cause to alter:

[1.] The second and third day of the week, read lectures as followeth:
To the first year at eight of the clock in the morning Logic the first three quarters, Physics the last quarter.

To the second year, at the ninth hour, Ethics and Politics at convenient distances of time.

To the third year at the tenth [hour] Arithmetic and Geometry the three first quarters, Astronomy the last.

Afternoon   The first year disputes at the second hour.
The second year at the third hour.
The third year at the fourth, everyone in his Art.
[2.] The fourth day read Greek.
To the first year the Etymology and Syntax at the eighth hour.
To the second at the ninth hour, Prosodia and Dialects.

Afternoon   The first year at second hour practice the precepts of Grammar in such authors as have a variety of words.

The second year at third hour practice in Poesy, Nonnus, Duport, or the like.

The third year perfect their Theory before noon, and exercise Style, Composition, Imitation, Epitome, both in Prose and Verse, afternoon.

[3.] The fifth day read Hebrew and the Eastern Tongues.
Grammar to the first year hour the eighth.
To the second, Chaldee at the ninth hour.
To the third, Syriac at the tenth hour.

Afternoon   The first year practice in the *Bible* at the second hour.
The second in Ezra and Daniel at the third hour.
The third at the fourth hour in Trostius's New Testament.
[4.] The sixth day read Rhetoric to all at the eighth hour.
Declamations at the ninth. So ordered that every scholar may declaim once a month. The rest of the day [free from studies].
[5.] The seventh day read Divinity Catechetical at the eighth hour.
Commonplaces at the ninth hour.

Afternoon   The first hour reads history in the winter, the nature of plants in the summer.

The sum of every lecture shall be examined before the new lecture be read.

Every scholar, that on proof is found able to read the originals of the Old and New Testament into the Latin tongue, and to resolve them logically, withal being of godly life and conversation, and at any public act hath the approbation of the Overseers and Master of the College, is fit to be dignified with his first degree.

Every scholar that giveth up in writing a system, or synopsis, or sum of Logic, Natural and Moral Philosophy, Arithmetic, Geometry and Astronomy, and is ready to defend his theses or positions, withal skilled in the originals as abovesaid, and of godly life and conversation, and so approved by the Overseers and Master of the College, at any public act, is fit to be dignified with his second degree.

Three Early New England Portraits

Our knowledge of the literate Puritans comes mostly from their own writings. But they left to posterity other kinds of evidence, including a number of individual portraits. The first is of a young boy, Henry Gibbs. Do you think he was really like that? Or do you think the portrait was a Puritan dream of what little boys should be like? What do you make of his clothing? What does the background—the tessellated floor—tell you about his society? The second portrait is a self-portrait of Thomas Smith. Do you think it is more revealing than young Henry's portrait? Why? What does the background say about his life, his concerns? The third portrait is of an ancient Puritan named Ann Pollard. Painted in 1721, she was one of the original settlers of Boston, coming over on one of the first ships as a "romping girl" of ten. She had outlived all her generation, and the portrait was done in honor of her one-hundredth birthday. Does she share any traits with young Henry Gibbs or with Thomas Smith?

"Henry Gibbs" (1670), Anonymous. *Collection of Mrs. David M. Giltinan/Photo by Richard Lee.*

Thomas Smith's Self-Portrait (ca. 1675).
Worcester Art Museum.

"Ann Pollard" (1721), Anonymous. *Massachusetts Historical Society/Photo by George M. Cushing.*

The Trial of Anne Hutchinson, 1637

The Puritans might indoctrinate small children with their Primer. *They might create tight rules at Harvard for the education of their ministers. But their world was full of dissent, despite their efforts. They never achieved their ideal of a community of Christian believers firm and secure in their shared faith. One of the sharpest controversies in Massachusetts erupted in the early 1630s and centered on a woman named Anne Hutchinson. Mrs. Hutchinson, a devout wife and mother of a large, well-to-do family, was in some ways a model Puritan. She studied scripture and listened intently to sermons. She held discussions with her neighbors in her home. But she began to argue, publicly, that the ministers were preaching too much about "works," or the behavioral obligations of Christians, and not enough about* grace: *God's free gift of salvation to the saved, a gift they could not earn through their own efforts. The leaders of the colony gradually recognized a threat to their authority and to the stability of their little society. They decided to try Anne Hutchinson and brought her into court in 1637. The colony's governor, John Winthrop, took the role of prosecutor. How would you describe Mrs. Hutchinson's attitude toward authority? toward law?*

November 1637

The Examination of Mrs. Anne Hutchinson at the Court of Newtown

MR. WINTHROP, GOVERNOR: Mrs. Hutchinson, you are called here as one of those that have troubled the peace of the commonwealth and the churches here; you are known to be a woman that hath had a great share in the promoting and divulging of those opinions that are causes of this trouble, and to be nearly joined not only in affinity and affection with some of those the court had taken notice of and passed censure upon, but you have spoken divers things as we have been informed very prejudicial to the honour of the churches and ministers thereof, and you have maintained a meeting and an assembly in your house that hath been condemned by the general assembly as a thing not tolerable nor comely in the sight of God nor fitting for your sex, and notwithstanding that was cried down you have continued the same, therefore we have thought good to send for you to understand how things are, that if you be in an erroneous way we may reduce you that so you may become a profitable member here among us, otherwise if you be obstinate in your course that then the court may take such course that you may trouble us no further, therefore I would intreat you to express whether you do not assent and hold in practice to those opinions and factions that

From Thomas Hutchinson, *The History of the Colony and Province of Massachusetts Bay*, Thomas and John Fleet, Boston, 1767, Vol. II, Appendix II, pp. 366–391.

have been handled in court already, that is to say, whether you do not justify Mr. Wheelwright's sermon and the petition.

MRS. HUTCHINSON: I am called here to answer before you but I hear no things laid to my charge.

GOV.: I have told you some already and more I can tell you.

MRS. H.: Name one, Sir.

GOV.: Have I not named some already?

MRS. H.: What have I said or done?

GOV.: Why for your doings, this you did harbour and countenance those that are parties in this faction that you have heard of.

MRS. H.: That's matter of conscience, Sir.

GOV.: Your conscience you must keep or it must be kept for you.

MRS. H.: Must not I then entertain the saints because I must keep my conscience?

GOV.: Say that one brother should commit felony or treason and come to his brother's house, if he knows him guilty and conceals him he is guilty of the same. It is his conscience to entertain him, but if his conscience comes into act in giving countenance and entertainment to him that hath broken the law he is guilty too. So if you do countenance those that are transgressors of the law you are in the same fact.

MRS. H.: What law do they transgress?

GOV.: The law of God and of the state.

MRS. H.: In which particular?

GOV.: Why in this among the rest, whereas the Lord doth say honour they father and thy mother.

MRS. H.: Ey Sir in the Lord. . . .

GOV.: Why do you keep such a meeting at your house as you do every week upon a set day?

MRS. H.: It is lawful for me to do so, as it is all your practices, and can you find a warrant for yourself and condemn me for the same thing? The ground of my taking it up was, when I first came to this land because I did not go to such meetings as those were, it was presently reported that I did not allow of such meetings but held them unlawful and therefore in that regard they said I was proud and did despise all ordinances, upon that a friend came unto me and told me of it and I to prevent such aspersions took it up, but it was in practice before I came, therefore I was not the first. . . .

GOV.: Well, we see how it is we must therefore put it away from you or restrain you from maintaining this course.

MRS. H.: If you have a rule for it from God's word you may.

GOV.: We are your judges, and not you ours and we must compel you to it.

MRS. H.: If it please you by authority to put it down I will freely let you for I am subject to your authority. . . .

DEP. GOV.: I would go a little higher with Mrs. Hutchinson. About three years ago we were all in peace. Mrs. Hutchinson from that time she came hath made a disturbance, and some that came over with her in the ship did inform me what she was as soon as she was landed. I being then in place dealt with the pastor and teacher of Boston and desired them to enquire of her, and then I was satisfied that she held nothing different from us, but within half a year after, she had vented divers of her strange opinions and had made parties in the country, and at length it comes that Mr. Cotton and Mr. Vane were of her judgment, but Mr. Cotton hath cleared himself that he was not of that mind, but now it appears by this woman's meeting that Mrs. Hutchinson hath so forestalled the minds of many by their resort to her meeting that now she hath a potent party in the country. Now if all these things have endangered us as from that foundation and if she in particular hath disparaged all our ministers in the land that they have preached a covenant of works, and only Mr. Cotton a covenant of grace, why this is not to be suffered, and therefore being driven to the foundation and it being found that Mrs. Hutchinson is she that hath depraved all the ministers and hath been the cause of what is fallen out, why we must take away the foundation and the building will fall.

MRS. H.: I pray Sir prove it that I said they preached nothing but a covenant of works. . . .

DEP. GOV.: I do but ask you this, when the ministers do preach a covenant of works do they preach a way of salvation?

MRS. H.: I did not come hither to answer to questions of that sort.

DEP. GOV.: Because you will deny the thing.

MRS. H.: Ey, but that is to be proved first.

DEP. GOV.: I will make it plain that you did say that the ministers did preach a covenant of works.

MRS. H.: I deny that.

DEP. GOV.: And that you said they were not able ministers of the new testament, but Mr. Cotton only.

MRS. H.: If ever I spake that I proved it by God's word.

COURT: Very well, very well. . . .

GOV.: Here are six undeniable ministers who say it is true and yet you deny that you did say that they did preach a covenant of works and that they were not able ministers of the gospel, and it appears plainly that you have spoken it. . . .

MRS. H.: That I absolutely deny. . . .

GOV.: Mrs. Hutchinson, the court you see hath laboured to bring you to acknowledge the error of your way that so you might be reduced, the time now grows late, we shall therefore give you a little more time to consider of it and therefore desire that you attend the court again in the morning.

The Next Morning

MRS. H.: If you please to give me leave I shall give you the ground of what I know to be true. Being much troubled to see the falseness of the constitution of the church of England, I had like to have turned separatist; whereupon I kept a day of solemn humiliation and pondering of the thing; this scripture was brought unto me—he that denies Jesus Christ to be come in the flesh is antichrist—This I considered of and in considering found that the papists did not deny him to be come in the flesh, nor we did not deny him—who then was antichrist? Was the Turk antichrist only? The Lord knows that I could not open scripture; he must by his prophetical office open it unto me. So after that being unsatisfied in the thing, the Lord was pleased to bring this scripture out of the Hebrews. He that denies the testament denies the testator, and in this did open unto me and give me to see that those which did not teach the new covenant had the spirit of antichrist, and upon this he did discover the ministry unto me and ever since, I bless the Lord, he hath let me see which was the clear ministry and which the wrong. Since that time I confess I have been more choice and he hath left me to distinguish between the voice of my beloved and the voice of Moses, the voice of John Baptist and the voice of antichrist, for all those voices are spoken of in scripture. Now if you do condemn me for speaking what in my conscience I know to be truth I must commit myself unto the Lord.

MR. NOWEL: How do you know that that was the spirit?

MRS. H.: How did Abraham know that it was God that bid him offer his son, being a breach of the sixth commandment?

DEP. GOV.: By an immediate voice.

MRS. H.: So to me by an immediate revelation.

DEP. GOV.: How! an immediate revelation.

MRS. H.: By the voice of his own spirit to my soul. . . .

GOV.: The case is altered. . . . The ground work of her revelations is the immediate revelation of the spirit and not by the ministry of the word, . . . and this hath been the ground of all these tumults and troubles, and I would that those were all cut off from us that trouble us, for this is the thing that hath been the root of all the mischief.

COURT: We all consent with you. . . .

DEP. GOV.: These disturbances that have come among the Germans have been all grounded upon revelations, and so they that have vented them have stirred up their hearers to take up arms against their prince and to cut the throats of one another, and these have been the fruits of them, and whether the devil may inspire the same into their hearts here I know not, for I am fully persuaded that Mrs. Hutchinson is deluded by the devil, because the spirit of God speaks truth in all his servants.

GOV.: I am persuaded that the revelation she brings forth is delusion.

All the court but some two or three ministers cry out we all believe it—we all believe it.

. . . GOV.: The court hath already declared themselves satisfied concerning the things you hear, and concerning the troublesomeness of her spirit and the danger of her course amongst us, which is not to be suffered. Therefore if it be the mind of the court that Mrs. Hutchinson for these things that appear before us is unfit for our society, and if it be the mind of the court that she shall be banished out of our liberties and imprisoned till she be sent away, let them hold up their hands.

All but three. . . .

GOV.: Mrs. Hutchinson, the sentence of the court you hear is that you are banished from out of our jurisdiction as being a woman not fit for our society, and are to be imprisoned till the court sends you away.

MRS. H.: I desire to know wherefore I am banished?

GOV.: Say no more, the court knows wherefore and is satisfied.

CHAPTER 4

The Have-Nots in Colonial Society

Once the colonies were established, colonial leaders faced a long-term problem. If they were to become rich, they had to recruit a labor force. Acquiring land was easy for a man of means, since land in America was so plentiful. But acquiring *labor* was a constant problem. The small farmer could rely on his family, but a man with broad acres needed extra hands. Where were they to be found?

One possible source was obviously the Indian. And colonists repeatedly tried to enslave the Indian. As late as 1708 South Carolina held 1400 red men in bondage as compared with 4100 Africans. But colonists found to their chagrin that enslaving the Indian was more trouble than it was worth. In any case, the supply of Indian labor was minute compared with the need. Since enslaving the Indians proved unworkable, the earliest planters had to look to Europe—particularly to England—for their solutions. The most immediate solution to the labor problem seemed to lie in the English practice of "indentured" or contractual servitude. The arrangement was basically simple: in return for a promise of some kind—a promise to be fed and housed and trained in some work, for example—men or women could bind themselves to work for a master for a period of years. The most common term in England, and then in the colonies, was seven years. An agreement, called an indenture, would then be written and signed, and for the agreed-upon period of years, the servant would become the virtual property of the master.

As it happened, England in the seventeenth century contained thousands of young men and women who were desperate enough to bind themselves into servitude and risk the hazards of the Atlantic crossing—all in return for little more than the vague hope that they would somehow be better off at the end of their term. It is impossible to know just how many came, but probably as many as half the immigrants of the seventeenth and eighteenth centuries came in bondage of one kind or another. Most were indentured servants; others were "redemptioners," who had to work off only the costs of their passage. But, no matter what the form, their servitude had much in common with slavery. Their contracts could be bought and sold. They could not live where they pleased, or marry without their masters' permission, or work for themselves. They had no guarantee of fair treatment or of decent food, clothing, and shelter.

Africans were first purchased as servants in 1619, only a dozen years after Jamestown was settled. But it was not until after 1700 that black slavery displaced white servitude as the dominant form of forced labor. Gradually—at first in Virginia and then in other colonies, both north and south—the legal status of slave was defined. Especially in the southern colonies where large-scale commercial agriculture was the way of life, slaves became *the* work force on many plantations. By 1750, the largest single stream of immigration into British North America was composed of black slaves from Africa.

To understand this development, it is necessary to realize that North America was always on the fringes of the immense slave trade that developed between West Africa and tropical America. The Spanish colonies and Portuguese Brazil began importing slaves in the early 1500s, and by the time Jamestown was settled in 1607 some 250,000 African slaves had been brought to the new world. It was primarily the need for labor on the sugar plantations of Brazil and the Caribbean that stimulated the growth of the Atlantic slave trade after 1700. As that trade skyrocketed, the number of slave ships that wandered as far north as Virginia also increased. Yet of the 6 million slaves who survived the Atlantic voyages between 1700 and 1810, less than 6 percent ended up in what is now the United States. So the growth of slavery in the thirteen colonies was only a small part of the growth of slavery in the new world.

It is also necessary to realize that very few people in colonial times had any qualms about slavery. Human bondage had been considered a part of the natural scheme of things since ancient times—and except for a few Quakers and kindred German sects, colonists everywhere accepted slavery as "normal." Even churches owned slaves. Indeed, the pious often bequeathed slaves to their ministers as tokens of affection. When the Reverend Cotton Mather, one of the leading New England ministers of his day, was honored with the gift of a slave, he recorded the event in his diary as "a smile from Heaven."

INTERPRETIVE ESSAY

Peter Kolchin

The Origin and Consolidation of Unfree Labor

The following selection comes from the opening chapter of Peter Kolchin's imaginative book comparing American slavery and Russian serfdom. The two systems of human bondage developed at roughly the same time, became firmly entrenched by the 1750s, and played similar economic and social roles in the two countries. In this extract, Kolchin confronts the question of why the American elite embraced forced labor. As you read it, you should keep several questions in mind: Why did the wealthier colonists continue to rely on European indentured servants long after the arrival of the first African slaves? And why did white indentured servitude in some colonies eventually give way to black slavery? What was the importance of race in all this? And, finally, why did the elite fear the "giddy multitude" before 1700—and "servile insurrection" after 1700? How significant was this change?

A shortage of laborers . . . plagued English settlers in the American colonies, and . . . this situation led to the use of physical compulsion to secure workers. A vast abundance of virgin land together with a paucity of settlers defined the problem in all the mainland colonies; everywhere, land was plentiful and labor scarce. To attract laborers, the colonists consequently found it necessary to pay wages that in Europe would have been considered exorbitant. "Poor People (both men and women) of all kinds, can here get three times the wages for their Labour they can in *England* or *Wales,*" reported an observer from Pennsylvania in 1698. In all the colonies complaints were rampant about the high cost of labor and about the resulting lack of submissiveness among the much-sought-after workers. The law of supply and demand rendered unsuccessful the early efforts of several colonial governments to legislate maximum wages, and both skilled and unskilled labor continued to command wages up to twice those prevalent in England.

The payment of high wages proved inadequate, however, to secure a sufficient number of workers, and in every colony highly paid free labor was supplemented by forced labor of one type or another. Like the Spaniards to the south, although with less success, the English forced Indians to work for them. Indian slavery was most prevalent in South Carolina, where in 1708 the governor estimated that there were 1400 Indian slaves in a population of 12,580, but Indians also served as house servants and occasional laborers in the other colonies: New Jersey wills reveal the continued presence of small numbers of Indian slaves in that colony as late as the middle of the eighteenth century.

For a variety of reasons, however, Indian slavery never became a major institution in the English colonies. The proximity of the wilderness and of friendly tribes made escape relatively easy for Indian slaves. The absence of a tradition of agricultural work among East Coast Indian males—women customarily performed the primary field labor—rendered them difficult to train as agricultural laborers. Because they were "of a malicious, surly and revengeful spirit; rude and insolent in their behavior, and very ungovernable," the Massachusetts legislature forbade the importation of Indian slaves in 1712. Finally, there were not enough Indians to fill the labor needs of the colonists. In New England, for example, most of the natives present when the Puritans arrived died from illness and war during the next half-century. The policy of eliminating the threat of Indian attack by eliminating the Indians themselves proved in the long run incompatible with the widespread use of Indians as slaves and necessitated the importation of foreign laborers.

For the greater part of the seventeenth century the colonists relied on the most obvious source for their labor: other Europeans. Although more prevalent in some colonies than in others, indentured servants were common everywhere in seventeenth-century America. Most served between four and seven years in exchange for free passage from Europe to America, although some were kidnapped and others transported as criminals. All found themselves highly prized commodities. In many colonies, such as Virginia, settlers received a headright—often fifty acres—for every person they imported. But even without such incentives, colonists eagerly snapped up newly arriving stocks of servants, who performed vital functions as agricultural laborers, domestics, and artisans. These immigrant servants, as well as colony-born Americans bound out for poverty, debt, or crime, were virtual slaves during their periods of indenture, bound to do as their masters ordered, subject to physical chastisement, forbidden to marry without permission, and liable to be bought and sold. Like slaves, some were forcibly separated from their relatives. Although a few servants became prosperous and influential in later life, for most the future was decidedly less rosy. In the mid-seventeenth century close to half the servants in Virginia and Maryland died before their terms of indenture were complete; once freed, many males continued to labor for others, living in their households and often—because of the excess of men over women—remaining unmarried.

Finally, the colonists turned to Africa for labor. As early as 1619 the forced labor of blacks supplemented that of whites in Virginia, and by the middle of the seventeenth century blacks were to be found in all the existing English colonies. Nevertheless, what is most striking about the early American labor force is the length of time it took for slavery to replace indentured servitude: throughout most of the seventeenth century white laborers, not black, prevailed in the English mainland colonies, and it was only between 1680 and 1730 that slaves became the backbone of the labor force in the south. This pattern raises two interrelated questions: why, despite the presence of some slaves, did the colonists continue for so long to rely primarily on indentured servants, and why, during the half-century beginning in the 1680s, did African slaves replace European servants in most of the colonies?

Despite the prevailing labor shortage, there were certain limitations on the colonists' demand for slaves. Very few could afford to buy them during the first three-quarters of the seventeenth century. Most early settlers were people of fairly modest means for whom the purchase of a servant—at one-third to one-half the price of an African slave—represented a substantial investment. Even if one could afford the initial outlay, the high mortality rate among the inhabitants of the early southern colonies made the purchase of slaves risky, and servants who were held for only a few years may have represented a better buy. Not only were servants cheaper than slaves, but their successful management required smaller investments of time and effort. They usually spoke the language—at least in the seventeenth century, when most of them came from the British Isles—and were at least partially familiar with the agricultural techniques practiced by the settlers. Given the circumstances, as long as European servants were readily available, their labor continued to make sense to most colonists.

Precisely such conditions prevailed during the first three-quarters of the seventeenth century, when the population of the colonies was small and the number of Englishmen anxious to come as servants was large. Readjustments in the English economy during the late sixteenth and early seventeenth centuries worked serious hardships on many British subjects, who suffered through periodic depressions and famines. Vagabondage, crime, and destitution all increased markedly, as did public awareness of these problems. Increased concern was expressed both by greater attention to charity and by savage repression of the criminal, the rowdy, and the idle. Impoverished Britons were only too anxious to start anew in America, where radically different conditions promised some hope of success and where they were actually wanted rather than regarded as a burden, but so too were many skilled and semiskilled workers who saw their opportunities decline at home. Recent studies of servant immigrants in the seventeenth century suggest that they were overwhelmingly young and male but represented a wide diversity of occupations with perhaps as many as one-half having some skill. The tide of immigration reached its peak in the third quarter of the seventeenth century when, spurred by a series of ten crop failures, political dislocations at home, and a strong colonial demand for labor, close to forty-seven thousand Englishmen came to Virginia alone.

If the supply of servants seemed abundant during most of the seventeenth century, that of slaves was limited at best. The English were latecomers to the African slave trade, which, throughout the first two-thirds of the century, was primarily in Portuguese and then Dutch hands. Only after the Anglo-Dutch war of 1664–1667 was English naval superiority established; shortly thereafter, in 1672, the Royal African Company, with a (theoretical) monopoly of the English slave trade, was formed. Even then, the supply of Africans remained limited. Despite the anguished cries of British planters in the West Indies (where the most lucrative colonies were located), the Royal African Company was unable to supply a sufficient quantity of slaves. West Indian planters mounted a vigorous attack on the company's monopoly, and even before 1698, when the monopoly was formally lifted, private traders illegally supplied a large portion of the islands' laborers. If there were not enough Africans for the West Indies, where the need was greatest, the number available for export to the mainland, which was of relatively small economic importance, was small indeed. Until the last third of the century, most of the slaves imported to the mainland colonies were probably bought from Dutch and other private merchants, so it is not surprising that New York, where the Dutch had early encouraged the importation of slaves, had a higher proportion of blacks in its population than any other English mainland colony except South Carolina as late as 1680.

During the half-century from 1680 to 1730 these conditions impeding the importation of slaves changed radically. The growing prosperity of many colonists meant that an increasing number of them were able to afford slaves. The growth in the number and wealth of large holdings was especially significant, because large planters, who could afford to make the initial investment and whose need for labor was greatest, were the principal purchasers of slaves. In Maryland, for example, the average net worth of the richest 10 percent of probated estates increased 241 percent between 1656–1683 and 1713–1719, far more than the increase among smaller estates; as a consequence the proportion of all wealth owned by the richest 10 percent increased from 43 to 64 percent.

Since servants were only temporarily bound and did not produce new servants, as the colonial population grew the number of servants imported would have had to increase sharply in order for them to form a constant proportion of the population. The 10,910 headrights issued in Virginia between 1650 and 1654 were the equivalent of more than 57 percent of the colony's estimated population in the former year; the 10,390 issued between 1665 and 1669 were only equal to about 29 percent of the population in 1670. Even if the number of immigrants had remained constant, they would have represented a continually decreasing percentage of the population and would soon have become inadequate to meet the colonies' labor needs.

In fact, the supply of English servants declined sharply at just the time that the demand for labor was increasing in many of the colonies. As the English social situation stabilized following the Restoration of 1660 and the British government adopted a strongly mercantilist policy, Englishmen no longer complained, as they had formerly, about an excess population; instead, with increasing economic productivity and well-being, a large population now seemed an asset in Britain's struggle for supremacy with other European powers. Although conditions for the poor remained hard, they no longer experienced the continual crises, famines, and unemployment of the early and middle seventeenth century. Conditions within the colonies also acted to discourage immigration. By the late seventeenth century land was no longer so easily acquired as it had been earlier; furthermore, generally declining tobacco prices may have led merchants to reduce intentionally their importation of servants to Maryland and Virginia.

The result was a rather abrupt decline in the number of British immigrants to the colonies. In no five-year period between 1650 and 1674 did the number of headrights issued for whites in Virginia fall below 7900; in none between 1675 and 1699 did it rise above 6000:

1650–1654:	10,910	1675–1679:	3,991
1655–1659:	7,926	1680–1684:	5,927
1660–1664:	7,979	1685–1689	4,474
1665–1669:	10,390	1690–1694	5,128
1670–1674:	9,876	1695–1699	4,251

The number of English servants thus declined precisely when more were needed. Although Britain continued to transport convict laborers to Maryland and a growing number of German and Irish servants settled in Pennsylvania, there simply were not enough Europeans willing to sell themselves into indentured servitude in America to continue filling the labor needs of the colonies.

At the same time that the supply of servants was decreasing, that of enslaved Africans was increasing, and it was this changing relative supply (and hence price) of labor in the face of high (indeed growing) demand that most simply explains the shift in the nature of the colonial labor force. With the founding of the Royal African Company in 1672, Britain became the foremost slave-trading country in the world. In 1713, by the Treaty of Utrecht, the English won the *asiento* or monopoly awarded by the Spanish government to supply the Spanish colonies with slaves. The eighteenth century was the golden era of the English slave trade, when British merchants provided slave labor for most of the world's colonies.

Given the heightened demand for labor and the new availability of Africans, planters who needed large, stable labor forces had good reason to prefer slaves to indentured servants, even had the supply of the latter not begun to dwindle. For one thing, slaves were held permanently—as were their children—while servants were freed after a definite term. As a consequence, although slaves required a larger initial investment, a plantation using slaves became a self-perpetuating concern, especially by the early eighteenth century, when slave fertility rates increased markedly, mortality rates declined, and the black population began to grow through natural reproduction as well as importation. A plantation using indentured servants, however, required the continual replenishment of the labor force.

Equally important, servants tended to disrupt the efficient working of a farm or plantation by running away. Although slaves too attempted to escape, it was more difficult for them to succeed. Their color made them easily identifiable and naturally suspect. White servants, on the other hand, had little trouble pretending to be free, and the shortage of labor rendered it easy for fugitives to find employment. As a result, the flight of indentured servants was a common and widely lamented occurrence. The colonies adopted stringent penalties for fugitives, usually involving their serving additional time and, for subsequent offenses, branding or mutilation. Newspaper advertisements for fugitives give evidence of both the scope of the problem and the treatment of servants. A typical notice in the Pennsylvania *Gazette* of 18 June 1752 offered a five-pound reward for the return to his West Jersey master of "an Irish servant man, named Thomas Bunn, a thick well set fellow, of middle stature, full faced, a little pock mark'd, and his hair cut off; he speaks pretty good English, and pretends to be something of a shoemaker, he has a scar on his belly, and is mark'd on the upper side of his right thumb with TB."

A comparison of the number of slaves and servants from New Jersey listed in newspaper advertisements with the number of slaves and servants listed in New Jersey wills suggests how much more often indentured servants escaped than did slaves. Although more than four times as many slaves as servants were listed in the wills of 1751–1760, in 1753 and 1754 there were fifty-four notices of fugitive servants and only seventeen of slaves. In other words, servants were apparently escaping at a rate about thirteen times as high as that of slaves. For planters this kind of discrepancy must have been a powerful argument in favor of using slaves.

Discontent with white laborers was not confined to the problem of fugitives. The prevalent labor shortage together with the availability of land encouraged an independent mode of thought on the part of supposedly subordinate white workers—who knew they would have little trouble finding employment no matter what their behavior—that was extremely distasteful to employers. After complaining about the high price of blacks, New York planter-politician Cadwallader Colden noted that "our chief loss is from want of white hands . . . The hopes of having land of their own & becoming independent of Landlords is what chiefly induces people into America, & they think they have never answer'd the design of their coming till they have purchased land which as soon as possible they do & begin to improve ev'n before they are able to mentain [*sic*] themselves." That slavery did not allow for the development of this kind of independence among the laboring class was one more consideration in its favor.

*   *   *

The key determinant of the kind of labor system that emerged in the American colonies was the degree to which agriculture was geared to market. Although the increased availability of Africans made *possible* the widespread adoption of slave labor after 1680, slavery became the backbone of the economy in some colonies while in others it made little or no advance. Where a basic subsistence agriculture was practiced (as in most of New England), farms were small, the labor of a farmer and his family—and perhaps one or two extra hands at harvest time—was quite sufficient, and there was little need for forced labor. Where crops were grown for export, planters sought to maximize their production and extend the acreage planted. In such areas, which included much but not all of the southern colonies, the demand for labor was great, and the indentured servitude that characterized agricultural operations prior to the 1680s gave way to slave labor. Where commercial agriculture was practiced on a smaller scale, as in the middle colonies, the labor system was less uniform: in some places, such as Pennsylvania, indentured servitude remained widespread; in others, families augmented their own labor with that of occasional hired hands; and in still others—most notably parts of New York—slavery was an institution of some importance.

*   *   *

A brief examination of the geographic distribution of slaves . . . illustrates the close connection between agricultural expansion and the spread of forced labor. In the British mainland colonies large-scale commercial agriculture developed first in the Chesapeake Bay region. As early as 1617 tobacco was grown "in the streets, and even in the market-place of Jamestown"; a Dutch traveler reported of Maryland and Virginia in 1679 that "tobacco is the only production in which the planters employ themselves, as if there were nothing else in the world to plant." Spurred by a seemingly insatiable European demand for the new weed and blessed with good soil, a mild climate, and an excellent system of water routes, Chesapeake Bay planters produced increasing quantities of tobacco throughout the seventeenth century; the 20,000 pounds exported in 1619 swelled to 175,590,000 in 1672 and 353,290,000 in 1697, after which, despite annual fluctuations varying with tobacco prices, average yields stabilized for the next generation.

With an abundance of land and a shortage of labor, the amount of tobacco a planter could raise depended primarily on the number of workers he could command. Relying throughout most of the seventeenth century on a continual supply of fresh indentured servants, beginning in the 1680s, when the number of white immigrants had begun to decline sharply and African slaves had become more readily available, planters turned to slave labor. Wesley Frank Craven's computation of slave imports into Virginia, based on the number of black headrights granted, shows a marked increase beginning in 1690:

1650–1654:	162	1675–1679:	115
1655–1659:	155	1680–1684:	388
1660–1664:	280	1685–1689:	231
1665–1669:	329	1690–1694:	804
1670–1674:	296	1695–1699:	1043

He suggests, however, that "the greatly expanded number of black headrights in the 1690s . . . is substantially representative of postponed claims for Negroes reaching the colony somewhat earlier." Corroborative evidence comes from a calculation that in York County, Virginia, the ratio of servants to slaves plummeted from 1.90 in 1680–1684 to 0.27 in 1685–1689 to 0.07 in 1690–1694; within a decade servants had virtually stopped coming to the county. By 1700, when more than one-quarter of Virginia's population was black, the revolution in the composition of the colony's labor force had been largely completed. In Maryland, too, the number of slaves increased markedly, although because large parts of Maryland were unsuited for tobacco growing and because the colony continued to receive substantial shipments of convict servants, the change occurred slightly later than in Virginia and was less dramatic.

Even more heavily dependent on slave labor, although later in development, was South Carolina. First settled by Europeans in the 1660s, it grew slowly as colonists sought in vain to find a staple that would play for them the same role that tobacco did in Virginia. They raised cattle and hogs for sale to the West Indies and also exported deerskins and naval stores. Because of the large role played by West Indian planters in the settling of South Carolina, the colony from the beginning had a higher percentage of slaves than the other mainland colonies, although as elsewhere from Pennsylvania south most of the early immigrants were white indentured servants.

Then, in the 1690s, Carolinians discovered rice, a crop that within a few years became as much a staple for them as tobacco was to planters of the Chesapeake. American rice shipments to England—almost all of which came from South Carolina (and from the middle of the eighteenth century, Georgia)—increased from less than 1 percent of the total value of American shipments to England in 1697–1705 to 12 percent in 1721–1730 and 24 percent in 1766–1775. Even more than in Virginia, South Carolina's commercial orientation created a society in which most heavy labor was coerced. With a population of only a little more than a thousand in 1680, the colony by 1740 claimed forty thousand residents, of whom approximately two-thirds were slaves.

Slavery was much less central in the northern colonies and consequently proved relatively easy to abolish without serious social dislocations in the late eighteenth and early nineteenth centuries; . . . Nevertheless, it is worth noting that unfree labor was of some importance in parts of the north as late as the middle of the eighteenth century. In Pennsylvania, spurred in part by an active propaganda campaign waged by William Penn and his agents who sought to convince impoverished Europeans of the boundless opportunities that awaited them in the colony, tens of thousands of indentured servants, many of them German, continued to perform a significant share of the agricultural labor. By far the largest concentration of slaves outside the southern colonies, however, was located in New York: as late as 1760 about one of every seven New Yorkers was a black slave.

Although both the Dutch, who ruled the colony as the New Netherlands until 1667, and the British who came after them actively promoted the importation of Africans, this policy would have met with little success had conditions there not been conducive to their employment. Wherever water transportation was available, especially on Long Island, Staten Island, and along the banks of the Hudson River, large planters—beneficiaries of huge land grants from both the Dutch and the English—grew a variety of crops for sale. The most important of these was wheat. "Wheat is the staple of this Province . . ." explained New York's governor in 1734; "it's generally manufactured into flower [sic] and bread, and sent to supply the sugar collonys." Slaves appeared wherever large quantities of wheat or other crops were raised for export; on Long Island, for example, they increased from 14 percent of the population in 1698 to 21 percent in 1738. Of course, some New Yorkers, especially in the city, employed slaves as house servants, and others possessed slaves who performed various trades. The typical owner, however, was a farmer with one to five slaves, who used them to supplement his family's labor and increase the amount of its product available for sale.

Slavery was least important in New England, where small farms and a largely self-sufficient agriculture required little labor that a farmer's family could not provide. In the seventeenth century the New England colonies contained relatively few indentured servants, and those few more often served as domestics and artisans than as agricultural laborers. In the early eighteenth century blacks constituted about 2 percent of the population in Connecticut, Massachusetts, and New Hampshire, and few of them were farm workers. They were a luxury for those who could afford them rather than an essential part of the economy.

The one area of New England where extensive use of slaves prevailed nicely illustrates the impact of commercially oriented agriculture on the labor system of colonial America. In the fertile flatlands of the Narragansett region of Rhode Island there arose a system of large-scale stock raising and dairy farming. There, on soil ideally suited for grazing, planters bred the famed Narragansett racehorses, raised herds of sheep and dairy cows, and developed an aristocratic lifestyle similar to that of Virginia and Carolina planters. Estates of hundreds and sometimes thousands of acres required a large, steady laboring population, and it is no accident that "slavery, both negro and Indian, reached a development in colonial Narragansett unusual in the colonies north of Mason and Dixon's line." In 1730 about 10 percent of Rhode Island's population was black, but this figure conceals widespread variations. In the Narragansett country townships of South Kingston and Jamestown from one-fifth to one-quarter of the inhabitants were black, and including Indians about one-third were slaves; in many other areas of Rhode Island blacks constituted no more than 3 or 4 percent of the population. As elsewhere in the colonies, slavery in Rhode Island was strong only where there was substantial market-oriented agriculture.

*   *   *

Over the course of the seventeenth and first part of the eighteenth centuries unfree labor gradually became entrenched and solidified in . . . the American south. If at first serfdom and slavery had emerged as institutions designed to help landholders cope with specific problems of labor shortage, by the middle of the eighteenth century they appeared part of the natural order, as God-given as government or agriculture itself. A central feature of this process of entrenchment was the hardening and clarification of class lines, so that . . . the welter of overlapping groups that still prevailed in much of the seventeenth century had coalesced by the eighteenth into well-delineated classes, the masters and their bondsmen. Of course, there remained intermediate groupings, people who did not fit into either of these major classes; these two, however, dominated society and gave shape to the social order.

It was not at first obvious that this would be so. In the English mainland colonies, class lines were still fluid during most of the seventeenth century, and a variety of laborers, ranging from slave through semifree to free, rubbed shoulders. Indentured servants continued to arrive and in some colonies—most notably Pennsylvania—continued to provide a large share of agricultural laborers well into the eighteenth century. There were still Indian slaves. Criminals and debtors were routinely bound out to work as servants, as were children learning a trade. Nor was the status of all blacks immediately clear: there were some who served as indentured servants, especially during the first two-thirds of the seventeenth century, and for several decades the notion persisted among some colonists that the conversion of African slaves to Christianity might necessitate their manumission. The very term *slave* lacked precision and was sometimes used for someone only temporarily deprived of freedom. In 1639, for example, a white man, "John Kempe, for filthy, uncleane attempts with 3 yong girles, was censured to bee whiped . . . very severely, and was committed for a slave." In this case and several others from the same period the slavery imposed was only temporary, but it is significant that the nature of slavery and freedom could remain so ill defined in the 1630s and 1640s. The early colonists were familiar with a continuum of unfree and semifree statuses and did not yet set the black slaves off from other laborers as an entirely separate class. Of course, the Africans were different and perceived as such, but so too were they differentiated from one another on the basis of national origins; among Carolina planters, for example, "Coromantes and Whydahs, because of their greater hardiness, were supposed to be especially desirable as field hands, whereas Ibos, Congos, and Angolas, allegedly weaker, were said to be more effective as house servants." The rigid dichotomy of later years between black and white, slave and free, did not yet exist.

A flexibility was evident in South Carolina slavery as late as the early years of the eighteenth century, when, although blacks were already a majority of the labor force, there was considerable leeway in what was expected of them. Until the 1720s "servants and masters shared the crude and egalitarian intimacies inevitable on a frontier." Because of the lack of white manpower in this frontier environment, slaves performed a multitude of jobs that would later be considered inappropriate and that sometimes involved considerable initiative, independence, and free association with whites. Thus, slaves served as hunters, trappers, guides, sailors, and fishermen; they were even used to fight Indians, as in the Yamassee war of 1715.

In Virginia, where until shortly before the turn of the century blacks were still a small proportion of the population and most unfree workers were white, racial lines seemed even less firmly drawn. Black and white agricultural laborers often worked together; in his 1705 description of Virginia Robert Beverley noted that "the male servants, and slaves of both sexes, are employed together in tilling and manuring the ground" although "some distinction indeed is made between them in their clothes, and food" and white women were no longer assigned field work. Black and white laborers also fraternized with one another, shared living accommodations, and sometimes ran away together. Indeed, black and white, slave, servant, and often ex-servant as well were all part of a general underclass, a "giddy multitude" that in the third quarter of the seventeenth century showed growing restiveness and caused considerable unease among the well-to-do.

Just how fluid class alliances still were was demonstrated by Bacon's Rebellion, a conflict that erupted in 1676 when Nathaniel Bacon led an uprising against the government of Governor William Berkeley, an uprising that achieved momentary success before its leader caught ill and died of the "bloody flux" and his forces disintegrated. One of a series of violent upheavals that shook the colonies in the 1670s and 1680s, Bacon's Rebellion seemed destined to bear out all the worst fears about the "giddy multitude." Although historians have disagreed sharply over the nature of the rebellion, what is significant here is not Bacon's goal so much as the composition of his forces, which cut across racial and class lines. Enlisted in Bacon's ranks was an incongruous medley of disaffected Virginians: slaves, indentured servants, debtors, ex-servants, frontiersmen chafing under Berkeley's restrained Indian policy, and political enemies of the governor. That such an alliance was possible and that the governor's supporters did not make an issue of the participation of blacks on the side of the rebels indicate how little slavery had yet shaped class attitudes.

Such a configuration of forces as was seen in Bacon's Rebellion would have been impossible in the southern colonies by the early eighteenth century. The rapid spread of slavery and the decline in the number of servant immigrants meant that blacks, instead of constituting one element of a complex, turbulent underclass, were now the backbone of the labor force. Class lines were coming more and more to approximate racial lines. The change was not just one of numbers: the social distance between blacks and whites increased too. As plantation labor came to be associated with slaves, there was a perceptible rise in the status, treatment, and economic well-being of most white colonists. Not only were fewer whites coming over as indentured servants, but those who did tended to be from a somewhat higher social rank, often possessing mechanical skills much in demand in the colonies. David W. Galenson, after examining the backgrounds of 2955 servants leaving England for Jamaica, Maryland, Pennsylvania, and Virginia between 1718 and 1759, found that most were skilled, 65 percent of the men were literate, and only 6 percent listed their occupations as "laborers."

Equally important were the changed conditions they met in the colonies. As fewer servants arrived, the colonists felt stronger pressure to treat them tolerably, because only by convincing prospective immigrants that they faced a bright future in America could the colonists generate continued immigration. Of course, even at the height of the immigration in the 1650s and 1660s the need to attract laborers had militated against treatment so harsh as to discourage other would-be servants from indenturing themselves; here is one reason, as Edmund Morgan has suggested, that indentured servants were never actually reduced to slaves. But when the economic and political dislocations leading Englishmen to flee their country had largely disappeared, the need to offer positive incentives to potential immigrants was much greater. The relatively few immigrants who continued to perform agricultural labor were increasingly differentiated from slaves, as Beverley noted in stressing differences in food, clothing, and treatment of women. The economic well-being of white immigrants in the colonies also improved. Not only were they employed more often in skilled trades, but as the general economic level of the colonies improved they were more able to translate the heavy demand for their services into better material conditions.

There was no such improvement in the status of blacks, who came to America involuntarily and did not have to be lured by attractive conditions. In fact, as the ranks of indentured servants diminished and as their condition improved, the blacks seemed increasingly different and threatening, and there was a decrease in the fraternization and sense of common cause that had once existed between black and white in the laboring underclass. Contributing to this growing isolation of black slaves was the fact that whereas previously most had spent time in the West Indies, where they had already been "seasoned" before coming to the United States, from the 1680s the majority were imported directly from Africa, spoke no English on arrival, and consequently seemed more alien to white Americans. By the turn of the century the pervasive fear of the "giddy multitude" had disappeared. Southern colonists of the eighteenth century dreaded rebellion too, but their fear was of a "servile insurrection," an uprising by black slaves against whites. The growing tide of slave imports and the changed relations between whites and blacks led to a sharp rise in white racial consciousness and widespread expressions of fear that too large a slave population threatened the peace of the community. As Virginia planter William Byrd—himself a large slaveowner—wrote to the Earl of Egmont in 1736, congratulating him on the (temporary) prohibition of slavery in the new colony of Georgia, "They import so many Negros hither, that I fear this Colony will some time or other be confirmed by the Name of New Guinea. . . . The farther [sic] Importation of them in Our Colonys should be prohibited lest they prove as troublesome and dangerous everywhere, as they have been lately in Jamaica."

The result was a rash of colonial legislation designed to regulate slaves. Codification of slavery lagged well behind its actual establishment. In Virginia blacks "had an uncertain legal status" until 1661, and it was only in 1664 that a Maryland law spelled out that "all Negroes and other slaves . . . shall serve Durante Vita"; so long as there were relatively few blacks in the colonies there seemed little need to pass elaborate legislation defining their status and regulating their behavior. During the late seventeenth and early eighteenth centuries, however, the southern colonies passed a series of laws designed to set blacks off from whites, legitimize slavery, and protect society from potential servile insurrections. These laws ranged from reassurances that conversion to Christianity did not require manumission, as in Virginia's act of 1667 and Maryland's of 1671, to measures prohibiting free blacks from voting, testifying in court against whites, or marrying whites, to the establishment of slave patrols to guard against suspicious behavior and the passage of duties in part designed to stem the importation of Africans and thus safeguard public security.

By the middle of the eighteenth century slavery was solidly entrenched as the labor system of the southern colonies, from Maryland to Georgia. Whereas a century earlier freedom was a vague concept, and the lot of most laborers, white and black, was to one extent or another unfree, now the assumption was practically universal among whites that slavery was the natural state of blacks and freedom that of whites. Blacks were simply different: "Kindness to a Negroe by way of reward for having done well is the surest way to spoil him although according to the general observation of the world most men are spurred on to diligence by rewards," wrote Virginia planter Landon Carter in 1770. Eight years later he expressed the same sentiment more bluntly: blacks "are devils," he proclaimed, "and to make them otherwise than slaves will be to set devils free."

*   *   *

SOURCES

Portraits of Poverty

The following pictures are eloquent testimony about one of the social conditions in England that had fateful consequences for the American colonies: poverty. The first is an engraving by the great satirist William Hogarth. How would you describe the attitude toward the poor the illustration suggests was dominant in the upper classes? The beggar in the second illustration is an Elizabethan figure. Does he look pitiful? Or threatening?

The Granger Collection.

The Folger Shakespeare Library.

The Experience of Bondage: Gottlieb Mittelberger's Account, 1754

One of our richest sources of information about the life of the white bondsmen and women is the following autobiographical account. It was written by Gottlieb Mittelberger, a German who came to Pennsylvania in 1750 and spent four years in bondage. Mittelberger was a schoolmaster, and we can see his education and intelligence at work in this story. But the conditions he encountered were probably typical of those met by other indentured servants. What kind of impression do you think Mittelberger is trying to make on his German audience? Why do you think Mittelberger uses the term serf?

Both in Rotterdam and in Amsterdam the people are packed densely, like herrings so to say, in the large sea vessels. One person receives a place of scarcely 2 feet width and 6 feet length in the bedstead, while many a ship carries four to six hundred souls; not to mention the innumerable implements, tools, provisions, water-barrels and other things which likewise occupy much space.

On account of contrary winds it takes the ships sometimes 2, 3, and 4 weeks to make the trip from Holland to Kaupp [Cowes] in England. But when the wind is good, they get there in 8 days or even sooner. Everything is examined there and the custom-duties paid, whence it comes that the ships ride there 8, 10 to 14 days and even longer at anchor, till they have taken in their full cargoes. During that time every one is compelled to spend his last remaining money and to consume his little stock of provisions which had been reserved for the sea; so that most passengers, finding themselves on the ocean where they would be in

From Gottlieb Mittelberger, *Journey to Pennsylvania in the Year 1750 and Return to Germany in the Year 1754,* J. J. McVey, Philadelphia, 1898, pp. 19–20, 22, 24.

greater need of them, must greatly suffer from hunger and want. Many suffer want already on the water between Holland and Old England.

When the ships have for the last time weighed their anchors near the city of Kaupp [Cowes] in Old England, the real misery begins with the long voyage. For from there the ships, unless they have good wind, must often sail 8, 9, 10 to 12 weeks before they reach Philadelphia. But even with the best wind the voyage lasts 7 weeks.

But during the voyage there is on board these ships terrible misery, stench, fumes, horror, vomiting, many kinds of seasickness, fever, dysentery, headache, heat, constipation, boils, scurvy, cancer, mouth-rot, and the like, all of which come from old and sharply salted food and meat, also from very bad and foul water, so that many die miserably.

Add to this want of provisions, hunger, thirst, frost, heat, dampness, anxiety, want, afflictions and lamentations, together with other trouble, as *c.v.* the lice abound so frightfully, especially on sick people, that they can be scraped off the body. The misery reaches the climax when a gale rages for 2 or 3 nights and days, so that every one believes that the ship will go to the bottom with all human beings on board. In such a visitation the people cry and pray most piteously. . . .

Many sigh and cry, "Oh, that I were at home again, and if I had to lie in my pigsty!" Or they say: "O God, if I only had a piece of good bread, or a good fresh drop of water." Many people whimper, sigh and cry piteously for their homes; most of them get home-sick. Many hundred people necessarily die and perish in such misery and must be cast into the sea, which drives their relatives, or those who persuaded them to undertake the journey, to such despair that it is almost impossible to pacify and console them. In a word, the sighing and crying and lamenting on board the ship continues night and day so as to cause the hearts even of the most hardened to bleed when they hear it. . . .

At length, when, after a long and tedious voyage, the ships come in sight of land, so that the promontories can be seen, which the people were so eager and anxious to see, all creep from below on deck to see the land from afar, and they weep for joy, and pray and sing, thanking and praising God. The sight of the land makes the people on board the ship, especially the sick and the half-dead, alive again, so that their hearts leap within them; they shout and rejoice, and are content to bear their misery in patience, in the hope that they may soon reach the land in safety. But alas!

When the ships have landed at Philadelphia after their long voyage, no one is permitted to leave them except those who pay for their passage or can give good security; the others, who cannot pay, must remain on board the ships till they are purchased, and are released from the ships by their purchasers. The sick always fare the worst, for the healthy are naturally preferred and purchased first; and so the sick and wretched must often remain on board in front of the city for 2 or 3 weeks, and frequently die, whereas many a one, if he could pay his debt and were permitted to leave the ship immediately, might recover and remain alive. . . .

The sale of human beings in the market on board the ship is carried on thus:

Every day Englishmen, Dutchmen and High-German people come from the city of Philadelphia and other places, in part from a great distance, say 20, 30, or 40 hours away, and go on board the newly arrived ship that has brought and offers for sale passengers from Europe, and select among the healthy persons such as they deem suitable for their business, and bargain with them how long they will serve for their passage money, which most of them are still in debt for. When they have come to an agreement, it happens that adult persons bind themselves in writing to serve 3, 4, 5, or 6 years for the amount due by them, according to their age and strength. But very young people, from 10 to 15 years, must serve till they are 21 years old.

Many parents must sell and trade away their children like so many head of cattle; for if their children take the debt upon themselves, the parents can leave the ship free and unrestrained; but as the parents often do not know where and to what people their children are going, it often happens that such parents and children, after leaving the ship, do not see each other again for many years, perhaps no more in all their lives. . . .

It often happens that whole families, husband, wife, and children, are separated by being sold to different purchasers, especially when they have not paid any part of their passage money.

When a husband or wife has died at sea, when the ship has made more than half of her trip, the survivor must pay or serve not only for himself or herself, but also for the deceased.

When both parents have died over halfway at sea, their children, especially when they are young and have nothing to pawn or to pay, must stand for their own and their parents' passage, and serve till they are 21 years old. When one has served his or her term, he or she is entitled to a new suit of clothes at parting; and if it has been so stipulated, a man gets in addition a horse, a woman, a cow.

When a serf has an opportunity to marry in this country, he or she must pay for each year which he or she would have yet to serve, 5 to 6 pounds. But many a one who has thus purchased and paid for his bride, has subsequently repented his bargain, so that he would gladly have returned his exorbitantly dear ware, and lost the money besides.

If some one in this country runs away from his master, who has treated him harshly, he cannot get far. Good provision has been made for such cases, so that a runaway is soon recovered. He who detains or returns a deserter receives a good reward.

If such a runaway has been away from his master one day, he must serve for it as a punishment a week, for a week a month, and for a month half a year. But if the master will not keep the runaway after he has got him back, he may sell him for so many years as he would have to serve him yet.

Wanted: Runaway Servants

*We have learned a considerable amount about colonial servitude from docu-
ments like the following. They are advertisements for runaway servants, placed
by their masters in eighteenth-century newspapers in Virginia, Georgia, and
South Carolina. Why did the masters describe the clothes their servants were
wearing when they ran away? Why would the servants not simply discard
those clothes for others? In terms of purchasing power, the rewards offered were
very large. What kinds of trades and skills did the runaways represent? These
advertisements were published in an area where black slavery was well established. Does that fact make any sense? If there were thousands of slaves, why
were there indentured servants?*

Virginia *Gazette,* April 16, 1767. Advertisement.

Run away from King William court-house, on the 14th of March last, three
apprentice boys, viz. James Axley, a carpenter, about 5 feet 8 inches high, and
wears his own black hair cued behind; had on when he went away a gray cloth
coat, without pockets or flaps, and a pair of leather breeches much daubed with
turpentine. William Arter, a carpenter, rather taller and better set than the former, of a dark complexion, has black hair, but his clothes no way remarkable.
William Kindrick, a bricklayer, which business he understands well, and is supposed to be gone with a view of carrying it on with the other boys; he is a fresh
complexioned youth, wears a cap, and had on a bearskin coat with metal buttons, a dark brown waistcoat, and a pair of lead coloured serge breeches. It is
supposed they are gone to Bedford, or into Carolina. Whoever brings the said
apprentices to King William or Hanover court-houses shall have forty shillings
reward for each, besides their expenses defrayed.

Francis Smith, Sen.-James Geddy

Virginia *Gazette,* Nov. 1767

Prince George, November 10, 1767

Supposed to be run away from the subscriber (having liberty about three
weeks ago to go up to Osborne's and Warwick, on James river, to look for work,
and not since heard of) an indented servant man named Alexander Cuthbert, by
trade a bricklayer, born in Perth in Scotland, but came last from London in one
Captain Grigg to Potowmack river. He is about 5 feet 6 or 7 inches high, about
22 years of age, wears his own hair of a dark brown colour, is a little pitted with
the smallpox, and, as he was some time in England, has not much of the Scotch
accent. Had with him when he went away a blue coarse cloth coat, blue and red

From U. B. Phillips, ed., "Plantation and Frontier," Part I in John R. Commons et al., eds., *A Documentary History of American Industrial Society.* Copyright 1909, 1937 by John R. Commons; copyright
1958 by Russell & Russell. Russell & Russell, New York, 1958, pp. 352–354, 346–348.

striped silk and cotton jacket, blue breeches, several white and check linen shirts, and many other articles of apparel. He carried with him his bricklayer's and plaistering tools, a sliding rule, some books of architecture and mensuration, etc. From the little time I have had him, he appeared a harmless inoffensive lad, entirely sober and obliging, and if he has gone off must have been advised to such a measure by some more designing than himself. It is probable he may make to the northward and so to Philadelphia, having been heard to speak of some acquaintances gone that way. Whoever takes up the said servant (if run away) and delivers him to the subscriber, shall have five pounds if taken within the colony, and ten pounds if taken at any considerable distance out of it, paid by

William Black

N.B. All masters of vessels are desired to be cautious of not carrying such a person out of the country.

Virginia *Gazette*, March 26, 1767

Run away from the subscriber, in Northumberland county, two Irish convict servants named William and Hannah Daylies, tinkers by trade, of which the woman is extremely good; they had a note of leave to go out and work in Richmond county and Hobb's Hole, the money to be paid to Job Thomas, in said county; soon after I heard they were run away. The man wore a light coloured coarse cloth frock coat, a blue striped satin jacket, and plaid one, a pair of leather breeches, a pair of Russia drill white stockings, a little brown bog wig, and his hat cocked up very sharp. He is about 5 feet 8 inches high, of a sandy complexion, and freckled; is a well made fellow, somewhat bow legged. The woman had on an old stuff gown and a light coloured petticoat, and under petticoat of cotton with a blue selvedge at the bottom, a blue striped satin gown, the same with his jacket, two check aprons, and a pair of pale blue calimanco shoes. They both wore white shirts, with very short ruffles, and white thread stockings. They had a complete set of tinkers tools. They were seen to have two English guineas and a good deal of silver, and said in Essex county they lived in Agusta, and inquired the road that way. Whoever will apprehend both or either of said servants, and brings them to me, shall have five pounds reward for each, and reasonable travelling charges allowed by

William Taite

Virginia *Gazette*, Feb. 26, 1767. Advertisement.

Run away from the subscriber in Augusta, on the 17th of January last, a convict servant man named John Jones, an Englishman, about 35 years of age, about 5 feet 7 inches high, of a fair complexion, and fair short hair; had on when he went away a blue homemade drugget jacket lined with striped linen, a blue broad cloth do. under it, leather breeches, coarse spun shirt made out of hemp linen, sheep gray stockings, and country made shoes; he has been a sailor, and I suppose will endeavour to get on board some vessel. I have heard that he has altered his name at Fredericksburg, and stole from thence a ruffed shirt, a pair of everlasting breeches, an old whitish coloured jacket, and two razors. Whoever takes up the said servant, and brings him to me, or John Briggs at Falmouth, or secures him in any county gaol so that I may get him again, shall have five pounds reward, paid by me or John Briggs.

Andrew Burd

N.B. As he is a very good scholar, it is imagined he will forge a pass.

Virginia *Historical Register,* vol. vi, 96–97, advertisements reprinted from the Virginia *Gazette* (Williamsburg), 1736–1737.

Ran away lately from the Bristol Company's Iron Works, in King George County, a servant man named James Summers, a West Country [i.e., Cornish] Man, and speaks thick, he is a short thick fellow, with short black hair and a ruddy complexion. Whoever secures the said servant and brings him to the said Iron Works, or to the Hon. John Taylor, Esq., in Richmond County, or gives notice of him, so as he may be had again, shall be well rewarded besides what the law allows.

Nansemond, July 14, 1737

Ran away some time in June last, from William Pierce of Nansemond County, near Mr. Theophilus Pugh's Merchant: a convict servant woman named Winifred Thomas. She is Welsh woman, short black Hair'd and young; mark'd on the Inside of her Right Arm with Gunpowder W. T. and the Date of the Year underneath. She knits and spins, and is supposed to be gone into North Carolina by the way of Cureatuck and Roanoke Inlet. Whoever brings her to her master shall be paid a Pistole besides what the law allows, paid by

William Pierce

South Carolina *Gazette* (Charleston), June 16 to 23, 1739. Advertisement. Savannah, May 7, 1739

Run away on the 5th Instant from Robert William's Plantation in Georgia, 3 Men Servants, one named James Powell, is a Bricklayer by Trade about Five Feet 9 inches high, a strong made man, born in Wiltshire, talks broad, and when he went away he wore his own short hair, with a White cap: Among his comrades he was call'd Alderman.

Another named Charles Gastril did formerly belong to the Pilot Boat at Pill near Bristol, is by Trade a Sawyer, about 5 feet 10 Inches high, of a thin spare make, raw boned, and has a Scar somewhere on his upper Lip, aged about 25.

The 3rd named Jenkin James, a lusty young fellow, about the same

Height as Gastrill, has a good fresh complection, bred by trade a Taylor, but of late has been used to Sawing, talks very much Welshly, and had on when he went away a coarse red coat and waistcoat, the Buttons and Button holes of the Coat black.

Any person or Persons who apprehend them, or either of them, and bring them to Mr. Thomas Jenys in Charleston, or to the said Mr. Robert Williams in Savannah shall receive 10 1. Currency of South Carolina for each.

Robert Williams

Besides the above mentioned Reward, there is a considerable sum allow'd by the Trustees [of the colony of Georgia] for taking run away Servants.

N.B. About a Fortnight ago, three other of the said Robert William's Servants run away, who are already advertized.

Portraits of Slavery

What follows is a collection of pictures representing the institution of black slavery, from its beginnings in Africa, through the horrors of the "middle passage," to life and suffering in the new world. What does the engraving of the slave being whipped suggest about the ways whites were able to keep discipline in the system? The slave ship shown is the infamous "négrier" (as it was called in French) La Vigilante de Nantes. *Do you think that spending weeks in such a suffocating prison would break down the human cargo psychologically, or would they be able to maintain a hold on sanity and on their cultural identity? Does the advertisement for a slave sale in South Carolina suggest that the owners of the cargo would be ruthless or careless with their human commodity, or would they have reason to guard their investment against spoilage? Finally, remember that all these pictures were produced by white men. Can you imagine how pictures left by the slaves themselves would have looked?*

Africans were smuggled into the United States between 1808 and 1860 in violation of a congressional act prohibiting new slaves. Here, they cram the upper decks of the bark *Wildfire*.
Culver Pictures

Bartering for Slaves on the Gold Coast.
Wilberforce Museum and Georgian Houses, Hull.

**Engraving by Alexander Ander-
son in Volume 2 of his scrap-
books.**
*Prints Division/New York Public
Library.*

Shock of Enslavement.
The Granger Collection

This is a diagram of the slave ship *La Vigilante de Nantes,* showing how 400 slaves could be crammed into a hold 36 feet in length and 3 1/2 feet in height.
New York Public Library at Lincoln Center.

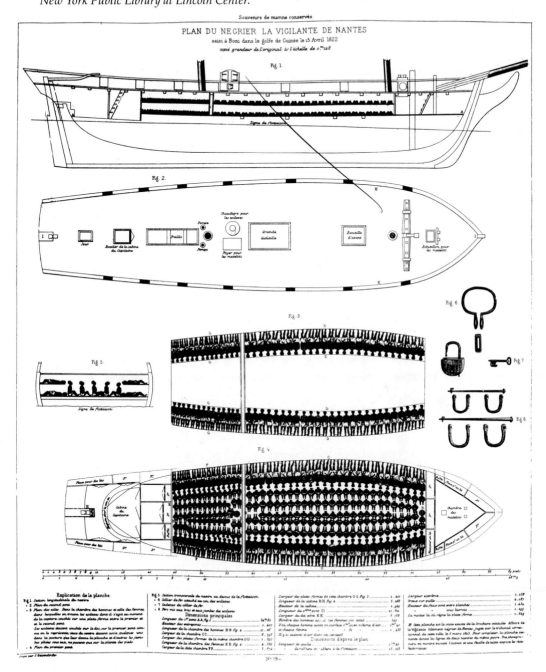

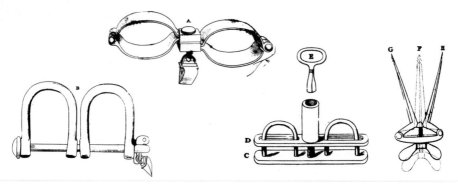

Standard Equipment for the Middle Passage. *A* is a pair of iron handcuffs by which one slave was padlocked to another. *B* is a pair of leg irons, also for two slaves. *C, D, E* is the thumbscrew, an instrument of torture; *F, G, H* is the mouth opener for slaves who refused to eat.
The History of the Abolition of the African Slave Trade by Thomas Clarkson.

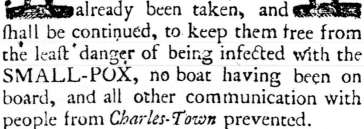

Advertisement in a Charleston, S.C., newspaper, 1766. Slaves from the Windward Coast were highly valued for their knowledge of growing rice. The Laurens of the commission merchants was Henry Laurens, later president of the Continental Congress.
Library of Congress.

Wanted: Runaway Slaves

Angry masters advertised for runaway slaves just as they did for runaway in-dentured servants. The following notices, published in southern newspapers between 1767 and 1808, contain some of our most detailed descriptions and ac-counts of slaves. They also reveal much of the masters' attitudes toward their "property" and their general insensitivity toward pain and brutality. What do these advertisements mean, really? Do they suggest that slaves were, on the whole, so broken by their experience that they became submissive? Can you generalize about the kinds of backgrounds the runaways had? Is John Brown interested only in getting his property back, or does he want punishment too? Notice that the last document in the set is signed with a famous name—An-drew Jackson, who was soon to become one of the nation's most popular presi-dents. Notice the reward offered and the additional payment Jackson offered to anyone who could whip this slave. Do these documents throw any additional light on the slave community? How do you think the owners could guess where the slaves might run to?

Advertisement from the Virginia *Gazette* (Williamsburg), March 26, 1767.

Run away about the 15th of December last, a small yellow Negro wench named Hannah, about 35 years of age; had on when she went away a green plains petticoat, and sundry other clothes, but what sort I do not know, as she stole many from the other Negroes. She has remarkable long hair, or wool, is much scarified under the throat from one ear to the other, and has many scars on her back, occasioned by whipping. She pretends much to the religion the Ne-groes of late have practised, and may probably endeavour to pass for a free woman, as I understand she intended when she went away, by the Negroes in the neighbourhood. She is supposed to have made for Carolina. Whoever takes up the said slave, and secures her so that I get her again, shall be rewarded ac-cording to their trouble, by

Stephen Dence

Advertisement from the Virginia *Gazette* (Williamsburg), April 23, 1767. Bounty on the head of an outlawed slave.

Run Away from the subscriber in Norfolk, about the 20th of October last, two young Negro fellows, viz. Will, about 5 feet 8 inches high, middling black, well made, is an outlandish fellow, and when he is surprised the white of his eye turns red; I bought him of Mr. Moss, about 8 miles below York, and imagine he is gone that way, or some where between York and Williamsburg. Peter, about 5 feet 9 inches high, a very black slim fellow, has a wife at Little Town, and a father at Mr. Philip Burt's quarter, near the half-way house between Williamsburg and York, he formerly belonged to Parson Fontaine, and I bough[t] him of Doctor James Carter. They are both outlawed; and Ten Pounds a piece offered to any person that will kill the said Negroes, and bring me their heads, or Thirty Shillings for each if brought home alive.

John Brown

Advertisement from the Virginia *Gazette* (Williamsburg), Nov. 5, 1767.

Taken up on the 26th of July last, and now in Newbern gaol, North Carolina, Two New Negro Men, the one named Joe, about 45 years of age, about 5 feet 6 inches high, much wrinkled in the face, and speaks bad English. The other is a young fellow, about 5 feet 10 inches high, speaks English better than Joe, who he says is his father, has a large scar on the fleshy part of his left arm, and says they belong to Joseph Morse, but can give no account where he lives. They have nothing with them but an old Negro cloth jacket, and an old blue sailors jacket without sleeves. Also on the 21st of September was committed to the said gaol a Negro man named Jack, about 23 years of age, about 5 feet 4 inches high, of a thin visage, blear eyed, his teeth and mouth stand very much out, has six rings of his country marks round his neck, his ears full of holes, and cannot tell his master's name. And on the 27th of September two other Negro men, one named Sampson, about 5 feet 10 inches high, about 25 years of age, well made, very black, and is much marked on his body and arms with his country marks. The other named Will, about 5 feet 4 inches high, about 22 years of age, and marked on the chin with his country marks*; they speak bad English, and cannot tell their masters names. Whoever own the said Negroes are desired to come and pay the fees and take them away.

Richard Blackledge, Sheriff

Advertisement from the Virginia *Gazette* (Williamsburg), Jan. 13, 1774.

TWENTY POUNDS REWARD. Run away from Subscriber, a Mullatto Man named Abel, about forty Years old, near six Feet high, has lost several of his Teeth, large Eyebrows, a Scar or two on some Part of his Face, occasioned by a Brick thrown at him by a Negro, is very apt to stroke his Hand over his Chin, and plays on the Violin. He is well known as a Pilot for York River and the Bay. As I have whipped him twice for his bad Behaviour, I believe Scars may be seen upon his Body. He can write so as to be understood, and once wrote a Pass for a Negro belonging to the Honourable Colonel Corbin, wherein he said the Fellow had served his Time honestly and truly. He has been to England, but the Captain he went with took Care to bring him back, and since his Return from that Country

---

*"Country marks" were the scars, tattooing, boring of ears, filing of teeth, etc., by which the Africans of certain tribes were accustomed to mark their persons.—ED.

is very fond of Liquor. He is gone off in a Boat with two Masts, Schooner rigged, once a Pilot Boat, but now the Property of the Magdalen Schooner of War, and was seen, I am told, fifty or sixty Leagues to the southward of Cape Henry, from which it is expected he intends for one of the Carolinas. He is a very great Rogue, and is so instructed by several Persons not far from Wormeley's Creek, York River; one of whom, he told me, said I was not worthy to be his Master. He had some Cash of my Son's, and an Order drawn by Captain Punderson on Richard Corbin, Esq; payable to Ralph G. Meredith or myself. A White Lad went off with him, whom I cannot describe, never having seen him to my Knowledge. Whoever secures said Servant, so that I might get him again, shall have the above Reward.

Samuel Meredith, Senior

King and Queen, November 16, 1773

Advertisement from the Virginia *Gazette,* April 21, 1774.
A talented and wily mulatto.

Run away from the Neabsco Furnace, on the 16th of last Month, a light coloured Mulatto Man named Billy or Will, the Property of the Honourable John Taylor, Esquire. When I tell the Publick that he is the same Boy who, for many Years, used to wait on me in my Travels through this and the neighbouring Province, and, by his Pertness, or rather Impudence, was well known to almost all my Acquaintances, there is the less Occasion for a particular Description of him. However, as he is now grown to the Size of a Man, and has not attended me for some Time past, I think it not amiss to say that he is a very likely young Fellow, about twenty Years old, five Feet nine Inches high, stout and strong made, has a remarkable Swing in his Walk, but is much more so by a surprising Knack he has of gaining the good Graces of almost every Body who will listen to his bewitching and deceitful Tongue, which seldom or ever speaks the Truth; has a small Scar on the right Side of his Forehead, and the little Finger of his right Hand is quite straight by a Hurt he got when a Child. He had on when he went away a blue Fearnaught and an under Jacket of green Baize, Cotton Breeches, Osnabrug Shirt, a mixed Blue Pair of Stockings, a pair of Country made Shoes, and yellow Buckles. From his Ingenuity, he is capable of doing almost any Sort of Business, and for some Years past has been chiefly employed as a Founder, a Stone Mason, and a Miller, as Occasion required; one of which Trades, I imagine, he will, in the Character of a Freeman, profess. I have some Reason to suspect his travelling towards James River, under the Pretence of being sent by me on Business. Whoever apprehends the said Mulatto Slave, and brings him to me, or his Master, the Honourable John Taylor of Mount Airy, or secures him so as to be had again, shall have double what the Law allows, and all reasonable Charges paid by

Thomas Lawson

Neabsco Furnace, April 1, 1774

Advertisement from the Georgia *Express* (Athens), Dec. 17, 1808.

Runaway from the subscriber living in Jackson county, on the Oconee river near Clarkesborough, on Sunday night the 13th of November last a mulatto man of the name of Joe. He is a very bright mulatto, almost white, about six feet high, tolerably well made, yellow gray eyes and yellow hair. He is branded on each cheek with the letter R, one of his upper fore teeth out, and, on examining under one of his arms there will be found a scar. He carried off with him clothes of different kinds, among them is a blue regimental coat turned up with red. He likewise took away with him a smooth bored gun. I suspect he will attempt to pass for a free man, and no doubt will aim northwardly or for the Indian Nation. Any person who will apprehend the above described negro, deliver him to me or confine him in jail shall be handsomely compensated.

Richard Thurmond

Advertisement from the Tennessee *Gazette & Mero District Advertiser* (Nashville), Nov. 7, 1804.

Andrew Jackson's way.

STOP THE RUNAWAY. FIFTY DOLLARS REWARD. Eloped from the subscriber, living near Nashville on the 25th of June last, a Mulatto Man Slave, about thirty years old, five feet and an inch high, stout made and active, talks sensible, stoops in his walk, and has a remarkably large foot, broad across the root of the toes—will pass for a free man, as I am informed he has obtained by some means, certificates as such—took with him a drab great-coat, dark mixed body coat, a ruffled shirt, cotton home spun shirts and overalls. He will make for Detroit, through the states of Kentucky and Ohio, or the upper part of Louisiana. The above reward will be given any person that will take him and deliver him to me or secure him in jail so that I can get him. If taken out of the state, the above reward, and all reasonable expenses paid—and ten dollars extra for every hundred lashes any person will give him to the amount of three hundred.

Andrew Jackson, near Nashville, State of Tennessee

CHAPTER 5

Toward Revolution

To Englishmen and colonists alike, the year 1763 was a great one. For almost a hundred years, the British had carried on an intense struggle with the French for the control of North America. For the colonists, this had meant involvement in one war after another, with Indians and their French allies sweeping down from Canada in raids on the New England and New York frontiers. Now, after the bloodiest of those wars, the French were finally beaten. Canada was British. In London and in all British North America, the loyal subjects of the now mighty British Empire ought to be able to look forward to peace and prosperity. Small wonder that proud colonists toasted the British monarch, George III, and swore their undying allegiance to king and Parliament. Small wonder, too, that authorities in London now saw a chance to put their governmental house in order and to extend a more efficient administration to their growing colonies across the Atlantic.

Twelve years later, the same loyal colonists were at war with the same authorities in England. Twelve years later, the names of George III and even of Parliament were cursed all up and down the North American seaboard.

This astonishing turn of events had its seeds in the situation of 1763. The British government came out of its long series of wars with France with a large debt. And the wish to extend efficient government across the Atlantic was in part a wish to make the colonies profitable through taxes—primarily taxes on trade, on the goods the colonists shipped to Europe, and the manufactured items they imported. Parliament began to add to the list of taxes and duties the colonists were supposed to pay, and to send over officials to administer the duties and collect the taxes. The colonists, who had been virtually untaxed, responded vigorously and angrily. They began to boycott English goods, mob Crown officers, quarrel relentlessly with their royal governors, and destroy British property. The outcome of a succession of crises and protests was open rebellion, followed by a full-scale war for independence.

Who rebelled and why? Historians have been grappling with these related

109

questions ever since the revolution began in 1775. The only thing we know for certain is that there are no simple and easy answers. A number of general guesses have been proposed over the years. One takes the colonists more or less at their word and suggests that the cause of the rebellion was the attempt of the British to undercut some of the "liberties" the colonists had enjoyed as "free-born" Englishmen. Another kind of answer has been that the colonists were reacting basically to their economic interests, trying to protect a trading position that was vulnerable to British attempts to regulate commerce. Still others have argued that the issue was not the relationship between the home country and the colonies at all, but within the *colonies,* and that the revolution was an *internal* revolution in which "radicals" in the colonies seized power from colonial elites who were dependent on their connection with authority in London. And within such general arguments, there are specific questions that still are unanswered. How much attention should be paid, for example, to the efforts of leading agitators like Sam Adams or Tom Paine? How important were the blundering shifts in policy in London, or the incompetence of British officials in the colonies?

Questions like these have made the interpretation of the American Revolution one of the most complicated and interesting of our historical problems. Underneath all the interpretations and disagreements lies a profoundly important question: Should the revolution be seen as an anticipation of modern political and social history, or as an event rooted in local quarrels and the concerns of British and American politicians at the time? Was it a violent family squabble, or was it, as Ralph Waldo Emerson called it, the "shot heard round the world"? Or was it somehow and mysteriously *both?*

INTERPRETIVE ESSAY

Gary B. Nash

The Growth of Urban Radicalism

Some of the best recent work on the coming of the revolution has been done by Gary B. Nash, a professor of history at UCLA. Nash takes issue with historians who rely on the role of ideas in explaining the revolution. He also disagrees with their claim that America was such a prosperous country that economic unrest and social discontent had little to do with the coming of the revolution. As you read this excerpt, notice how Nash builds his case. Is he convincing? Why, in his view, did American colonists rebel?

Recent studies of the American Revolution have relied heavily on the role of ideas to explain the advent of the American rebellion against England. The gist of the ideological interpretation of the revolution is that colonists, inheriting a tradition of protest against arbitrary rule, became convinced in the years after 1763 that the English government meant to impose in America "not merely misgovernment and not merely insensitivity to the reality of life in the British overseas provinces but a deliberate design to destroy the constitutional safeguards of liberty, which only concerted resistance—violent resistance if necessary— could effectively oppose." It was this conspiracy against liberty that "above all else . . . propelled [the colonists] into Revolution."

An important corollary to this argument, which stresses the colonial defense of constitutional rights and liberties, is the notion that the material conditions of life in America were so generally favorable that social and economic factors deserve little consideration as a part of the impetus to revolution. "The outbreak of the Revolution," writes Bernard Bailyn, a leading proponent of the ideological school, "was not the result of social discontent, or of economic disturbances, or of rising misery, or of those mysterious social strains that seem to beguile the imaginations of historians straining to find peculiar predispositions to upheaval." Nor, asserts Bailyn, was there a "transformation of mob behavior or of the lives of the 'inarticulate' in the pre-Revolutionary years that accounts for the disruption of Anglo-American politics." Another historian, whose focus is economic change and not ideas, writes that "whatever it might have been, the American Revolution was not a rising of impoverished masses—or merchants—in search of their share of the wealth. The 'predicament of poverty,' in Hannah Arendt's phrase, was absent from the American scene"—so much so that even though the "secular trend in the concentration of wealth created an in-

Gary B. Nash, "Social Change and the Growth of Prerevolutionary Urban Radicalism," in THE AMERICAN REVOLUTION. Edited by Alfred F. Young. © 1976 Northern Illinois University Press. Used with permission of the publisher.

creasing gulf between the rich and the poor over the years separating 1607 and 1775, the fact remains that not only were the rich getting richer but the poor were also, albeit at a slower rate."

One of the purposes of this essay is to challenge these widely accepted notions that the "predicament of poverty" was unknown in colonial America, that the conditions of everyday life among "the inarticulate" had not changed in ways that led toward a revolutionary predisposition, and that "social discontent," "economic disturbances," and "social strains" can generally be ignored in searching for the roots of the Revolution. I do not suggest that we replace an ideological construction with a mechanistic economic interpretation, but argue that a popular ideology, affected by rapidly changing economic conditions in American cities, dynamically interacted with the more abstract Whig ideology borrowed from England. These two ideologies had their primary appeal within different parts of the social structure, were derived from different sensibilities concerning social equity, and thus had somewhat different goals. The Whig ideology, about which we know a great deal through recent studies, was drawn from English sources, had its main appeal within upper levels of colonial society, was limited to a defense of constitutional rights and political liberties, and had little to say about changing social and economic conditions in America or the need for change in the future. The popular ideology, about which we know very little, also had deep roots in English culture, but it resonated most strongly within the middle and lower strata of society and went far beyond constitutional rights to a discussion of the proper distribution of wealth and power in the social system. It was this popular ideology that undergirded the politicization of the artisan and laboring classes in the cities and justified the dynamic role they assumed in the urban political process in the closing decades of the colonial period.

It is toward understanding this popular ideology and its role in the upsurge of revolutionary sentiment and action in the 1760s that this essay is devoted. Our focus will be on the three largest colonial cities—Boston, New York, and Philadelphia. Other areas, including the older, settled farming regions and backcountry, were also vitally important to the upwelling of revolutionary feeling in the fifteen years between 1776 and in the struggle that followed. But the northern cities were the first areas of revolutionary ferment, the communication centers where newspapers and pamphlets spread the revolutionary message, and the arenas of change in British North America where most of the trends overtaking colonial society in the eighteenth century were first and most intensely felt.

To understand how this popular ideology swelled into revolutionary commitment within the middle and lower ranks of colonial society, we must first comprehend how the material conditions of life were changing for city dwellers during the colonial period and how people at different levels of society were affected by these alterations. We cannot fathom this process by consulting the writings of merchants, lawyers, and upper-class politicians, because their business and political correspondence and the tracts they wrote tell us almost nothing about those below them in the social hierarchy. But buried in more obscure documents are glimpses of the lives of both ordinary and important people— shoemakers and tailors as well as lawyers and merchants. The story of changing conditions and how life in New York, Philadelphia, and Boston was experienced can be discerned, not with perfect clarity but in general form, from tax, poor relief, and probate records.

I

The most generally recognized alteration in eighteenth-century urban social structures is the long-range trend toward a less even distribution of wealth. Tax lists for Boston, Philadelphia, and New York, ranging over nearly a century prior to the Revolution, make this clear. By the early 1770s the top 5 percent of Boston's taxpayers controlled 49 percent of the taxable assets of the community, whereas they had held only 30 percent in 1687. In Philadelphia the top twentieth increased its share of wealth from 33 to 55 percent between 1693 and 1774. Those in the lower half of society, who in Boston in 1687 had commanded 9 percent of the taxable wealth, were left collectively with a mere 5 percent in 1771. In Philadelphia, those in the lower half of the wealth spectrum saw their share of wealth drop from 10.1 to 3.3 percent in the same period. It is now evident that the concentration of wealth had proceeded very far in the eighteenth-century cities.

Though city dwellers from the middle and lower ranks could not measure this redistribution of economic resources with statistical precision, they could readily discern the general trend. No one could doubt that upper-class merchants were amassing fortunes when four-wheeled coaches, manned by liveried Negro slaves, appeared in Boston's crooked streets, or when urban mansions, lavishly furnished in imitation of the English aristocracy, rose in Philadelphia and New York. Colonial probate records reveal that personal estates of £5000 sterling were rare in the northern cities before 1730, but by 1750 the wealthiest town dwellers were frequently leaving assets of £20,000 sterling, exclusive of real estate, and sometimes fortunes of more than £50,000 sterling— equivalent in purchasing power to about 2.5 million dollars today. Wealth of this magnitude was not disguised in cities with populations ranging from about 16,000 in Boston to about 25,000 in New York and Philadelphia and with geographical expanses half as large as public university campuses today.

While urban growth produced a genuinely wealthy upper class, it simultaneously created a large class of impoverished city dwellers. All the cities built almshouses in the 1730s in order to house under one roof as many of the growing number of poor as possible. . . .

Beginning in Boston in the 1740s and in New York and Philadelphia somewhat later, poverty scarred the lives of a growing part of the urban populations. Among its causes were periodic unemployment, rising prices that outstripped wage increases, and war taxes, which fell with unusual severity on the lower classes. In Boston, where the Overseers of the Poor had expended only £25–35 sterling per thousand inhabitants in the 1720s and 1730s, per capita expenditures for the poor more than doubled in the 1740s and 1750s, and then doubled again in the last fifteen years of the colonial period. Poor relief rose similarly in Philadelphia and New York after 1750. . . . The data on poor relief leaves little room for doubt that the third quarter of the eighteenth century was an era of severe economic and social dislocation in the cities, and that by the end of the colonial period a large number of urban dwellers were without property, without opportunity, and, except for public aid, without the means of obtaining the necessities of life.

The economic changes that redistributed wealth, filled the almshouses to overflowing, and drove up poor rates, also hit hard at the lower part of the middle class in the generation before the Revolution. These people—master artisans rather than laborers, skilled shipwrights rather than merchant seamen, shopkeepers rather than peddlers—were financially humbled in substantial numbers in Boston beginning in the 1740s and in Philadelphia and New York a dozen years later.

In Boston, this crumbling of middle-class economic security can be traced in individual cases through the probate records and in aggregate form in the declining number of "taxables." In that city, where the population remained nearly static, at about 15,500 from 1735 to the Revolution, the number of "rateable polls" declined from a high of more than 3600 in 1735, when the city's economy was at its peak, to a low of about 2500 around mid-century. By 1771, Boston's taxables still numbered less than 2600. This decline of more than a thousand taxable adults was not caused by loss of population but by the sagging fortunes of more than 1000 householders—almost one-third of the city's taxpaying population. . . .

In Philadelphia, the decay of a substantial part of the "middling sort" similarly altered the urban scene, though the trend began later and did not proceed as far as in Boston. City tax collectors reported the names of each taxable inhabitant from whom they were unable to extract a tax, and the survival of their records allows for some precision in tracing this phenomenon. Taxpayers dropped from the rolls because of poverty represented less than 3 percent of the taxables in the period before 1740, but they increased to about 6 to 7 percent in the two decades beginning in 1740, and then to one in every ten taxpayers in the fifteen years before the Revolution.

The probate records of Boston and Philadelphia tell a similar tale of economic insecurity hovering over the middle ranges of urban society. . . . Though many city dwellers had made spectacular individual ascents from the bottom, in the manner of Benjamin Franklin of Philadelphia or Isaac Sears of New York, the statistical chances of success for those beginning beneath the upper class were considerably less after the first quarter of the eighteenth century than before. The dominating fact of late colonial life for many middle-class as well as most lower-class city folk was not economic achievement but economic frustration.

II

Understanding that the cities were becoming centers of frustrated ambition, propertylessness, genuine distress for those in the lower strata, and stagnating fortunes for many in the middle class makes comprehensible much of the violence, protest, and impassioned rhetoric that occurred in the half-generation before the colonial challenge to British regulations began in 1764. Upper-class colonists typically condemned these verbal attacks and civil disorders as the work of the "rabble," the "mob," the "canaille," or individuals "of turbulent disposition." These labels were used to discredit crowd activity, and historians have only recently recognized that the "rabble" often included a broad range of city dwellers, from slaves and servants through laborers and seamen to artisans and shopkeepers—all of whom were directly or indirectly expressing grievances. Cutting across class lines, and often unified by economic conditions that struck at the welfare of both the lower and middle classes, these crowds began to play a larger role in a political process that grew more heated as the colonial period came to an end. This developing consciousness and political sophistication of ordinary city dwellers came rapidly to fruition in the early 1760s and thereafter played a major role in the advent of the Revolution.

Alienation and protest had been present in the northern cities, especially during periods of economic difficulty, since the early eighteenth century. In Boston, between 1709 and 1713, townspeople protested vigorously and then took extralegal action when Andrew Belcher, a wealthy merchant, refused to stop exporting grain during a bread shortage in the city. . . . Rank had no privileges, as even the lieutenant-governor was shot when he tried to intervene. Bostonians of meager means learned that through concerted action, the powerless could become powerful, if only for the moment. Wealthy merchants who would not listen to pleas from the community could be forced through collective action to subordinate profits to the public need. . . .

In Philadelphia, economic issues also set the mechanic and laborer against the rich as early as the 1720s. When a business recession brought unemployment and a severe shortage of specie (the only legal circulating medium), leading merchant-politicians argued that the problem was moral in nature. If the poor were unemployed or hungry, they had their own lack of industry and prudence to thank, wrote James Logan, a thriving merchant and land speculator. "The Sot, the Rambler, the Spendthrift, and the Slip Season," he charged, were at the heart of the slump. Schemes for reviving the economy with emissions of paper money were reckless attempts to cheat those who worked for their money instead of drinking their time away.

But, as in Boston, the majority of people were not fooled by such high-toned arguments. Angry tracts appeared on both sides of the debate concerning the causes and cure for recession. Those who favored paper money and called for restrictions on land speculators and monopolizers of the money market made an attack on wealth itself an important theme. Logan found bricks flying through his windows and a crowd threatening to level his house. . . .

The "moral economy of the crowd," as E. P. Thompson has called it—the people's sense that basic rules of equity in social relations had been breached—had intervened when the rich would do nothing to relieve suffering in a period of economic decline.

In Boston, resentment against the rich, focusing on specific economic grievances, continued to find voice in the middle third of the century. Moreover, since the forming of the caucus a generation before, well-coordinated street action channeled the wrath of townspeople against those who were thought to act against the interest of the commonality. In the 1730s an extended debate erupted on establishing a public market where prices and marketing conditions would be controlled. Many Bostonians in the lower and middle strata regarded a regulated public market as a device of merchants and fiscal conservatives to drive small retailers from the field and reap the profits of victualing Boston themselves. . . .

The timbers of the public market that fell before the night raiders in 1737 showed how widely held was the conviction that only this kind of civil disobedience would "deliver the poor oppressed and distressed People out of the Hands of the Rich and Mighty." . . .

The growing sentiment in the cities against the wealthy was nourished by the Great Awakening—the outbreak of religious enthusiasm throughout the colonies beginning in the late 1730s. Although this eruption of evangelical fervor is identified as a primarily rural phenomenon, it also had powerful effects in the cities, where fiery preachers such as George Whitefield and Gilbert Tennant had their greatest successes. We have no study as yet of the Great Awakening in the cities, but clues abound that one important reason for its urban appeal was the fact that the evangelists took as one of their primary targets the growth of wealth and extravagance, accompanied by a dwindling of social concern in colonial America. Nowhere was this manifested more noticeably than in the cities.

The urban dwellers who thronged to hear George Whitefield in Philadelphia in 1739 and 1741 and those who crowded the Common in Boston to hear Whitefield and the vituperative James Davenport in the early 1740s were overwhelmingly from the "lower orders," so far as we can tell. What accounts for their "awakening" is the evangelists' presentation of a personal religion wherein humble folk might find succor from debt, daily toil, sickness, and want, and might express deeply felt emotions in an equality of fellowship. At the same time, the revivalist preachers spread a radical message concerning established authority. City dwellers were urged to partake in mass revivals, where the social distance between clergyman and parishioner and among worshipers themselves was obliterated. They were exhorted to be skeptical toward dogma and to participate in ecclesiastical affairs rather than bow passively to established hierarchy.

Through the Great Awakening, doctrinal controversy and attacks on religious leaders became widely accepted in the 1740s. In Boston the itinerant preacher James Davenport hotly indicted the rich and powerful and advised ordinary people to break through the crust of tradition in order to right the wrongs of a decaying society. It was the specter of unlearned artisans and laborers assuming authority in this manner that frightened many upper-class city dwellers and led them to charge the revivalists with preaching levelism and anarchy. "It is . . . an exceedingly difficult, gloomy time with us . . . ," wrote one conservative clergyman from Boston. "Such an enthusiastic, factious, censorious Spirit was never known here. . . . Every low-bred, illiterate Person can resolve Cases of Conscience and settle the most difficult Points of Divinity better than the most learned Divines."

Such charges were heard repeatedly during the Great Awakening, revealing the fears of those who trembled to see the "unthinking multitude" invested with a new dignity and importance. Nor could the passing of the Awakening reverse the tide, for this new sense of power remained a part of the social outlook of ordinary people. In fact, the radical transformation of religious feeling overflowed into civil affairs. The new feeling of autonomy and importance was bred in the churches, but now it was carried into the streets. Laboring people in the city learned "to identify the millenium with the establishment of governments which derived their power from the people, and which were free from the great disparities of wealth which characterized the old world."

III

The crescendo of urban protest and extralegal activity in the prerevolutionary decades cannot be separated from the condition of people's lives. Of course those who authored attacks on the growing concentration of wealth and power were rarely artisans or laborers; usually they were men who occupied the middle or upper echelons of society, and sometimes they were men who sought their own gain—installment in office, or the defeat of a competitor for government favors. But whatever their motives, their sharp criticisms of the changes in urban society were widely shared among humbler townspeople. . . . A rising tide of class antagonism and political consciousness, paralleling important economic changes, was a distinguishing feature of the cities at the end of the colonial period.

It is this organic link between the circumstances of people's lives and their political thought and action that has been overlooked by historians who concentrate on Whig ideology, which had its strongest appeal among the educated and well-to-do. The link had always been there, as detailed research into particular communities is beginning to show. But it became transparently clear in the late colonial period, even before England began demanding greater obedience and greater sacrifices in the colonies for the cause of the British Empire. The connection can be seen in New York in the 1760s, where the pleas of the impoverished against mercenary landlords were directly expressed in 1762, and where five years later the papers were pointing out that while the poor had vastly increased in recent years and while many families were selling their furniture at vendue to pay their rent, carriage owners in the city had grown from five to seventy. The link can also be seen in Philadelphia, where growing restlessness at unemployment, bulging almshouses, rising poor taxes, and soaring prices for food and firewood helped to politicize the electorate and drew unprecedented numbers of people to the polls in the last decade of the colonial period.

However, it was in Boston, where poverty had struck first, cut deepest, and lasted longest, that the connection between changing urban conditions and rising political radicalism is most obvious. That it preceded the post-1763 imperial debate, rather than flowing from it, becomes apparent in a close examination of politics in that city between 1760 and 1765. . . .

The bitter Otis-Hutchinson fight of the early 1760s, carried on *before* English imperial policy became an issue in Massachusetts, revolved around a number of specific issues, including the replacement of William Bollan as provincial agent, the establishment of an Anglican mission in the shadow of Harvard College, the multiple offices held by Hutchinson and his relatives, the writs of assistance, and other problems. But more fundamentally, the struggle matched two incompatible conceptions of government and society. Developed during the controversies of preceding decades, these conceptions were spelled out in an outpouring of political rhetoric in the early 1760s and in the crystallization of two distinct factions.

James Otis, Samuel Adams, Royall Tyler, Oxenbridge Thacher, and a host of other Bostonians, linked to the artisans and laborers through a network of neighborhood taverns, fire companies, and the Caucus, espoused a vision of politics that gave credence to laboring-class views and regarded as entirely legitimate the participation of artisans and even laborers in the political process. This was not a new conception of the rightful political economy, but a very old one. The leaders of this movement were merely following in the footsteps of earlier popular leaders—from John Noyes to Elisha Cooke to James Allen. The town meeting, open to almost all property owners in the city and responsive to the propertyless as well, was the foundation of this system. By no means narrowly based, the "popular" party included many of the city's merchants, shopkeepers, lawyers, doctors, clergymen, and other well-to-do men. They provided leadership and filled the most important elective offices—overseers of the poor, tax assessors, town selectmen, and delegates to the House of Representatives. Lesser people filled minor offices and voiced their opinions at the town meetings where they were numerically dominant.

For the conservative merchants and lawyers, led and personified by Thomas Hutchinson, the old system spelled only chaos. "Reform" for these men meant paring back the responsibilities of the town meeting, substituting appointive for elective officeholders, restricting the freedom of the press, and breaking down the virulent anti-Anglican prejudice that still characterized the popular party. Like their opponents, members of the "prerogative" party had suffered as Boston's economy stagnated after 1740. But they saw the best hope for reviving the economy in handing over the management of town government to the wealthy and well-born exclusively. To see Otis address the crowd and to witness "the Rage of Patriotism . . . spread so violently . . . thro' town and country, that there is scarce a cobler or porter but has turn'd mountebank in politicks and erected his stage near the printing-press" was their vision of hell.

Between 1761 and 1764 proponents of the "popular" and "prerogative" conceptions of politics engaged in a furious battle of billingsgate that filled the columns of the *Gazette* and *Evening-Post.* It is easy to be diverted by the extreme forms that the scurrility took. Charges of "Racoon," "stinking Skunk," "Pimp," "wild beast," "drunkard," and dozens of other choice titles were traded back and forth in verbal civil war. But more important than this stream of epithets was the deep-seated, class-tinged animosity that the polemical pieces exposed: hatred and suspicion of laboring people on the part of the Hutchinsonians; suspicion and hatred of the wealthy, Anglican, prerogative elite held by the common people. . . .

This reciprocal animosity and mistrust, suffusing the newspapers and pamphlets of the late colonial period, reveals the deeply rooted social tensions that Bostonians would carry into the revolutionary era. These tensions shaped the ways in which different social groups began to think about *internal* political goals once the conflict against *external* authority began. In the end, the Hutchinson faction, looking not to the future but staring into the distant past, faced an impossible task—to convince a broad electorate that the very men who had accumulated fortunes in an era when most had suffered were alone qualified to govern in the interest of the whole community. Lower- and middle-class Bostonians had heard fiscal conservatives and political elitists pronounce the same platitudes for half a century. Even now, a generation before James Madison formally enunciated an interest-group theory of politics, they understood that each group had its particular interest to promote and that aristocratic politicians who claimed to work for the commonweal were not to be trusted. Such men employed the catchwords of the traditional system of politics—"public good," "community," "harmony," and "public virtue"—to cloak their own ambitions for aggrandizing wealth and power. The growing inequalities of wealth in Boston, which could be readily seen in the overcrowded almshouse and flocks of outreliefers in contrast to the urban splendor of men like Hutchinson and Oliver, were proof enough of that.

IV

Only by understanding the long animosity that the common people of Boston held for Thomas Hutchinson and his clique can sense be made of the extraordinary response to the Stamp Act in Boston in August 1765—the systematic destruction of the houses of Hutchinson and other wealthy and conservative Boston officials—and of the course of revolutionary politics in the city in the years that followed. It is possible, of course, to revert to the explanation of Peter Oliver, who, at the time, argued that "the People in general . . . were like the Mobility of all Countries, perfect Machines, wound up by any Hand who might first take the winch." In this view, the crowd was led by the nose by middle- and upper-class manipulators such as Otis and Samuel Adams, and used to further their own political ambitions. In this Newtonian formulation, the crowd could never be self-activating, for thought and planned action could have their source only in the minds of educated persons.

Such explanations, however, bear no relationship to the social realities in Boston at the time or to the long history of popular protest in the city. Again and again in the eighteenth century the Boston crowd had considered its interest, determined its enemies, and moved in a coordinated and discriminating way to gain its ends through street action. It was frequently supported in this by men higher up on the social scale—men who shielded the crowd leaders from subsequent attempts of the authorities to punish them. Thus, several socioeconomic groups, with interests that often coincided but sometimes diverged, found it profitable to coordinate their actions.

The attacks on Andrew Oliver's house on the evening of August 14, 1765, and on Hutchinson's house twelve days later, were entirely consistent with this pattern of politics. On the evening of August 14, the crowd, led by the shoemaker Ebenezer MacIntosh, culminated a day of protest against the Stamp Act by reducing Oliver's mansion to a shambles. Accompanied by the sheriff, Hutchinson attempted to stop the property destruction. For his trouble, he was driven off with a hailstorm of stones. Less than two weeks later it was Hutchinson's turn. Forcing him and his family to flee, the crowd smashed in the doors with axes, reduced the furniture to splinters, stripped the walls bare, chopped through inner partitions until the house was a hollow shell, destroyed the formal gardens behind the house, drank the contents of the wine cellar, and carried off every movable object of value except some of Hutchinson's books and papers, which were left to scatter in the wind. Not a person in Boston, neither private citizen nor officer of the law, attempted to stop the crowd. Its members worked through the night with almost military precision to raze the building, spending three hours alone "at the cupola before they could get it down," according to Governor Bernard.

Historians agree that in destroying the Boston mansions of Oliver and Hutchinson, the crowd was demonstrating against the Stamp Act. Oliver had been appointed Stamp Collector, and Hutchinson, though he publicly expressed his view that the act was unwise, had vowed to use his authority as lieutenant-governor to see it executed. But in conducting probably the most ferocious attack on private property in the history of the English colonies, the crowd was demonstrating against far more than Parliamentary policy. Stamp collectors were intimidated and handled roughly in many other cities. But nowhere else did the crowd choose to destroy property on such a grand scale and with such exacting thoroughness. The full meaning of these attacks can be extracted only by understanding the long-standing animus against the Oliver-Hutchinson circle. Beyond intimidating British officialdom, the crowd was giving vent to years of hostility at the accumulation of wealth and power by the aristocratic, Hutchinson-led prerogative faction. Behind every swing of the ax and every hurled stone, behind every shattered plate and splintered mahogany chair lay the fury of a Bostonian who had read or heard the repeated references to the people as "rabble," and who had suffered economic hardship while others grew rich. . . .

Seen in the context of three generations of social and economic change in Boston, and set against the drive for power of the Hutchinson-Oliver faction in Massachusetts, the Stamp Act riots provide a revealing example of the "moral economy of the crowd" in the early stages of the revolutionary movement. Members of the Boston "mob" needed no upper-class leaders to tell them about the economic stagnation of the late colonial period that had been affecting their lives and the structure of opportunity in the town. Nor did they need to destroy the homes of Oliver and Hutchinson in order to obtain the promise of these officeholders to hold the Stamp Act in abeyance. Instead, the crowd paid off some old debts and served notice on those whom it regarded as enemies of its interests. It was the culminating event of an era of protest against wealth and oligarchic power that had been growing in all the cities. In addition, it demonstrated the fragility of the union between protesting city dwellers of the laboring classes and their more bourgeois partners, for in the uninhibited August attacks on property, the Boston crowd went much farther than Caucus leaders such as James Otis and Samuel Adams had reckoned or wished to countenance.

V

In the other cities the growing resentment of wealth, the rejection of an elitist conception of politics, and the articulation of artisan- and laboring-class interests also gained momentum after 1765. These were vital developments in the revolutionary period. Indeed, it was the extraordinary new vigor of urban laboring people in defining and pursuing their goals that raised the frightening specter of a radicalized form of politics and a radically changed society in the minds of many upper-class city dwellers, who later abandoned the resistance movement against England that they had initially supported and led.

That no full-fledged proletarian radical ideology emerged in the decade before the revolution should not surprise us, for this was a preindustrial society in which no proletariat yet existed. Instead, we can best understand the long movement of protest against concentrated wealth and power, building powerfully as social and economic conditions changed in the cities, as a reflection of the disillusionment of laborers, artisans, and many middle-class city dwellers against a system that no longer delivered equitable rewards to the industrious. "Is it equitable that 99, rather 999, should suffer for the Extravagance or Grandeur of one," asked a New Yorker in 1765, "especially when it is considered that Men frequently owe their Wealth to the impoverishment of their Neighbors?" Such thoughts, cutting across class lines, were gaining force among large parts of the urban population in the late colonial period. They were directed squarely at outmoded notions that only the idle and profligate could fail in

America and that only the educated and wealthy were entitled to manage political affairs.

But the absence of clearly identifiable class consciousness and of organized proletarian radicalism does not mean that a radical ideology, nurtured within the matrix of preindustrial values and modes of thought, failed to emerge during the revolution. Though this chapter in the history of the revolution is largely unwritten, current scholarship is making it clear that the radicalization of thought in the cities, set in motion by economic and social change, advanced very rapidly once the barriers of traditional thought were broken down. A storm of demands, often accompanied by crowd action to ensure their implementation, rose from the urban "tradesmen" and "mechanicks": for the end of closed assembly debates and the erection of public galleries in the legislative houses; for published roll-call votes that would indicate how faithfully elected legislators followed the wishes of their constituents; for open-air meetings where laboring men could help devise and implement public policy; for more equitable laying of taxes; for price controls instituted by and for the laboring classes to shield them from avaricious men of wealth; and for the election of mechanics and other ordinary people at all levels of government.

How rapidly politics and political ideology could be transformed, as colonists debated the issue of rebellion, is well illustrated by the case of Philadelphia. In one brief decade preceding the revolution the artisanry and laboring poor of the city moved from a position of clear political inferiority to a position of political control. They took over the political machinery of the city, pushed through the most radical state constitution of the period, and articulated concepts of society and political economy that would have stunned their predecessors. By mid-1776, laborers, artisans, and small tradesmen, employing extralegal measures when electoral politics failed, were in clear command in Philadelphia. Working with middle-class leaders such as James Cannon, Timothy Matlack, Thomas Young, and Thomas Paine, they launched a full-scale attack on wealth and even on the right to acquire unlimited private property. By the summer of 1776 the militant Privates Committee, which probably represented the poorest workers, became the foremost carrier of radical ideology in Pennsylvania. It urged the voters, in electing delegates for the constitutional convention, to shun "great and overgrown rich men [who] will be improper to be trusted, [for] they will be too apt to be framing distinctions in society, because they will reap the benefits of all such distinctions." Going even further, they drew up a bill of rights for consideration by the convention, which included the proposition that "an enormous proportion of property vested in a few individuals is dangerous to the rights, and destructive of the common happiness, of mankind; and therefore every free state hath a right by its laws to discourage the possession of such property." For four years, in an extremely fluid political scene, a radicalized artisanry shaped—and sometimes dominated—city and state politics, while setting forth the most fully articulated ideology of reform yet heard in America.

These calls for reform varied from city to city, depending on differing conditions, past politics, and the qualities of particular leaders. Not all the reforms were implemented, especially those that went to the heart of the structural problems in the economy. Pennsylvania, for example, did not adopt the radical limitation on property holding. But that we know from hindsight that the most radical challenges to the existing system were thwarted, or enjoyed only a short period of success, does not mean that they are not a vital part of the revolutionary story. At the time, the disaffected in the cities were questioning some of the most fundamental tenets of colonial thought. Ordinary people, in bold opposition to their superiors, to whom custom required that they defer, were creating power and suggesting solutions to problems affecting their daily lives. . . . How far these calls for radical reform extended and the success they achieved are matters that historians have begun to investigate only lately. But this much is clear: even though many reforms were defeated or instituted briefly and then abandoned, political thought and behavior would never again be the same in America.

SOURCES

George III

The American Revolution had many victims—the dead and wounded, the loyalists who went into exile, and a host of others. But perhaps the most dramatic victim (though the loss was bloodless) was the habitual reverence the king's loyal subjects felt for His Majesty. In fact, it was only at the moment of revolution that Americans could bring themselves to stop complaining about Parliament, or the Board of Trade, and to address their complaints directly to their revered monarch, George III. You can gather something about the completeness of the shift by comparing these two illustrations. The first is a woodcut that appeared in a schoolbook published in America in 1770. The second shows a mob attacking a statue of the same king just five years later. Do the two pictures seem to you to have implications about social class as well as politics? How would you characterize the dress and expression attributed to George III in the first picture? What generalization can you make about the dress and manner of the mob in the second picture? Do the pictures add anything to Nash's essay on urban unrest? Do they challenge his interpretation?

Woodcut Frontispiece to Watt's
Speller, **1770.**
The Granger Collection.

GEORGE III. by the Grace of GOD, of GREAT-BRITAIN, FRANCE and IRELAND, King, Defender of the Faith.

In ev'ry Stroke, in ev'ry Line,
Does fome exalted Virtue fhine ;
And *Albion*'s Happinefs we trace,
In every Feature of his Face.

Pulling Down the Statue of
George III.
Prints Division/New York Public Library.

Thomas Paine

Common Sense, 1776

No one who wrote about the revolution had an influence even remotely compa-
rable to that of Thomas Paine, an English radical who had come to Philadelphia
only in 1774. Paine's pamphlet Common Sense, *published in 1776, was*
quickly an astonishing success. Within months, it had sold 150,000 copies.
Paine's success was a result, in part, of his rhetorical skills. He was simply a
master propagandist. But Common Sense *was significant for another reason,*
too: Paine realized before many of his countrymen that the time for reason had
passed. And so had the time for emotional appeals to British sentiment. The
colonies were at war, and Common Sense *was a war document that intended*
to fasten words like brute *and* savage *on the enemy. For whom do you think*
Paine thought he was writing? Englishmen or Americans? Or was he ad-
dressing what he called "Mankind"?

. . . Volumes have been written on the subject of the struggle between England and America . . . but all have been ineffectual, and the period of debate is
closed. Arms, as the last resource, decide the contest; the appeal was the choice
of the king, and the continent hath accepted the challenge. . . .

I have heard it asserted by some, that as America hath flourished under her
former connexion with Great-Britain, that the same connexion is necessary towards her future happiness. . . . Nothing can be more fallacious than this kind
of argument. We may as well assert that because a child has thrived upon milk,
that it is never to have meat, or that the first twenty years of our lives is to become a precedent for the next twenty. But even this is admitting more than is
true, for I answer roundly, that America would have flourished as much, and
probably much more, had no European power had any thing to do with her. The
commerce, by which she hath enriched herself, are the necessaries of life, and
will always have a market while eating is the custom of Europe.

But she has protected us, say some. . . .

Alas, we have been long led away by ancient prejudices, and made large
sacrifices to superstition. We have boasted the protection of Great-Britain, without considering, that her motive was *interest* not *attachment;* that she did not protect us from *our enemies* on *our account,* but from *her enemies* on *her own account,*
from those who had no quarrel with us on any *other account,* and who will always be our enemies on the *same account.* Let Britain wave her pretensions to the
continent, or the continent throw off the dependance, and we should be at peace
with France and Spain were they at war with Britain. . . .

But Britain is the parent country, say some. Then the more shame upon her
conduct. Even brutes do not devour their young, nor savages make war upon

From Thomas Paine, *Common Sense* (1776) in Moncure Daniel Conway, ed., *The Writings of Thomas Paine,* Putnam, New York, 1894, Vol. I, pp. 67–120.

their families; . . . but it happens not to be true, or only partly so. . . . Europe, and not England, is the parent country of America. This new world hath been the asylum for the persecuted lovers of civil and religious liberty from *every part* of Europe. Hither have they fled, not from the tender embraces of the mother, but from the cruelty of the monster; and it is so far true of England, that the same tyranny which drove the first emigrants from home, pursues their descendants still. . . .

But admitting, that we were all of English descent, what does it amount to? Nothing. Britain, being now an open enemy, extinguishes every other name and title: And to say that reconciliation is our duty is truly farcical. The first king of England, of the present line (William the Conqueror) was a Frenchman, and half the Peers of England are descendants from the same country; wherefore, by the same method of reasoning, England ought to be governed by France. . . .

I challenge the warmest advocate for reconciliation, to shew a single advantage that this continent can reap by being connected with Great-Britain. I repeat the challenge, not a single advantage is derived. Our corn will fetch its price in any market in Europe, and our imported goods must be paid for buy them where we will.

But . . . any submission to, or dependance on Great-Britain, tends directly to involve this continent in European wars and quarrels; and sets us at variance with nations, who would otherwise seek our friendship, and against whom we have neither anger nor complaint. As Europe is our market for trade, we ought to form no partial connection with any part of it. It is the true interest of America to steer clear of European contentions, which she never can do, while by her dependance on Britain, she is made the make-weight in the scale of British politics.

Europe is too thickly planted with kingdoms to be long at peace, and whenever a war breaks out between England and any foreign power, the trade of America goes to ruin, *because of her connection with Britain.* The next war may not turn out like the last, and should it not, the advocates for reconciliation now, will be wishing for separation then, because, neutrality in that case, would be a safer convoy than a man of war. Every thing that is right or natural pleads for separation. The blood of the slain, the weeping voice of nature cries, 'TIS TIME TO PART. Even the distance at which the Almighty hath placed England and America is a strong and natural proof that the authority of the one, over the other, was never the design of Heaven. The time likewise at which the continent was discovered adds weight to the argument, and the manner in which it was peopled encreases the force of it. The reformation was preceded by the discovery of America, as if the Almighty graciously meant to open a sanctuary to the persecuted in future years, when home should afford neither friendship nor safety.

The authority of Great-Britain over this continent, is a form of government, which sooner or later must have an end: And a serious mind can draw no true pleasure by looking forward, under the painful and positive conviction, that what he calls "the present constitution" is merely temporary. . . .

As to government matters, it is not in the power of Britain to do this continent justice: The business of it will soon be too weighty, and intricate, to be managed with any tolerable degree of convenience, by a power so distant from us, and so very ignorant of us; for if they cannot conquer us, they cannot govern us. To be always running three or four thousand miles with a tale or a petition, waiting four or five months for an answer, which when obtained requires five or six more to explain it in, will in a few years be looked upon as folly and childishness—There was a time when it was proper, and there is a proper time for it to cease.

Small islands not capable of protecting themselves are the proper objects for kingdoms to take under their care; but there is something very absurd in supposing a continent to be perpetually governed by an island. In no instance hath nature made the satellite larger than its primary planet, and as England and America, with respect to each other, reverses the common order of nature, it is evident they belong to different systems; England to Europe, America to itself. . . .

But admitting that matters were now made up, what would be the event? I answer, the ruin of the continent. And that for several reasons.

First. The powers of governing still remaining in the hands of the king, he will have a negative over the whole legislation of this continent. And as he hath shewn himself such an inveterate enemy to liberty, and discovered such a thirst for arbitrary power; is he, or is he not, a proper man to say to these colonies, *"You shall make no laws but what I please."* And is there any inhabitant in America so ignorant, as not to know, that according to what is called the *present constitution,* that this continent can make no laws but what the king gives leave to; and is there any man so unwise, as not to see, that (considering what has happened) he will suffer no law to be made here, but such as suit *his* purpose. We may be as effectually enslaved by the want of laws in America, as by submitting to laws made for us in England. After matters are made up (as it is called) can there be any doubt, but the whole power of the crown will be exerted, to keep this continent as low and humble as possible? Instead of going forward we shall go backward, or be perpetually quarrelling or ridiculously petitioning.—We are already greater than the king wishes us to be, and will he not hereafter endeavour to make us less? To bring the matter to one point. Is the power who is jealous of our prosperity, a proper power to govern us? Whoever says No to this question, is an *independant,* for independancy means no more, than, whether we shall make our own laws, or whether the king, the greatest enemy this continent hath, or can have, shall tell us *"there shall be no laws but such as I like."*

But the king you will say has a negative in England; the people there can make no laws without his consent. In point of right and good order, there is something very ridiculous, that a youth of twenty-one (which hath often happened) shall say to several millions of people, older and wiser than himself, I forbid this or that act of yours to be law. But in this place I decline this sort of reply, though I will never cease to expose the absurdity of it, and only answer, that England being the King's residence, and America not so, makes quite another case. The king's negative *here* is ten times more dangerous and fatal than it can be in England, for *there* he will scarcely refuse his consent to a bill for putting England into as strong a state of defence as possible, and in America he would never suffer such a bill to be passed. . . .

Secondly. That as even the best terms, which we can expect to obtain, can amount to no more than a temporary expedient, or a kind of government by guardianship, which can last no longer than till the colonies come of age, so the general face and state of things, in the interim, will be unsettled and unpromising. Emigrants of property will not choose to come to a country whose form of government hangs but by a thread, and who is every day tottering on the brink of commotion and disturbance; and numbers of the present inhabitants would lay hold of the interval, to dispose of their effects, and quit the continent.

But the most powerful of all arguments, is, that nothing but independance, i.e. a continental form of government, can keep the peace of the continent and preserve it inviolate from civil wars. I dread the event of a reconciliation with Britain now, as it is more than probable, that it will be followed by a revolt somewhere or other, the consequences of which may be far more fatal than all the malice of Britain.

Thousands are already ruined by British barbarity; (thousands more will probably suffer the same fate) Those men have other feelings than us who have nothing suffered. All they *now* possess is liberty, what they before enjoyed is sacrificed to its service, and having nothing more to lose, they disdain submission. . . .

But where, says some, is the King of America? I'll tell you. Friend, he reigns above, and doth not make havoc of mankind like the Royal Brute of Britain. Yet that we may not appear to be defective even in earthly honors, let a day be solemnly set apart for proclaiming the charter; let it be brought forth placed on the divine law, the word of God; let a crown be placed thereon, by which the world may know, that so far we approve of monarchy, that in America THE LAW IS KING. For as in absolute governments the King is law, so in free countries the law *ought* to be King; and there ought to be no other. But lest any ill use should afterwards arise, let the crown at the conclusion of the ceremony, be demolished, and scattered among the people whose right it is.

A government of our own is our natural right: And when a man seriously reflects on the precariousness of human affairs, he will become convinced, that it is infinitely wiser and safer, to form a constitution of our own in a cool deliberate manner, while we have it in our power, than to trust such an interesting event to time and chance. . . .

Ye that tell us of harmony and reconciliation, can ye restore to us the time that is past? Can ye give to prostitution its former innocence? Neither can ye reconcile Britain and America. The last cord now is broken, the people of England are presenting addresses against us. There are injuries which nature cannot forgive; she would cease to be nature if she did. As well can the lover forgive the ravisher of his mistress, as the continent forgive the murders of Britain. The Almighty hath implanted in us these unextinguishable feelings for good and wise purposes. They are the guardians of his image in our hearts. They distinguish us from the herd of common animals. The social compact would dissolve, and justice be extirpated from the earth, or have only a casual existence were we callous to the touches of affection. The robber, and the murderer, would often escape unpunished, did not the injuries which our tempers sustain, provoke us into justice.

O ye that love mankind! Ye that dare oppose, not only the tyranny, but the tyrant, stand forth! Every spot of the old world is overrun with oppression. Freedom hath been hunted round the globe. Asia, and Africa, have long expelled her—Europe regards her like a stranger, and England hath given her warning to depart. O! receive the fugitive, and prepare in time an asylum for mankind. . . .

CHAPTER 6

The American Revolution

After festering for a decade or more, discontent in the American colonies erupted in violence on April 19, 1775, at Lexington and Concord. Months later, when news of the Battle of Bunker Hill reached London, George III and his advisers decided that they had no alternative but to use force to put down the insurrection. The king was confident that the insurrection would be quickly over "when once these rebels have felt a smart blow." Britain, after all, was the greatest empire since Rome, and the colonial militia were "raw, undisciplined, cowardly men."

There was good reason for the confidence of George III and his advisers. So far as they knew, violent resistance to British authority had been confined to the area around Boston. No doubt the colonies to the south would behave as they had in the past and place their own local interests above those of any neighbor. And surely, even in Boston, the rebellion had been the work of a minority of citizens, led astray by a few agitators. It would be easy for the British army and its navy, the most powerful in the world, to occupy strategic centers like Boston and New York, Philadelphia and Charleston. And since the colonists depended economically on trade with Europe, whoever held those trading centers would control the fate of North America.

The king, in his determination and optimism, obviously overlooked some formidable problems. Surpassing all others, perhaps, was the immense distance between England and the rebellious colonies. Every musket and every soldier had to be shipped across 3000 miles of Atlantic. At least 10 percent of the soldiers, and perhaps a higher percentage of animals, died on these crossings. And beyond the water lay the vast American wilderness, which only the best axmen in the world could conquer. The British soldier was no match for the American with an ax. There was, moreover, no chance of striking a single crushing blow. All the major seats of government—Boston, New York, and Philadelphia—were held at one time or another by British troops without much damage to the rebel cause. There was simply no great political center in America like Paris or London, whose loss might have been totally demoralizing to Americans. And even if Washington's Continental Army were totally crushed, that alone would not guarantee victory. For there was always the chance that Washington, or some other rebel, could raise another army among the thousands of guerrillas that swarmed the countryside.

In retrospect, the outcome may seem almost inevitable. But it did not appear very likely in 1775, either in London or to those Americans who understood fully that they were committing treason and, if they lost, would have nothing to look forward to but the noose.

What stood between the leaders of the revolution and the gallows was a process that we could call today mobilization. The Spirit of '76 was a necessary ingredient, and so were the words of men like Paine presented in the preceding chapter. But the spirit and the words would count for nothing if they could not be backed up with a mobilized population.

Mobilization had three phases. The first, and most obvious, was raising and supplying an army in the field to resist the introduction of British troops all along the seaboard. The second was the enforcement of discipline and revolutionary order in the great stretches of land the British did not occupy—a task that was partly political, partly military. The third was the repression of dissent, the silencing and driving out of those called Tories, who remained loyal to the crown.

The material in this chapter bears on all these phases of mobilization. You may find it useful to think of them as an examination of the ways the Spirit of '76 had to be given meaning amid the Realities of '78 or '80.

INTERPRETIVE ESSAY

John Shy

Mobilizing Armed Force in the American Revolution

What kind of men could Washington count on? Fourth of July orators would have us believe that the woods and fields were swarming with "minutemen" who were willing and able to bear arms against the redcoats. True enough, perhaps, for the short haul, for an engagement at Lexington or Concord, or on Bunker Hill—then home to the farm. But what of the long run? Who was willing to shoulder a musket, camp in the snows of Valley Forge, and face death month in and month out to "secure these liberties"? In the following essay, John Shy tries to come to terms with that question. In so doing, he tells us much about the character of the American Revolution. As you read the essay, pay particular attention to the distinctions Shy makes between the types of men who served year after year in the regular army and the others who served from time to time in the militia. You should note, too, the ways that social class was reflected in the military experience of Americans. What place does Shy give to ideology—to belief, political theory, philosophical attitudes? What is your guess about what, in the long run, motivated "Long Bill" Scott? Can you make any connection between his career and, say, the excerpt from Common Sense *in the preceding chapter? If you cannot, is the problem yours, or is it Shy's? Or was it Long Bill's?*

Armed force, and nothing else, decided the outcome of the American Revolution. Without armed force mobilized on a decisive scale, there would not today be a subject for discussion; shorn even of its name, the revolution would shrink to a mere rebellion—an interesting episode perhaps, but like dozens of others in the modern history of western societies. Crude, obvious, and unappealing as this truism may be, it is still true. And its truth needs to be probed and understood if we are to understand the revolution, because that revolution overcame the armed resistance of one of the two militarily strongest powers in the eighteenth-century world.

If the subject of mobilizing armed force in the American Revolution is important, it is also an exceptionally difficult one. Violence, with all its ramifications, remains a great mystery for students of human life, while the deeper motivational sources of human behavior—particularly behavior under conditions of stress—are almost equally mysterious. When these two mysteries come together, as they do in wars and revolutions, then the historian faces a problem full of traps and snares for the unwary, a problem that challenges his ability to

From John Shy, "Mobilizing Armed Force in the American Revolution," in John Parker and Carol Urness, eds., *The American Revolution: A Heritage of Change,* Associates of the James Ford Bell Library, Minneapolis, 1975, pp. 96–106. Reprinted by permission.

know *anything* about the past. A certain humility is obviously in order. Any of us who are tempted not to be humble might recall how recently intelligent, well-informed American leaders spoke glibly about winning the "hearts and minds" of another few million people caught up by war and revolution. That is our subject: the hearts and minds of Americans whose willingness to engage in violence, two centuries ago, fundamentally changed the course of history.

Ideas on our subject, as opposed to analysis based solidly on evidence, come cheap. Writing about an earlier revolutionary war, Thomas Hobbes expressed a cynical view of the relationship between armed force and mere public opinion—like that in the Declaration of Independence—when he said that "covenants without swords are but words." But a century later David Hume tempered Hobbes's cynicism with realism: "As Force is always on the side of the governed," Hume wrote, "the governors have nothing to support them but opinion." Perhaps Hume's view has lost some of its validity in our own time, when technology vastly multiplies the amount of force that a few people can wield, but it certainly held good for the eighteenth century, when even the best weapons were still relatively primitive and widely available. If Hobbes—like all his fellow cynics down through history—is right in believing that public opinion is a fairly fragile flower, which can seldom survive the hot wind of violence, Hume reminds us that no one uses force without being moved to do so. John Adams put his finger on this matter of motivation when he said that the real American Revolution, the revolution that estranged American hearts from old British loyalties and readied American minds to use (and to withstand) massive violence, was over before the war began. Adams also opined that a third of the American people supported the revolutionary cause, another third remained more or less loyal to Britain, and that the rest were neutral or apathetic. Clearly, even Adams conceded that not all hearts and minds had been affected in the same way. Many British observers thought that the real American revolutionaries were the religious dissenters, Congregationalists and Presbyterians who had always been secretly disloyal to the crown because they rejected the whole Anglican Establishment, whose head was the king; and that these revolutionaries persuaded poor Irishmen, who had poured into the American colonies in great numbers during the middle third of the eighteenth century, to do most of the dirty business of actual fighting. American observers, on the other hand, generally assumed that all decent, sane people supported the revolution, and that those who did not could be categorized as timid, vicious, corrupt, or deluded. Each of these ideas on our subject contains a measure of truth; but they seem to contradict one another, and they do not carry us very far toward understanding.

Like these stock ideas, we have two standard images of the popular response to revolutionary war. One is of whole towns springing to arms as Paul Revere carries his warning to them in the spring of 1775. The other is of a tiny, frozen, naked band of men at Valley Forge, all that are left when everyone else went home in the winter of 1778. Which is the true picture? Both, evidently. But that answer is of no use at all when we ask whether the revolution succeeded only by the persistence of a very small group of people, the intervention of France, and great good luck; or whether the revolution was—or became—

unbeatable because the mass of the population simply would not give up the struggle, and the British simply could not muster the force and the resolution to kill them all or break their will or sit on all, or even any large proportion, of them. Who actually took up arms and why? How strong was the motivation to serve, and to keep serving in spite of defeat and other adversities? What was the intricate interplay and feedback between attitude and behavior, events and attitude? Did people get war-weary and discouraged, or did they become adamant toward British efforts to coerce them? If we could answer these questions with confidence, not only would we know why the rebels won and the government lost, but we would also know important things about the American society that emerged from seven years of armed conflict.

A suitably humble approach to these staggering questions lies readily to hand in a book written by Peter Oliver, who watched the revolution explode in Boston. Oliver descended from some of the oldest families of Massachusetts Bay, he was a distinguished merchant and public official, and he became a bitter Tory. His book, *The Origin and Progress of the American Rebellion*, not published until 1961 and [available] in paperback, is a fascinatingly unsympathetic version of the revolution, and in it Oliver makes an attempt to answer some of our questions. Using the technique, perfected by S. L. A. Marshall during the Second World War, of the after-action interview, Oliver asked a wounded American lieutenant, who had been captured at Bunker Hill, how he had come to be a rebel. The American officer allegedly replied as follows:

> The case was this Sir! I lived in a Country Town; I was a Shoemaker, & got my Living by my Labor. When this Rebellion came on, I saw some of my Neighbors get into Commission, who were no better than myself. I was very ambitious, & did not like to see those Men above me. I was asked to enlist, as a private Soldier. My Ambition was too great for so low a Rank; I offered to enlist upon having a Lieutenants Commission; which was granted. I imagined myself now in a way of Promotion: if I was killed in Battle, there would be an end of me, but if my Captain was killed, I should rise in Rank, & should still have a Chance to rise higher. These Sir! were the only Motives of my entering into the Service; for as to the Dispute between great Britain & the Colonies, I know nothing of it; neither am I capable of judging whether it is right or wrong.

Those who have read U.S. government publications over the last decade will find this POW interrogation familiar; during the Vietnam war, the State and Defense Department[s] published many like it, and more than one Vietcong prisoner is said to have spoken in the vein of the wounded American lieutenant so long ago.

Now the lieutenant was not a figment of Oliver's embittered imagination. His name is given by Oliver as Scott, and American records show that a Lieutenant William Scott, of Colonel Paul Sargent's regiment, was indeed wounded and captured at the battle of Bunker Hill. Scott turns out, upon investigation, to have been an interesting character. Perhaps the first thing to be said about him is that nothing in the record of his life down to 1775 contradicts anything in Oliver's account of the interview. Scott came from Peterborough, New Hampshire, a town settled in the 1730s by Irish Presbyterians. Scott's father had served in the famous Rogers' Rangers during the French and Indian War. At the news of the outbreak of fighting in 1775, a cousin who kept the store in Peterborough recruited a company of local men to fight the British. Apparently the cousin tried to enlist our William Scott—known to his neighbors as "Long Bill," thus distinguishing him from the cousin, "Short Bill." But "Long Bill"—our Bill—seems to have declined serving as a private, and insisted on being a lieutenant if cousin "Short Bill" was going to be a captain. "Short Bill" agreed. So far the stories as told by Oliver and as revealed in the New Hampshire records check perfectly. Nor is there any reason to think that "Long Bill" had a deeper understanding of the causes of the revolution than appear in Oliver's version of the interview.

What Peter Oliver never knew was the subsequent life history of this battered yokel, whose view of the American rebellion seemed so pitifully naive. When the British evacuated Boston, they took Scott and other American prisoners to Halifax, Nova Scotia. There, after more than a year in captivity, Scott somehow managed to escape, to find a boat, and to make his way back to the American army just in time for the fighting around New York City in 1776. Captured again in November, when Fort Washington and its garrison fell to a surprise British assault, Scott escaped almost immediately, this time by swimming the Hudson River at night—according to a newspaper account—with his sword tied around his neck and his watch pinned to his hat. He returned to New Hampshire during the winter of 1777 to recruit a company of his own; there, he enlisted his two oldest sons for three years or the duration of the war. Stationed in the Boston area, he marched against Burgoyne's invading army from Canada, and led a detachment that cut off the last retreat just before the surrender near Saratoga. Scott later took part in the fighting around Newport, Rhode Island. But when his light infantry company was ordered to Virginia under Lafayette in early 1781, to counter the raiding expedition led by Benedict Arnold, Scott's health broke down; long marches and hot weather made the old Bunker Hill wounds ache, and he was permitted to resign from the army. After only a few months of recuperation, however, he seems to have grown restless, for we find him during the last year of the war serving as a volunteer on a navy frigate.

What would Scott have said if Oliver had been able to interview him again, after the war? We can only guess. Probably he would have told Oliver that his oldest son had died in the army, not gloriously, but of camp fever, after six years of service. Scott might have said that in 1777 he had sold his Peterborough farm in order to meet expenses, but that the note which he took in exchange turned into a scrap of paper when the dollar of 1777 became worth less than two cents by 1780. He might also have said that another farm, in Groton, Massachusetts, slipped away from him, along with a down payment that he had made on it, when his military pay depreciated rapidly to a fraction of its nominal value. He might not have been willing to admit that when his wife died he simply turned their younger children over to his surviving elder son, and then set off to beg a pension or a job from the government. Almost certainly he would not have told Oliver that when the son—himself sick, his corn crop killed by a late frost, and saddled with three little brothers and sisters—begged his father for help, our hero told him that, if all else failed, he might hand the children over to the selectmen of Peterborough.

In 1792, "Long Bill" Scott once more made the newspapers: he rescued eight people from drowning when their small boat capsized in New York harbor. But heroism did not pay very well. At last, in 1794, Secretary of War Henry Knox made Scott deputy storekeeper at West Point; and a year later General Benjamin Lincoln took Scott with him to the Ohio country, where they were to negotiate with the Indians and survey the land opened up by Anthony Wayne's victory at Fallen Timbers. At last he had a respectable job, and even a small pension for his nine wounds; but Lincoln's group caught something called "lake fever" while surveying on the Black River, near Sandusky. Scott, ill himself, guided part of the group back to Fort Stanwix, New York, then returned for the others. It was his last heroic act. A few days after his second trip, he died, on September 16, 1796.

Anecdotes, even good ones like the touching saga of "Long Bill" Scott, do not make history. But neither can a subject like ours be treated in terms of what Professor Jesse Lemisch has referred to as the lives of Great White Men—Washington, Adams, Jefferson, Hamilton, and the handful like them. Scott's life, in itself, may tell us little about how armed force and public opinion were mobilized in the revolution; yet the story of his life leads us directly—and at the level of ordinary people—toward crucial features of the process.

Peterborough, New Hampshire, in 1775 had a population of 549. Town, state, and federal records show that about 170 men were credited to Peterborough as performing some military service during the revolution. In other words, almost every adult male, at one time or another, carried a gun in the war. Of these 170 participants, less than a third performed really extensive service; that is, service ranging from over a year up to the whole eight years of the war. Only a fraction of these—less than two dozen—served as long as Bill Scott. In Scott we are not seeing a typical participant, but one of a small "hard core" of revolutionary fighters—men who stayed in the army for more than a few months or a single campaign. As we look down the list of long-service soldiers from Peterborough, they seem indeed to be untypical people. A few, like Scott and his cousin "Short Bill" and James Taggert and Josiah Munroe, became officers or at least sergeants, and thereby acquired status and perhaps some personal satisfaction from their prolonged military service. But most of the hard core remained privates, and they were an unusually poor, obscure group of men, even by the rustic standards of Peterborough. Many—like John Alexander, Robert Cunningham, William Ducannon, Joseph Henderson, Richard Richardson, John Wallace, and Thomas Williamson—were recruited from outside the town, from among men who never really lived in Peterborough. Whether they lived *anywhere*—in the strict legal sense—is a question. Two men—Zaccheus Brooks and John Miller—are simply noted as "transients." At least two—James Hackley and Randall McAllister—were deserters from the British army. At least two others—Samuel Weir and Titus Wilson—were black men, Wilson dying as a prisoner of war. A few, like Michael Silk, simply appear to join the army, then vanish without a documentary trace. Many more reveal themselves as near the bottom of the socioeconomic ladder: Hackley, Benjamin Allds, Isaac Mitchell, Ebenezer Perkins, Amos Spofford, Jonathan Wheelock, and Charles White were legal paupers after the revolution; Joseph Henderson was a landless day-laborer; Samuel Spear was jailed for debt; and John Millet was mentally deranged.

We can look at the whole Peterborough contingent in another way, in terms of those in it who were, or later became, prominent or at least solid citizens of the town. With a few exceptions like "Short Bill" Scott and "Long Bill's" son John, who survived frost-killed corn and a parcel of unwanted siblings to become a selectman and a leader of the town, these prominent men and solid citizens had served in the war for only short periods—a few months in 1775, a month or two in the Burgoyne emergency of 1777, maybe a month in Rhode Island or a month late in the war to bolster the key garrison of West Point. The pattern is clear, and it is a pattern that reappears wherever the surviving evidence has permitted a similar kind of inquiry. Lynn, Massachusetts; Berks County, Pennsylvania; Colonel Smallwood's recruits from Maryland in 1782; several regiments of the Massachusetts Line; a sampling of pension applicants from Virginia—all show that the hard core of Continental soldiers, the Bill Scotts who could not wangle commissions, the soldiers at Valley Forge, the men who shouldered the heaviest military burden, were something less than average colonial Americans. As a group, they were poorer, more marginal, less well anchored in the society. Perhaps we should not be surprised; it is easy to imagine men like these actually being attracted by the relative affluence, comfort, security, prestige, and even the chance for satisfying human relationships offered by the Continental army. Revolutionary America may have been a middle-class society, happier and more prosperous than any other in its time, but it contained a large and growing number of fairly poor people, and many of them did much of the actual fighting and suffering between 1775 and 1783: a very old story.

The large proportion of men, from Peterborough and other communities, who served only briefly might thus seem far less important to our subject than the disadvantaged minority who did such a large part of the heavy work of revolution. This militarily less active majority were of course the militiamen. One could compile a large volume of pithy observations, beginning with a few dozen from Washington himself, in which the value of the militia was called into question. The nub of the critique was that these part-time soldiers were untrained, undisciplined, undependable, and very expensive, consuming pay, rations, clothing, and weapons at a great rate in return for short periods of active service. By the end of the war, the tendency of many Continental officers, like Colonel Alexander Hamilton, to disparage openly the military performance of the militia was exacerbating already strained relations between state and Continental authorities. And indeed there were a number of cases in which the failure of militia to arrive in time, to stand under fire, or to remain when they were needed, either contributed to American difficulties or prevented the exploitation of American success. But the revolutionary role of the men from Peterborough and elsewhere who did *not* serve as did Bill Scott, but whose active military service was rather a sometime thing, is easily misunderstood and underestimated if we look at it only in terms of traditional military strategy and set-piece battles.

To understand the revolutionary militia and its role, we must go back to the year before the outbreak of fighting at Lexington and Concord. Each colony, except Pennsylvania, had traditionally required every free white adult male, with a few minor occupational exceptions, to be inscribed in a militia unit, and to take part in training several times a year. These militia units seldom achieved any degree of military proficiency, nor were they expected to serve as actual fighting formations. Their real function might be described as a hybrid of draft board and modern reserve unit—a modicum of military training combined with a mechanism to find and enlist individuals when they were needed. But the colonial militia did not simply slide smoothly into the revolution. Militia officers, even where they were elected, held royal commissions, and a significant number of them were not enthusiastic about rebellion. Purging and restructuring the militia was an important step toward revolution, one that deserves more attention than it has had.

When in early 1774, the news reached America that Parliament would take a very hard line in response to the Boston Tea Party, and in particular had passed a law that could destroy economically and politically the town of Boston, the reaction in the colonies was stronger and more nearly unanimous than at any time since the Stamp Act. No one could defend the Boston Port Act; it was an unprecedented, draconian law the possible consequences of which seemed staggering. Radicals, like Sam Adams, demanded an immediate and complete break in commercial relations with the rest of the empire. Boycotts had worked effectively in the past, and they were an obvious response to the British hard line. More moderate leaders, however, dreaded a hasty confrontation that might quickly escalate beyond their control, and they used democratic theory to argue that nothing ought to be done without a full and proper consultation of the popular will. Like the boycott, the consultative congress had a respectable pedigree, and the moderates won the argument. When the Continental Congress met in September 1774, there were general expectations in both Britain and America that it would cool and seek to compromise the situation.

Exactly what happened to disappoint those expectations is even now not wholly clear; our own sense that Congress was heading straight toward revolution and independence distorts a complex moment in history, when uncertainty about both ends and means deeply troubled the minds of most decision-makers. Congress had hardly convened when it heard that the British had bombarded Boston. For a few days men from different colonies, normally suspicious of one another, were swept together by a wave of common fear and apprehension. Though the report was quickly proved false, these hours of mutual panic seem to have altered the emotional economy of the Congress. Soon afterward it passed without any serious dissent a resolution in favor of the long-advocated boycott, to be known as the Association. Local committees were to gather signatures for the Association, and were to take necessary steps to enforce its provisions. The Association was the vital link in transforming the colonial militia into a revolutionary organization.

For more than a year, a tenuous line of authority ran directly from the Continental Congress to the grass roots of American society. The traditional, intermediate levels of government, if they did not cooperate fully, were bypassed. Committees formed everywhere to enforce the Association, and sympathetic men volunteered to assist in its enforcement. In some places, like Peterborough, the same men who were enrolled in the militia became the strong right arm of the local committee; reluctant militia officers were ignored because, after all, not the militia as such but a voluntary association of militia members was taking the action. In other places, like parts of the Hudson Valley and Long Island, reluctance was so widespread that men opposed to the Association actually tried to take over the committee system in order to kill it; when meetings were called to form the new armed organization of Associators, loyal militiamen packed the meetings and re-elected the old, royally commissioned lieutenants and captains. But even where the Association encountered heavy opposition, it effectively dissolved the old military structure and created a new one based on consent, and whose chief purpose was to engineer consent, by force if necessary. The new revolutionary militia might look very much like the old colonial militia, but it was, in its origins, less a draft board and a reserve training unit than a police force and an instrument of political surveillance. Although the boycott could be defended to moderate men as a constitutional, nonviolent technique, its implementation had radical consequences. Adoption by Congress gave it a legitimacy and a unity that it could have gained in no other way. Ordinary men were forced to make public choices, and thus to identify themselves with one side or the other. Not until the Declaration of Independence clarified the hazy status of the traditional levels of government did the local committees, acting through the new militia, relinquish some of their truly revolutionary power.

It is difficult to overestimate the importance of what happened in 1775 to engage mass participation on the side of the revolution. The new militia, which was repeatedly denying that it was in rebellion and proclaimed its loyalty to the crown, enforced a boycott intended to make Britain back down; Britain did not back down, but the attempt drew virtually everyone into the realm of politics. Enlistment, training, and occasional emergencies were the means whereby dissenters were identified, isolated, and dealt with. Where the new militia had trouble getting organized, there revolutionary activists could see that forceful intervention from outside might be needed. Connecticut units moved into the New York City area; Virginia troops moved into the Delmarva peninsula; in Pennsylvania, men from Reading and Lancaster marched into Bucks County. Once established, the militia became the infrastructure of revolutionary government. It controlled its community, whether through indoctrination or intimidation; it provided on short notice large numbers of armed men for brief periods of emergency service; and it found and persuaded, drafted or bribed, the smaller number of men needed each year to keep the Continental army alive. After the first months of the war, popular enthusiasm and spontaneity could not have sustained the struggle; only a pervasive armed organization, in which almost everyone took some part, kept people constantly, year after year, at the hard task of revolution. While Scott and his sons, the indigent, the blacks, and the otherwise socially expendable men fought the British, James and Samuel Cunningham, Henry Ferguson, John Gray, William McNee, Benjamin Mitchell, Robert Morison, Alexander and William Robbe, Robert Swan, Robert Wilson, and four or five men named Smith—all militiamen, but whose combined active service hardly equaled that of "Long Bill" Scott alone—ran Peterborough, expelling a few Tories, scraping up enough recruits for the Continental army to meet the town's quota every spring, taking time out to help John Stark destroy the Germans at the battle of Bennington.

The mention of Tories brings us, briefly, to the last aspect of our subject. Peterborough had little trouble with Tories; the most sensational case occurred when the Presbyterian minister, the Reverend John Morrison, who had been having trouble with his congregation, deserted his post as chaplain to the Peterborough troops and entered British lines at Boston in June 1775. But an informed estimate is that about a half million Americans, about a fifth of the population, can be counted as loyal to Britain. Looking at the absence of serious loyalism in Peterborough, we might conclude that Scotch-Irish Presbyterians almost never were Tories. That, however, would be an error of fact, and we are impelled to seek further for an explanation. What appears as we look at places, like Peterborough, where Tories are hardly visible, and at other places were Toryism was rampant, is a pattern—not so much an ethnic, religious, or ideological pattern, but a pattern of raw power. Wherever the British and their allies were strong enough to penetrate in force—along the seacoast, in the Hudson, Mohawk, and lower Delaware Valleys, in Georgia, the Carolinas, and the transappalachian west—there Toryism flourished. But geographically less exposed areas, if population density made self-defense feasible—most of New England, the Pennsylvania hinterland, and piedmont Virginia—where the enemy hardly appeared or not at all, there Tories either ran away, kept quiet, even serving in the rebel armies, or occasionally took a brave but hopeless stand against revolutionary committees and their gunmen. After the war, of course, men remembered their parts in the successful revolution in ways that make it difficult for the historian to reconstruct accurately the relationship between what they thought and what they did.

The view which I have presented of how armed force and public opinion were mobilized may seem a bit cynical—a reversion to Thomas Hobbes. True, it gives little weight to ideology, to perceptions and principles, to grievances and aspirations, to the more admirable side of the emergent American character. Perhaps that is a weakness; perhaps I have failed to grasp what really drove Bill Scott. But what strikes me most forcibly in studying this part of the revolution is how much in essential agreement almost all Americans were in 1774, both in their views of British measures and in their feelings about them. What then is puzzling, and thus needs explaining, is why so many of these people behaved in anomalous and in different ways. Why did so many, who did not intend a civil war or political independence, get so inextricably involved in the organization and use of armed force? Why did relatively few do most of the actual fighting? Why was a dissenting fifth of the population so politically and militarily impotent, so little able to affect the outcome of the struggle? Answers to these questions cannot be found in the life of one obscure man, or in the history of one backwoods town. But microscopic study does emphasize certain features of the revolution: the political structuring of resistance to Britain, the play of social and economic factors in carrying on that resistance by armed force, and the brutally direct effects on behavior, if not on opinions, of military power.

SOURCES

A Spy's View of Washington's Army, 1775

What do contemporary sources tell us about Washington's army? What follows is an eyewitness version—written by a spy. He was a New Englander named Benjamin Thompson, in the pay of the British. He was, in other words, a British patriot, who later moved to Europe, where he became famous as a scientist and philosopher known to the world as Count Rumford. As you read, note that Rumford's observations were made at about the same time that Peter Oliver interviewed William Scott (see p. 135). Do Rumford's observations seem believable to you? What do you think his attitude toward "lower-class" soldiers was? Would it surprise you to know that Washington might have agreed with most of what Rumford says? What do you think lies behind Rumford's attempt to puncture the myth of the deadly accuracy of American riflemen? It might all be simply true, of course. But could it also reflect his desire to cause the British officials to be confident in their capacity to defeat the Americans militarily? Or could this opinion have something to do with social class? What would you suppose was the class status of the riflemen? Of Rumford?

Observations by Benjamin Thompson

Boston, November 4, 1775

. . . The army in general is not very badly accoutered, but most wretchedly clothed, and as dirty a set of mortals as ever disgraced the name of a soldier. They have had no clothes of any sort provided for them by the Congress (except the detachment of 1133 that are gone to Canada under Col. Arnold, who had each of them a new coat and a linen frock served out to them before they set out), tho' the army in general, and the Massachusetts forces in particular, had encouragement of having coats given them by way of bounty for inlisting. And the neglect of the Congress to fulfill their promise in this respect has been the source of not a little uneasiness among the soldiers.

They have no women in the camp to do washing for the men, and they in general not being used to doing things of this sort, and thinking it rather a disparagement to them, choose rather to let their linen, etc., rot upon their backs than to be at the trouble of cleaning 'em themselves. And to this nasty way of life, and to the change of their diet from milk, vegetables, etc., to living almost

From "Miscellaneous Observations upon the State of the Rebel Army," in Great Britain Historical Manuscripts Commission, Report on the Manuscripts of Mrs. Stopford-Sackville, 2 vols., H. M. Stationery Office, London, by Mackie, 1904–1910, Vol. II, pp. 15–18.

intirely upon flesh, must be attributed those putrid, malignant and infectious disorders which broke out among them soon after their taking the field, and which have prevailed with unabating fury during the whole summer.

The leading men among them (with their usual art and cunning) have been indefatigable in their endeavors to conceal the real state of the army in this respect, and to convince the world that the soldiers were tolerably healthy. But the contrary has been apparent, even to a demonstration, to every person that had but the smallest acquaintance with their camp. And so great was the prevalence of these disorders in the month of July that out of 4207 men who were stationed upon Prospect Hill no more than 2227 were returned fit for duty.

The mortality among them must have been very great, and to this in a great measure must be attributed the present weakness of their regiments; many of which were much stronger when they came into the field. But the number of soldiers that have died in the camp is comparatively small to those vast numbers that have gone off in the interior parts of the country. For immediately upon being taken down with these disorders they have in general been carried back into the country to their own homes, where they have not only died themselves, but by spreading the infection among their relatives and friends have introduced such a general mortality throughout New England as was never known since its first planting. Great numbers have been carried off in all parts of the country. Some towns 'tis said have lost near one-third of their inhabitants; and there is scarce a village but has suffered more or less from the raging virulence of these dreadful disorders. . . .

The soldiers in general are most heartily sick of the service, and I believe it would be with the utmost difficulty that they could be prevailed upon to serve another campaign. The Continental Congress are very sensible of this, and have lately sent a committee to the camp to consult with the general officers upon some method of raising the necessary forces to serve during the winter season, as the greatest part of the army that is now in the field is to be disbanded upon the last day of December.

Whether they will be successful in their endeavours to persuade the soldiers to re-inlist or not, I cannot say, but am rather inclined to think that they will. For as they are men possessed of every species of cunning and artifice, and as their political existence depends upon the existence of the army, they will leave no stone unturned to accomplish their designs.

Notwithstanding the indefatigable endeavours of Mr. Washington and the other generals, and particularly of Adjutant General Gates, to arrange and discipline the army, yet any tolerable degree of order and subordination is what they are totally unacquainted with in the rebel camp. And the doctrines of independence and levellism have been so effectually sown throughout the country, and so universally imbibed by all ranks of men, that I apprehend it will be with the greatest difficulty that the inferior officers and soldiers will be ever brought to any tolerable degree of subjection to the commands of their superiors.

Many of their leading men are not insensible of this, and I have often heard them lament that the existence of that very spirit which induced the common people to take up arms and resist the authority of Great Britain, should induce them to resist the authority of their own officers, and by that means effectually prevent their ever making good soldiers.

Another great reason why it is impossible to introduce a proper degree of subordination in the rebel army is the great degree of equality as to birth, fortune, and education that universally prevails among them. For men cannot bear to be commanded by others that are their superiors in nothing but in having had the good fortune to get a superior commission, for which perhaps they stood equally fair. And in addition to this, the officers and men are not only in general very nearly upon a par as to birth, fortune, etc., but in particular regiments are most commonly neighbours and acquaintances, and as such can with less patience submit to that degree of absolute submission and subordination which is necessary to form a well-disciplined corps.

Another reason why the army can never be well united and regulated is the disagreement and jealousies between the different troops from the different Colonies; which must never fail to create disaffection and uneasiness among them. The Massachusetts forces already complain very loudly of the partiality of the General to the Virginians, and have even gone so far as to tax him with taking pleasure in bringing their officers to court martials, and having them cashiered that he may fill their places with his friends from that quarter. The gentlemen from the Southern Colonies, in their turn, complain of the enormous proportion of New England officers in the army, and particularly of those belonging to the province of Massachusetts Bay, and say, as the cause is now become a common one, and the experience is general, they ought to have an equal chance for command with their neighbours.

Thus have these jealousies and uneasiness already begun which I think cannot fail to increase and grow every day more and more interesting, and if they do not finally destroy the very existence of the army (which I think they bid very fair to do), yet must unavoidably render it much less formidable than it otherways might have been.

Of all useless sets of men that ever incumbered an army, surely the boasted riflemen are certainly the most so. When they came to the camp they had every liberty and indulgence allowed them that they could possibly wish for. They had more pay than any other soldiers; did not duty; were under no restraint from the commands of their officers, but went when and where they pleased, without being subject to be stopped or examined by any one, and did almost intirely as they pleased in every respect whatever. But they have not answered the end for which they were designed in any one article whatever. For instead of being the best marksmen in the world, and picking off every regular that was to be seen, there is scarsely a regiment in camp but can produce men that can beat them at shooting, and the army is now universally convinced that the continual fire which they kept up by the week and month together has had no other effect than to waste their ammunition and convince the King's troops that they are not really so formidable adversaries as they would wish to be thought. . . .

Three Views Of The
American Soldier

Here are three representations of the American soldier. The first is an English caricature. The second is a painting by Charles Willson Peale (a soldier himself) that shows the highest ideal the Americans had of soldierly appearance and conduct, George Washington. The Marquis de Lafayette is the center figure, and to the right is Washington's aide, General Tench Tilghman. The third is a French painting showing two infantrymen, a rifleman, and an artilleryman. (Each is wearing a different uniform, not just because they serve in different branches of the army but because they come from different colonies.)

As you examine these three pictures, keep these points and questions in mind. Patrick Henry's famous remark, "Give me liberty or give me death," is mocked in the British picture. But what is the effect of reversing the order of the words? Notice the clothing, stance, and the facial expression of Washington. What kinds of class values and attitudes do you think Peale is trying to depict here? In the French picture, do the soldiers look "American" at all, or do they conform more to your image of a typical European soldier of the Napoleonic period? Or is there a mixture?

British Caricature.
Metropolitan Museum of Art. Bequest of Charles Allen Munn, 1924.

THE AMERICAN RIFLE MEN.

Washington, with the Marquis de Lafayette. By the American artist Charles Willson
Peale.
M. E. Warren Photography/Photo Researchers.

A Contemporary French Painting.
Anne S. K. Brown Military Collection/Brown University Library.

Silencing the Tories

The following documents tell us something about the American treatment of Tories, who probably constituted about 20 percent of the population—potentially a powerful and dangerous force. The first is a cartoon drawn in London mocking the way the rebels treated John Malcomb, a crown official who had tried to collect the tea tax in Boston in 1774. What do the clothes tell you about the kinds of people the British thought were in rebellion? Look at the facial features. How does the cartoonist try to convince us that John Malcomb is made of finer stuff than the men who have tarred and feathered him?

The second document is part of the letter from a Tory woman, Ann Hulton, a Bostonian, about another 1774 tarring and feathering; the third is a rebel description of a similar event in New York about a year later. Which document do you find more convincing? Taken together, do they support Shy's point about the importance of using military and quasi-military force to keep revolutionary order? Or do they hint at a rabble acting in undisciplined anger?

The BOSTONIAN'S Paying the EXCISE-MAN, or TARRING & FEATHERING

Library of Congress.

Ann Hulton to Mrs. Lightbody.

Boston, January 31, 1774

. . . But the most shocking cruelty was exercised a few nights ago, upon a poor old man, a tidesman, one Malcolm. He is reckoned creasy, a quarrel was picked with him, he was afterward taken and tarred and feathered. There's no law that knows a punishment for the greatest crimes beyond what this is of cruel torture. And this instance exceeds any other before it. He was stript stark naked, one of the severest cold nights this winter, his body covered all over with tar, then with feathers, his arm dislocated in tearing off his cloaths. He was dragged in a cart with thousands attending, some beating him with clubs and knocking him out of the cart, then in again. They gave him several severe whippings, at different parts of the town. This spectacle of horror and sportive cruelty was exhibited for about five hours.

The unhappy wretch they say behaved with the greatest intrepidity and fortitude all the while. Before he was taken, [he] defended himself a long time against numbers, and afterwards when under torture they demanded of him to curse his masters, the King, Governor, etc., which they could not make him do, but he still cried, "Curse all traitors!" They brought him to the gallows and put a rope about his neck, saying they would hang him. He said he wished they would, but that they could not, for God was above the Devil. The doctors say that it is impossible this poor creature can live. They say his flesh comes off his back in stakes.

It is the second time he has been tarred and feathered and this is looked upon more to intimidate the judges and others than a spite to the unhappy victim tho' they owe him a grudge for some things particularly. He was with Govr. Tryon in the battle with the Regulators and the Governor has declared that he was of great servise to him in that affair, by his undaunted spirit encountering the greatest dangers.

Govr. Tryon had sent him a gift of ten guineas just before this inhuman treatment. He has a wife and family and an aged father and mother who, they say, saw the spectacle which no indifferent person can mention without horror.

These few instances amongst many serve to shew the abject state of government and the licentiousness and barbarism of the times. There's no majestrate that dare or will act to suppress the outrages. No person is secure. There are many objects pointed at, at this time, and when once marked out for vengeance, their ruin is certain.

The judges have only a week's time allowed them to consider whether they will take the salaries from the Crown or no. Govr. Hutchinson is going to England as soon as the season will permit.

We are under no apprehension at present on our own account but we can't look upon our safety secure for long.

From Ann Hulton, *Letters of a Loyalist Lady* . . . *1767–1776*, Cambridge, Mass., 1927, pp. 70–72.

From the records of the Committee of Safety.

New York, December 28, 1775

The 6th of December, at Quibbletown, Middlesex County, Piscataway Township, New-Jersey, Thomas Randolph, cooper, who had publickly proved himself an enemy to his country, by reviling and using his utmost endeavours to oppose the proceedings of the Continental and Provincial Conventions and Committees, in defence of their rights and liberties; and he, being judged a person of not consequence enough for a severer punishment, was ordered to be stripped naked, well coated with tar and feathers, and carried in a wagon publickly round the town; which punishment was accordingly inflicted. And as he soon became duly sensible of his offence, for which he earnestly begged pardon, and promised to atone, as far as he was able, by a contrary behaviour for the future, he was released, and suffered to return to his house in less than half an hour. The whole was conducted with that regularity and decorum that ought to be observed in all publick punishments.

From Peter Force, ed., *American Archives: Fourth Series,* 6 vols., M. St. Clair Clarke and Peter Force, Washington, D.C., 1837–1846, Vol. IV, p. 203.

CHAPTER 7

Creating the Constitution

The new nation brought into being by the revolution stretched from the Atlantic to the Mississippi. It was a huge wilderness by European standards, six times the size of England and Wales combined, but thinly populated. Although most of the 3 to 4 million inhabitants lived near the Atlantic, the population had begun to move into the forests beyond the seaboard, farther and farther away from the centers of communication. So poor were communications and so rudimentary were transportation facilities that the country was little more than a collection of isolated communities. There were only six cities with over 8000 inhabitants. The largest was Philadelphia, with some 40,000, followed by New York, Boston, Charleston, Baltimore, and Salem. Ninety-five percent of the population lived elsewhere, on isolated farms or in small villages, scattered from Maine to Georgia.

How could 3 to 4 million people, dispersed over a vast wilderness, be governed? That question was faced by every state in the revolutionary period, and also by the new nation. But it was never really resolved. Laws were passed and orders were given, but there was simply no way that a handful of government officials could force a scattered—and somewhat unruly—population to obey the law. And few officials were foolish enough to try.

Instead, America's leaders were content to fashion a new system of government. And that, to them, was exciting. They saw themselves as daring innovators, creating a republic in a world of monarchies, establishing a new government not only for themselves but "for millions yet unborn." Wrote John Adams in 1776: "You and I, my dear friend, have been sent into life at a time when the greatest lawgivers of antiquity would have wished to live. How few of the human race have enjoyed an opportunity of making an election of government for themselves or their children."

It would be foolish to ignore this self-perception. But it would be equally foolish to forget that nine-tenths of those who had the chance to mold the new government were men of property, members of the colonial elite, old hands at government. Clearly, their vision of the new order was tempered by experience. But was it also tempered by self-interest? That question has been raised particularly in regard to the men who met in Philadelphia in 1787, destroyed the first system of federal government, and established the present system.

INTERPRETIVE ESSAY

Alfred F. Young

The Framers and the People

The modern debate over the nature of the Constitutional Convention has been dominated by two opinions. One is that the Founding Fathers were men of detached and lofty perceptions, men of principle who tried to embody those principles in a frame of government they hoped would endure for generations. The other is that the members of the convention were men of property whose actions were tied directly to their own economic stake in the outcome. In the following selection, Alfred F. Young takes a somewhat different stance. He agrees that the founders of the Constitution represented the interests of slaveholding planters, merchants, and "monied men." But they accommodated the "genius" of the people, not because they were saints but because they feared the wrath of ordinary citizens. As you read, try to determine what these accommodations were. And what, if anything, these accommodations cost the governing elite.

On June 18, 1787, about three weeks into the Constitutional Convention at Philadelphia, Alexander Hamilton delivered a six-hour address that was easily the longest and most conservative the Convention would hear. Gouverneur Morris, a delegate from Pennsylvania, thought it was "the most able and impressive he had ever heard."

Beginning with the premise that "all communities divide themselves into the few and the many," "the wealthy well born" and "the people," Hamilton added the corollary that the "people are turbulent and changing; they seldom judge or determine right." Moving through history, the delegate from New York developed his ideal for a national government that would protect the few from "the imprudence of democracy" and guarantee "stability and permanence": a president and senate indirectly elected for life ("to serve during good behavior") to balance a house directly elected by a popular vote every three years. This "elective monarch" would have an absolute veto over laws passed by Congress. And the national government would appoint the governors of the states, who in turn would have the power to veto any laws by the state legislatures.

If others quickly saw a resemblance in all of this to the king, House of Lords, and House of Commons of Great Britain, with the states reduced to colonies ruled by royal governors, they were not mistaken. The British constitution, in Hamilton's view, remained "the best model the world has ever produced."

Three days later a delegate reported that Hamilton's proposals "had been praised by everybody," but "he has been supported by none." Acknowledging

Alfred F. Young, "The Framers of the Constitution and the 'Genius' of the People," *Radical History Review*, 42 (Fall 1988), pp. 8–18. Reprinted with permission from C MARHO: The Radical Historians' Organization. Originally published in *Radical History Review*, vol. 42, Fall 1988.

that his plan "went beyond the ideas of most members," Hamilton said he had brought it forward not "as a thing attainable by us, but as a model which we ought to approach as near as possible." When he signed the Constitution the framers finally agreed to on September 17, 1787, Hamilton could accurately say, "no plan was more remote from his own."

Why did the framers reject a plan so many admired? To ask this question is to go down a dark path into the heart of the Constitution few of its celebrants care to take. We have heard so much in our elementary and high school civics books about the "great compromises" within the Convention—between the large states and the small states, between the slaveholders and nonslaveholders, between north and south—that we have missed the much larger accommodation that was taking place between the delegates as a whole at the Convention and what they called "the people out of doors."

The Convention was unmistakably an elite body. The official exhibit for the bicentennial, "Miracle at Philadelphia," opens appropriately enough with a large oil portrait of Robert Morris, a delegate from Philadelphia, one of the richest merchants in America, and points out elsewhere that eleven out of fifty-five delegates were business associates of Morris's. The fifty-five were weighted with merchants, slaveholding planters and "monied men" who loaned money at interest. Among them were numerous lawyers and college graduates in a country where most men and only a few women had the rudiments of a formal education. They were far from a cross section of the 4 million or so Americans of that day, most of whom were farmers or artisans, fishermen or seamen, indentured servants or laborers, half of whom were women and about 600,000 of whom were African-American slaves.

I. THE FIRST ACCOMMODATION

Why did this elite reject Hamilton's plan that many of them praised? James Madison, the Constitution's chief architect, had the nub of the matter. The Constitution was "intended for the ages." To last it had to conform to the "genius" of the American people. "Genius" was a word eighteenth-century political thinkers used to mean spirit: we might say character or underlying values.

James Wilson, second only to Madison in his influence at Philadelphia, elaborated on the idea. "The British government cannot be our model. We have no materials for a similar one. Our manners, our law, the abolition of entail and primogeniture," which made for a more equal distribution of property among sons, "the whole genius of the people, are opposed to it."

This was long-range political philosophy. There was a short-range political problem that moved other realistic delegates in the same direction. Called together to revise the old Articles of Confederation, the delegates instead decided to scrap [them] and frame an entirely new constitution. It would have to be submitted to the people for ratification, most likely to conventions elected especially for the purpose. Repeatedly, conservatives recoiled from extreme proposals for which they knew they could not win popular support.

In response to a proposal to extend the federal judiciary into the states, Pierce Butler, a South Carolina planter, argued, "the people will not bear such innovations. The states will revolt at such encroachments." His assumption was "we must follow the example of Solomon, who gave the Athenians not the best government he could devise but the best they would receive."

The suffrage debate epitomized this line of thinking. Gouverneur Morris, Hamilton's admirer, proposed that the national government limit voting for the House to men who owned a freehold, i.e., a substantial farm, or its equivalent. "Give the vote to people who have no property and they will sell them to the rich who will be able to buy them," he said with some prescience. George Mason, author of Virginia's Bill of Rights, was aghast. "Eight or nine states have extended the right of suffrage beyond the freeholders. What will people there say if they should be disfranchised?"

Benjamin Franklin, the patriarch, speaking for one of the few times in the convention, paid tribute to "the lower class of freemen" who should not be disfranchised. James Wilson explained, "it would be very hard and disagreeable for the same person" who could vote for representatives for the state legislatures "to be excluded from a vote for this in the national legislature." Nathaniel Gorham, a Boston merchant, returned to the guiding principle: "the people will never allow" existing rights to suffrage to be abridged. "We must consult their rooted prejudices if we expect their concurrence in our propositions."

The result? Morris's proposal was defeated and the convention decided that whoever each state allowed to vote for its own assembly could vote for the House. It was a compromise that left the door open and in a matter of decades allowed states to introduce universal white male suffrage.

II. GHOSTS OF YEARS PAST

Clearly there was a process of accommodation at work here. The popular movements of the revolutionary era were a presence at the Philadelphia Convention even if they were not present. The delegates, one might say, were haunted by ghosts, symbols of the broadly based movements elites had confronted in the making of the revolution from 1765 to 1775, in waging the war from 1775 to 1781, and in the years since 1781 within their own states.

The first was the ghost of Thomas Paine, the most influential radical democrat of the revolutionary era. In 1776 Paine's pamphlet *Common Sense* (which sold at least 150,000 copies), in arguing for independence, rejected not only King George III but the principle of monarchy and the so-called checks and balances of the unwritten English constitution. In its place he offered a vision of a democratic government in which a single legislature would be supreme, the executive minimal, and representatives would be elected from small districts by a broad electorate for short terms so they could "return and mix again with the voters." John Adams considered *Common Sense* too "democratical," without even an attempt at "mixed government" that would balance "democracy" with "aristocracy."

The second ghost was that of Abraham Yates, a member of the state senate of New York typical of the new men who had risen to power in the 1780s in the state legislatures. We have forgotten him; Hamilton, who was very conscious of him, called him "an old Booby." He had begun as a shoemaker and was a self-taught lawyer and warm foe of the landlord aristocracy of the Hudson Valley into which Hamilton had married. As James Madison identified the "vices of the political system of the United States" in a memorandum in 1787, the Abraham Yateses were the number-one problem. The state legislatures had "an itch for paper money" laws, laws that prevented foreclosure on farm mortgages, and tax laws that soaked the rich. As Madison saw it, this meant that "debtors defrauded their creditors" and "the landed interest has borne hard on the mercantile interest." This, too, is what Hamilton had in mind when he spoke of the "depredations which the democratic spirit is apt to make on property" and what others meant by the "excess of democracy" in the states.

The third ghost was a very fresh one—Daniel Shays. In 1786 Shays, a captain in the revolution, led a rebellion of debtor farmers in western Massachusetts that the state quelled with its own somewhat unreliable militia. There were "combustibles in every state," as George Washington put it, raising the specter of "Shaysism." This Madison enumerated among the "vices" of the system as "a want of guaranty to the states against internal violence." Worse still, Shaysites in many states were turning to the political system to elect their own kind. If they succeeded they would produce legal Shaysism, a danger for which the elites had no remedy.

The fourth ghost we can name the ghost of Thomas Peters, although he had a thousand other names. In 1775, Peters, a Virginia slave, responded to a plea by the British to fight in their army and win their freedom. He served in an "Ethiopian Regiment," some of whose members bore the emblem "Liberty to Slaves" on their uniforms. After the war the British transported Peters and several thousand escaped slaves to Nova Scotia from whence Peters eventually led a group to return to Africa and the colony of Sierra Leone, a long odyssey to freedom. Eighteenth-century slaveholders, with no illusions about happy or contented slaves, were haunted by the specter of slaves in arms.

III. ELITE DIVISIONS

During the revolutionary era elites divided in response to these varied threats from below. One group, out of fear of "the mob" and then "the rabble in arms," embraced the British and became active loyalists. After the war most of them went into exile. Another group who became patriots never lost their obsession with coercing popular movements.

"The mob begins to think and reason," Gouverneur Morris observed in 1774. "Poor reptiles, they bask in the sunshine and ere long they will bite." A snake had to be scotched. Others thought of the people as a horse that had to be whipped. This was coercion.

Far more important, however, were those patriot leaders who adopted a strategy of "swimming with a stream which it is impossible to stem." This was the metaphor of Robert R. Livingston, Jr., like Morris, a gentleman with a large tenanted estate in New York. Men of his class had to learn to "yield to the torrent if they hoped to direct its course."

Livingston and his group were able to shape New York's constitution, which some called a perfect blend of "aristocracy" and "democracy." John Hancock, the richest merchant in New England, had mastered this kind of politics and emerged as the most popular politician in Massachusetts. In Maryland Charles Carroll, a wealthy planter, instructed his anxious father about the need to "submit to partial losses" because "no great revolution can happen in a state without revolutions or mutations of private property. If we can save a third of our personal estate and all of our lands and Negroes, I shall think ourselves well off."

The major leaders at the Constitutional Convention in 1787 were heirs to both traditions: coercion and accommodation—Hamilton and Gouverneur Morris to the former, James Madison and James Wilson much more to the latter.

They all agreed on coercion to slay the ghosts of Daniel Shays and Thomas Peters. The Constitution gave the national government the power to "suppress insurrections" and protect the states from "domestic violence." There would be a national army under the command of the president and authority to nationalize the state militias and suspend the right of habeas corpus in "cases of rebellion or invasion." In 1794 Hamilton, as secretary of the treasury, would exercise such powers fully (and needlessly) to suppress the Whiskey Rebellion in western Pennsylvania.

Southern slaveholders correctly interpreted the same powers as available to shackle the ghost of Thomas Peters. As it turned out, Virginia would not need a federal army to deal with Gabriel Prosser's insurrection in 1800 or Nat Turner's rebellion in 1830, but a federal army would capture John Brown after his raid at Harpers Ferry in 1859.

But how to deal with the ghosts of Thomas Paine and Abraham Yates? Here Madison and Wilson blended coercion with accommodation. They had three solutions to the threat of democratic majorities in the states.

Their first was clearly coercive. Like Hamilton, Madison wanted some kind of national veto over the state legislatures. He got several very specific curbs on the states written into fundamental law: no state could "emit" paper money or pass "laws impairing the obligation of contracts." Wilson was so overjoyed with these two clauses that he argued that if they alone "were inserted in the Constitution I think they would be worth our adoption."

But Madison considered the overall mechanism adopted to curb the states "short of the mark." The Constitution, laws, and treaties were the "supreme law of the land" and ultimately a federal court could declare state laws unconstitutional. But this, Madison lamented, would only catch "mischiefs" after the fact. Thus they had clipped the wings of Abraham Yates but he could still fly.

The second solution to the problem of the states was decidedly democratic. They wanted to do an end-run around the state legislatures. The Articles of Confederation, said Madison, rested on "the pillars" of the state legislatures who elected delegates to Congress. The "great fabric to be raised would be more stable and durable if it should rest on the solid grounds of the people themselves"; hence, there would be popular elections to the House.

Wilson altered only the metaphor. He was for "raising the federal pyramid to a considerable altitude and for that reason wanted to give it as broad a base as possible." They would slay the ghost of Abraham Yates with the ghost of Thomas Paine.

This was risky business. They would reduce the risk by keeping the House of Representatives small. Under a ratio of one representative for every 30,000 people, the first house would have only 65 members; in 1776 Thomas Paine had suggested 390. But still, the House would be elected every two years, and with each state allowed to determine its own qualifications for voting, there was no telling who might end up in Congress.

There was also a risk in Madison's third solution to the problem of protecting propertied interests from democratic majorities: "extending the sphere" of government. Prevailing wisdom held that a republic could only succeed in a small geographic area; to rule an "extensive" country, some kind of despotism was considered inevitable.

Madison turned this idea on its head in his since famous *Federalist* essay No. 10. In a small republic, he argued, it was relatively easy for a majority to gang up on a particular "interest." "Extend the sphere," he wrote, and "you take in a greater variety of parties and interests." Then it would be more difficult for a majority "to discover their own strength and to act in unison with each other."

This was a prescription for a noncolonial empire that would expand across the continent, taking in new states as it dispossessed the Indians. The risk was there was no telling how far the "democratic" or "leveling" spirit might go in such likely would-be states as frontier Vermont, Kentucky, and Tennessee.

IV. DEMOCRATIC DIVISIONS

In the spectrum of state constitutions adopted in the revolutionary era, the federal Constitution of 1787 was, like New York's, somewhere between "aristocracy" and "democracy." It therefore should not surprise us—although it has eluded many modern critics of the Constitution—that in the contest over ratification in 1787–1788, the democratic minded were divided.

Among agrarian democrats there was a gut feeling that the Constitution was the work of an old class enemy. "These lawyers and men of learning and monied men," argued Amos Singletary, a working farmer at the Massachusetts ratifying convention, "expect to be managers of this Constitution and get all the power and all the money into their own hands and then will swallow up all of us little folks . . . just as the whale swallowed up Jonah."

Democratic leaders like Melancton Smith of New York focused on the small size of the proposed House. Arguing from Paine's premise that the members of the legislature should "resemble those they represent," Smith feared that "a substantial yeoman of sense and discernment will hardly ever be chosen" and the

government "will fall into the hands of the few and the great." Urban democrats, on the other hand, including a majority of the mechanics and tradesmen
of the major cities who in the revolution had been a bulwark of Paineite radicalism, were generally enthusiastic about the Constitution. They were impelled
by their urgent stake in a stronger national government that would advance
ocean-going commerce and protect American manufacturers from competition.
But they would not have been as ardent about the new frame of government
without its saving graces. It clearly preserved their rights to suffrage. And the
process of ratification, like the Constitution itself, guaranteed them a voice. As
early as 1776 the New York Committee of Mechanics held it as "a right which
God has given them in common with all men to judge whether it be consistent
with their interest to accept or reject a constitution."

Mechanics turned out en masse in the parades celebrating ratification,
marching trade by trade. The slogans and symbols they carried expressed their
political ideals. In New York the upholsterers had a float with an elegant "Federal Chair of State" flanked by the symbols of Liberty and Justice that they identified with the Constitution. In Philadelphia the bricklayers put on their banner
"Both buildings and rulers are the work of our hands."

Democrats who were skeptical found it easier to come over because of the
Constitution's redeeming features. Thomas Paine, off in Paris, considered the
Constitution "a copy, though not quite as base as the original, of the form of the
British government." He had always opposed a single executive and he objected
to the "long duration of the Senate." But he was so convinced of "the absolute
necessity" of a stronger federal government that "I would have voted for it myself had I been in America or even for a worse, rather than have none." It was
crucial to Paine that there was an amending process, the means of "remedying
its defects by the same appeal to the people by which it was to be established."

V. THE SECOND ACCOMMODATION

In drafting the Constitution in 1787 the framers, self-styled Federalists, made
their first accommodation with the "genius" of the people. In campaigning for
its ratification in 1788 they made their second. At the outset, the conventions in
the key states—Massachusetts, New York, and Virginia—either had an anti-
Federalist majority or were closely divided. To swing over a small group of
"antis" in each state, Federalists had to promise that they would consider
amendments. This was enough to secure ratification by narrow margins in
Massachusetts, 187 to 168; in New York, 30 to 27; and in Virginia, 89 to 79.

What the anti-Federalists wanted were dozens of changes in the structure of
the government that would cut back national power over the states, curb the
powers of the presidency as well as protect individual liberties. What they got
was far less. But in the first Congress in 1789, James Madison, true to his pledge,
considered all the amendments and shepherded twelve amendments through
both houses. The first two of these failed in the states; one would have enlarged
the House. The ten that were ratified by December 1791 were what we have

since called the Bill of Rights, protecting freedom of expression and the rights of the accused before the law. Abraham Yates considered them "trivial and unimportant." But other democrats looked on them much more favorably. In time the limited meaning of freedom of speech in the First Amendment was broadened far beyond the framers' original intent. Later popular movements thought of the Bill of Rights as an essential part of the "constitutional" and "republican" rights that belonged to the people.

VI. THE "LOSERS'" ROLE

There is a cautionary tale here that surely goes beyond the process of framing and adopting the Constitution and Bill of Rights from 1787 to 1791. The Constitution was as democratic as it was because of the influence of popular movements that were a presence, even if not present. The losers helped shape the results. We owe the Bill of Rights to the opponents of the Constitution, as we do many other features in the Constitution put in to anticipate opposition.

In American history popular movements often shaped elites, especially in times of crisis when elites were concerned with the "system." Elites have often divided in response to such threats and according to their perception of the "genius" of the people. Some have turned to coercion, others to accommodation. We run serious risk if we ignore this distinction. Would that we had fewer Gouverneur Morrises and Alexander Hamiltons and more James Madisons and James Wilsons to respond to the "genius" of the people.

•   •   •

SOURCES

Ratification

*There was considerable agreement on at least the major point among the mem-
bers of the Constitutional Convention: a stronger central government was
needed to replace the Confederation of the States. But when the Constitution
was sent out to the country, not even this initial assumption was widely
shared. The result was that after sailing through four or five state ratifying conventions with ease, the Constitution ran into bitter opposition in such key
states as Massachusetts, Virginia, and New York. In those states the supporters of the Constitution, as Young noted, were able to win majorities only by
promising a host of amendments to the Constitution. The most exciting fight
was in New York, where the Constitution squeaked through by a mere three
votes. The map on page 163, and the table giving the order of ratification, will
give you some idea of how the Constitution fared from state to state. Do you see
any patterns in the vote? Is it fair to say that the seaboard was for the Constitution and the back country was generally against it? What would have happened if New York, Virginia, or Massachusetts had gone the other way? It took
only nine states to ratify the Constitution, but could the new government have
survived without one of these key states?*

Order of Ratification

State	Date	Vote in Convention	Rank in Population	1790 Population
1. Delaware	Dec. 7, 1787	Unanimous	13	59,096
2. Pennsylvania	Dec. 12, 1787	46 to 23	3	433, 611
3. New Jersey	Dec. 18, 1787	Unanimous	9	184,139
4. Georgia	Jan. 2, 1788	Unanimous	11	82,548
5. Connecticut	Jan. 9, 1788	128 to 40	8	237,655
6. Massachusetts (incl. Maine)	Feb. 7, 1788	187 to 168	2	475,199
7. Maryland	Apr. 28, 1788	63 to 11	6	319,728
8. South Carolina	May 23, 1788	149 to 73	7	249,073
9. New Hampshire	June 21, 1788	57 to 46	10	141,899
10. Virginia	June 26, 1788	89 to 79	1	747,610
11. New York	July 26, 1788	30 to 27	5	340,241
12. North Carolina	Nov. 21, 1789	195 to 77	4	395,005
13. Rhode Island	May 29, 1790	34 to 32	12	69,112

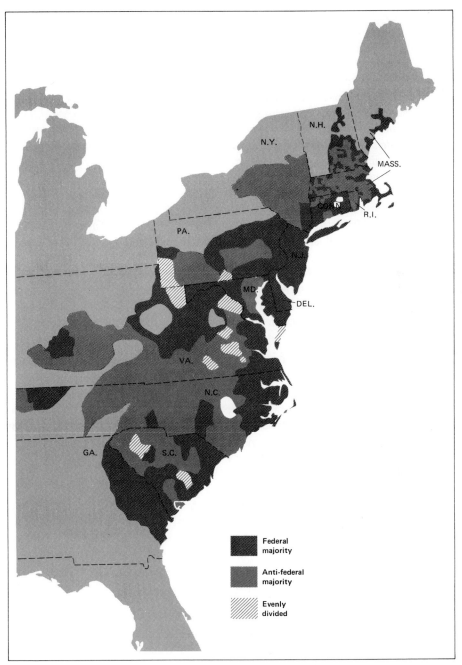

Voting for Ratification.

The Virginia Debates

Proud Virginia, the biggest and most populous state, was sharply divided over the Constitution. Only by promising a Bill of Rights, and by making good use of the knowledge that Washington would undoubtedly be the first president, were the supporters of the Constitution able to win by an 89 to 79 vote.

Here are some selections from one of the significant debates in Virginia. What opinions divided the proponents of the Constitution (who seized the name Federalists for themselves) from its opponents (who seem to have been left with the uninspired title of anti-Federalists)?

Some historians, notably Charles Beard early in the twentieth century, have argued that the Constitution was a political maneuver by the elite designed to protect their economic position and interests. Other historians have disagreed and have seen the Constitution as an able response to a political, not an economic or social, problem. What evidence can you find in the following debate to support either point of view?

Many years later, Abraham Lincoln argued that the nation had been conceived in liberty and dedicated to the proposition that all men are created equal. Which of these two values, liberty or equality, can you find expressed in the debate between Mason and Pendleton?

Mr. George Mason.   Mr. Chairman, whether the Constitution be good or bad, the present clause clearly discovers that it is a national government, and no longer a Confederation. I mean that clause which gives the first hint of the general government laying direct taxes. The assumption of this power of laying direct taxes does, of itself, entirely change the confederation of the states into one consolidated government. This power, being at discretion, unconfined, and without any kind of control, must carry every thing before it. The very idea of converting what was formerly a confederation to a consolidated government, is totally subversive of every principle which has hitherto governed us. This power is calculated to annihilate totally the state governments. Will the people of this great community submit to be individually taxed by two different and distinct powers? Will they suffer themselves to be doubly harassed? These two concurrent powers cannot exist long together; the one will destroy the other: the general government being paramount to, and in every respect more powerful than the state governments, the latter must give way to the former. . . . Was there ever an instance of a general national government extending over so extensive a country, abounding in such a variety of climates, &c., where the people retained their liberty? I solemnly declare that no man is a greater friend to a firm union of the American states than I am; but, sir, if this great end can be obtained without hazarding the rights of the people, why should we recur to such dangerous principles? . . .

From Jonathan Elliott, ed., *The Debates in the Several State Conventions on the Adoption of the Federal Constitution,* Jonathan Elliott, Washington, D.C., 1836, Vol. 3, pp. 29–38, 80–84.

The mode of levying taxes is of the utmost consequence; and yet here it is to be determined by those who have neither knowledge of our situation nor a common interest with us, nor a fellow-feeling for us.

Why should we give up this dangerous power of individual taxation? Why leave the manner of laying taxes to those who, in the nature of things, cannot be acquainted with the situation of those on whom they are to impose them, when it can be done by those who are well acquainted with it? . . .

. . . There is one thing in it which I conceive to be extremely dangerous. Gentlemen may talk of public virtue and confidence; we shall be told that the House of Representatives will consist of the most virtuous men on the continent, and that in their hands we may trust our dearest rights. This, like all other assemblies, will be composed of some bad and some good men; and, considering the natural lust of power so inherent in man, I fear the thirst of power will prevail to oppress the people.

But my principal objection is, that the Confederation is converted to one general consolidated government, which, from my best judgment of it, (and which perhaps will be shown, in the course of this discussion, to be really well founded,) is one of the worst curses that can possibly befall a nation. Does any man suppose that one general national government can exist in so extensive a country as this? I hope that a government may be framed which may suit us, by drawing a line between the general and state governments, and prevent that dangerous clashing of interest and power, which must, as it now stands, terminate in the destruction of one or the other. When we come to the judiciary, we shall be more convinced that this government will terminate in the annihilation of the state governments: the question then will be, whether a consolidated government can preserve the freedom and secure the rights of the people.

Mr. Pendleton.   Mr. Chairman, my worthy friend has expressed great uneasiness in his mind, and informed us that a great many of our citizens are also extremely uneasy, at the proposal of changing our government; but that, a year ago, before this fatal system was thought of, the public mind was at perfect repose. It is necessary to inquire whether the public mind was at ease on the subject, and if it be since disturbed, what was the cause. What was the situation of this country before the meeting of the federal Convention? Our general government was totally inadequate to the purpose of its institution; our commerce decayed; our finances deranged; public and private credit destroyed: these and many other national evils rendered necessary the meeting of that Convention. If the public mind was then at ease, it did not result from a conviction of being in a happy and easy situation: it must have been an inactive, unaccountable stupor. The federal Convention devised the paper on your table as a remedy to remove our political diseases. What has created the public uneasiness since? Not public reports, which are not to be depended upon; but mistaken apprehensions of danger, drawn from observations on government which do not apply to us. When we come to inquire into the origin of most governments of the world, we shall find that they are generally dictated by a conqueror, at the point of the sword, or are the offspring of confusion, when a great popular leader, taking advantage of circumstances, if not producing them, restores order at the expense of liberty, and becomes the tyrant over the people. It may well be supposed that, in forming a government of this sort, it will not be favorable to liberty: the conqueror will take care of his own emoluments, and have little concern for the interest of the people. In either case, the interest and ambition of a despot, and not the good of the people, have given the tone to the government. A government thus formed must necessarily create a continual war between the governors and governed.

Writers consider the two parties (the people and tyrants) as in a state of perpetual warfare, and sound the alarm to the people. But what is our case? We are perfectly free from sedition and war: we are not yet in confusion: we are left to consider our real happiness and security: we want to secure these objects: we know they cannot be attained without government. Is there a single man, in this committee, of a contrary opinion? What was it that brought us from a state of nature of society, but to secure happiness? And can society be formed without government? Personify government: apply to it as a friend to assist you, and it will grant your request. This is the only government founded in real compact. There is no quarrel between government and liberty; the former is the shield and protector of the latter. The war is between government and licentiousness, faction, turbulence, and other violations of the rules of society, to preserve liberty. Where is the cause of alarm? We, the people, possessing all power, form a government, such as we think will secure happiness: and suppose, in adopting this plan, we should be mistaken in the end; where is the cause of alarm on that quarter? . . .

But an objection is made to the form: the expression, We, the people, is thought improper. Permit me to ask the gentlemen who made this objection, who but the people can delegate powers? Who but the people have a right to form government? The expression is a common one, and a favorite one with me. The representatives of the people, by their authority, is a mode wholly inessential. If the objection be, that the Union ought to be not of the people, but of the state governments, then I think the choice of the former very happy and proper. What have the state governments to do with it? Were they to determine, the people would not, in that case, be the judges upon what terms it was adopted.

But the power of the Convention is doubted. What is the power? To propose, not to determine. This power of proposing was very broad; it extended to remove all defects in government: the members of that Convention, who were to consider all the defects in our general government, were not confined to any particular plan. Were they deceived? This is the proper question here. Then the question must be between this government and the Confederation. The latter is no government at all. It has been said that it has carried us, through a dangerous war, to a happy issue. Not that Confederation, but common danger, and the spirit of America, were bonds of our union: union and unanimity, and not that insignificant paper, carried us through that dangerous war. "United, we stand; divided, we fall!" echoed and reëchoed through America—from Congress to the drunken carpenter—was effectual, and procured the end of our wishes, though

now forgotten by gentlemen, if such there be, who incline to let go this strong-
hold, to catch at feathers; for such all substituted projects may prove.

Mr. Madison then arose. . . .

Before I proceed to make some additions to the reasons which have been ad-
duced by my honorable friend over the way, I must take the liberty to make
some observations on what was said by another gentleman, (Mr. Patrick Henry.)
He told us that this Constitution ought to be rejected because it endangered the
public liberty, in his opinion, in many instances. Give me leave to make one answer to that observation: Let the dangers which this system is supposed to be
replete with be clearly pointed out: if any dangerous and unnecessary powers
be given to the general legislature, let them be plainly demonstrated; and let us
not rest satisfied with general assertions of danger, without examination. If
powers be necessary, apparent danger is not a sufficient reason against conceding them. He has suggested that licentiousness has seldom produced the loss of
liberty; but that the tyranny of rulers has almost always effected it. Since the
general civilization of mankind, I believe there are more instances of the abridg-
ment of the freedom of the people by gradual and silent encroachments of those
in power, than by violent and sudden usurpations; but, on a candid examination of history, we shall find that turbulence, violence, and abuse of power, by
the majority trampling on the rights of the minority, have produced factions and
commotions, which, in republics, have, more frequently than any other cause,
produced despotism. If we go over the whole history of ancient and modern republics, we shall find their destruction to have generally resulted from those
causes. If we consider the peculiar situation of the United States, and what are
the sources of that diversity of sentiment which pervades its inhabitants, we
shall find great danger to fear that the same causes may terminate here in the
same fatal effects which they produced in those republics. This danger ought to
be wisely guarded against. Perhaps, in the progress of this discussion it will appear that the only possible remedy for those evils, and means of preserving and
protecting the principles of republicanism, will be found in that very system
which is now exclaimed against as the parent of oppression.

I must confess I have not been able to find his usual consistency in the gentleman's argument on this occasion. He informs us that the people of the country are at perfect repose—that is, every man enjoys the fruits of his labor peace-
ably and securely, and that every thing is in perfect tranquility and safety. I wish
sincerely, sir, this were true. If this be their happy situation, why has every state
acknowledged the contrary? Why were deputies from all the states sent to the
general Convention? Why have complaints of national and individual dis-
tresses been echoed and reëchoed throughout the continent? Why has our general government been so shamefully disgraced, and our Constitution violated?
Wherefore have laws been made to authorize a change, and wherefore are we
now assembled here? A federal government is formed for the protection of its
individual members. Ours has attacked itself with impunity. Its authority has
been disobeyed and despised. I think I perceive a glaring inconsistency in another of his arguments. He complains of this Constitution, because it requires

the consent of at least three-fourths of the states to introduce amendments which shall be necessary for the happiness of the people. The assent of so many he urges as too great an obstacle to the admission of salutary amendments, which, he strongly insists, ought to be at the will of a bare majority. We hear this argument, at the very moment we are called upon to assign reasons for proposing a constitution which puts it in the power of nine states to abolish the present inadequate, unsafe, and pernicious Confederation! In the first case, he asserts that a majority ought to have the power of altering the government, when found to be inadequate to the security of public happiness. In the last case, he affirms that even three-fourths of the community have not a right to alter a government which experience has proved to be subversive of national felicity! nay, that the most necessary and urgent alterations cannot be made without the absolute unanimity of all the states! Does not the thirteenth article of the Confederation expressly require that no alteration shall be made without the unanimous consent of all the states? Could any thing in theory be more perniciously improvident and injudicious than this submission of the will of the majority to the most trifling minority? Have not experience and practice actually manifested this theoretical inconvenience to be extremely impolitic? Let me mention one fact, which I conceive must carry conviction to the mind of any one: the smallest state in the Union has obstructed every attempt to reform the government; that little member has repeatedly disobeyed and counteracted the general authority; nay, has even supplied the enemies of its country with provisions. Twelve states had agreed to certain improvements which were proposed, being thought absolutely necessary to preserve the existence of the general government; but as these improvements, though really indispensable, could not, by the Confederation, be introduced into it without the consent of every state, the refractory dissent of that little state prevented their adoption. The inconveniences resulting from this requisition, of unanimous concurrence in alterations in the Confederation, must be known to every member in this Convention; it is therefore needless to remind them of them. Is it not self-evident that a trifling minority ought not to bind the majority? Would not foreign influence be exerted with facility over a small minority? Would the honorable gentleman agree to continue the most radical defects in the old system, because the petty state of Rhode Island would not agree to remove them? . . .

Charles Cotesworth Pinckney and James Wilson

The Meaning of the Slave Trade Provision

One of Young's arguments is that the Founding Fathers were canny politicians who knew the hopes and fears of their constituents. The following speeches were made by two members of the 1787 convention, in defense of the same clause of the Constitution—the provision that Congress could not prohibit the international slave trade until after 1808. In the first speech, Charles Cotesworth

*Pinckney defends the clause to a proslavery audience in his home state of South
Carolina. In the second, Pennsylvanian James Wilson tells his audience why
they should accept the provision. As you read the two speeches, note the extent
to which each man defends the clause as the best compromise that could be
achieved in the circumstances. Does this seem consistent with Young's way of
characterizing the convention? If you thought the Constitution was a bundle
of just such compromises, would you still regard it as a great document?*

SOUTH CAROLINA

Gen. Charles Cotesworth Pinckney . . . then said he would make a few observations on the objections which the gentleman had thrown out on the restrictions
that might be laid on the African trade after the year 1808. On this point your
delegates had to contend with the religious and political prejudices of the Eastern and Middle States, and with the interested and inconsistent opinion of Virginia, who was warmly opposed to our importing more slaves. I am of the same
opinion now as I was two years ago, when I used the expressions the gentleman
has quoted—that, while there remained one acre of swamp-land uncleared of
South Carolina, I would raise my voice against restricting the importation of negroes. I am as thoroughly convinced as that gentleman is, that the nature of our
climate, and the flat, swampy situation of our country, obliges us to cultivate our
lands with negroes, and that without them South Carolina would soon be a
desert waste.

You have so frequently heard my sentiments on this subject, that I need not
now repeat them. It was alleged, by some of the members who opposed an unlimited importation, that slaves increased the weakness of any state who admitted them; that they were a dangerous species of property, which an invading
enemy could easily turn against ourselves and the neighboring states; and that,
as we were allowed a representation for them in the House of Representatives,
our influence in government would be increased in proportion as we were less
able to defend ourselves. "Show some period," said the members from the Eastern States, "when it may be in our power to put a stop, if we please, to the importation of this weakness, and we will endeavor, for your convenience, to restrain the religious and political prejudices of our people on this subject." The
Middle States and Virginia made us no such proposition; they were for an immediate and total prohibition. We endeavored to obviate the objections that
were made in the best manner we could, and assigned reasons for our insisting
on the importation, which there is no occasion to repeat, as they must occur to
every gentleman in the house: a committee of the states was appointed in order
to accommodate this matter, and, after a great deal of difficulty, it was settled on
the footing recited in the Constitution.

From Jonathan Elliott, ed., *The Debates in the Several State Conventions on the Adoption of the Federal
Constitution,* Jonathan Elliott, Washington, D.C., 1836, Vol. 2, p. 452; Vol. 4, pp. 285–286.

By this settlement we have secured an unlimited importation of negroes for twenty years. Nor is it declared that the importation shall be then stopped; it may be continued. We have a security that the general government can never emancipate them, for no such authority is granted; and it is admitted, on all hands, that the general government has no powers but what are expressly granted by the Constitution, and that all rights not expressed were reserved by the several states. We have obtained a right to recover our slaves in whatever part of America they may take refuge, which is a right we had not before. In short, considering all circumstances, we have made the best terms for the security of this species of property it was in our power to make. We would have made better if we could; but, on the whole, I do not think them bad.

PENNSYLVANIA

Mr. JAMES WILSON. . . . With respect to the clause restricting Congress from prohibiting the *migration or importation of such persons* as any of the states now existing shall think proper to admit, prior to the year 1808, the honorable gentleman says that this clause is not only dark, but intended to grant to Congress, for that time, the power to admit the importation of *slaves.* No such thing was intended. But I will tell you what was done, and it gives me high pleasure that so much was done. Under the present Confederation, the states may admit the importation of slaves as long as they please; but by this article, after the year 1808, the Congress will have power to prohibit such importation, notwithstanding the disposition of any state to the contrary. I consider this as laying the foundation for banishing slavery out of this country; and though the period is more distant than I could wish, yet it will produce the same kind, gradual change, which was pursued in Pennsylvania. It is with much satisfaction I view this power in the general government, whereby they may lay an interdiction on this reproachful trade: but an immediate advantage is also obtained; for a tax or duty may be imposed on such importation, not exceeding ten dollars for each person; and this, sir, operates as a partial prohibition; it was all that could be obtained. I am sorry it was no more; but from this I think there is reason to hope, that yet a few years and it will be prohibited altogether; and in the mean time, the *new* states which are to be formed will be under the control of Congress in this particular, and slaves will never be introduced amongst them. . . .

Designing the Nation's Capitol

After the Constitution was ratified, the creative effort was not over with. It was followed by another bold plan, the creation of the city of rulers that the world today knows as Washington. Within four years of the ratification of the Constitution, the leaders of the new government, who met first at New York and then at Philadelphia, made plans to turn wetlands along the Potomac into the nation's capital. The plans were no less detailed than the Constitution, and they provide eloquent testimony about the kind of government that many of the Founding Fathers envisaged.

Consider, for example, the Capitol building, the home of the Senate and the House of Representatives, and until 1935 of the Supreme Court. In 1791 George Washington and other political leaders agreed with the French architect Pierre Charles L'Enfant that the Capitol should be located at the crest of Jenkins' Hill, the highest point in the envisioned city. And in 1792 the government offered a prize of $500 and a piece of property in the District of Columbia to whomever submitted the best design.

Below are some of the designs that were offered. You will notice that the designers, most of whom were rank amateurs, emphasized symmetry, domes, monumentality. Why do you think they did that? And why do you think the nation's leaders chose William Thornton's design as best suited for a community of republican rulers? Etienne Hallet's plan as second best? What do the winning plans tell you about the kind of government that the Founding Fathers envisaged?

This design, submitted by Samuel Dobie, included three enormous statues on the building's roof.
Library of Congress.

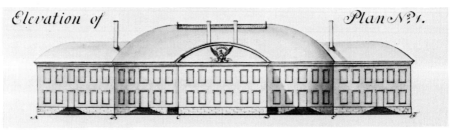

Contemporaries felt that the design submitted by Charles Wintersmith lacked elegance.
The Maryland Historical Society.

Etienne Hallet's plan placed second in the competition, but he was chosen to supervise the actual construction according to Thornton's design.
Library of Congress.

James Diamond capped his building with an enormous weathercock.
Library of Congress.

William Thornton's design was praised by President Washington for its "Grandeur, Simplicity and Convenience." It called for a central rotunda flanked by two identical wings, one for the Senate and the other for the House of Representatives. The above drawing is a slightly revised version of his first plan, which has been lost.
Library of Congress.

William Thornton.
Library of Congress.

CHAPTER 8

Federalists and Republicans

The Constitution created only the framework of the new government. The details still had to be worked out. At first the Federalists, under Presidents George Washington and John Adams, tried to build a consolidated and aristocratic nation. They were convinced that the fear of disunity and anarchy was so great that Americans would accept almost any sort of strong national government. They were dead wrong. Their goals ran against the grain of the revolutionary impulse. Indeed, they were so out of touch with the realities of American life that they came close to provoking a second revolution. Only the electoral victory of the Republican opposition in 1800 ended this threat.

The very existence of a Republican opposition pointed to a serious problem on which the Constitution had been totally silent: the problem of political parties. To the men who wrote the Constitution, the idea of parties and factions was an evil one—as evil as the idea of democracy. Their conception of a successful government was one in which there *were* no factions. To a few sophisticated men, especially to James Madison, faction seemed to be an inevitable feature of human society. But, Madison believed, a well-framed government was one in which faction could *not* express itself in party.

The problem with political parties, of course, was that they led to disunity and disruption. They fed the ambitions of unscrupulous men. They gave demagogues a chance to excite the masses, and so led toward mob rule and an anarchic democracy. Madison, in a famous paper in the series known as *The Federalist*, had even argued that the republic ought to be large, so that no faction could easily seize control of it. In short, the leaders of the first period of American history were still committed to the idea of a society in which status and deference were more fundamental than ideology or faction.

In his famous Farewell Address, Washington spent much more time warning against the spirit of faction and party than he did trying to persuade his fellow citizens not to become involved in entangling alliances with European powers. And the warning was well taken. Washington, during his second administration especially, had watched while a faction developed into a party, a party of opposition to the very policies that he and his successor, John Adams, pursued.

The opposition leader was Thomas Jefferson, Washington's secretary of state, who lost the presidency to John Adams in 1796, but defeated him in 1800. He has been portrayed most vividly as an ideologist who feared both national and presidential power; who believed that states' rights should be predominant; that the small farmer was the foundation of the good society; that the threat to American life was the growth of big cities, industrialization, national banking, an urban proletariat, and a consolidated national government; that the best governments were those that governed least. He has also been portrayed as a revolutionary dreamer who made radical statements such as this about the need for revolutions every twenty years or so: "The tree of liberty must be refreshed from time to time with the blood of patriots and tyrants. It is its natural manure."

INTERPRETIVE ESSAY

Forrest McDonald

Washington and Jefferson

What was the presidency to be like? The Constitution provided only a rough outline. The actual office had to be created by its first occupants. And in this respect the presidencies of George Washington and Thomas Jefferson were decisive. The two men were the towering figures of their age, larger than life, virtual monuments long before their likenesses were carved in stone. Washington was treated like a god even before his presidency, and Jefferson was worshiped by many during and after his eight years in office. Both men, as Forrest McDonald explains in the following essay, set lasting precedents. The office also took its toll on both men, leaving one in anguish, the other in agony. As you read this essay, you will notice that McDonald likes to make provocative statements, to say things that are certain to irritate some of his readers. But what about his basic arguments? Do you think that they are valid? And which man, Washington or Jefferson, do you think had the more lasting impact on the presidency?

The presidencies of George Washington and Thomas Jefferson were as different as those of John F. Kennedy and Richard Nixon. The two men represented fiercely hostile parties, their ideologies were polar opposites, their administrative methods were studies in contrast, their styles were strikingly antithetical. Apart from being Virginians, they seemingly had nothing in common but their red hair, and even on that score they differed, for Washington never appeared in public without a powdered wig and Jefferson scrupulously disdained that affectation.

If, however, their periods of incumbency are viewed in institutional perspective—if one considers their presidencies not as administrations but as experiences in the office—one is struck by similarities rather than differences. Moreover, certain inherent and enduringly relevant characteristics of the presidency itself become manifest.

One such characteristic is that the presidency is dual in nature, entailing two functions so different from one another that the ability to perform them both is rarely to be found in a single person. One function is administrative and executive, and is involved in the formulation and implementation of policy. The other is ritualistic and ceremonial, and though we think of that part of the presidency as being of secondary importance when we bother to think about it at all, it is at least as important as the governing function—and possibly a good deal more so. Indeed, scholars have often misunderstood the presidency because they ig-

From Forrest McDonald, "A Mirror for Presidents," *Commentary*, Vol. 62, December 1976, pp. 34–41. Reprinted from COMMENTARY, December 1976 by permission; all rights reserved. McDonald is the author of *The American Presidency: An Intellectual History* (University Press of Kansas, 1994).

nored or underestimated the purely ceremonial aspect of the office; and no small number of gifted men have failed as president because they did likewise, or were adept at one of the functions but not the other.

To justify and explain that observation, it is necessary to begin with colonial and even precolonial times. We derived our perception of the executive branch of government from the English, who unfortunately were not at all gifted in dealing with executive authority. For some centuries before the accession of the Tudors in 1485, the English tried to get along with home-grown kings, and they underwent a continuing succession of rebellions, civil wars, regicides, and usurpations. The Tudors, who were Welsh, not English, provided stability in the crown until 1603, though with a great deal of attendant social, religious, and economic upheaval. Then came the Stuarts and along with them another century of rebellion, regicide, civil war, and revolution. At last, in 1714, the English found a king they could live with—George I of the small German principality of Hanover, who understood neither the English government nor the English language, and spent his entire reign unhappily wishing he could return to his beloved fatherland. The Hanoverians have occupied the British throne ever since, down to and including Elizabeth II.

It was under the first two Hanoverians (George I and George II, 1714–1760) that the English worked out a permanently viable monarchy—and, significantly, it was then that Anglo-Americans came to political maturity. The English solution to their problem was at once ingenious and ingenuous: they simply divided the two sets of royal functions and entrusted them to two separate sets of persons. Those functions that had to do with the exercise of power—defending the nation against alien enemies, enforcing domestic order and justice, and formulating and implementing governmental policy—became the province of the ministry, which was composed of members of Parliament and headed by the chancellor of the Exchequer. The ritualistic and ceremonial functions remained the province of the crown. Removed from the actual work of government, the English crown became the symbol of the nation—its mystical embodiment— and as such the object of reverence, awe, veneration, even love. In English America, things were somewhat different: whereas the ministry in the mother country was recognized and obeyed as the government, tension continued to exist in the colonies between executive authority, as embodied in the royal governors and their councils, and the colonial assemblies, representing the colonial subjects. But the Americans professed as much reverence for the crown in the person of the king as did their brethren in the home country, and except in parts of New England those professions reflected deeply felt sentiments. On both sides of the water, a people formerly given to killing their kings had now become willing to fight and die for them.

Then came an aberration, the third George, who attempted to reunite the two royal functions—with, for a time, a considerable measure of success. The Anglo-Americans reacted strongly against that effort, and the story of the American presidency, as well as the independence of the United States, begins with their reaction. The Americans' sense of betrayal is reflected in the Declaration of Independence: apart from a bit of stirring propaganda at the beginning and end, that document is little more than a recitation in dreary detail of George III's alleged abuses of executive authority. The same sentiment was expressed more tangibly in the revolutionary constitutions: the governors of the several states were mere figureheads, and the Confederation Congress had no executive arm at all.

Yet the Americans did not abandon their habit of ceremonial reverence toward the crown, despite the Founding Fathers' fervent protestations in favor of republicanism. To have done so would have been to cast off generations of social conditioning overnight, if indeed not to deny a basic human need. Instead, the Americans kept the monarchical habit alive through various surrogates. Thus, for instance, they vested the state governors with responsibility for performing many of the traditional royal rituals; in lieu of celebrating George's birthday they celebrated that of their "deliverer," Louis XVI of France; and when the French dauphin was born in the 1780s they celebrated the event with public balls, firing of cannon, displays of fireworks, and dancing in the streets.

Meanwhile, the political experience of the immediate postwar years convinced most thinking Americans that they had overreacted against executive power in 1776—and, indeed, that government without an executive branch is no government at all. The subject was still so touchy, however, that the delegates to the Constitutional Convention of 1787 spent more time debating the proper construction of the executive branch than they did on the legislative and judicial branches combined. In the end, they merely sketched the duties and description of the office in broad outlines, and left it for the first incumbent to fill in the details.

They were willing to do so—and, in fact, were willing to create the presidency at all—only because George Washington was available to serve as the first president. The virtual deification of Washington in his own time, not merely by the multitudes but by sophisticated and hard-nosed politicians and businessmen as well, is something of a wonder. Part of the explanation is that he was the nation's military hero, though some other American commanders were abler and had better records. He also looked like a leader: he was cool and aloof, and tall, broad-shouldered, and narrow-hipped; and in a country populated mainly by people who were hot-tempered and overly confidential, and short and fat, such attributes were not to be taken lightly. Moreover, he quite self-consciously played the part of the impeccably upright Father of his Country. And, finally, there was the unspoken (and unspeakable) but nevertheless very real popular craving for a king.

Therein lay Washington's greatest contribution to the presidency and to the perdurance of republican institutions in America. He provided a halfway house between monarchy and republicanism; he made it possible (and safe) for Americans to indulge their traditional reverence for the crown without reneging on their commitment to a republican form of government. The way he played his role was a product of studied design, and he devoted far more time and thought to matters of ceremony than to matters of state. From all advisers that he trusted he solicited suggestions for rules of conduct that would strike a balance between "too free an intercourse and too much familiarity" (which would reduce the dignity of the office) and "an ostentatious show" of monarchical aloofness (which would be improper in a republic). Rules were worked out, and so effectively did Washington follow them that no less skeptical a person than Abigail Adams, wife of the vice president and a veteran of receptions at Versailles and the Court of St. James, was almost moonstruck upon meeting the president. Washington, she gushed, moved and handled himself "with a grace, dignity, and ease that leaves Royal George far behind him."

As to carrying out the executive functions of government, Washington looked to the Constitution as a guide and took the document quite literally, almost as if it were a manual of instructions. For several years, for instance, he did not meet with his department heads in cabinet sessions; rather, as the Constitution directed, he "required their opinions in writing," even on the most trivial of matters, which added greatly to their work loads. As to the formulation of legislative policy, Washington scrupulously avoided having any part of it, for that, he believed, would have involved an improper violation of the doctrine of the separation of powers: he would no more have proposed a law, for example, than he would have vetoed a bill on grounds of policy. Even in regard to foreign affairs he tried for a time to follow the Constitution literally; once, he sauntered into a session of the Senate to seek its "advice and consent" regarding some Indian treaties, and occasioned a great deal of confused embarrassment in the doing.

Such methods of procedure left a considerable void in the actual wielding of executive power, and under those circumstances the United States moved rapidly, albeit temporarily, toward a version of the ministerial system then used in England. Secretary of the Treasury Alexander Hamilton—acting, it will be recalled, neither on his own initiative nor on orders from the president, but upon instructions from Congress—submitted his two great reports on the public debt, then his report on the Bank, and then his report on manufactures, and accompanied them all with lengthy drafts of proposed legislation. Moreover, he worked intimately with congressmen in steering his proposals into law; and, with congressional cooperation, he continued to formulate and see to the enactment of legislation throughout his tenure as secretary. Clearly he conceived of his "ministry" as the "government," and thought of himself as the prime minister. Even after he retired, Hamilton continued for some time more or less to direct the government, more or less through a ministry.

The Jeffersonian Republicans objected to the Federalists' approach to government on quite a number of grounds, central among them being the Federalists' conception of the executive. Jefferson and his followers not only believed Hamilton to be a monarchist but even regarded him as the agent of an international monocratic conspiracy. They castigated Washington for indulging in royal pageantry and for wallowing, kinglike, in popular adulation; they denounced Hamilton for introducing, extraconstitutionally, the corrupt British ministerial system. And yet the Republicans' own conception of a proper executive branch was curiously mixed. On the one hand, they insisted that executive power was and should be strictly limited by the written Constitution, and that it should be absolutely separate from the legislative branch. On the other hand, in their hearts they did not trust paper Constitutions, and they looked to Jefferson to be an elected version of what the English Tory Viscount Bolingbroke had called a patriot king: one who would rally the entire nation to his banner, and then, in an act of supreme wisdom and virtue, voluntarily restrain himself and thus restore the ancient system of the separation of powers.

When the Jeffersonians came to power in 1801, they promptly refashioned the executive in accordance with their ideological precepts. As to the ceremonial—or what we might properly call the monarchical—functions of the office, Jefferson seemingly rejected them entirely. What he actually did, however, was to republicanize them. He ostentatiously forswore ostentation and display, pomp and protocol. He gave no public balls and held no levees, and no one celebrated his birthday. He abandoned the monarchical ritual (which had been followed by Washington and Adams and all state governors) of appearing in person before the legislative branches, and afterward exchanging formal messages about the executive message; instead, when Jefferson had anything to say to Congress he sent a written note, and kept it as brief as possible. He staged no entertainments for the public; instead, his doors were open to every citizen at all times. Finally, he never held "court" for government officials or foreign ministers. Instead, he held a continuous succession of small, informal dinner parties, at which the wines were superb and the cuisine was prepared by a French chef, but the atmosphere was one of studied casualness. Unwigged, dressed in frayed homespun and rundown slippers, Jefferson captivated his guests with the folksy, open hospitality of a country squire and with dazzling conversation that ranged from art, architecture, and archeology through mathematics and music to philosophy and zoology.

This was not merely a republican affectation adopted as a counterfoil to monarchical affectation, nor was it a form of reverse snobbery. Rather, it reflected a calculated design on Jefferson's part, and accomplished just what he expected it to accomplish. By stripping everyone of the possibility of pretense and the trappings of status, and by dealing with people only in intimate gatherings where he was host and master of the house, he established a setting in which he was utterly without peers. In those circumstances he stood towering as the first among equals.

By that means—and through the instrumentality of a well-organized Republican press, which had only to describe him as he truly was—Jefferson became immensely popular. He became, in fact, quite as popular as Washington had been at the time of his inauguration, before partisan attacks began to tarnish his previously spotless reputation. There was, however, a crucial difference between Jefferson's popularity and that of Washington. Whereas Washington had been revered as a demigod and the symbol of the nation, Jefferson made the transition from monarchy to republicanism complete by humanizing the presidency and serving as a symbol not of the nation but of the people. That was an achievement of profound significance, for as the American people became democratized and spread their society over a vast continent, they sorely needed a symbolic monarch if they were to remain a single nation, and yet they could tolerate one only if he bore the peculiarly democratic stamp that Jefferson had coined.

As to the executive function, the "Revolution of 1800," as Jefferson called it, took place on several levels and in several stages. Administratively, the government was purged of "irreconcilable monarchists" (that is, staunch Hamiltonians) and in choosing their replacements Jefferson employed an artful blend of patronage and meritocracy. The actual conduct of administration was put mainly in the charge of Secretary of the Treasury Albert Gallatin, who had the twin tasks of dismantling Hamilton's elaborate fiscal machinery and of instituting methodical procedures and strict accounting in place of the slipshod and cavalier ways that had been followed by the Federalists. Gallatin also served as the middleman between the president and Congress. That made it possible for Jefferson to influence legislation without interfering directly in the legislative process, and thus to preserve the form of strict separation of powers; and it gave Jefferson all the flexibility of Hamilton's independent ministerial system while leaving the president in command.

Jefferson presided over the administration with the easy, relaxed, informal manner that he employed at his congressional dinner parties, and with equal success. He conducted cabinet meetings as a democracy of equals, and allowed Congress to operate with no overt presidential direction and only the gentlest of presidential guidance; and yet, until almost the very end, he ran Congress more successfully and more completely than Hamilton had ever done and few succeeding presidents ever would do, and the cabinet always reflected his will except when he had no firm opinions on a matter. Moreover, he did so without using any of the techniques that are usually associated with "strong" presidents—popular pressure, naked power, bribery, flattery, cajolery, blackmail, or shrewd trading. Rather, his achievements all flowed from the force of his intellect, his character, and his personality.

But that, perversely, was a grave weakness in the Republican scheme of things: administratively, the system could be made to work only with a Thomas Jefferson at the helm, and so far we have never had another. When Jefferson himself faltered, as he did on several occasions during his presidency, government almost stopped functioning except in the routine operations of Gallatin's Treasury machinery. When Jefferson left office, the shortcomings of his method of administration rapidly became manifest. The cabinet became the center of petty bickering and continuous cabalizing, and Congress split into irreconcilable factions and repeatedly asserted its will against that of the president.

In other words, the Jeffersonians destroyed the English-*cum*-Washingtonian/Hamiltonian split system of the presidency, and erected no viable alternative in its place. The resulting problem has plagued us throughout the nation's history. The most popular presidents in their own time—those who most successfully fulfilled the monarchical function of the office—were men like Theodore Roosevelt and John F. Kennedy, who obviously put on a swell show but never accomplished much of anything, or like Andrew Jackson, who won popular adulation while wreaking irreparable destruction. Others were extremely able at getting things done—I make no comment here about the merits of what they were doing, and have in mind such presidents as Taft, Hoover, Johnson, and Nixon—but were so totally incompetent in fulfilling the monarchical function of the presidency that they were virtually ridden out of the office on a rail. The big winners in the history books are those who—like Lincoln, Wilson, and Harry Truman—were shrewd, devious, unscrupulous, and successful operators, unloved and unlovable in their own times, but whom the historians can enshrine as retroactively lovable after all memory of their personalities has disappeared.

So much for the first characteristic of the presidency. A second characteristic has to do with the exercise, structure, and psychic cost of presidential power, and is a bit more involved. . . . As it happens, both Washington and Jefferson could have been re-elected for a third term had they so chosen, but it took a great deal of persuasion to get Washington to serve even a second term, and Jefferson announced shortly after his re-election that he would follow Washington's precedent and retire at the end of his second. By Madison's time the two-term limit had already hardened into a hoary tradition.

Given that tradition, the relations between a president and his party and Congress change profoundly between his first and second terms. Politically they are interdependent during the first term, for each can help the other to re-election. After the president is re-elected, they no longer have such a relationship: the president, not coming up for a third election, has no further political need for the congressmen of his party, and he is of no future political use to them. The resulting mutual estrangement is exacerbated by a peculiarity of American political history. That is, though the president is cut off from his power base in government by reason of his lame-duck status, he almost invariably has the illusion of increased power because he almost invariably wins bigger when running for re-election than he did when being elected the first time.

This shifting of political relationships has major implications, one of which is that the president's followers, no matter how loyal and honorable they may have been during the first term, tend to start jockeying for positions in the race to become his successor four years hence—even though such activity may be clearly inimical to the national interest. Throughout Washington's first term, for instance, Jefferson and Hamilton behaved with some civility toward one another in their roles as secretaries of state and the treasury; but during the second term they were the leading rivals to succeed him, and all restraint was abandoned. Hamilton spent more time attacking (or, actually, counterattacking) Jefferson than he did attending to his duties, and eventually he more or less forced Jefferson to resign. Meanwhile, Jefferson entirely neglected his duties in the State Department, attempted to sabotage the administration's foreign policy, vilified his rival incessantly, and finally destroyed Hamilton as a presidential prospect with a lurid exposé of his extramarital indiscretions.

A decade later, after Jefferson himself had been elected for a second term, he was a hapless witness to an even more destructive version of the game. His secretary of the Navy, supported by factions in the House and the Senate, sought to undermine the administration's foreign policy so as to discredit Secretary of State James Madison as a prospective successor to the presidency. They backed James Monroe, who was then minister to England; and Madison, for his part, deliberately hewed to a policy that created a serious danger of war with Britain rather than allow Monroe to negotiate a treaty that would insure peace but also greatly increase Monroe's pretensions to the presidency. Toward the end of Jefferson's second term, the maneuvering for future advantage took on extreme proportions: for instance, William Branch Giles of Virginia, who for fifteen years had been an unwaveringly loyal Republican, began to sabotage Gallatin's Treasury administration when he learned that Gallatin (instead of himself) might be Madison's own choice for secretary of state.

Other implications of the shifting of relationships in the second term more directly affect the president and the presidency. One is that the president, no matter how humble his behavior before, tends to emerge from his triumphant reelection with a sense of power that borders on arrogance, if indeed he does not suffer delusions that he is God or superman. . . .

Washington, shortly after his re-election, was faced with mounting criticism from informal oppositionist political clubs called Democratic-Republican societies. He regarded the societies much as the late Senator Joseph McCarthy regarded "cells" of the American Communist party—namely, as agents of a foreign power and of an international revolutionary conspiracy—but was at first unable to do much to suppress them. Then a group of moonshiners in the mountains of Pennsylvania tarred and feathered a "revenooer," so to speak—actually they besieged and burned the house of a collector of the federal excise tax on whiskey—and Washington proclaimed the action to be the handiwork of Jacobin subversives, the Democratic-Republican societies. He assembled a force of 15,000 militiamen and personally marched at their head to crush the so-called insurrection. That episode was typical of his toleration for political opposition during his second administration.

But if Washington's second administration was intolerant, that of the Father of American Liberty, Thomas Jefferson, was a nightmare of repression. Among other things, Jefferson attempted to have the Supreme Court purged of Federalists through impeachment on purely political grounds; he sanctioned the suspension of *habeas corpus*, the wholesale arrest of citizens without charges, and the forcible removal of accused persons from the district in which they had a constitutional right to trial; he declared large regions in insurrection and under martial law for the legal violations of a handful of persons; he became the only president prior to modern times who bypassed the courts and used the army in the routine enforcement of the laws; he sought, received, and personally enforced legislation depriving whole classes of people of their property, not only without due process of law but without even the possibility of a trial; he denounced a critical press with an almost paranoid sense of persecution, and attempted by legal and extralegal means to suppress newspapers that opposed him. Finally, he attempted during his last year in office to supervise, with minute and personal attention, not only what his fellow citizens should eat—this is quite literally true—but how much they should eat as well.

In the face of all this, his party became split into two ideological wings. One, concentrated in the House and led by John Randolph of Roanoke, veered to the extreme position of the doctrinaire libertarian who would abide the subversion of government and of society itself before willingly jeopardizing the rights and liberties of a single citizen. The other, concentrated in the Senate and led by William Branch Giles, adhered to a form of Republicanism that might be styled totalitarian libertarianism: believing that government in their hands was dedicated to preserving human liberty, they saw legal protection of the civil rights of accused persons only as subterfuges behind which traitors and other enemies of liberty could hide. Jefferson almost uniformly sided with this latter group. Among the fruits of their labors was a bill, passed in the Senate but rejected in the House, which would have prescribed the death penalty for any person who "resisted the general execution of any public law." . . .

Still another aspect of the problem is that in his second term the president becomes fair prey for every manner of vilification: once the reality of his lame-duck status begins to penetrate the popular consciousness, press and politicians move in like so many hyenas gathering around a wounded lion. It has been so since the beginning. Washington, who had been utterly sacrosanct before, had scarcely been re-elected when the personal attacks began. Early in 1793 Philip Freneau's *National Gazette* (an opposition newspaper secretly financed by Jefferson out of State Department funds) opened the barrage by describing the celebration of Washington's birthday as a "monarchical farce," and by sneering that his sycophants fawned upon him as if he were "Virtue's self." The attacks mounted in shrillness and intensity in the ensuing months, and by year's end a New York Republican journal was emboldened to charge that Washington's education had consisted mainly of "gambling, reveling, horse racing, and horse whipping"; that he was "infamously niggardly" in private dealings; and that, despite his pretended religious piety, he was a "most horrid swearer and blasphemer." Before long, if John Adams's recollections are to be believed, "ten thousand people in the streets of Philadelphia, day after day, threatened to drag Washington out of his house, and effect a revolution in the government." For the next two years, as the attacks continued and increased (he was accused of stealing from the Treasury and even of having secretly been a traitor during the revolution), Washington repeatedly interrupted cabinet meetings to indulge himself in tirades against the press or in fits of self-pity. When he finally left office, Benjamin Bache—grandson of Franklin and editor of the Philadelphia *Aurora*—penned this stirring eulogy: "If ever there was a period for rejoicing, this is the moment. Every heart [that is] in unison with the freedom and happiness of the people ought to beat high with exultation that the name of Washington from this day ceases to give a currency to political iniquity and to legalized corruption."

Jefferson's story was somewhat different, for he had been exposed to some pretty juicy scurrility through much of his public career. Already before he became president he had been widely castigated as an atheist, a coward, a bloodthirsty revolutionary, a hypocrite, a liar, a demagogue, and a fop; and during his first term his improper advances toward the wife of a close friend were revealed in the newspapers, and it was charged (or exposed, depending upon which historians you believe) that he had long had a slave as a concubine and had sired several children by her. Throughout all this, however, he maintained his aplomb, and at least publicly maintained his posture as the unqualified champion of freedom of the press.

It was in the second term that newspaper attacks finally and deeply began to wound him—or, to put it another way, that his critics became so vicious that they were at last able to find his vulnerable spots. Curiously, he proved to be relatively insensitive to attacks on his personal behavior or morality but hypersensitive to charges regarding his public conduct. Charges that he was an agent or lackey of Napoleon, or was excessively secretive, or dictated to Congress sent him into fits of rage or fits of depression. And his enemies, once they got the knife in, twisted it unmercifully. Jefferson's response was much as Washington's had been, except perhaps that it was more so. He had once written that a free press was more vital to public happiness than good government, and that faced with a mutually exclusive choice he would readily opt for the press; now he resurrected the oppressive ancient doctrine of common-law indictment for seditious libel, and attempted to whip the press into line by instituting what he called "a few wholesome prosecutions." When that failed to stop the onslaught, he could only fulminate and whimper and rage. "Nothing can now be believed which is seen in a newspaper," he wrote again and again. He remarked repeatedly that it was a "melancholy truth" that suppression of the press would be no worse than the press's own "abandoned prostitution to falsehood." He wailed that "our printers raven on the agonies of their victims, as wolves do on the blood of the lamb."

Along with attacks by the press, there is usually, toward the end, some sort of open rebellion by Congress. This does not always apply, but it is almost invariable with what political scientists used to call "strong" presidents. . . .

With Washington, the rebellion came in 1796, and arose in the House of Representatives. The keystone in Washington's foreign policy was [John] Jay's treaty with Great Britain, signed in the winter of 1794–1795 and approved by the Senate, after an intensive campaign and by the narrowest of constitutional margins, in a special session in the summer of 1795. When the full Congress reconvened in December, House Republicans (who vehemently opposed the treaty) sought to chastise the administration and cut the House in on foreign-policy decisions in the future. Taking the position that the House's exclusive power to initiate appropriations (without which no treaty could be implemented) gave it a voice in foreign policy co-equal to the Senate's power to approve or reject treaties, the House demanded that the president turn over all papers relating to Jay's mission. Those papers contained some politically damaging documents, and (quite in addition to his objection to the constitutional challenge) Washington was loath to surrender them. He brooded over the demand; and then, summoning what was left of his great personal dignity, he sent his answer. The papers, he said, were not "relative to any purpose under the cognizance of the House of Representatives, except that of an impeachment; which the resolution had not expressed," and on that ground he refused. Despite everything, no congressman was willing to go that far, and the matter died.

Jefferson, for his part, did not fare as well. During the last congressional session of his presidency, the Senate rose to reassert its claim to a role in foreign affairs, particularly in ways designed to prevent Jefferson's successor from having a free hand in continuing Jefferson's policies. Then both houses decided to scuttle the embargo, on which Jefferson had staked his all as an instrument of foreign policy, and they did so in a way that was at least partly a deliberate insult: they voted that the embargo should expire on March 4, so that Jefferson's presidency and his favorite policy should die together. Finally, the Senate took a cheap shot that was a matter of calculated cruelty aimed at the fallen president. Some months earlier Jefferson had appointed an old friend, William Shot, to a legally nonexistent post as minister to Russia, expecting that the Senate would routinely confirm the appointment and thus support a pet project that he had worked long and diligently for, the opening of diplomatic relations with Czar Alexander I. For political reasons, he held back an announcement of the appointment until the last minute; and when the senators received it, they summarily and unanimously rejected it.

My final point should by now be obvious. It is simply that the burden of presidential power over a period of two terms—the psychic cost of the office—is greater than any reasonable man can be expected to bear.

The presidency left Washington a broken and beaten man—embittered, given to almost insane rages, possessed of little memory or judgment, and convinced that a conspiracy had undermined his presidency and was hounding him to his grave. Perhaps the most telling testimony as to what the office had cost him is the angry, defensive, and self-pitying draft of a final message that he composed early in 1796—that is, before Hamilton wrote for him the immortal document that was actually released as his Farewell Address. This is how Washington's own version read:

> As this address, fellow citizens, will be the last I shall ever make to you, and as some of the gazettes of the United States have teemed with all the invective that disappointment, ignorance of facts, and malicious falsehoods could invent, to misrepresent my politics and affections—to wound my reputation and feelings—and to weaken, if not entirely destroy, the confidence you have been pleased to repose in me; it might be expected at the parting scene of my public life that I should take some notice of such virulent abuse. But, as heretofore, I shall pass them over in utter silence.

The rest of the draft was an itemized denial of the charges.

And if Washington's presidency ended in anguish, Jefferson's ended in agony. Jefferson had remarked that Washington suffered during his second term "more than any person I ever yet met with," but Jefferson's own suffering in the same circumstances was even greater. He came to regard each session of Congress as an unbearable ordeal; he repeatedly referred to the presidency as his prison; during his last two years in office he was periodically afflicted with migraine headaches that kept him shut alone in a darkened room for weeks on end; in his final year he collapsed under what used to be called a nervous breakdown—a total paralysis of will. At last the ordeal was done, and on March 4, 1809, he was at Madison's side as Chief Justice John Marshall administered the oath of office to the president-elect. He remained in Washington a week, packing his belongings, before quitting the place forever. Then the sixty-five-year-old Father of American Liberty mounted a horse, to ride through snow and storm for three days and nights until he regained the sanctuary of his home at Monticello. In the seventeen years that remained of his life, he never again left the foothills of the Blue Ridge Mountains.

SOURCES

Roughhouse Politics

On all sides, Americans were apparently convinced that party politics mobilized the worst passions of men. And it did seem to be true. In the early years of the republic, party politics was a roughhouse affair. Gentlemen fought in the streets, in taverns, and even in Congress itself. Here is a cartoon lampooning a famous brawl in the House of Representatives in February 1798. In the chair, wearing the silliest possible grin, is Speaker of the House Jonathan Dayton. The principals are, on the left, Republican Matthew Lyon, and, suitably on the right, Federalist representative Roger Griswold. What is the clerk at the lower left doing? Does any member have dignity, or are all shown as either involved or behaving almost as absurdly as Lyon and Griswold? Compare this picture with the Peale painting of Washington in Chapter 6 (p. 147). If the clothing of the members of Congress shown here identifies them with Washington as members of the republic's elite, what sets them apart? How have they failed? What connection can you draw between this cartoon and Jefferson's famous remark, after his victory in 1800, "We are all Republicans—we are all Federalists"?

Picture Collection/New York Public Library.

He in a trice struck Lyon thrice   Who seized the tongs to ease his wrongs,
Upon his head, enraged sir.   And Griswold thus engaged, sir.

Truth Versus Treason

American politics eventually was founded on the assumption that contests between major political parties are not struggles for control of the nation, but are contests between two groups, both *legitimate and loyal,* both *with valid programs,* both *with patriotic voter support. In the early stages, however, this was not the assumption at all. The governing idea was simple: one party represented the real interests of the nation, the other was so misguided as to be downright treasonable. The following documents illustrate the point nicely. In the first, Washington is leading an army to put down a rebellion in Pennsylvania—the so-called Whiskey Rebellion of 1794–1795. He is, in short, saving the country. But in this Federalist depiction, Jefferson is shown to be giving traitorous aid and comfort to the enemy. In fact, he is made to speak in pidgin French: "Stop de wheels of de gouvernement," thus supporting the Federalist opinion that Jefferson was little better than an American agent of the French Revolution. On the other hand, the Republican handbills of 1804 and 1807 depict the Federalists as* British *agents, the servants of George III, and as men who would undo the hard-won triumphs of the revolution.*

New-York Historical Society.

REPUBLICANS

Turn out, turn out and save your Country from ruin !

From an *Emperor*—from a *King*—from the iron grasp of a *British Tory Faction*—an unprincipled banditti of British speculators.   The hireling tools and emissaries of his majesty king George the 3d have thronged our city and diffused the poison of principles among us.

DOWN WITH THE TORIES, DOWN WITH THE BRITISH FACTION,

Before they have it in their power to enslave you, and reduce your families to distress by heavy taxation. Republicans want no Tribute-liars—they want no ship Ocean-liars—they want no Rufus King's for Lords —they want no Varick to lord it over them—they want no Jones for senator, who fought with the British against the Americans in time of the war.—But they want in their places such men as

Jefferson & Clinton,

who fought their Country's Battles in the year '76

New-York Historical Society.

The finifhing

STROKE.

Every Shot's a Vote,

And every Vote

KILLS A TORY !

DO YOUR DUTY, REPUBLICANS,

Let your exertions this day

Put down the Kings

AND TYRANTS OF BRITAIN.

LAST DAY.

April, 1807.

New-York Historical Society.

Thomas Jefferson and John Adams

The Nature of American Aristocracy, 1813

When John Adams lost the presidency to Jefferson in the "revolution" of 1800, he was so embittered that he refused to stay in Washington to see Jefferson inaugurated. But many years later, after Jefferson had also retired from the presidency, the two men began corresponding. The letters that follow are part of their exchange on the nature of American government, and particularly on the relationship between the idea of popular government and the equally attractive idea of aristocracy. Both men believe that aristocracy is "natural." But how does each one think that this fact ought to be reflected in government? What do you think Jefferson means by the phrase "pseudo-aristocracy"? Adams by "artificial aristocracy"? Are they talking about the same thing? If so, how do they think the republic can best be protected?

JEFFERSON TO ADAMS, OCTOBER 28, 1813

. . . I agree with you that there is a natural aristocracy among men. The grounds of this are virtue and talents. Formerly, bodily powers gave place among the aristoi. But since the invention of gunpowder has armed the weak as well as the strong with missile death, bodily strength, like beauty, good humor, politeness and other accomplishments, has become but an auxiliary ground of distinction. There is also an artificial aristocracy, founded on wealth and birth, without either virtue or talents; for with these it would belong to the first class. The natural aristocracy I consider as the most precious gift of nature, for the instruction, the trusts, and government of society. And indeed, it would have been inconsistent in creation to have formed man for the social state, and not to have provided virtue and wisdom enough to manage the concerns of the society. May we not even say, that that form of government is the best, which provides the most effectually for a pure selection of these natural aristoi into the offices of government? The artificial aristocracy is a mischievous ingredient in government, and provision should be made to prevent its ascendency. On the question, what is the best provision, you and I differ; but we differ as rational friends, using the free exercise of our own reason, and mutually indulging its errors. You think it best to put the pseudo-aristoi into a separate chamber of legislation, where they may be hindered from doing mischief by their co-ordinate branches, and where, also, they may be a protection to wealth against the agrarian and plundering enterprises of the majority of the people. I think that to give them power in order to prevent them from doing mischief, is arming them for it, and increasing instead of remedying the evil. For if the co-ordinate branches can arrest their ac-

The texts of both letters are taken from Andrew A. Lipscomb and Albert E. Bergh, eds., *The Writings of Thomas Jefferson*, 20 vols., Washington, D.C., 1905, Vol. 13, pp. 394–403; Vol. 14, pp. 1–10.

tion, so may they that of the co-ordinates. Mischief may be done negatively as well as positively. Of this, a cabal in the Senate of the United States has furnished many proofs. Nor do I believe them necessary to protect the wealthy; because enough of these will find their way into every branch of the legislation, to protect themselves. From fifteen to twenty legislatures of our own, in action for thirty years past, have proved that no fears of an equalization of property are to be apprehended from them. I think the best remedy is exactly that provided by all our constitutions, to leave to the citizens the free election and separation of the aristoi from the pseudo-aristoi, of the wheat from the chaff. In general they will elect the really good and wise. In some instances, wealth may corrupt, and birth blind them; but not in sufficient degree to endanger the society.

It is probable that our difference of opinion may, in some measure, be produced by a difference of character in those among whom we live. From what I have seen of Massachusetts and Connecticut myself, and still more from what I have heard, and the character given of the former by yourself, who know them so much better, there seems to be in those two States a traditionary reverence for certain families, which has rendered the offices of the government nearly hereditary in those families. I presume that from an early period of your history, members of those families happening to possess virtue and talents, have honestly exercised them for the good of the people, and by their services have endeared their names to them. In coupling Connecticut with you, I mean it politically only, not morally. For having made the Bible the common law of their land, they seem to have modeled their morality on the story of Jacob and Laban. But although this hereditary succession to office with you, may, in some degree, be founded in real family merit, yet in a much higher degree, it has proceeded from your strict alliance of Church and State. These families are canonized in the eyes of the people on common principles, "you tickle me, and I will tickle you." In Virginia we have nothing of this. Our clergy, before the revolution, having been secured against rivalship by fixed salaries, did not give themselves the trouble of acquiring influence over the people. Of wealth, there were great accumulations in particular families, handed down from generation to generation, under the English law of entails. But the only object of ambition for the wealthy was a seat in the King's Council. All their court then was paid to the crown and its creatures. . . . Hence they were unpopular; and that unpopularity continues attached to their names. A Randolph, a Carter, or a Burwell must have great personal superiority over a common competitor to be elected by the people even at this day. At the first session of our legislature after the Declaration of Independence, we passed a law abolishing entails. And this was followed by one abolishing the privilege of primogeniture, and dividing the lands of intestates equally among all their children, or other representatives. These laws, drawn by myself, laid the axe to the foot of pseudo-aristocracy. And had another which I prepared been adopted by the legislature, our work would have been complete. It was a bill for the more general diffusion of learning. This proposed to divide every county into wards of five or six miles square, like your townships; to establish in each ward a free school for reading, writing and common arithmetic; to provide for the annual selection of the best subjects from these schools, who might receive, at the public expense, a higher degree of education at a district school; and from these district schools to select a certain number of the most promising subjects, to be completed at an university, where all the useful sciences should be taught. Worth and genius would thus have been sought out from every condition of life, and completely prepared by education for defeating the competition of wealth and birth for public trusts. . . .

With respect to aristocracy, we should further consider, that before the establishment of the American States, nothing was known to history but the man of the old world, crowded within limits' either small or overcharged, and steeped in the vices which that situation generates. A government adapted to such men would be one thing; but a very different one, that for the man of these States. Here every one may have land to labor for himself, if he chooses; or, preferring the exercise of any other industry, may exact for it such compensation as not only to afford a comfortable subsistence, but wherewith to provide for a cessation from labor in old age. Every one, by his property, or by his satisfactory situation, is interested in the support of law and order. And such men may safely and advantageously reserve to themselves a wholesome control over their public affairs, and a degree of freedom, which, in the hands of the *canaille* of the cities of Europe, would be instantly perverted to the demolition and destruction of everything public and private. The history of the last twenty-five years of France, and of the last forty years in America, nay of its last two hundred years, proves the truth of both parts of this observation.

But even in Europe a change has sensibly taken place in the mind of man. Science had liberated the ideas of those who read and reflect, and the American example had kindled feelings of right in the people. An insurrection has consequently begun, of science, talents, and courage, against rank and birth, which have fallen into contempt. It has failed in its first effort, because the mobs of the cities, the instrument used for its accomplishment, debased by ignorance, poverty, and vice, could not be restrained to rational action. But the world will recover from the panic of this first catastrophe. Science is progressive, and talents and enterprise on the alert. Resort may be had to the people of the country, a more governable power from their principles and subordination; and rank, and birth, and tinsel-aristocracy will finally shrink into insignificance, even there. This, however, we have no right to meddle with. It suffices for us, if the moral and physical condition of our own citizens qualifies them to select the able and good for the direction of their government, with a recurrence of elections at such short periods as will enable them to displace an unfaithful servant, before the mischief he mediates may be irremediable. . . .

ADAMS TO JEFFERSON, NOVEMBER 15, 1813

. . . We are now explicitly agreed upon one important point, viz., that there is a natural aristocracy among men, the grounds of which are virtue and talents. . . . But though we have agreed in one point, in words, it is not yet certain that we are perfectly agreed in sense. Fashion has introduced an indeterminate use of the word talents. Education, wealth, strength, beauty, stature, birth, marriage, graceful attitudes and motions, gait, air, complexion, physiognomy, are talents, as well as genius, science, and learning. Any one of these talents that in fact commands or influences two votes in society, gives to the man who possesses it the character of an aristocrat, in my sense of the word. Pick up the first hundred men you meet, and make a republic. Every man will have an equal vote; but when deliberations and discussions are opened, it will be found that twenty-five, by their talents, virtues being equal, will be able to carry fifty votes. Every one of these twenty-five is an aristocrat in my sense of the word; whether he obtains his one vote in addition to his own, by his birth, fortune, figure, eloquence, science, learning, craft, cunning, or even his character for good fellowship, and a *bon vivant*.

. . . Your distinction between natural and artificial aristocracy, does not appear to me founded. Birth and weight are conferred upon some men as imperiously by nature as genius, strength, or beauty. The heir to honors, and riches, and power, has often no more merit in procuring these advantages, than he has in obtaining a handsome face, or an elegant figure. When aristocracies are established by human laws, and honor, wealth and power are made hereditary by municipal laws and political institutions, then I acknowledge artificial aristocracy to commence; but this never commences till corruption in elections becomes dominant and uncontrollable. But this artificial aristocracy can never last. The ever-lasting envies, jealousies, rivalries, and quarrels among them; their cruel rapacity upon the poor ignorant people, their followers, compel them to set up Caesar, a demagogue, to be a monarch, a master; *pour mettre chacun `a sa place.* Here you have the origin of all artificial aristocracy, which is the origin of all monarchies. And both artificial aristocracy and monarchy, and civil, military, political, and hierarchical despotism, have all grown out of the natural aristocracy of virtues and talents. We, to be sure, are far remote from this. Many hundred years must roll away before we shall be corrupted. Our pure, virtuous, public-spirited, federative republic will last forever, govern the globe, and introduce the perfection of man; his perfectability being already proved by Price, Priestley, Condorcet, Rousseau, Diderot, and Godwin. Mischief has been done by the Senate of the United States. I have known and felt more of this mischief, than Washington, Jefferson, and Madison all together. But this has been all caused by the constitutional power of the Senate, in executive business, which ought to be immediately, totally, and essentially abolished. Your distinction between the aristoi and pseudo aristoi will not help the matter. I would trust one as well as the other with unlimited power. The law wisely refuses an oath as a witness in his own case, to the saint as well as the sinner. No romance would be more amusing than the history of your Virginian and our New England aristocratical families. Yet even in Rhode Island there has been no clergy, no church, and I had almost said no State, and some people say no religion. There has been a constant respect for certain old families. Fifty-seven or fifty-eight years ago, in company with Colonel, Counsellor, Judge, John Chandler, whom I have quoted before, a newspaper was brought in. The old sage asked me to look for the news from Rhode Island, and see how the elections had gone there. I read the list of

Wantons, Watsons, Greens, Whipples, Malbones, etc. "I expected as much," said the aged gentleman, "for I have always been of opinion that in the most popular governments, the elections will generally go in favor of the most ancient families." . . .

You suppose a difference of opinion between you and me on the subject of aristocracy. I can find none. I dislike and detest hereditary honors, offices, emoluments, established by law. So do you. I am for excluding legal, hereditary distinctions from the United States as long as possible. So are you. I only say that mankind have not yet discovered any remedy against irresistible corruption in elections to offices of great power and profit, but making them hereditary.

But will you say our elections are pure? Be it so, upon the whole; but do you recollect in history a more corrupt election than that of Aaron Burr to be President, or that of DeWitt Clinton last year? By corruption here, I mean a sacrifice of every national interest and honor to private and party objects. I see the same spirit in Virginia that you and I see in Rhode Island and the rest of New England. In New York it is a struggle of family feuds—a feudal aristocracy. Pennsylvania is a contest between German, Irish and Old England families. When Germans and Irish unite they give 30,000 majorities. There is virtually a white rose and a red rose, a Caesar and a Pompey, in every State in this Union, and contests and dissensions will be as lasting. The rivalry of Bourbons and Noailleses produced the French Revolution, and a similar competition for consideration and influence exists and prevails in every village in the world. Where will terminate the *rabies agri?* The continent will be scattered over with manors much larger than Livingston's, Van Rensselaer's or Philips's; even our Deacon Strong will have a principality among you southern folk. What inequality of talents will be produced by these land jobbers. Where tends the mania of banks? At my table in Philadelphia, I once proposed to you to unite in endeavors to obtain an amendment of the Constitution prohibiting to the separate States the power of creating banks; but giving Congress authority to establish one bank with a branch in each State, the whole limited to ten millions of dollars. Whether this project was wise or unwise, I know not, for I had deliberated little on it then, and have never thought it worth thinking of since. But you spurned the proposition from you with disdain. This system of banks, begotten, brooded and hatched by Duer, Robert and Gouverneur Morris, Hamilton and Washington, I have always considered as a system of national injustice. A sacrifice of public and private interest to a few aristocratical friends and favorites. My scheme could have had no such effect. Verres plundered temples, and robbed a few rich men, but he never made such ravages among private property in general, nor swindled so much out of the pockets of the poor, and middle class of people, as these banks have done. No people but this would have borne the imposition so long. . . .

CHAPTER 9

The Transformation of Northern Society

Thomas Jefferson wanted America to remain a nation of farmers. Identifying corruption and vice with the "dark satanic mills" of Europe, he hoped that America would never have an industrial revolution. There was a need, he acknowledged, for small rural mills to provide useful employment for "a few women, children and invalids, who could do little on the farm." But large industrial cities would destroy the moral fiber of the American people. Farming had to remain the basis of American life.

The south remained true to Jefferson's vision much longer than the north. Even though southerners moved west and turned to cotton as their cash crop, the basic structure of southern society changed very little after Jefferson's death in 1826. The south continued to be an agrarian society with few industries of its own and a small urban population. And, as always, the great planters ran things. In contrast the north—and particularly the northeast—underwent something of a metamorphosis. New York became a huge city. Factories sprang up throughout New England, New York, and Pennsylvania. Boatloads of Irish and German workers descended upon Boston, New York, Philadelphia, and other port cities. And between 1800 and 1850 the portion of the northern labor force in agriculture declined from 70 percent to 40 percent.

Our own society is so much a product of the industrial revolution that we sometimes find it difficult to appreciate just how deep the transformation went, just how disconcerting and exciting the process of "modernization" really was. Much of what a modern society is we take for granted and treat almost as "natural" or "human." But, though much lingered on from the past, the society that Americans were building in the first half of the nineteenth century was fundamentally new. And the newness reached into every detail of life. The ways Americans dressed and the ways they decorated their houses changed. So too did their ideas about childrearing and education, domestic architecture, and even diet. The nature and pace of work were altered in ways everyone knew about, but few understood.

Amid all the excitement about "progress" and "growth," there was a good deal of fear. Many Americans responded to change by trying to find ways to hold on to old values and habits. Religious revivalism, which swept across the nation in the period, was one way of trying to preserve inherited values. So was a rash of reform movements. But even the attempt to resist change employed the methods of modernity. Revivalists and reformers appealed to mass constituencies through the most modern means of communication. And they organized themselves in ways that paralleled the ways the new corporations were discovering to reach their markets.

All in all, the society that Lincoln would later look back on across his "fourscore and seven years" was a society in which little or nothing stood still. The south might still exhibit many eighteenth-century features, and might dress itself out as a kind of feudal scene of romance, but the reality was one of transformation.

INTERPRETIVE ESSAY

John F. Kasson

Civilizing the Machine

Today, we normally think of cities when we think of factories; but in the early nineteenth century water power dictated the location of factories and hence factories were often located in rural areas. This was especially true of New England, where almost overnight cow pastures were turned into mill towns. Of these the most famous was Lowell, Massachusetts, which grew from nothing to 28,000 in just two decades. Founded by rich Boston merchants, it was purposely laid out to take advantage of the peaceful rural setting as well as the water power of the Merrimack River. The town, in fact, became something of a tourist attraction, and everybody of importance—from Charles Dickens to the legendary Davy Crockett—came to see the "factory girls of Lowell."

Here is a modern account of the famous Lowell "system." It was written by John F. Kasson, a historian who is primarily interested in the question of whether it was possible to have industrial cities and still maintain the values of Jefferson's America.

The question of what social environment American manufacturers would create went to the heart of the republican venture. The introduction of new manufacturing centers portended dramatic changes in the structure of society. Their impact upon the character of American life was an issue of national concern. Could a system of manufactures be established that would nurture and protect the health, intelligence, independence, and virtue of their operatives, qualities essential to a republic? Or would factories breed disease, ignorance, dependence, and corruption? Would industrialization provide new prosperity and comfort for all levels of society? Or would industrialization prove an instrument of economic and political repression and social cleavage? In short, was the revolutionary ideal of a republican civilization compatible with rapid industrial development? On the answer to these questions much of the nation's future depended.

Americans in the early nineteenth century united in admiration of English machine technology; smuggling British industrial secrets and mechanics was the sincerest form of flattery. However, there was considerably less enthusiasm for the social consequences of the English factory system. Jefferson found cause to revise his earlier opposition to the promotion of domestic manufactures, but not his horror of the "mobs" of workmen in European cities. In the late eighteenth and early nineteenth centuries, factory town sprang up in England at unprecedented rates, stimulated by the colossal expansion in cotton manufactures in Lancashire. The capital of the cotton industry, Manchester, expanded from an ancient town of 17,000 people in 1770 to over 70,000 by 1801, 142,000 in 1831, and over 250,000 by midcentury, with more than an additional 150,000 in the sprawling towns that surrounded it. It stood as the "shock city" of the age, attracting numerous visitors from both England and abroad anxious to confront the symbol and embodiment of the new industrial order. Manchester's contrasts both fascinated and repelled: the advanced technology and immense productivity of its factories; the unbelievably primitive, cramped, and diseased hovels; the vitality of its magnates; the feebleness and despair of its workers. Wrestling with its conflicting characteristics during a visit in 1835, the astute social critic Alexis de Tocqueville concluded: "From this foul drain the greatest stream of human industry flows out to fertilise the whole world. From this filthy sewer pure gold flows. Here humanity attains its most complete development and its most brutish; here civilisation works its miracles, and civilised man is turned back almost into a savage." . . .

Such reports confirmed the popular American image of English factory towns in the first half of the nineteenth century as centers of advanced technology and productivity but also as cancers against both nature and society, producing an oppressed, ignorant, and debauched working class and threatening the civilization as a whole. Could the United States develop a system of manufactures that would avoid a similar fate? If American technology could indeed, as its proponents from Coxe to Everett claimed, integrate the country socially and politically and buttress its republican virtue, it would have to prove it first at the local level in the nation's new manufacturing towns. Here more than anywhere else would be the testing ground of the new republican industrial order.

No one was more aware of this challenge than American manufacturers themselves. The merchant-entrepreneurs who created the leading industrial towns of the nineteenth century shared their fathers' sense of republican mission and distrust of aristocratic Europe. Though some advocates of manufactures took heart in reports that pauperism pervaded England's agricultural counties to a much greater extent than her manufacturing ones, they were not generally inclined to dispute the sordid reputation of English factory towns. Many of them had observed firsthand what Nathan Appleton called the "misery and poverty" of English industrial workers, and they resolved that American manufactures must never be allowed to take a similar course. Manufacturing itself need not be debilitating, they reasoned. Many of the social and moral evils of the English system, they believed, stemmed from the establishment of factories in large cities, in which vice thrived and unchecked and a debased proletariat perpetuated itself. They shared the faith of some of the earliest American planners of industrial towns, including Tench Coxe and Alexander Hamilton, that by locating American manufactures in the countryside and instituting a strict system of moral supervision, the health and virtue of operatives would be protected. Thus situated, manufactures would harmoniously complement agricultural life, and the nation's agrarian character would remain undisturbed.

However, the leading American factory towns of the first half of the nineteenth century were shaped in response not only to the English factory system but to events in America as well. As we have seen, technology was absorbed into a conservative ideology of republicanism as early as the 1780s in part as an instrument of social order and control against both the insidious influences of European manufactures and symptoms of social discord and rebellion at home. As Americans advanced into the nineteenth century, pressures on a deferential society continued and the problems of republican order increased. The whole country surged with dramatic volatility and energy. The nation's population, which had more than doubled every twenty-five years in the eighteenth century, continued to grow at the same phenomenal rate through the first half of the nineteenth. People migrated restlessly not only along the vast new frontier but within the rapidly mushrooming urban centers as well. And the concept of republicanism, instead of controlling and containing this expansion, became in the hands of new egalitarian forces a weapon with which to challenge established authority in politics, religion, law, commerce—virtually every aspect of society. Social conservatives rubbed their eyes to see a reversion in American life from civilization to barbarism as the whole social order upon which the republican experiment was premised appeared to be collapsing around them. Some recent scholars, including Stanley Elkins and David Donald, have in effect supported their perception, arguing that ante-bellum America suffered from a general "institutional breakdown" and "an excess of democracy" that ultimately paved the way for Civil War. . . .

To the total institution, then, turned a group of merchants known as the Boston associates, who would become America's leading manufacturers before the Civil War, as they sought an alternative to the poverty and neglect of English industrial conditions and a safeguard against the fluidity and potential corruption of an expanding American society. Beginning in Waltham, Massachusetts, in 1815, they established a successful pattern of textile manufactures and extended it rapidly. By 1850 the Boston associates controlled mills in operation in Chicopee, Taunton, and Lawrence, Massachusetts; Manchester, Dover, Somersworth, and Nashua, New Hampshire; and Saco and Biddeford, Maine; and were making active preparations for new mills in Holyoke, Massachusetts. But the queen city of their system and the leading producer of cotton goods, the nation's largest industry before the Civil War, was Lowell, Massachusetts. Lowell's fame rested not only on its industrial capacity but even more on its reputed social achievement. One of the most important and influential of all total institutions of republican reform in the ante-bellum period, Lowell promised to resolve the social conflict between the desire for industrial progress and the fear of a debased and disorderly proletariat. Its founding sprang from the conviction that, given the proper institutional environment, a factory town need not be a byword for vice and poverty, but might stand as a model of enlightened republican community in a restless and dynamic nation. Lowell offers a dramatic example of the effort to put this conservative faith into practice. Its story is particularly interesting because within a few years of its founding, the basic assumptions of the Lowell factory system and its conception of republican community were challenged on both ideological and institutional grounds by the working class and their spokesmen. Branding Lowell's directors as a repressive new aristocracy, dissident workers increasingly rejected what they regarded as a manipulative social structure and an exploitative industrial capitalism. Against the conservative view of republicanism of Lowell's directors, protesting workers interpreted the American Revolution as the beginning of a continuing struggle toward a radical egalitarianism. The early history of Lowell thus provides an encapsulated version of the debate over the meaning of republicanism in an industrial society and the attempt to give that meaning institutional shape.

Lowell was conceived in the second decade of the nineteenth century by a trio of innovative and energetic young Boston merchants: Francis Cabot Lowell, Nathan Appleton, and Patrick Tracy Jackson. Touring Great Britain in 1810 and 1811 for his health, F. C. Lowell visited a large iron works in Edinburgh and grew excited over the enormous possibilities such large-scale manufacturing had for America. While in Edinburgh, he also met Nathan Appleton, his friend and fourth cousin, and the merchants discussed the idea of establishing cotton manufacture employing English technology in the United States. At the same time Lowell was corresponding on the subject with his business partner and brother-in-law, P. T. Jackson, and he determined, before his return to America, to study thoroughly the cotton mills at Manchester and Birmingham. He spent weeks in these factories, applying his keen mathematical and mechanical skill and questioning engineers eager to accommodate a wealthy potential customer. Thus Lowell circumvented stringent regulations against the exportation of English machinery or mechanical drawings and smuggled into America valuable mental baggage. His contemporaries would later acclaim him a hero and a genius, who had performed an act of patriotic espionage to rank with Samuel Slater's a generation earlier.

Shortly after Lowell's return from Europe, he and Jackson bought a water-power site in Waltham, obtained a charter of incorporation from the Massachusetts legislature for their new Boston Manufacturing Company, and sought investors for the enterprise within their circle of friends and relatives among Boston's merchants. Some of Lowell's relations, including the Cabots whose pioneering 1787 cotton factory at Beverly had failed, attempted to dissuade him from what they considered "a visionary and dangerous scheme, and thought him mad." Nathan Appleton himself warily agreed to invest only five thousand dollars, half the amount Lowell and Jackson requested, "in order to see the experiment fairly tried." The two merchants also enlisted the financial support of Patrick Jackson's brothers; Israel Thorndike and his son; Uriah Cotting; James Lloyd; and two of Lowell's brothers-in-law, Benjamin Gorham and Warren Dutton.

Lowell hired a talented engineer, Paul Moody, and quickly set about a series of reinventions based upon his observations of English machinery and contemporary American developments. Of these the most important was the power loom, which promised to free American mills from dependence on neighborhood weavers and to permit the organization of all manufacturing processes from raw cotton to finished cloth within a single integrated mill complex. When

Nathan Appleton first saw Lowell's loom in 1814, he was stupefied by its significance and, in a "state of admiration and satisfaction," sat with Lowell "by the hour, watching the beautiful movement of this new and wonderful machine, destined as it evidently was, to change the character of all textile industry." To exploit the capacity of large-scale mechanized production to its fullest extent while relying on unskilled labor, Lowell decided to concentrate production on standardized inexpensive cotton cloths, sheetings, and shirtings. Later, as new corporations arose at the town of Lowell and elsewhere, each manufactured a different type of cotton goods to avoid duplication and competition with fellow companies. Mills were designed to facilitate the flow of materials from one stage of processing to the next. Cotton was carded on the first floor, spun on the second, woven on the third and fourth, while machine shops resided in the basement. In the next fifteen years New England inventors would build upon this structure and introduce a series of labor-saving technological innovations which equaled or excelled British methods and machinery and mechanized all the basic processes of cloth manufacturing except spooling and warping. Even before some of these refinements, however, Lowell's system achieved dramatic gains in production. According to one technological historian, from its first years of operation the Waltham mill could with the same number of employees produce three and a half times as much as other American factories still operating according to pre-1812 methods. The achievement of Lowell and his colleagues, sometimes known as the "Massachusetts system," thus marked a significant stage in the development of modern mass production.

As a final stroke in his grand design, Lowell turned his attention to politics. Competition with British textiles had in the past been the bane of the American industry. Thus when Congress began deliberations over a new tariff measure in 1816, Lowell rushed to Washington to lobby for his cause. He adroitly steered through Congress a minimum valuation tariff that helped to establish the principle of protection to American industry and sheltered his own company's products from foreign competition, while leaving exposed rival manufacturers of more expensive cotton goods. Lowell made a powerful impression even on opponents of the protective tariffs, such as Daniel Webster, then a representative from New Hampshire. Only two years earlier, discussing another tariff measure Webster had declared he was "not in haste to see Sheffields and Birminghams in America." The grim image of English industrial towns dominated his thinking on the subject, and he gestured with foreboding toward the day "when the young men of the country shall be obliged to shut their eyes upon external nature, upon the heavens and the earth, and immerse themselves in close and unwholesome workshops; when they shall be obliged to shut their ears to the bleating of their own flocks, upon their own hills, and to the voice of the lark that cheers them at the plough, that they may open them in dust, and smoke, and steam, to the perpetual whirl of spools and spindles, and the grating of rasps and saws." Lowell helped Webster to change his opinion and to convert him gradually to the protectionist position. Webster's ambition was outgrowing New Hampshire, and he soon moved to Boston, where Lowell supplied him with letters of introduction. Such ministrations, including a later offer to obtain stock in the Boston associates' new enterprise at the town of Lowell, ultimately won Webster's services as a major apologist for American industrial interests.

In the eyes of his contemporaries, however, Lowell's greatest achievement lay in neither his technological success, nor his political skill, nor his business acumen. The special reverence with which his name was spoken in the period before the Civil War emerged from the sense that he had conceived a manufacturing system that concerned itself as much with the health, character, and well-being of its operatives as it did with profits. By allegedly protecting the integrity of America's workers, he had in important measure safeguarded the character of the republic itself. From the beginning, Lowell and his associates were mindful of the condition of European workers and particularly concerned to avoid a similar fate here. As Appleton recalled their earnest discussions, "The operatives in the manufacturing cities of Europe, were notoriously of the lowest character, for intelligence and morals. The question therefore arose, and was deeply considered, whether this degradation was the result of the peculiar occupation, or of other and distinct causes. We could not perceive why this peculiar description of labor should vary in its effects upon character from all other occupation."

Their solution was to organize the factory as a total institution, so that the company might exercise exclusive control over the environment. Unlike most English cotton factories of this time, which were powered by steam, American mills depended upon water power; and the necessity to locate the plant near an important rapids further insured that the community would be placed in the country, apart from urban contamination. But where Lowell's plan differed radically from both earlier English and American factory settlements was in his decision to establish a community with a rotating rather than a permanent population; this was central to the conception. Previous American factory settlements had retained the English system of hiring whole families, often including school-aged children. Lowell and his associates opposed the idea of a long-term residential force that might lead to an entrenched proletariat. They planned to hire as their main working force young, single women from the surrounding area for a few years apiece. For a rotating work force such women were an obvious choice. Able-bodied men could be attracted from farming only with difficulty, and their hiring would raise fears that the nation might lose her agrarian character and promote resistance to manufactures. Women, on the other hand, had traditionally served as spinners and weavers when textiles had been produced in the home, and they constituted an important part of the family economy. However, imports of European manufactured fabrics were eroding American household industry. At the same time, southern New England farmers were gradually shifting from subsistence to commercial agriculture. By employing young farm women in American factories on a relatively short-term basis, the Lowell system in effect extended and preserved the family economy while at the same time avoiding incorporation into the factory of the family as a whole. Factory work, then, would not become a lifetime vocation or mark of caste, passed on from parent to child in the omnipresent shadow of the mill. Rather it might form an honorable stage in a young woman's maturation, allowing her to supplement her family's income or earn a dowry, before assuming what the founders regarded as "the higher and more appropriate responsibilities of her sex" in a domestic capacity. Her factory experience would be a moral as well as an economic boon, numerous spokesmen for American manufactures maintained, rescuing her from idleness, and vice, pauperism, possibly even confinement in an almshouse or penitentiary. Instead, in the cotton mill, under the watchful eyes of supervisors, she would receive a republican education, imbibing "habits of order, regularity and industry, which lay a broad and deep foundation of public and private future usefulness." During her term at Lowell, the worker would be protected *in loco parentis* by strict corporate supervision, lodged in company boardinghouses kept by upright matrons, and provided compulsory religious services. Such stringent standards of moral scrutiny and company control would serve a treble purpose: to attract young women and overcome the reluctance of their parents, most of them farmers; to provide optimal factory discipline and management control of the operatives; and to maintain an intelligent, honorable, and exemplary republican work force. Though Lowell's founders never regarded their efforts as utopian, they aimed to establish an ideal New England community, which would stand not as a blight but a beacon of republican prosperity and purity upon the American landscape.

Recently, however, some scholars have questioned the extent to which the Lowell system actually stemmed from any grand social vision or solicitude in behalf of the workers. How much choice, they ask, did Lowell's founders really have in developing their vaunted system? According to the economist Howard M. Gitelman, the complexity of the early power-driven machinery employed at Lowell and elsewhere made child labor unfeasible, and thus the economies of a family labor system were not a viable option for the founders. Moreover, he contends, the rural location of Waltham, Lowell, and similar mill towns was dictated mainly by considerations of available water power; company housing then had to be provided in order to staff the mills. Concerned parents and an aroused community, Gitelman speculates, would in any case have insisted upon supervised company housing and a strict system of rules and regulations for the operatives. Economic necessity, not employer magnanimity, so the argument runs, compelled the shape of Lowell.

But to conclude that because the Boston associates were not altruistic reformers, they were therefore simply capitalists following the line of least economic resistance clearly ignores a broad middle ground. A fuller, more satisfactory explanation of the founding of Lowell would recognize *both* commercial and social and ideological motives. For the Boston associates and many of their colleagues were in fact both capitalists and concerned citizens, hard-dealing merchants and public-spirited philanthropists, entrepreneurs and ideologues. Even as they helped to transform New England's economy, they sought to preserve a cohesive social order by adhering tenaciously to a rigorous code of ethics and responsibility. They took seriously their role as republican leaders, and the public turned to them for leadership. The Unitarian reformer Theodore Parker expressed the sense of gratitude of many when he praised the development of manufactures and improvements in transportation as helping to "civilize, educate, and refine men." "These are men," he concluded, "to whom the public owes a debt which no money could pay, for it is a debt of life." Whether it was sufficient payment or not, obviously these manufacturers received a great deal of money for their services. Nevertheless, they insisted both publicly and privately that wealth was not their goal. "My mind has always been devoted to many other things rather than moneymaking," Nathan Appleton declared toward the end of his life. "Accident, and not effort, has made me a rich man." Amos Lawrence, who with his brother Abbott joined forces with Lowell's investors in 1830, filled his diary and letters with reminders of the stewardship and public trust that wealth entailed. From 1829 through 1852 he personally and meticulously made charitable gifts of $639,000 in cash, as well as clothing, food, books, and other articles. He once wrote a factory agent, "We must make a good thing out of this establishment, unless you ruin us by working on Sundays. Nothing but works of necessity should be done in holy time." Boston's leading merchants generally scorned a narrowly acquisitive view of their role and participated in a wide variety of public affairs. They were active and influential in Federalist and later Whig politics and held important offices on both state and national levels. Their contributions to numerous charities and philanthropies, including hospitals, orphanages, and asylums, as well as libraries, historical societies, schools and colleges, helped to make Boston a center of social and cultural institutions in the nineteenth century. Such enterprises, they believed, were essential to the solidity and progress of society. As Francis Cabot Lowell's son John Lowell declared in establishing a series of public lectures, the Lowell Institute, in 1835, "The prosperity of my native land, New England, which is sterile and unproductive, must depend . . . 1st on the moral qualities and 2dly on the intelligence and information of its inhabitants."

Concern with the social consequences of Lowell, Massachusetts, as a tight-knit, carefully regulated republican community, then, was certainly consistent with the values and activities of the founders and their associates in a variety of other fields. Moreover, their philanthropic and industrial pursuits were related both historically and institutionally. Nineteenth-century textile mills were direct descendants of the manufacturing societies formed in various American colonies in the eighteenth century and more distant relatives of the work houses of the seventeenth century. Institutions such as the Boston Society for Encouraging Industry and Employing the Poor, established in 1751 and one of the colonies' most important prerevolutionary factories, had, as its name indicates, a dual purpose: not only to stimulate American manufactures but to provide work for the destitute; to encourage industry in both senses of the word, under official supervision. Undoubtedly, with increased mechanization in the textile industry, commercial motives were uppermost in the establishment of Lowell and other mill towns in the nineteenth century, but at the same time one should not lose sight of the social vision that accompanied them. Of course Lowell's founders and directors were not always as idealistic as they professed. But in instituting their factory system, they did not have to choose between their ethical and ideological convictions and their economic advantage as entrepreneurs—

not in the beginning at least. The Lowell system united advanced technology, factory discipline, and conservative republicanism; and when it was eventually challenged, protest came on both economic and ideological grounds.

F. C. Lowell lived only until 1817, long enough to see the success of his Waltham experiment but before practical plans for the city that would bear his name had begun. Yet despite his premature death, he remained, in Nathan Appleton's words, "the informing soul, which gave direction and form to the whole proceeding." To carry on his work, Appleton and Jackson selected as agent Kirk Boott, a trained engineer with an autocratic personality who had perhaps acquired his rigorous standards of discipline and strong class-consciousness in his service in the British army under the Duke of Wellington. They purchased the Pawtucket canal on the Merrimack in what was then the town of Chelmsford, together with four hundred acres of farmland, in the fall of 1821. Boott quickly set about the planning and construction of the industrial town according to F. C. Lowell's general conception, opening the first factory complex, the Merrimack Manufacturing Company, for production in September 1823. The company's six factory buildings were grouped in a spacious quadrangle bordering the river and landscaped with flowers, trees, and shrubs. They were dominated by a central mill, crowned with a Georgian cupola. Made of brick, with flat, plain walls, and white granite lintels above each window space, the factories presented a neat, orderly, and efficient appearance, which symbolized the institution's goals and would be emulated by many of the penitentiaries, insane asylums, orphanages, and reformatories of the period. Beyond the counting house at the entrance to the mill yard stretched the company dormitories. Their arrangement reflected a Federalist image of proper social structure. The factory population of Lowell was rigidly defined into four groups, and their hierarchy immutably preserved in the town's architecture. As chief agent for the corporation, most of whose stockholders resided in Boston, Boott and the other company agents formed the unquestioned aristocracy of the community; a Georgian mansion with an imposing Ionic portico just below the original factory in Lowell powerfully symbolized Boott's authority. Beneath this class stood the overseers, who lived in simple yet substantial quarters at the ends of the rows of boardinghouses where the operatives resided, thus providing a secondary measure of surveillance. In the boardinghouses themselves lived the female workers, who outnumbered male employees roughly three to one. Originally these apartments were constructed in rows of double houses, at least thirty girls to a unit, with intervening strips of lawn. Later, in the 1830s, as companies expanded and proliferated, the houses were strung together, blocking both light and air. These quarters were intended to serve essentially as dormitories and offered few amenities beyond dining rooms and bedrooms, each of the latter shared by as many as six or eight girls, two to a bed. Boardinghouse keepers were responsible for both the efficient administration of the buildings and for enforcing company regulations as to the conduct of the workers. Similar tenements were provided for male mechanics and their families. At the bottom of this hierarchy were the Irish day laborers, who built the canals and mills and made possible the continuing expansion of Lowell. Significantly, no housing had been planned for this group, and they lived in hundreds of little shanties next to a small Catholic church in an area called "New Dublin" and the "Acre." This early corporate insensitivity to the needs of the immigrant presaged Lowell's response to the great mass of immigrants later on.

The adjustment of workers to factory life marked a critical juncture in America's transition to a mature industrial society. Many of Lowell's operatives had known long hours and hard tasks before in farms or shops; but the regularity and discipline of factory work were altogether new. They no longer labored at their own speeds in completing of a task, but to the clock at the pace of the machine. The employer aimed to standardize irregular labor rhythms and to make time the measurement of work. Thus the cupolas that crowned Lowell mills were not simply ornamental; their bells insistently reminded workers that time was money. Operatives worked a six-day week, approximately twelve hours a day, and bells tolled them awake and to their jobs (lateness was severely punished), to and from meals, curfew, and bed. Other factory owners also demanded long hours, even while they simultaneously claimed that the factory system had in large measure repealed the primeval curse "In the sweat of thy face shalt thou eat bread." In the hands of their operatives, they believed, leisure meant mischief; idleness at best; at worst vicious amusements, drink, gambling, and riot. Hence the resistance to shorter working hours throughout the nineteenth century and into the twentieth; work was a form of social control. Lowell's managers shared this perception and wove it into the entire social order. They established an elaborate structure of social deterrents and incentives, insisting at all times upon "respectability" and defining it to suit their needs. Here the heritage of the Puritan ethic served employers especially well. Many Lowell women had been raised in a strongly evangelical atmosphere, which placed heavy emphasis upon personal discipline and restraint. Injunctions to industry and the redemption of time pervaded their home communities, and their reading of popular didactic literature, from Isaac Watts's "How doth the little busy Bee," and Poor Richard's *Way to Wealth,* to the writings of Hannah More, reinforced these teachings. Company officials appropriated these values and adapted them to the imperatives of industrial capitalism. The Lawrence Company regulations, for example, stipulated that all employees "must devote themselves assiduously to their duty during working hours" and "on all occasion, both in their words and in their actions, show they are penetrated by a laudable love of temperance and virtue, and animated by a sense of their moral and social obligations."

A policy of strict social control, implicit in the residential architecture, enforced this code of factory discipline. The factory as a whole was governed by the superintendent, his office strategically placed between the boardinghouses and the mills at the entrance to the mill yard. From this point, as one spokesman enthusiastically reported, his "mind regulates all; his character inspires all; his plans, matured and decided by the directors of the company, who visit him every week, control all." Beneath his watchful eye in each room of the factory, an overseer stood responsible for the work, conduct, and proper management of the operatives therein. Should he choose to exercise it, an overseer possessed formidable power. The various mill towns of New England participated in a "black list" system. A worker who bridled at employers' demands was charged with an offense of character, such as "insubordination," "profanity," or "improper conduct." Issued a "dishonorable discharge," she would be unable to find similar work elsewhere. Supervision was thus constant. If the lines of social division occasionally relaxed on special occasions, it was only because the hierarchical authority of the community, which formed the basis of factory discipline, remained so indisputable.

In addition to these powerful institutional controls, corporate authorities relied upon the factory girls to act as moral police over one another. The ideal, as described by an unofficial spokesman of the corporation, represented a tyranny of the majority that would have made Tocqueville shudder. Declared the Rev. Henry A. Miles of Lowell, "Among the virtuous and high-minded young women, who feel that they have the keeping of their characters and that any stain upon their associates brings reproach upon themselves, the power of opinion becomes an ever-present, and ever-active restraint. A girl, *suspected* of immoralities, or serious improprieties of conduct, at once loses caste." As Miles approvingly described the ostracism, the girl's fellow-boarders would threaten to leave the house unless the housekeeper dismissed the offender. They would shun her on the street, refuse to work with her, and point her out to their companions. "From their power of opinion, there is no appeal." Eventually the outcast would submit to her punishment and leave the community. Even if, as one suspects, Miles overestimated the moral severity of Lowell women, his description nevertheless represented the official standard of behavior. On no account did employers wish to encourage independence of character, for it threatened the stability of the entire factory system.

During its first two decades of operation, Lowell's reputation as a model factory town, offering economic opportunity in a wholesome moral and intellectual atmosphere, proved notably successful in attracting labor. Eager and intelligent young women flocked to the city, mostly from farms in New Hampshire, Vermont, Massachusetts, and Maine. Though their pay was not great and declined relative to the general economy over the years, manufacturing initially offered the greatest income of any occupation open to women at the time; domestic service in particular suffered as a result. Women came for manifold reasons: for money to assist their families, to support a brother's education, or to earn a dowry, and in some cases to gain independence from family life. Often Lowell women offered more romantic explanations as well: a failed family fortune, infidel parents, a cruel mistress, a lover's absence. As Lowell operatives reported their experiences and the community's reputation spread, many came for an informal education and the stimulation of their peers in an urban setting. In addition, company recruiters traveled through New England painting glowing pictures of the life and wages to be enjoyed at Lowell and collecting a commission for each young woman they persuaded. With the construction of new factories and the rise of a middle class in the town to serve the needs of the enterprise, Lowell's population expanded rapidly: From roughly 200 in 1820, it climbed to 6477 in 1830, 21,000 in 1840, and over 33,000 in 1850. For many young women away from home and family for the first time, the factory town appeared overwhelming at first, though most soon adapted to the new industrial environment and institutional life. Some even found the community rather snug and reassuring. With memories tinged by the nostalgia of old age, Harriet Robinson described the early days of Lowell as a life of "almost Arcadian simplicity," and Lucy Larcom recalled "a frank friendliness and sincerity in the social atmosphere," a purposefulness and zest for life that contrasted warmly with her early days as a child on the Massachusetts seacoast. Despite Lowell's swelling population and the lack of public parks until the mid-1840s, the town retained at least suggestions of a rural life. House plants in windows often gave corners of the mills the effect of a bower, and some of the overseers cultivated flower gardens behind the factories as well. According to Miss Larcom, "Nature came very close to the mill gates . . . in those days. There was green grass all around them; violets and wild geraniums grew by the canals; and long stretches of open land between the corporation buildings and the street made the town seem countrylike."

Gradually, most of these young women adjusted to the demands of factory life. Probably the greatest challenge confronting them was the machinery itself. "The buzzing and hissing and whizzing of pulleys and rollers and spindles and flyers"—as one ex-worker described them—often proved bewildering and oppressive for people completely unaccustomed to such devices. As they mastered their machines' intricacies, they learned to defy the noise and tedium by distancing themselves from their work through private thoughts and daydreams. Furthermore, before operatives were given more looms to attend and the machines speeded up in the mid-1840s, they often had long periods of idleness between catching broken threads. Regulations prohibited books in the mill, but women frequently cut out pages or clippings from the newspaper and evaded the edict. Others worked on compositions in their spare moments or spent the time lost in contemplation. Thus they attempted to give meaning to the time that their work denied and to cultivate a mental separation from their activities and surroundings.

In the two or three hours they had remaining at the end of a long working day, and on Sundays, many Lowell women relentlessly pursued an education. They borrowed books from lending libraries, attended the lyceum at which Edward Everett, John Quincy Adams, and Ralph Waldo Emerson spoke, met in church groups, and organized a number of "Improvement Circles," two of which produced their own periodicals, the *Operatives' Magazine* (1841–1842) and, most famous, the *Lowell Offering* (1840–1845), and its successor, the *New England Offering* (1848–1850). Writers in these journals were self-conscious of their position as "factory girls" and eager to vindicate their reputations. As they endeavored "to remove unjust prejudice—to prove that the female operatives of Lowell were, as a class, intelligent and virtuous"—they offered impressive support for the Lowell system as a model republican community. Factory life at Lowell, a number of writers maintained, did not injure their health or degrade their morals. On the contrary, they asserted, the conscientious worker's "intellect is strengthened, her moral sense quickened, her manners refined, her whole character elevated and improved, by the privileges and discipline of her factory life." To those who chafed against this regimen and thought of returning to the country, various authors replied that Lowell presented the most stimulating moral and intellectual climate, the most authentic republican community, in the land. Declared one woman in the *Lowell Offering:* "I believe there is no place where there are so many advantages within the reach of the laboring class of people, as exist here; where there is so much equality, so few aristocratic distinctions, and such good fellowship, as may be found in this community." A contributor to the *Operatives' Magazine* agreed: "We are, in fact, a truly republican community, or rather we have among us the only aristocracy which an intelligent people should sanction—an aristocracy of worth." While the stress of these remarks was more egalitarian than the conception of Lowell's founders, they effectively supported the existing system. The icon of the *Lowell Offering*'s title page depicted the symbolic landscape in which the operative stood: "the school girl, near her cottage home, with a bee-hive, as emblematical of industry and intelligence, and, in the background, the Yankee school-house, church and factory." With school and church, the factory thus formed a triad of republican instruction and uplift.

As Lowell's fame spread in the 1830s, 1840s, and 1850s, countless visitors made the pilgrimage to the town, were conducted through its factories by representatives of the corporations, and emerged awe-stricken by its technological splendor and moral sublimity. Their rhapsodic testimonies overwhelmingly endorsed the policies of F. C. Lowell, his associates, and successors. Not only did the town appear to sustain the nation's highest standards of health, intellect, prosperity, and character; its success was such that in many respects it presented a model for American communities. . . .

American enthusiasm over Lowell was eminently shared by European visitors. The town quickly emerged as the celestial countertype to infernal Manchester. By the 1830s it had become an obligatory stop on foreign itineraries, as distinctively a republican innovation as the American penitentiary, as established a landmark as Niagara Falls. Despite Lowell's international reputation, each traveler retained a European conception of factory towns that left him unprepared for what he saw. The dramatic natural setting along the banks of the Merrimack, nestled in the hills, with views reputedly as far as the White Mountains, no less than the crisp, clean aspect of the town itself, gave Lowell an air of "rural freshness" that dazzled foreign guests. As a result, each took his first glimpse of Lowell in amazement, even an air of disbelief. Viewing the city from a hilltop one winter evening, the Swedish novelist Fredrika Bremer compared it to "a magic castle on the snow-covered earth." Upon closer inspection she exclaimed, "To think and to know that these lights were not *ignes fatui,* not merely pomp and show, but that they were actually symbols of a healthful and hopeful life." Alexander Mackay found himself searching in vain for "the tall chimneys and the thick volumes of black smoke" that characterized English manufacturing towns. Lowell's appearance of newness overwhelmed Charles Dickens in the early 1840s, so that it seemed to him created only yesterday. And the perspicacious French engineer Michel Chevalier, who had earlier experienced "the delusive splendor" of the great Manchester mills, approached Lowell warily. His sense of pleasure at the town, "new and fresh like an opera scene," warred with his fear of its eventual decline, causing him to ponder, "Will this become like Lancashire?" Only gradually, watching Lowell operatives passing neatly through the streets and learning of their wages, did he wholly credit the enormous gulf between Lowell and Manchester. . . .

Lowell's planners and directors might thus have felt deservedly proud of their accomplishment. For in Lowell and its sister cities—Chicopee, Holyoke, Lawrence, Manchester, Saco, and the rest—they had apparently built a productive, cohesive, and harmonious community based upon the earlier ideological fusion of technology and republicanism. Lowell promised not to compromise the nation's agrarian commitment, but rather to supplement it, to strengthen the country economically, socially, and morally. The factory town ostensibly reconciled the myth of the American garden with a new myth of the machine. Safely removed from Boston yet connected by the railroad, Lowell represented in the public mind a region in the middle distance, between city and wilderness. In this setting among the hills and on the banks of the Merrimack River, the town at once partook of the purifying influences of nature, yet—unwilling totally to submit to its siren song and reel as debauchees of dew—retained the beneficial discipline of the factory. The flowers in factory windows, so often noted by visitors, provided a fitting token of the community's premise, that an oasis of harmony and joy was attainable only through the maintenance of rigid moral standards and the fulfillment of hard work. One may protest that this represented a vitiated pastoralism, hardly worthy of the name; but this mythic fusion reconfirmed America's self-image as a natural yet disciplined republic and a land of abundance and opportunity. Prosperity and republicanism, the directors might have congratulated one another, had—despite John Adams's anguished cry—indeed been reconciled in a temperate and industrious community. This was the stunning achievement of Lowell. But was it?

Alongside the proud affirmations of company officials, the hosannas of industrial spokesmen and technological enthusiasts, and the admiring testimonies of European visitors, the 1830s and 1840s saw an insurgent attack upon the basic assumptions of the Lowell factory system and its conception of republican community. This assault was launched by members of the working class and their spokesmen, who, with the emergence of the labor movement, protested their oppressive working conditions and the hierarchical conception of society that sustained them. Probably their sentiments were not shared by the preponderance of Lowell workers, many of whom shunned political opinions of any sort. But if these dissidents were a minority, they were nonetheless significant. Their very existence contradicted Lowell's image as a uniquely happy and harmonious community, and their arguments brought a radically different perspective to the institutionalization of the Lowell ideology and to the course of American technological development. Instead of remaining content in their station and allowing the social machinery to run smoothly, these workers rejected the notion that they shared a community of interests with mill-owners and called for the secret class war that was being waged against them to be fought in the open. The contrast between American and English factory systems did not appear to them so impressively distinct, and they were hardly inclined to join Whig politicians like Edward Everett in proclaiming Lowell as the fulfillment of the American Revolution and a model of republicanism. Quite the reverse; the more extreme among them charged that the manufacturing elite had betrayed everything the revolution stood for and were following in the footsteps of the luxury-loving and tyrannical British. Under the guise of humanitarian concern for the republic, they contended, Lowell's supporters were busily erecting a repressive new aristocracy. . . .

The attack against the Lowell factory system gained momentum . . . as Lowell women began to demonstrate on behalf of reform. In 1834 they participated in their first "turn-out," a demonstration and short-lived strike. Their numbers were estimated from "nearly eight hundred" (*Lowell Journal*) to two thousand (*The Man*), varying with the sympathies of newspaper reporters. The workers issued a proclamation asking the support of all "who imbibe the spirit of our patriotic ancestors," and ending with the verse:

> Let oppression shrug her shoulders,
>   And a haughty tyrant frown,
> And little upstart Ignorance
>   In mockery look down.
> Yet I value not the feeble threats
>   Of Tories in disguise,
> While the flag of Independence
>   O'er our noble nation flies.

The immediate occasion of the "turn-out" was the announcement of a 15 percent reduction in wages, but it represented as well a protest against Lowell's paternalism as unrepublican. As one of the demonstrators announced, "We do not estimate our liberty by dollars and cents; consequently it was not the reduction of wages alone which caused the excitement, but that haughty, overbearing disposition, that purse-proud insolence, which was becoming more and more apparent." Two and a half years later, in October 1836, Lowell women struck against an increase in the price of board in company houses, amounting to a one-eighth cut in wages. Again they fortified their resolution by reminding one another of the revolutionary struggle against tyranny: "As our fathers resisted unto blood the lordly avarice of the British ministry," they declared, "so we, their daughters, never will wear the yoke which has been prepared for us."

Thus, despite the founders' best efforts and most stringent regulations, the radical, egalitarian strain of republicanism they had hoped to suppress broke out within the fortress of Lowell itself. Like other dissident workers throughout the nineteenth century, Lowell operatives returned repeatedly to the American Revolution and particularly to the Declaration of Independence to fortify and articulate their protest against what they regarded as a repressive social and in-

dustrial system. They insisted that since they were "created with certain un-
alienable rights," their labor could not simply be reduced to a commodity of
which they were denied the fruits; human rights, "life, liberty, and the pursuit
of happiness," took precedence over property rights. Lowell's leading investors
were also acutely conscious of the revolution. Though Amos Lawrence, for example, was not born until 1786, so steeped was he in stories of that event that he
felt himself "an actor in the scenes described," and a simple incident like the
sound of a gunshot in 1843 instantly transported him back to the battles of Lexington and Concord in 1775. But the moral he and other manufacturers drew
from the revolution was very different from the workers'. As his biographer
Freeman Hunt wrote shortly after Lawrence's death, "In all [the revolution's]
phases it was of a conservative character, aiming to maintain what was, and not
seeking the development of fanciful theories. Our ancestors had no projects for
the colonization of Utopia. The revolutionists were all on the other side." So the
revolutionists must have seemed again in the 1830s and 1840s. Lowell's directors and other manufacturers were not about to surrender to these dangerous
new visionaries. Prior to 1860 in Massachusetts not a single strike ended in victory for the workers or checked the reduction of wages.

The workers were handicapped not only in the lack of union organization;
the very institutional character of the Lowell factory system placed immense obstacles in the way of labor resistance. As George Frederickson and Christopher
Lasch have observed in considering the problem of resistance against another
total institution, plantation slavery, "all total institutions are set up in such a
way as to preclude any form of politics based on consent." In such a situation
the conditions for organized and sustained resistance were meager. The authority of Lowell's staff was directed not just at the workers' productive performance but at their private activities and feelings as well; and traditional moral
values were appropriated to reinforce the purposes and perspective of the institution. Political agitation not only smacked of "insubordination" but was also
considered "unladylike" in the dominant culture. In this respect, extremely
valuable allies to company management in quelling dissent were the much pub-
licized journals that Lowell women produced themselves. The *Lowell Offering*,
the *Operatives' Magazine*, and the *New England Offering*, though all nominally independent, served in effect as house organs, expressing solidarity between
workers and management, and they were covertly encouraged by Lowell's directors. Wishing to elevate the reputation of the factory girl and to prove her
virtue and intelligence, these periodicals rigidly excluded criticism of factory
conditions or management policies and resolutely presented cheerful expressions to the public. Occasionally, an editor would sharply rebuke those who violated their decorous image. "Constant abuse of those from whom one is voluntarily receiving the means of subsistence," Harriet Farley lectured dissident
workers, was "something more than bad taste." If an operative really wished to
improve her condition, Miss Farley suggested, she should leave the mills altogether. A character in Lucy Larcom's poem *An Idyl of Work* supported this point
of view when she asked:

> Why should we,
> Battling oppression, tyrants be ourselves,
> Forcing mere brief concession to our wish?
> Are not employers human as employed?
> Are not our interests common? If they grind
> And cheat as brethren should not, let us go
> Back to the music of the spinning-wheel,
> And clothe ourselves at hand-looms of our own,
> As did our grandmothers.

This theme that rather than protest, the dissatisfied worker should go elsewhere and seek a separate peace recurred in the pages of the *Offering*. If wages should finally drop too sharply, another young woman grandiloquently declared, "I fear not for the crust of black bread, the suppliant voice, and bended knee; for then the inducement to remain will be withdrawn. Our broad and beautiful country will long present her spreading prairies, verdant hills, and smiling vales, to all who would rather work than starve." In the last analysis, this supposedly "voluntary" character of Lowell and the fact that employment was temporary by design, encouraged cooperation between workers and management and mitigated against the formation of a class consciousness. High job turnover rates alone would have inhibited the development of a sense of solidarity among workers and of united opposition to their employers. In addition, as women who regarded their work in the mills as transient rather than a career, most Lowell workers were not disposed toward collective solutions to factory abuses.

Other obstacles also stood in the way of Lowell's protesting workers. The Panic of 1837 and subsequent depressions threw an estimated one-third of American laborers out of work and seriously damaged the union movement. With jobs scarce, workingmen's organizations came to regard the system of female labor as doubly pernicious; not only did it harm the women themselves, it brought women in competition with men, thereby either throwing the latter out of work or reducing their wages. In light of this situation, the National Trades' Union suggested in 1839 that the solution to the female labor problem might be to keep women at home where they belonged. Women operatives, clearly, could no longer depend upon male labor spokesmen always to uphold their position.

In spite of these impediments, however, resistance to the Lowell factory system gradually increased. By December 1844 Lowell's dissident workers, led by the redoubtable Sarah Bagley, had achieved sufficient strength to form an organization of their own, the Lowell Female Labor Reform Association. Its ranks swelled quickly: within three months it numbered three hundred members and by the end of 1845 it claimed six hundred workers in Lowell alone, plus branches in all major New England textile centers. Now workers were able to establish connections outside Lowell to the labor movement and hence to some degree to subvert institutional pressures. Immediately, they formed their own journal, *Factory Tracts*, and soon formed an alliance with the *Voice of Industry*, a new labor weekly newspaper, and brought it to Lowell. Denouncing the *Lowell Offering* as a "mouthpiece of the corporations," these dissident workers powerfully inveighed against the oppressive character of factory life. Like Luther and Douglas, they pointed with horror to the specter of a degenerate race, spawned in the mills to serve as slaves to a manufacturing aristocracy. And as in earlier appeals to labor, they attempted to rally and organize workers by applying the language and lessons of 1776 to their own times. "Is not," the *Voice of Industry* asked, "the same secret fawning, devouring monster, wilely [sic] drawing his fatal folds around us as a nation which has crushed the freedom, prosperity and existence of other republics whose sad fate, history long ago recorded. . . .?" In such conspiracies, the paper charged, industrious and virtuous labor was inevitably targeted as the first victim. Every year its burdens grew more grievous, and the *Voice of Industry* demanded for all workingmen their God-given right to " 'life, liberty, and the pursuit of happiness.' " The fact that conditions of European operatives might be even worse, the paper argued, was essentially irrelevant: "The American workingmen and women, will not long suffer this gradual system of *republican* encroachment, which is fast reducing them to dependence, vassalage and slavery; because the English, Irish or French operatives are greater slaves, their condition more deplorable or English capitalists and task masters have the power to be more tyrannical and oppressive." An article in *Factory Tracts* similarly appealed to America's true nobility, its workers, to cast off the yoke of tyranny from about their necks before their country became "one great hospital, filled with worn out operatives and colored slaves!" It closed defiantly, "EQUAL RIGHTS, or death to the corporations."

Such rhetoric reasserted the radical egalitarianism of the republican message which conservatives had been struggling to contain ever since the revolution. References to the possibility of violent revolution formed a recurrent theme in the writings of Luther, Douglas, and other labor spokesmen of the period; now such phrases were being shouted outside the very mills of Lowell. How seriously is one to take them? Certainly no laborers were stockpiling arms and actively preparing for an insurrection. But neither should one dismiss such talk as a kind of verbal spice utterly without significance. In part, of course, it was intended to goad manufacturers toward reforms. Yet one cannot help but feel that it had an opposite effect: that such language only reconfirmed in Lowell's managers and stockholders their sense of the violence and chaos that would erupt should their institutional controls be removed. Of equal if not greater significance, this rhetorical violence also represented tacit admission of the immense gulf between labor reformers' vision of life in an ideal technological society, freed from the exigencies of industrial capitalism, and the formidable obstacles they encountered even to such minimal reforms as the ten-hour day. Indeed, the primacy of the ten-hour movement, as one historian has suggested, only reflects the extent to which workers accepted and fought within their employers' categories of time and work discipline. From this point of view, one might speculate that the apocalyptic rhetoric of dissident laborers and other ante-bellum reformers signaled, not the weakness of American institutions, but their strength and the difficulty of gaining any real leverage for resistance. While continuing to affirm their faith in the ballot box, they summoned forth the image of revolution not only because it made another link in the carefully elaborated analogy between nineteenth-century workers and the American revolutionists, but because it provided a vague yet powerful metaphor by which the bleak conditions of the present might suddenly be wrenched to their conception of the future.

Whatever efficacy the workers' protests had, then, was as symbolic rather than instrumental action; whatever gains they achieved were expressive rather than substantial. Efforts at specific reforms encountered powerful resistance. Workers from several mill towns had petitioned the Massachusetts legislature for establishment of a ten-hour day and other factory reforms as early as 1842, with no response. The petition of 1600 workers from Lowell and elsewhere the next year met a similar fate. In 1844 a third petition was tabled until the next session; so that at last in 1845 a legislative committee held hearings on labor conditions for the first time. In the absence of an existing labor committee, the task was assigned to William Schouler, publisher of the *Lowell Courier* and a staunch supporter of the corporations. Sarah Bagley and the Lowell Female Labor Reform Association feverishly circulated new petitions to support the ten-hour cause and gained over two thousand signatures, half of them from Lowell. Two conflicting groups of witnesses then paraded before the committee. Spokesmen for the employers defended the healthful environment of the mills, while Miss Bagley and a group of operatives personally testified that Lowell workers endured overlong work days for insufficient pay to the detriment of health, mind, and spirit. To examine conditions firsthand, a portion of the committee went to Lowell, and they returned substantially impressed. Of their visit to the Massachusetts and Boott Mills, they reported, "The rooms are large and well-lighted, the temperature, comfortable, and in most of the window sills were numerous shrubs and plants, such as geraniums, roses, and numerous varieties of the cactus. These were the pets of the factory girls, and they were to the Committee convincing evidence of the elevated moral tone and refined taste of the operatives." Thus Lowell's technological version of pastoral proved remarkably resilient; even in the midst of protest, legislators found confirmation of the essential rightness of the enterprise in a single whiff of a potted flower.

The committee as a whole affirmed the healthfulness of existing conditions and further shied away from a ten-hour law as jeopardizing Massachusetts' industry with respect to its neighbors. Paying left-handed tribute to Lowell's petitioners, the committee declared, "Labor is intelligent enough to make its own bargains, and look out for its own interests without any interference from us." While it acknowledged that hours should be lessened, mealtimes extended, ventilation improved, and other reforms instituted, the committee contended, "the remedy is not with us. We look for it in the progressive improvement in art and science, in a higher appreciation of man's destiny, in a less love for money, and a more ardent love for social happiness and intellectual superiority." The *Lowell Offering* could not have put it better. Protesting workers did gain official support in Dr. Josiah Curtis's report on public hygiene for 1849 and the minority report of the legislature's special committee on labor for 1850. Finally, the Lowell corporation voluntarily shortened the work day to eleven hours in 1853. But no ten-hour legislation was passed in Massachusetts until 1874. . . .

. . . The failure of the ten-hour movement added to discontent. When prof-

its declined and new wage cuts were announced in 1848, the turnover of operatives rose sharply; at one of the most prosperous companies, the Merrimack,
average workers' tenure dropped to nine months. In the past, the city's mystique had proved a powerful agent of employee recruitment. Now, as mechanization spread to other industries, such as boots and clothing, and other employment opportunities rivaled the textile mills, Lowell's companies appeared
in danger of losing their command over their labor force.

Nevertheless, when the Lowell factory system was suddenly transformed
in the late 1840s and 1850s, it was from quite another source than capitulation to
workers' demands. At just the moment when company control of its traditional
labor pool was growing shaky, Ireland's terrible potato famine that had begun
in 1845 and the subsequent eviction of Irish peasants by their landlords triggered a massive immigration to America, over one and a half million people before the Civil War. As a major ship and railroad terminus, Boston received tens
of thousands of these Irish immigrants. Upon arriving, however, they encountered a constricted social and economic life with little receptivity to foreigners.
Nativist prejudice combined with the newcomers' lack of training and capital to
shut them out of all but unskilled occupations. In such a position, Irish immigrants offered textile factories at Lowell and neighboring mill towns a ready and
abundant supply of labor, and the incentive to accommodate demands of native
workers diminished. Almost immediately, Irish began to take the places of departing New Englanders in the mills; once established, their presence further
hastened the flow of native workers to other jobs and discouraged the entrance
of other New England women into the industry. Only 7 percent of the operatives
in Lowell mills were Irish in 1845, but by the early 1850s their proportion was
estimated as one-half, and it grew still higher year by year. Later in the century,
the labor force would be supplemented by French-Canadians and other immigrant groups. Instead of predominantly single women, the Irish came as families. As adult males were discriminated against, Irish women and, increasingly,
children went to the mills, the last receiving lower wages than ever. High
turnover rates thus persisted. But if the work force was not immobile, neither
was the work force in Britain; it was certainly not the kind of circulatory labor
force able to enter and leave the industrial economy at will with which the Lowell system had begun. Most lived not in company boardinghouses to be supervised by alien authority, but with family or friends in the town at large. With a
different culture, training, aspirations, and status from earlier Lowell workers,
the Irish obviously did not immerse themselves in improvement circles and lit-
erary magazines. And the Lowell mills, which had eagerly received credit for
the talents and accomplishments of earlier operatives, now found themselves
without their trophies. In less than a decade Lowell lost its prized population of
well-educated and temporary New England women and with it the factory system's very rationale. Suddenly the basis that Lowell's founders and most ardent
defenders had insisted constituted the principal difference between this city and
English manufacturing towns and upon which its welfare would stand or fall—
its lack of an established proletariat—was totally overthrown. . . .

The early history of Lowell, like that of other institutional innovations during this period, thus revealed complexities far beyond the shaping powers or expectations of its confident founders. The factory system they established, no matter how benign in intention, was still based upon a hierarchical and manipulative model in which workers were passive agents, tied to the demands of machine production and industrial capitalism as a whole. Ironically, Lowell's very success in attracting educated and independent New England women meant that at least an outspoken minority would refuse to accept the management's conception of "republicanism," inherent in its strict factory discipline, and insist upon a true egalitarian order. Reliance upon temporary workers, in any case, only postponed the question of what accommodations industry should make for a permanent labor force. But the arrival of the Irish triggered not a new concern upon the part of corporate officials and a re-examination of their conception of republican community, but, on the contrary, increased apathy. . . .

By the 1850s the possibility of an integrated and harmonious republican community seemed farther off than ever. Even while Lowell's praises echoed, its founders' optimistic vision lay tarnished, and its most ardent defenders were forced on the defensive. The problems of urban and industrial growth and social disorder that Lowell was established to correct had spread to the community itself.

SOURCES

Henry A. Miles

Lowell: As It Was and As It Is, 1845

When the owners of Lowell came under attack, they took pains to refute the charges made against them. Beginning in the 1840s they published articles, pamphlets, and books that defended Lowell's leading investors and company officials. Of these one of the most important was Lowell, As It Was and As It Is *by Henry A. Miles, a Unitarian minister at Lowell. Do you think he succeeded in convincing his fellow citizens that he was an impartial observer? That the influences going forth from Lowell were not "pernicious"?*

Lowell has been highly commended by some, as a model community, for its good order, industry, and general freedom from vice. It has been strongly condemned, by others, as a hotbed of corruption, tainting the whole land. We all, in New England, have an interest in knowing what are the exact facts of the case. We are destined to be a great manufacturing people. The influences that go forth from Lowell will go forth from many other manufacturing villages and cities. If these influences are pernicious, we have a great calamity impending over us. Rather than endure it, we should prefer to have every factory destroyed.

If, on the other hand, a system has been introduced, carefully provided with checks and safeguards, and strong moral and conservative influences, it is our duty to see that this system be faithfully carried out, so as to prevent the disastrous results which have developed themselves in the manufacturing towns of other countries. Hence the topics assume the importance of the highest moral questions. The author writes after a nine years' residence in this city, during which he has closely observed the working of the factory system, and has gathered a great amount of statistical facts which have a bearing upon this subject. He believes himself to be unaffected by any partisan views, as he stands wholly aside from the sphere of any interested motives.

A LOWELL BOARDINGHOUSE

Each of the long blocks of boardinghouses is divided into six or eight tenements, and are generally three stories high. These tenements are finished off in a style much above the common farmhouses of the country, and more nearly resemble the abodes of respectable mechanics in rural villages. These are constantly kept

From Henry A. Miles, *Lowell, As It Was and As It Is*, Powers and Bagley, Lowell, Mass., 1845, pp. 62–63, 66–67, 100–103, 128–135, 140–147.

clean, the buildings well painted, and the premises thoroughly whitewashed every spring, at the corporation's expense.

As one important feature in the management of these houses, it deserves to be named that male operatives and female operatives do not board in the same tenement; and the following regulations, printed by one of the companies, and given to each keeper of their houses, are here subjoined, as a simple statement of the rules generally observed by all the corporations.

> Regulations to be observed by persons occupying the boardinghouses belonging to the Merrimack Manufacturing Company.
>
> They must not board any persons not employed by the company, unless by special permission.
>
> No disorderly or improper conduct must be allowed in the houses.
>
> The doors must be closed at ten o'clock in the evening.
>
> Those who keep the houses, when required, must give an account of the number, names, and employment of their boarders; also with regard to their general conduct, and whether they are in the habit of attending public worship.
>
> The buildings, both inside and out, and the yards about them, must be kept clean, and in good order.

The hours of taking meals in these houses are uniform throughout all the corporations in the city. The time allowed for each meal is thirty minutes for breakfast, when that meal is taken after beginning work; for dinner, thirty minutes.

The food that is furnished in these houses is of a substantial and wholesome kind, is neatly served, and in sufficient abundance. Operatives are under no compulsion to board in one tenement rather than another. And then, as to the character of these boardinghouse keepers themselves, on no point is the superintendent more particular than on this. Applications for these situations are very numerous. The rents of the company's houses are purposely low, averaging only from one-third to one-half of what similar houses rent for in the city. There is no intention on the part of the corporation to make any revenue from these houses. They are a great source of annual expense. But the advantages of supervision are more than an equivalent for this.

The influence which this system of boardinghouses has exerted upon the good order and good morals of the place, has been vast and beneficent. To a very great degree the future condition of Lowell is dependent upon a faithful adhesion to this system.

The following table shows the average hours per day of running the mills, throughout the year, on all the corporations in Lowell.

In addition to the above, it should be stated that lamps are never lighted on Saturday evening, and that four holidays are followed in the year, viz. Fast Day, Fourth of July, Thanksgiving Day, and Christmas Day.

The average daily time of running the mills is twelve hours and ten minutes. Arguments are not needed to prove that toil, if it be continued for this length of time, each day, month after month, and year after year, is excessive, and too

Hours of Labor

	H.	M.		H.	M.
January	11	24	July	12	45
February	12	00	August	12	45
March	11	52	September	12	23
April	13	31	October	12	10
May	12	45	November	11	56
June	12	45	December	11	24

much for the tender frames of young women to bear. No one can more sincerely desire than the writer of this book, that they had more leisure time for mental improvement and social enjoyment. It must be remembered, however, that their work is comparatively light. All the hard processes, not conducted by men, are performed by machines, the movements of which female operatives are required merely to oversee and adjust.

MORAL POLICE OF THE CORPORATIONS

The productiveness of these works depends upon one primary and indispensable condition—the existence of an industrious, sober, orderly, and moral class of operatives. Without this, the mills in Lowell would be worthless. Profits would be absorbed by cases of irregularity, carelessness, and neglect; while the existence of any great moral exposure in Lowell would cut off the supply of help from the virtuous homesteads of the country. Public morals and private interests, identical in all places, are here seen to be linked together in an indissoluble connection. Accordingly, the sagacity of self-interest, as well as more disinterested considerations, has led to the adoption of a strict system of moral police.

The female operatives in Lowell do not work, on an average, more than four and a half years in the factories. They then return to their homes, and their places are taken by their sisters, or by other female friends from their neighborhood.

To obtain this constant importation of female hands from the country, it is necessary to secure *the moral protection of their characters while they are resident in Lowell.* This, therefore, is the chief object of that moral police.

No persons are employed on the corporations who are addicted to intemperance, or who are known to be guilty of any immoralities of conduct. As the parent of all other vices, intemperance is most carefully excluded.

In respect to discharged operatives, there is a system observed. Any person wishing to leave a mill is at liberty to do so, at any time, after giving a fortnight's notice. The operative so leaving, if of good character, and having worked a year, is entitled, as a matter of right, to an honorable discharge.

That form is as follows:

Mr. or Miss _____, has been employed by the _____ Manufacturing Company, in a _____ room, _____ years _____ months, and is hon-
orably discharged.

_____, Superintendent.

LOWELL, _____   _____

This discharge is a letter of recommendation to any other mill in the city,
and not without its influence in procuring employment in any other mill in New
England. Those dishonorable have another treatment. The names of all persons
dismissed for bad conduct, or who leave the mill irregularly, are also entered in
a book, and these names are sent to all the counting rooms of the city. *Such persons obtain no more employment throughout the city.*
      Any description of the moral care, studied by the corporations, would be
defective if it omitted a reference to the overseers. Every room in every mill has
its first and second overseer. At his small desk, near the door, where he can see
all who go out or come in, the overseer may generally be found, and he is held
responsible for the good order, and attention to business, of the operatives of
that room. Hence, this is a post of much importance. It is for this reason that peculiar care is exercised in their appointment. The overseers are almost universally married men, with families; and as a body, numbering about one hundred
and eighty in all, are among the most permanent residents, and most trustworthy and valuable citizens of the place. The guiding and salutary influence which
they exert over the operatives is one of the most essential parts of the moral machinery of the mills.
      It may not be out of place to present here the regulations, which are ob-
served alike on all the corporations, which are given to the operatives when they
are first employed, and are posted up conspicuously in all the mills. They are as
follows:

*Regulations to be observed by all persons employed by the Manufacturing Company, in
the factories.*
Every overseer is required to be punctual himself, and to see that those employed under him are so.
      The overseers may, at their discretion, grant leave of absence to those em-
ployed under them, when there are sufficient spare hands in the room to supply their place; but when there are not sufficient spare hands, they are not allowed to grant leave of absence unless in cases of absolute necessity.
      All persons are required to observe the regulations of the room in which
they are employed. They are not allowed to be absent from their work without
the consent of their overseer, except in case of sickness, and then they are required to send him word of the cause of their absence.
      All persons are required to board in one of the boardinghouses belonging

to the company, and conform to the regulations of the house in which they board.

All persons are required to be constant in attendance on public worship, at one of the regular places of worship in this place.

Persons who do not comply with the above regulations will not be employed by the company.

Persons entering the employment of the company are considered as engaging to work one year.

All persons intending to leave the employment of the company are required to give notice of the same to their overseer, at least two weeks previous to the time of leaving.

Anyone who shall take from the mills, or the yard, any yarn, cloth, or other article belonging to the company will be considered guilty of *stealing*—and prosecuted accordingly.

The above regulations are considered part of the contract with all persons entering the employment of the _____ Manufacturing Company. All persons who shall have complied with them, on leaving the employment of the company, shall be entitled to an honorable discharge, which will serve as a recommendation to any of the factories in Lowell. No one who shall not have complied with them will be entitled to such a discharge.

_____ _____, Agent.

Portraits of Industrialism

The following documents illustrate some important features of the mental picture of industrialism that Americans began to form around the Lowell experience. The first is an engraving, a "View of Lowell." The second is the title page of the Lowell Offering *of 1845, a collection of the writings of some of the young women who worked in the textile mill there. The third is an engraving by the famous painter Winslow Homer of workers in the nearby mill town of Lawrence. And the last is an artist's sketch of one of the most famous strikes of the century, the strike of 800 women shoemakers of Lynn, Massachusetts, in 1860. As you look at the pictures, think about the ways in which the artists have tried to resolve any potential contradiction between industry and nature, between industry and ordinary community life, between industry and femininity. Have the mills intruded on the landscape in its greenery, or do the artists create the impression that factories and trees can be integral parts of one harmonious landscape? What kind of relationship is suggested between the new factories and the traditional high points of a New England skyline, the church steeples? And what kind of relationship is suggested between the workers and the communities in which they lived? Notice the sign in the strike picture, comparing workers with slaves. Notice also that the Lynn City Guards, the local militia, preceded the striking women. What do you think middle-class women would have said upon seeing this picture?*

View of Lowell, Massachusetts
Prints Division/New York Public Library.

The Title Page of the *Lowell Offering.*
The Bettmann Archive.

Textile Workers of Lawrence, Massachusetts. Engraving by Winslow Homer.
Culver Pictures.

Striking Women and Local Militia.
Culver Pictures.

CHAPTER 10

Jacksonian Democracy

The dramatic changes that took place in the northern economy after the War of 1812 were accompanied by equally dramatic changes in national politics. Under President James Monroe (1817–1825) the party system that Jefferson helped to fashion fell apart. The Federalists dropped out of presidential politics after losing to Monroe in the election of 1816. The victorious Jeffersonian Republicans split into warring factions. Party leaders lost control of the political arena, and suddenly the most divisive issues of the day—slavery and southern power—came to dominate congressional debate when Missouri in 1819 asked to be admitted to the Union as a slave state. By 1824 Jefferson's party was in hopeless disarray. Instead of running one man for president, the party was unable to make a binding nomination, and four men—all calling themselves Jeffersonian Republicans—ran for the presidency. None of the four received the necessary majority of electoral votes, and hence the election went to the House of Representatives. There, after much wheeling and dealing, Andrew Jackson lost the presidency to John Quincy Adams. The outcome, said Jackson, was due to "bargain and corruption."

Along with the old party system went the old style of politics. James Monroe was the last president to dress like an aristocrat, powder his hair, and wear the knee-length pantaloons and white-topped boots of Washington's day. His successor, John Quincy Adams, wore long pants and was the least ostentatious of our early presidents. But he too was identified with the old style of politics in which ordinary citizens were expected to defer to their "betters." However, a new style was developing in which politicians sang the praises of "democracy," lauded the natural instincts of the ordinary white man, and even pretended to be just common folk. The new style came to be identified with General Andrew Jackson, the hero of the Battle of New Orleans, who defeated Adams in the election of 1828.

Historians have debated the meaning of Jacksonian democracy almost as vigorously as they have the American Revolution or the Civil War. The Jacksonian movement has seemed to some the expression of the spirit of the rise of

226

democracy along the frontier, north and south. To others, the new democracy has appeared to be something even newer and more remarkable: the politics of a new urban working class in the north. Others, content enough with the label "Jacksonian," have doubted the element of democracy. To them, Jackson was a conservative who might manipulate the rhetoric of the "common man," but a conservative nonetheless, a slaveholder with all the political instincts of a member of the southern elite.

INTERPRETIVE ESSAY

Richard H. Brown

Slavery and the Jacksonians

The following selection, written by Richard H. Brown, has generated much controversy. Historians have long known that large-scale slaveholders played dominant roles in the early Republic, including George Washington, "father of his country," and Thomas Jefferson, who proclaimed in the Declaration of Independence that "all men are created equal." They have also been well aware that eight of the first twelve presidents were slaveholders. In recent years, however, only a few scholars have made much of these facts. Brown is one of the exceptions. In Brown's judgment the decision of northern congressmen in 1819 to oppose the admission of Missouri as a slave state, to insist that slavery in Missouri be gradually abolished, was momentous. It not only touched off a bitter congressional debate but also proved to everyone that the old Jeffersonian coalition had lost control of the political agenda. To have Missouri admitted into the union as a slave state, southern congressmen first had to ward off blistering attacks against slavery and southern power, and then they had to accept a "compromise" that admitted Maine as a free state and barred slavery from the northern half of the Louisiana Purchase. That experience, argues Brown, terrified the plantation south and provided the "wellsprings" from which the Jacksonian movement developed. Some historians think that Brown has made too much of the slavery issue. Others think that his article is right on the mark or close to it. What do you think? Does he provide enough facts to back up his argument? Are there any obvious holes in his argument? How else might one account for the fact that slaveholders exercised far more power than their numbers would warrant?

From the inauguration of Washington until the Civil War the south was in the saddle of national politics. This is the central fact in American political history to 1860. To it there are no exceptions, not even in that period when the "common man" stormed the ramparts of government under the banner of Andrew Jackson. In Jackson's day the chief agent of southern power was a northern man with southern principles, Martin Van Buren of New York. It was he who put together the party coalition that Andrew Jackson led to power. That coalition had its wellsprings in the dramatic crisis over slavery in Missouri, the first great public airing of the slavery question in ante-bellum America.

I

More than anything else, what made southern dominance in national politics possible was a basic homogeneity in the southern electorate. In the early nineteenth century, to be sure, the south was far from monolithic. In terms of economic interest and social classes it was scarcely more homogeneous than the north. But under the diversity of interests that characterized southern life in most respects there ran one single compelling idea that virtually united all southerners, and that governed their participation in national affairs. This was that the institution of slavery should not be dealt with from outside the south. Whatever the merits of the institution—and southerners violently disagreed about this, never more than in the 1820s—the presence of the slave was a fact too critical, too sensitive, too perilous for all of southern society to be dealt with by those not directly affected. Slavery must remain a southern question. In the ante-bellum period a southern politician of whatever party forgot this at his peril. A northern politician might perceive it to his profit. There had been, Martin Van Buren noted with satisfaction late in life, a "remarkable consistency in the political positions" of southern public men. With characteristic insouciance the Little Magician attributed this consistency to the natural superiority of republican principles, which led them to win out in a region relatively untainted by the monied interest. But his partisan friend Rufus King, Van Buren admitted, ascribed it to the "black strap" of southern slavery.

The insistence that slavery was uniquely a southern concern, not to be touched by outsiders, had been from the outset a *sine qua non* for southern participation in national politics. It underlay the Constitution and its creation of a government of limited powers, without which southern participation would have been unthinkable. And when in the 1790s Jefferson and Madison perceived that a constitution was only the first step in guaranteeing southern security, because a constitution meant what those who governed under it said it meant, it led to the creation of the first national political party to protect that Constitution against change by interpretation. The party that they constructed converted a southern minority into a national majority through alliance with congenial interests outside the south. Organically, it represented an alliance between New York and Virginia, pulling between them Pennsylvania, and after them North Carolina, Georgia, and (at first) Kentucky and Tennessee, all states strongly subject to Virginia's influence. At bottom it rested on the support of people who lived on that rich belt of fertile farmland that stretched from the Great Lakes across upstate New York and Pennsylvania, southward through the southern piedmont into Georgia, entirely oblivious of the Mason-Dixon line. North as well as south it was an area of prosperous, well-settled small farms. More farmers than capitalists, its residents wanted little from government but to be let alone. Resting his party on them, Jefferson had found a formula for national politics which at the same time was a formula for southern pre-eminence. It would hold good to the Civil War.

So long as the Federalists remained an effective opposition, Jefferson's party worked as a party should. It maintained its identity in relation to the opposition by a moderate and pragmatic advocacy of strict construction of the Constitution. Because it had competition, it could maintain discipline. It responded to its constituent elements because it depended on them for support. But eventually its very success was its undoing. After 1815, stirred by the nationalism of the postwar era, and with the Federalists in decline, the Republicans took up Federalist positions on a number of the great public issues of the day, sweeping all before them as they did. The Federalists gave up the ghost. In the Era of Good Feelings that followed, everybody began to call himself a Republican, and a new theory of party amalgamation preached the doctrine that party division was bad and that a one-party system best served the national interest. Only gradually did it become apparent that in victory the Republican party had lost its identity—and its usefulness. As the party of the whole nation it ceased to be responsive to any particular elements in its constituency. It ceased to be responsive to the south.

When it did, and because it did, it invited the Missouri crisis of 1819–1820, and that crisis in turn revealed the basis for a possible configuration of national parties that eventually would divide the nation free against slave. As John Quincy Adams put it, the crisis had revealed "the basis for a new organization of parties . . . here was a new party ready formed, . . . terrible to the whole Union, but portentously terrible to the South—threatening in its progress the emancipation of all their slaves, threatening in its immediate effect that Southern domination which has swayed the Union for the last twenty years." Because it did so, Jefferson, in equally famous phrase, "considered it at once as the knell of the Union."

Adams and Jefferson were not alone in perceiving the significance of what had happened. Scarcely a contemporary missed the point. Historians quote them by the dozens as prophets—but usually *only* as prophets. In fact the Missouri crisis gave rise not to prophecy alone, but to action. It led to an urgent and finally successful attempt to revive the old Jeffersonian party and with it the Jeffersonian formula for southern pre-eminence. The resuscitation of the party would be the most important story in American politics in the decades that followed.

II

In Jefferson's day the tie between slavery, strict construction of the Constitution, and the Republican party was implicit, not explicit. After Missouri it was explicit, and commented upon time and again in both public and private discussion. Perceptive southerners saw (1) that unless effective means were taken to quiet discussion of the question, slavery might be used at any time in the future to force the south into a permanent minority in the Union, endangering all its interests; and (2) that if the loose constitutional construction of the day were allowed to prevail, the time might come when the government would be held to have the power to deal with slavery. Vital to preventing both of these—to keeping the slavery question quiet and to gaining a reassertion of strict construction principles—was the re-establishment of conditions which would make the party in power responsive once again to the south. . . .

Because they shaped the context of what was to come, the reactions to the Missouri crisis in the two citadels of Old Republican power, Richmond and Albany, were significant. Each cast its light ahead. As the donnybrook mounted in Congress in the winter of 1820, the Virginia capital was reported to be as "agitated as if affected by all the Volcanic Eruptions of Vesuvius." At the heart of the clamor were the Old Republicans of the Richmond Junto, particularly Thomas Ritchie's famous *Enquirer*, which spoke for the Junto and had been for years the most influential newspaper in the south. Associates of Jefferson, architects of southern power, the Old Republicans were not long in perceiving the political implications of the crisis. Conviction grew in their minds that the point of northern agitation was not Missouri at all but to use slavery as an anvil on which to forge a new party that would carry either Rufus King or DeWitt Clinton of New York to the presidency and force the south from power forever. But what excited them even more was the enormity of the price of peace, which alone seemed likely to avert the disaster. This was the so-called Thomas Proviso, amending the Missouri bill to draw the ill-fated 36°30´ line across the Louisiana Purchase, prohibiting slavery in the territory to the north, giving up the lion's share to freedom.

No sooner had the proviso been introduced in Congress than the temper of the Old Republicans boiled over, and with prescient glances to the future they leapt to the attack. Ritchie challenged the constitutionality of the proviso at once in the *Enquirer*, a quarter century before Calhoun would work out the subtle dialectic of a southern legal position. Nathaniel Macon agreed. "To compromise is to acknowledge the right of Congress to interfere and to legislate on the subject," he wrote; "this would be acknowledging too much." Equally important was the fact that, by prohibiting slavery in most of the West, the proviso forecast a course of national development ultimately intolerable to the south because, as Spencer Roane put it to Monroe, southerners could not consent to be "dammed up in a land of Slaves." As the debates thundered to their climax, Ritchie in two separate editorials predicted that if the proviso passed, the south must in due time have Texas. "If we are cooped up on the north," he wrote with grim prophecy, "we must have elbow room to the west."

When finally the southern Old Republicans tacitly consented to the Missouri Compromise, it was therefore not so much a measure of illusion about what the south had given up, as of how desperately necessary they felt peace to be. They had yielded not so much in the spirit of a bargain as in the spirit of a man caught in a holdup, who yields his fortune rather than risk his life in the hope that he may live to see a better day and perhaps even to get his fortune back. As Ritchie summed it up when news of the settlement reached Richmond, "Instead of joy, we scarcely ever recollect to have tasted of a bitterer cup." That they tasted it at all was because of the manipulative genius of Henry Clay, who managed to bring up the separate parts of the compromise separately in the House, enabling the Old Republicans to provide him his margin of victory on the closely contested Missouri bill while they saved their pride by voting to the end against the Thomas Proviso. They had not bound themselves by their votes to the proviso, as Ritchie warned they should not. If it was cold comfort for the moment, it was potent with significance for the future. . . .

Equally important to the reaction in Richmond was what went on in Albany. There command of the state's Old Republicans was in the hands of the Bucktails, a group of which State Senator Martin Van Buren, at thirty-eight, was already master spirit. Opposed to the Bucktails was Governor DeWitt Clinton, an erstwhile Republican who drew a good deal of his support from former Federalists. With the Bucktails committed to the old Virginia-New York alliance, the Missouri question offered Clinton a heaven-sent opportunity; indeed there were those who suspected the ambitious governor of playing God himself and helping to precipitate the crisis. Whether or not this was true, Clinton tried desperately while the storm was raging in Washington to get a commitment from the Bucktails that would stamp them as proslavery, but the Bucktails acted cautiously. When a large meeting was called in Albany to indorse the prohibition of slavery in Missouri, Van Buren found it convenient to be off on circuit. When the Clintonians whipped a resolution endorsing the restriction through the legislature, not a Bucktail raised a voice in dissent. But for all their caution against public commitment it was generally understood both in Washington and New York that the Bucktails were anxious for peace, and that they supported the corporal's guard of northern Republicans in Congress who, retreating finally from the Missouri prohibition, made peace possible. Several of the Bucktail newspapers said as much, and despite the lack of public commitment on the part of party leaders, more than one Clintonian newspaper would brand them the "Slave Ticket" in the legislative elections that followed.

In private, Van Buren left no doubt [as to] where he stood, or where he meant to go once the storm had passed. No sooner had the compromise been adopted in Washington than the Little Magician got off a letter to his friendly rival Rufus King, promising at "some future day" to give that veteran Federalist his own views on the expediency of making slavery a party question, and remarking meanwhile that notwithstanding the strong public interest in the Missouri question, "the excitement which exists in regard to it, or which is likely to arise from it, is not so great as you suppose." . . .

Twenty months after that, in the late fall of 1821, Van Buren set off for Washington as a newly elected United States senator. With his party having taken the measure of Clinton in the meantime, he carried with him into the lion's den of presidential politics effective command of the thirty-six uncommitted electoral votes of New York. If he would be the most disinterested statesmen in all the land, he could not avoid for long the responsibility that went with that power. It was an opportunity to be used for large purposes or small, as a man might chose, and the Little Magician lost no time in indicating his intended course. Within weeks of his arrival he was pulling the strings of the New York delegation in the House to bring about return of the speakership to the slave states, from whom it had been wrested by a straight sectional vote upon Clay's retirement the year before. The new speaker was P. P. Barbour of Virginia, a leader of the Old Republican reaction in the south. Three months after that Van Buren was on his way to Richmond to plan the resurrection of the Old Republican Party. . . .

III

In the long history of the American presidency no election appears quite so formless as that of 1824. With no competing party to force unity on the Republicans, candidates who could not command the party nomination were free to defy it. They did so, charging that "King Caucus" was undemocratic. Eventually no fewer than four candidates competed down to the wire, each a Republican, every man for himself. Because they divided the electoral votes between them, none came to close to a majority, and the election went to the House of Representatives. There, with the help of Henry Clay, John Quincy Adams outpolled the popular Andrew Jackson and the caucus nominee, William H. Crawford of Georgia, and carried off the prize.

Historians, viewing that election, look at King Caucus too much through the eyes of its opponents, who stated that the caucus represented an in-group of political officeholders attached to Crawford and anxious to preserve their own political power. In fact it was the Old Republicans who organized the caucus, not so much to sustain Crawford and preserve power as to revive the Virginia-New York party and regain power. They took up Crawford unenthusiastically because he came closest to the Old Republican pattern, and because he alone of all the candidates could hope to carry Virginia. They took up the caucus at the behest of Van Buren after two years of searching for a method of nominating which would command the support of all, because four years after Missouri the only hope of winning New York for a Southern candidate was to present him, however unpopularly, as the official party nominee.

Hidden in the currents and crosscurrents of that campaign was the reiterated issue of party versus amalgamation. Behind it, in turn, were repeated pleas by Old Republican presses, North and South alike, that unless genuine Republicans agreed on a method of choosing a candidate the division must be along sectional lines, in which case a Federalist or proto-Federalist might sneak into the White House. Behind it too was the repeated warning that party organization alone would make democracy work. Without it, the Old Republicans correctly prophesied, the election would end up in the House of Representatives, subject to the worst kind of political intrigue, and with the votes of the smallest states the equals of those of populous Virginia and New York. . . .

In the campaign of 1824 and the years immediately following, the slavery issue was never far below the surface. The Denmark Vesey conspiracy for an insurrection in Charleston (now a subject of controversy among historians) was to contemporaries a grim reminder of the Missouri debates, and it was attributed publicly to Rufus King's speeches on the Missouri question. In 1823–1824 some southerners suspected that an attempt by Secretary of State Adams to conclude a slave trade convention with Great Britain was an attempt to reap the benefit of northern antislavery sentiment; and some, notably Representative John Floyd of Virginia, sought to turn the tables on Adams by attacking him for allegedly ceding Texas to Spain in the Florida treaty, thus ceding what Floyd called "two slaveholding states" and costing "the Southern interest" four senators.

Old Republicans made no bones about their concern over the issue, or their fear that it might be turned against them. In the summer of 1823 an illuminating editorial debate broke out between the New York *American,* which spoke the thoughts of the old Federalists in New York, and the Richmond *Enquirer.* So vehemently had the *American* picked up a report of a plan to revise the Illinois constitution to admit slavery that Ritchie charged its editors with reviving the slave question to put New York into the lap of the "Universal Yankee Nation" and to put the south under the "ban of the Empire." "Call it the Missouri question, the Illinois question, what you please; it was the *Slave question*," Ritchie shrilled, which the *American* was seeking to get up for political purposes. Shortly, the Albany *Argus* got into the argument. The *Argus,* which got its signals from Van Buren and spoke the thoughts of New York's Old Republicans, charged the *American* with trying to revive the slave question to "abrogate the old party distinctions" and "organize new ones, founded in the territorial prejudices of the people." "The more general question of the North and South," the *Argus* warned, "will be urged to the uttermost, by those who can never triumph when they meet the democracy of the country, openly, and with the hostility they bear towards it." Over and over the debate rang out the argument that the attempt to revive party distinctions was an attempt to allay sectional prejudices, and by the time the debate was over only the most obtuse citizen could have missed the point. . . .

IV

. . . When finally it rode to power, the Jacksonian party was made up of two clearly discernible and distinct wings. One comprised the original Jacksonians, those who had supported him in 1824 when he ran on his own, bereft, like all the rest, of party, and nearly of allies. As measured in that election this strength was predominantly in the west. It spilled over into a few states east of the mountains, most notably Pennsylvania, where the chaos of the existing political structure enabled Jackson as military hero to ride roughshod over all the rest. But this was all. The western vote, especially when shared with Clay, amounted in electoral terms to little. Even with the votes of the Carolinas, thrown to him gratuitously by Calhoun and counting one-quarter of his total, he was far short of an electoral majority. To get even this much he had been formally before the public for two years, and all his considerable natural appeal as a westerner and a hero had gone into the bargain.

After 1824 Jackson found himself the candidate of a combined opposition. The concrete measure of difference between defeat in 1824 and victory in 1828 was the Old Republican strength of the South Atlantic states and New York, brought to the Jackson camp carefully tended and carefully drilled by Van Buren. Nearly equal in size to the original Jackson following, they constituted a political faction far older, far more permanent, far more purposeful, far better led, and in the long run far more important. Their purposes were set forth by Van Buren in a notable letter to Ritchie in January 1827, proposing support of the old hero. Such support, as the New Yorker put it, would be "the best and probably the only practicable mode of concentrating the entire vote of the opposition & of effecting what is of still greater importance, the substantial reorganization of the Old Republican Party." It would "restore a better state of things, by combining Genl Jackson's personal popularity with the portion of old party feeling yet remaining." It would aid Republicans of the north and middle states "by substituting *party principle* for *personal preference* as one of the leading points in the contest. . . . Instead of the question being between a northern and Southern man, it would be whether or not the ties, which have hitherto bound together a great political party should be severed." Most important, its effects would be highly salutary for the south:

> We must always have party distinctions and the old ones are the best of which the nature of the case admits. Political combinations between the inhabitants of the different states are unavoidable & the most natural & beneficial to the country is that between the planters of the South and the plain Republicans of the north. The country has once flourished under a party thus constituted & may again. It would take longer than our lives (even if it were practicable) to create new party feelings to keep those masses together. If the old ones are suppressed, geographical divisions founded on local interests or, what is worse prejudices between free and slave holding states will inevitably take their place. Party attachment in former times furnished a complete antidote for sectional prejudices by producing counteracting feelings. It was not until that deference had been broken down that the clamour agt. Southern Influence and African Slavery could be made effectual in the North. . . . Formerly, attacks upon Southern Republicans were regarded by those of the north as assaults upon their political brethren & resented accordingly. This all powerful sympathy has been much weakened, if not, destroyed by the amalgamating policy. . . . it can & ought to be revived.

Lastly, Van Buren noted, a Jackson administration brought to power by the "concerted effort of a political party, holding in the main, to certain tenets & opposed to certain prevailing principles" would be a far different thing from one brought to power by the popularity of a military hero alone. An administration brought to power by Old Republican votes would be governed by Old Republican principles. Van Buren would make himself the guarantor of that. . . .

No less important, it was the structure of the Jackson party that gave meaning to—and dictated the course of—that struggle between Van Buren and Calhoun which bulks so large in the politics of the Jackson years. It was far more than the empty struggle for the succession. Its essence was competition between two conflicting ideas as to how best to protect southern security in the Union, and thus, inferentially, how to preserve the Union itself. One of those ideas was the old Jeffersonian idea, resuscitated by Van Buren, sustained by the Jackson party and by the Democratic party until the Civil War. It was that southern security rested ultimately on the maintenance in national office of a political party that would be responsive to the south because dependent on it for election. A political answer, not a doctrinaire one, it was product of the practical, pragmatic, and thoroughly political minds of Thomas Jefferson and Martin Van Buren. It depended for its success on the winning of national elections by a party that would maintain its identity in relation to the opposition as a states' rights-strict construction party, but which would at the same time be moderate, flexible, pragmatic in tone, able to win support in the north as well as the south if it would serve its purpose.

Counter to this was the proposition developed by John C. Calhoun. . . . This was that southern security was dependent in the last analysis on the mainte-

nance of an effective southern power to veto anything it didn't like—thus nullification—and that failing, on the right to secede. In contrast to the political and
moderate remedy of the Old Republicans, this was a constitutional remedy,
product of the brilliant legal, doctrinaire, and essentially nonpolitical mind of
the great Carolinian.

That Van Buren won out over Calhoun in the Jackson years . . . had everything to do with the fact that the Old Republican moderates controlled the
south, all but South Carolina, almost that, in the twenties. While Calhoun
brought only South Carolina and some personal support in Congress to the
Jackson fold, Van Buren brought all the rest of the south, and New York as well.
The fact was not lost on Jackson or his Tennessee friends, either before his election or after. Van Buren's triumph over Calhoun was won not on Washington
backstairs after 1829 but on the southern hustings in the early twenties. Two
years before it came to power the Jackson party was already, in fact, a Jackson-
Van Buren party.

V

There were postscripts, too, that harked back to the structure of the Jackson
party, to the Missouri question, and to the political prophecies of Thomas
Ritchie, woven into the very fabric of the party by the skilled political weaver
from New York. First of these was that the Jackson party, the issue once raised,
was committed to Texas. When in 1844 a new drumfire of antislavery sentiment
in the north made it impossible for Van Buren to honor that commitment,
Ritchie and Van Buren, after nearly a quarter century of fruitful political team-
work, would part company, and Van Buren would give up leadership of the
party he had created. After 1844 the party of the Jeffersonian formula sustained
itself in the face of the rising slavery issue by giving vent to its expansionist ten-
dencies; and the northern man with southern principles who replaced Van
Buren was in fact a northwestern man with southern principles, Stephen A.
Douglas of Illinois. It was to be Douglas, governed by the irresistible logic of the
party structure, who carried through Congress finally, in 1854, the repeal of the
Missouri Compromise. And when three years after that the Supreme Court in
the Dred Scott decision held the Thomas Proviso of the Missouri Compromise
unconstitutional, as Ritchie and Nathaniel Macon had said it was thirty-seven
years before, who were the judges who comprised the majority? Of six, one had
been appointed in 1846 by "Young Hickory" James K. Polk, a second in 1853 by
the next successful Democrat, Franklin Pierce. The four others were James M.
Wayne of Georgia, coadjutor of Van Buren's Georgia lieutenant John Forsyth,
appointed to the court by Jackson in 1835; Roger B. Taney of Maryland, appointed by Jackson in 1836; John Catron, Van Buren campaign manager in Tennessee, appointed by Jackson in 1837; and Peter V. Daniel of Virginia, long-time
member of the Richmond Junto, confidante of Thomas Ritchie, appointed in
1841 by Van Buren.

SOURCES

The Election of 1828

The opposition fought Jackson with cartoons and broadsides as well as with speeches. In the 1828 election they made much of Jackson's violent nature, his street fights, and his many executions of army deserters and enemies. Do you think such propaganda had any effect on the voters? Undoubtedly it made little difference in states that Jackson either won or lost by big margins. But what about the close states? Who do you think would be influenced by such appeals? One thing is missing in the coffin handbill: the many duels Jackson had fought. Why do you think the opposition decided not to emphasize dueling?

The Bettmann Archive.   *"Jackson is to be President, and you will be HANGED."*

Some Account of some of the Bloody Deeds of
GEN. JACKSON.

Jacob Webb. David Morrow. John Harris. Henry Lewis. David Hunt. Edward Lindsey.

A brief account of the Execution of the Six Militia Men.

MOURNFUL TRAGEDY.

FRANKLIN, Tenn. September 10, 1818.

New-York Historical Society.

And here is how the voters responded to Jackson. Do the results support or un-
dermine Brown's analysis? .

The Election of 1828.

"King Andrew"

Later, when Jackson was president and vetoed more bills than all his predecessors combined and simply ignored the Supreme Court, the opposition tried to portray him as a tyrannical monarch. The first cartoon below, which is quite famous, has Jackson placing his will above that of the Constitution, the courts, and the good of the country. The second cartoon draws upon violent episodes from Jackson's military past and likens him to the English monarch Richard III, who was accused of murdering two young princes in the Tower of London. Which of the two cartoons do you think was more effective?

The
Bettmann
Archive.

*American
Antiquarian
Society.*

Davy Crockett

The Art of Democratic Politics

Jackson was a rich Tennessee planter with over one hundred slaves, but sometimes he was portrayed by his followers as a man of the people, an unlettered hero of the west, who spoke common sense and easily routed the learned eastern establishment. To counter this propaganda, anti-Jacksonians eventually found good copy in Davy Crockett, who had served in Congress since 1826 and had roasted Jackson for betraying the backwoodsmen of western Tennessee. Crockett played the role of a comic backwoods hero who claimed to be half-alligator, half-horse, with a touch of the snapping turtle. Here Crockett explains to a Little Rock audience the tricks of democratic politics.

From David Crockett, *The Life of Colonel David Crockett*, Porter and Coates, Philadelphia, 1865, pp. 275–278.

Having gone through with the regular toasts, the president of the day drank, "Our distinguished guest, Col. Crockett," which called forth a prodigious clattering all around the table, and I soon saw that nothing would do, but I must get up and make them a speech. I had no sooner elongated my outward Adam, than they at it again, with renewed vigor, which made me sort of feel that I was still somebody, though no longer a member of Congress.

In my speech I went over the whole history of the present administration; took a long shot at the flying deposites, and gave an outline, a sort of charcoal sketch, of the political life of "the Government's" heir-presumptive. I also let them know how I had been rascaled out of my election, because I refused to bow down to the idol; and as I saw a number of young politicians around the table, I told them, that I would lay down a few rules for their guidance, which, if properly attended to, could not fail to lead them on the highway to distinction and public honor. I told them, that I was an old hand at the business, and as I was about to retire for a time I would give them a little instruction gratis, for I was up to all the tricks of the trade, though I had practiced but few.

"Attend all public meetings," says I, "and get some friends to move that you take the chair; if you fail in this attempt, make a push to be appointed secretary; the proceedings of course will be published, and your name is introduced to the public. But should you fail in both undertakings, get two or three acquaintances, over a bottle of whisky, to pass some resolutions, no matter on what subject; publish them even if you pay the printer—it will answer the purpose of breaking the ice, which is the main point in these matters. Intrigue until you are elected an officer of the militia; this is the second step towards promotion, and can be accomplished with ease, as I know an instance of an election being advertised, and no one attending, the innkeeper at whose house it was to be held, having a military turn, elected himself colonel of his regiment." Says I, "You may not accomplish your ends with as little difficulty, but do not be discouraged—Rome wasn't built in a day.

"If your ambition or circumstances compel you to serve your country, and earn three dollars a day, by becoming a member of the legislature, you must first publicly avow that the constitution of the state is a shackle upon free and liberal legislation; and is, therefore, of as little use in the present enlightened age, as an old almanac of the year in which the instrument was framed. There is policy in this measure, for by making the constitution a mere dead letter, your headlong proceedings will be attributed to a bold and unshackled mind; whereas, it might otherwise be thought they arose from sheer mulish ignorance. 'The Government' has set the example in his attack upon the constitution of the United States, and who should fear to follow where 'the Government' leads?

"When the day of election approaches, visit your constituents far and wide. Treat liberally, and drink freely, in order to rise in their estimation, though you fall in your own. True, you may be called a drunken dog by some of the clean shirt and silk stocking gentry, but the real rough necks will style you a jovial fellow, their votes are certain, and frequently count double. Do all you can to appear to advantage in the eyes of the women. That's easily done you have but to kiss and slabber their children, wipe their noses, and pat them on the head; this cannot fail to please their mothers, and you may rely on your business being done in that quarter.

"Promise all that is asked," said I, "and more if you can think of anything. Offer to build a bridge or a church, to divide a county, create a batch of new offices, make a turnpike, or anything they like. Promises cost nothing, therefore deny nobody who has a vote or sufficient influence to obtain one.

"Get up on all occasions, and sometimes on no occasion at all, and make long-winded speeches, though composed of nothing else than wind—talk of your devotion to your country, your modesty and disinterestedness, or on any such fanciful subject. Rail against taxes of all kinds, office-holders, and bad harvest weather; and wind up with a flourish about the heroes who fought and bled for our liberties in the times that tried men's souls. To be sure you run the risk of being considered a bladder of wind, or an empty barrel, but never mind that, you will find enough of the same fraternity to keep you in countenance.

"If any charity be going forward, be at the top of it, provided it is to be advertised publicly; if not, it isn't worth your while. None but a fool would place his candle under a bushel on such an occasion.

"These few directions," said I, "if properly attended to, will do your business; and when once elected, why a fig for the dirty children, the promises, the bridges, the churches, the taxes, the offices, and the subscriptions, for it is absolutely necessary to forget all these before you can become a thoroughgoing politician, and a patriot of the first water."

My speech was received with three times three, and all that; and we continued speechifying and drinking until nightfall, when it was put to vote, that we would have the puppet show over again, which was carried *nem. con.* The showman set his wires to work, just as "the Government" does the machinery in his big puppet show; and we spent a delightful and rational evening. We raised a subscription for the poor showman; and I went to bed, pleased and gratified with the hospitality and kindness of the citizens of Little Rock. There are some first-rate men there, of the real half horse, half alligator breed, with a sprinkling of the steamboat, and such as grow nowhere on the face of the universal earth, but just about the back bone of North America.

The Election of 1840

By 1840, political strategists of all stripes were willing to try what one newsman called the "Davy Crockett Line" and portray their candidates as simple backwoodsmen who had been raised on possum fat and hominy. The Harrison campaign for president in 1840 probably carried political hoopla to an extreme. As you look at the picture below, and read the newspaper account of a St. Louis political rally that follows, you will begin to understand not only why Harri-son won but also why the election brought 78 percent of the electorate out to vote. In many ways the Harrison campaign was the first modern political cam-paign.

F.D.R. Library.

Rally for William Henry Harrison in St. Louis, Missouri

We cannot believe that any friend of Harrison could, in his most sanguine moments, have anticipated so glorious a day, such a turn-out of the people, as was witnessed on Tuesday last in this city. Everything was auspicious. The heavens, the air, the earth all seemed to have combined to assist in doing honor to the services, the patriotism and the virtues of William Henry Harrison. Never have we seen so much enthusiasm, so much honest, impassioned and eloquent feeling displayed in the countenances and bursting from the lips of freemen. It was a day of jubilee. The people felt that the time had come when they could breathe freely—when they were about to cast from them the incubus of a polluted and abandoned party, and when they could look forward to better and happier days in store for them and for the country.

Preparations had been made for the reception and entertainment of the company, by the proper committees, at Mrs. Ashley's residence. The extensive park was so arranged as to accommodate the throng of persons who were expected. Seats were erected for the officers of the day, for the speakers and for the ladies. At the hour appointed by the marshal of the day, the people commenced to assemble at the court house, and several associations and crafts were formed in the procession as they advanced on the ground. While this was going on, the steamboats bringing delegations from St. Charles, Hannibal, Adams county, Ill., and Alton, arrived at the wharf, with banners unfurled to the breeze, and presenting a most cheering sight. The order of procession, so far as we have been able to obtain it, was as follows:

Music: Brass band.

1. Banner, borne by farmers from the northern part of St. Louis township. This banner represented the "Raising of the Siege of Fort Meigs" and bore as its motto, "It Has Pleased Providence, We Are Victorious." (Harrison's dispatch.)

2. Officers and members of the Tippecanoe club, preceded by the president, Col. John O'Fallon, with a splendid banner, representing a hemisphere surmounted by an American eagle, strangling with his beak a serpent, its fold grasped within its talons, and its head having the face of a fox in the throes of death.

3. Log cabin committee, six abreast.

4. Soldiers who served under Harrison in the late war—in a car, adorned with banners on each side—one, a view of a steamboat named Tippecanoe, with a sign board, "For Washington City."

6. Invited guests in carriages.

7. Citizens on foot, six abreast, bearing banners inscribed, "Harrison, the Friend of Pre-emption Rights," "One Term for the Presidency," "Harrison, the People's Candidate;" "Harrison, the People's Sober Second Thought;" "Harri-

From "Rally for William Henry Harrison in St. Louis, Missouri," as reported by the St. Louis *New Era*, in A. B. Norton, ed., *The Election of 1840*, Vol. I, 1888, pp. 141–146.

son, He Never Lost a Battle;" "Harrison, the Protector of the Pioneers of the West;" "Harrison, Tyler and Reform;" "Harrison, the Poor Man's Friend;" "Harrison, the Friend of Equal Laws and Equal Rights."

    8. Citizens on horseback, six abreast.

    9. Delegation from Columbia Bottom.

    10. Canoe, "North Bend."

    11. Boys with banners, upon one of which was inscribed, "Our Country's Hope," and on another, "Just as the Twig is Bent, the Tree's Inclined."

    12. Laborers, with their horses and carts, shovels, picks, etc., with a banner bearing the inscription, "Harrison, the Poor Man's Friend—We Want Work."

    13. A printing press on a platform with banners, and the pressman striking off Tippecanoe songs, and distributing them to the throng of people as they passed along, followed in order by the members of the craft.

    14. Drays, with barrels of hard cider.

    15. A log cabin mounted on wheels, and drawn by six beautiful horses, followed by the craft of carpenters in great numbers. Over the door of the cabin, the words, "The String of the Latch Never Pulled In."

    16. The blacksmiths, with forge, bellows, etc., mounted on cars, the men at work. Banner, "We Strike for Our Country's Good."

    17. The joiners and cabinet-makers; a miniature shop mounted on wheels; men at work; the craft following it.

    18. A large canoe, drawn by six horses, and filled with men.

    19. Two canoes, mounted, and filled by sailors.

    20. Fort Meigs, in miniature, 40 by 15 feet, drawn by nine yoke of oxen.

    Arrived at the southern extremity of the park, the procession halted and formed in open order, the rear passing to the front.

    The people were then successively addressed by Mr. John Hogan, of Illinois.

    Colonial John O'Fallon was then called for, and mounted on Fort Meigs, he thus addressed the people:

My Fellow Citizens:

    I feel deeply sensible of the honor you confer upon me by calling me to address this vast concourse of intelligent freemen.

    I had the honor of serving under General Harrison at the battle of Tippecanoe, during the siege of Fort Meigs, and at the battle of the Thames. I can say that, from the commencement to the termination of his military services in the last war, I was almost constantly by his side. I was familiar with his conduct as governor and superintendent of Indian affairs of the Territory of Indiana, and after the return of peace, as commissioner to treat with all the hostile Indians of the last war in the Northwest, for the establishment of a permanent reconciliation and peace. I saw also much of General Harrison whilst he was in the Congress of the United States.

    Opportunities have thus been afforded me of knowing him in all the relations of life, as an officer and as a man, and of being enabled to form a pretty correct estimate of his military and civil services, as well as his qualifications and fitness for office.

    As a military man, his daring, chivalrous courage inspired his men with confidence and spread dismay and terror to his enemies. In all his plans he was successful. In all his engagements he was victorious. He has filled all the various civil and military offices committed to him by his country, with sound judgment and spotless fidelity. In every situation he was cautious and prudent, firm and energetic, and his decisions always judicious. His acquirements as a scholar are varied and extensive, his principles as a statesman sound, pure and republican.

If chosen President he will be the President of the people rather than of a party. The Government will then be administered for the general good and welfare.

His election will be drawn of a new era! The reform of the abuses of a most corrupt, profligate and oppressive Government. Then will end the ten years' war upon the currency and institutions of the country. The hard-money cry and and hard times will disappear altogether. Then will cease further attempts to increase the wages of the officeholders and reduce the wages of the people to the standard of European labor.

Then shall we see restored the general prosperity of the people, by giving them a sound local currency, mixed with a currency of a uniform value throughout the land. The revival of commerce, of trade, enterprise and general confidence. Then the return of happier, more peaceful and more prosperous days, when cheerfulness and plenty will, once more, smile around the poor man's table.

George Caleb Bingham

The Artist's View of Politics

What were ordinary elections like? Fortunately, the painter George Caleb Bingham of Missouri provided some answers to this question. He broke into Western politics in 1840 as an enthusiastic young orator for Harrison, and he eventually won a seat in the Missouri House of Representatives. He knew that every vote counted; he won one election by a mere three votes and another by twenty-five votes.

He painted these memorable political scenes out of his own experience. The first one, called "Canvassing for a Vote," shows a campaigner with a saddlebag full of literature trying to win a vote outside a highway tavern. The second, "County Election," shows the voters lined up to cast their ballots verbally, with candidates on top of the steps tipping their hats politely, and the inevitable barrel of cider (or whiskey) on the left. The third, "Verdict of the People," shows a clerk reading election results aloud from the steps of the courthouse. The fourth, "Stump Speaking," is Bingham's masterpiece. It shows an experienced politician who has grown gray in the pursuit of office trying to influence a crowd. The man taking notes is his opponent, and the fat man at the far left is the former governor of Missouri, Meredith Miles Marmaduke. He was so angry when he saw this painting that he challenged Bingham to a duel.

Compare these pictures with some earlier ones on pages 146–149 and 188. Do they help you understand why Jacksonian politics was regarded as being new and different? Was it really a complete break with the past? Or can you see some carry-over from earlier days?

Canvassing for a Vote. By George Bingham.
Nelson Gallery—Atkins Museum.

County Election. By George Bingham.
St. Louis Mercantile Library Association/City Art Museum.

Verdict of the People. By George Bingham.
Collection of the Boatman's National Bank of St. Louis.

Stump Speaking. By George Bingham.
Collection of the Boatman's National Bank of St. Louis.

CHAPTER 11

Antislavery

There was one issue that leaders of both parties, Whigs and Democrats alike, wanted to keep out of politics. And that issue was slavery. Politicians of all stripes knew that slavery could easily shatter their national parties—and perhaps the Union itself. They preferred to fight over "safe" political issues like banking, tariffs, roads, and canals. And they fought over such issues year in and year out. In working to keep slavery out of the limelight, of course, politicians were effectively supporting slavery, which was an old and well-established institution by Jackson's time.

Keeping slavery out of politics, however, became increasingly difficult. For one thing, the old institution of slavery, which had been "normal" throughout the Atlantic world since the 1500s, began to give way rapidly after the American Revolution. By 1804 all northern states had either freed their slaves or adopted programs of gradual emancipation. And by the time of Jackson's second administration (1833–1837) programs to abolish slavery had been adopted in Haiti, Argentina, Chile, Colombia, Central America, Mexico, Bolivia, and the British West Indies. The American South was beginning to stand out as a sore thumb.

For another thing, "reform" was in the air after the War of 1812, especially in the north, where all sorts of reformers suddenly emerged and tromped across the countryside. In contrast to the south, where one could go for weeks without hearing the cry of reform, there were parts of New England, upstate New York, and the Ohio Valley that seemed to be overrun with revivalists, reformers, and enthusiasts espousing one cause or another.

Why? The answers have been almost as numerous as the reformers and abolitionists. One point of view is that the reformers, especially the men and women who came out against slavery, were simply working out the logic of modern egalitarianism. Did not the Declaration of Independence assert simply the equality of all men? How could such a faith coexist with slavery? Other historians have argued that reform, especially in its connection with revivalism, was a product of the experience of the frontier. Others have claimed that the reform leaders were members of an old elite that was afraid of being displaced by a new class of people whose wealth came from business, and so turned to reform to relieve their anxiety at losing control of the nation's social and political life.

Another point of view is that the prime recruits for reform movements were to be found among people whose ethnic and regional identities led them to undergo conversion to a militant Protestant revivalism. Immigrants from England and Wales, and migrants from New England to the west, so this argument goes, were the people most likely to answer the evangelical preachers' calls that they dedicate their lives to Christ. Out of this wave of revival, on both sides of the Atlantic, came an army of hundreds of thousands of converts. And it was from among them that a tiny minority was chosen, a minority who turned now to try to perfect society in the image of Christ, and in so doing to try to perfect themselves.

INTERPRETIVE ESSAY

James Brewer Stewart

The Commitment to Immediate Emancipation

The following essay, by the historian James Brewer Stewart, examines the relationship between nineteenth-century Protestantism and the commitment to the immediate end of slavery. There were a variety of antislavery positions, some favoring gradual abolition, others immediate; some advocating sending ex-slaves to Africa; others involving paying their former owners something like their market value. The most radical position, which gained ground after 1830, was the uncompromising demand for the immediate, unconditional emancipation of the slaves without compensation to their owners—and without regard for the consequences. Only a minority of Americans with antislavery opinions adopted this position, and this selection is a guide to understanding who they were and why they embarked on such a course.

American society in the late 1820s presented the pious, well-informed Yankee with tremendous challenges. For the better part of a decade, Protestant spokesmen had warned him against the nation's all-absorbing interest in material wealth, geographic expansion, and party politics. Infidelity, he was told, flourished on the western and southern frontiers; vice reigned supreme in the burgeoning eastern cities. In politics, he was exhorted to combat atheist dema-gogues called Jacksonians who insisted on popular rule and further demanded that the clerical establishment be divorced from government. Urban working-men and frontier pioneers, morally numbed by alcoholism and illiteracy, were being duped in massive numbers by the blandishments of these greedy politi-cos. America, he was assured, faced moral bankruptcy and the total destruction of its Christian identity. Exaggerated as such claims may seem, they had some grounding in reality. Yankee Protestantism was indeed facing immense new challenges from a society in the throes of massive social change. As Protestants struggled to overcome these adversities, the abolitionists' crusade for immedi-ate emancipation also took form.

By the end of the 1820s, America was in the midst of unparalleled economic growth. Powerful commercial networks were coming to link all sections of the country; canals, mass-circulation newspapers, and (soon) railroads reinforced this thrust toward regional interdependency. Northern business depended as never before on trade with the south. The "cotton revolution" that swept the Mississippi-Alabama-Georgia frontier in turn stimulated textile manufacturing and shipping in the northeast. In the northwest, yet another economic boom took shape as businessmen and farmers in Ohio, Indiana, and Illinois developed lucrative relationships with the eastern seaboard, and the population of northern cities grew apace. Politicians organized party machines that catered to these new interests and to the "common man's" mundane preferences.

The cosmopolitan forces of economic interdependence, urbanization, democratic politics, and mass communication posed major challenges to provincial New England culture. The Protestant response, in John L. Thomas's apt phrase, was "to fight democratic excess with democratic remedies." Throughout the 1820s New Englanders mounted an impressive counterattack against the forces of "immorality" by commandeering the tools of their secular opponents: the printing press, the rally, and the efficiently managed bureaucratic agency. With the hope of renovating American religious life, the American Tract Society spewed forth thousands of pamphlets that exhorted readers to repent. The Temperance Union carried a similar message to the nation's innumerable hard drinkers. Various missionary societies sent witnesses to backcountry settlements, the waterfront haunts of Boston's seamen, the bordellos of New York City. These societies envisioned a reassertion of traditional New England values on a national scale. At the same time, although unintentionally, these programs for Christian restoration were stimulating in pious young men and women stirrings of spiritual revolt.

All of these reform enterprises drew their vitality from revivalistic religion. Once again, social discontent and political alienation found widespread expression through the conversion experience; the Great Revivals announced the Protestant resurgence of the 1820s. Like their eighteenth-century predecessors, powerful evangelists such as Charles G. Finney and Lyman Beecher urged their audiences that man, though a sinner, should nonetheless strive for holiness and choose a new life of sanctification. Free will once again took precedence over original sin, which was again redefined as voluntary selfishness. As in the 1750s, God was pictured as insisting that the "saved" performed acts of benevolence, expand the boundaries of Christ's kingdom, and recognize a personal responsibility to improve society. Men and women again saw themselves playing dynamic roles in their own salvation and preparing society for the millennium. By the thousands they flocked to the Tract Society, the Sunday School Union, the temperance and peace organizations, and the Colonization Society. Seeking prevention, certainly not revolution, evangelicals thus dreamed of a glorious era of national reform: rid of liquor, prostitution, atheism, and popular politics, the redeemed masses of America would gladly submit to the leadership of Christian statesmen. So blessed, Americans would no longer fall prey to the blandishments of that hard-drinking gambler, duelist, and unchurched slaveowner, President Andrew Jackson.

From this defensive setting sprang New England's crusade against slavery. Indeed, radical reformers of all varieties, not just abolitionists, traced their activism to the revivals of the 1820s. . . .

While revivalism's ambiguities stimulated anxiety in the 1820s, its network of benevolent agencies opened opportunities for young Americans that their eighteenth-century counterparts could never have foreseen. The missionary agencies and even the revivals themselves were organized along complex bureaucratic lines. Volunteers were always needed to drum up donations or to organize meetings. New careers were also created. For the first time in American history, young people could regard social activism as a legitimate profession. Earnest ministerial candidates began accepting full-time positions as circuit riders, regional agents, newspaper editors, and schoolteachers, with salaries underwritten by the various benevolent agencies. One important abolitionist-to-be, Joshua Leavitt, spent his first years after seminary editing the *Seaman's Friend*, an evangelical periodical for sailors. Another, Elizur Wright, Jr., was employed by the American Tract Society.

Most important to abolitionism was the effect of revivalism on the ministry itself. Once open to only an elite, the ministry had by the 1820s become a common profession. Spurred by expanding geography, seminaries increased their enrollments as they attracted young New Englanders who burned to aid in America's regeneration. Included were some destined to number among abolitionism's dominant figures: Samuel J. May, Amos A. Phelps, Theodore D. Weld, Joshua Leavitt, and Stephen S. Foster, to name only a few. First as seminarians, then as volunteers, paid agents, clergymen, and teachers, many pious young Americans dedicated themselves to fighting sin and disbelief. Given the intensity of the evangelical temperament, the results of such experiences were to suggest, to some, far more radical courses of action, and there can be no question that these abolitionists-to-be took their responsibilities in deadly earnest.

There is some persuasive evidence that family background and upbringing predisposed young New Englanders toward a radical outlook. Over twenty years ago, David Donald gathered information that suggests the influence of parental guidance on abolitionism's most prominent spokesmen. Abolitionism, he reported, was a revolt of youth raised by old New England families of farmers, teachers, ministers, and businessmen. The parents of abolitionists were usually well-educated Presbyterians, Congregationalists, Quakers, and Unitarians who participated heavily in revivalism and its attendant benevolent projects. Many scholars have effectively criticized Donald's methods and have raised serious questions about the reliability of his evidence regarding the movement's rank-and-file. Donald also erred in concluding that commitments to abolitionism were reactions to a loss of social status to nouveau riche neighbors. Actually, abolitionism flourished among groups with rising social prospects during the 1830s. Nevertheless, Donald's findings remain extremely suggestive as to the influence of parental guidance of abolitionism's most prominent leaders.

In such families, as numerous biographers have since attested, a stern emphasis on moral uprightness and social responsibility generally prevailed. In the words of Bertram Wyatt-Brown, young men and women "learned that integrity came not from conformity to the ways of the world, but to the principles by which the family tried to live." Parents were usually eager to inculcate a high degree of religious and social conscience. In their reminiscences, abolitionists commonly paid homage to strong-minded mothers or fathers who intense religious fervor dominated their households. In his early years, Wendell Phillips constantly turned to his mother for instruction, and after her death he confessed that "whatever good is in me, she is responsible for." Thomas Wentworth Higginson, Arthur and Lewis Tappan, and William Lloyd Garrison became, like Phillips, leading abolitionists and also internalized the religious dictates of dominating mothers. Sidney Howard Gay, James G. Birney, Elizur Wright, Jr., and Elijah P. Lovejoy are examples of abolitionists who modeled their early lives to fit the intentions of exacting fathers. Young women who were to enter the movement usually sought the advice of their fathers, as in the cases of Elizabeth Cady Stanton and Maria Weston Chapman. Yet whatever the child's focus, the expectations of parents seldom varied. Displays of conscience and upright behavior brought the rewards of parental love and approval.

Children also learn that sexual self-control was a vital part of righteous living. Parents stressed prayer and benevolent deeds as substitutes for "carnal thoughts" and intimacy; they associated sexual sublimation with family stability and personal redemption. During his years at boarding school and later at Harvard, Wendell Phillips strove to satisfy his mother on all these counts. Lewis Tappan, too, remembered how hard he had worked "to be one of the best scholars, often a favorite with the masters, and a leader among the boys in our plays." When he was twenty and living away from home, Tappan still received admonitions from his mother about the pitfalls of sex. Recalling a dream, she wrote, "Methought you had, by frequenting the theatre, been drawn into the society of lewd women, and had contracted a disease that was preying upon your constitution." For his part, Tappan had already sworn to "enjoy a sound mind and body, untainted by vice." A strong sense of their individuality, a deadly earnestness about moral issues, confidence in their ability to master themselves and to improve the world—these were the qualities that so often marked abolitionists in their early years. Above all, these future reformers believed in their own superiority and fully expected to become leaders.

Of course, not all children of morally assertive New England parents became radical abolitionists. William Lloyd Garrison's brother, for example, emerged from his mother's tutelage and lapsed into alcoholism. Still, the predisposition to rebellion remains hard to dismiss. Alienation and self-doubt certainly ran especially deep among these sensitive, socially conscious young people. Besides, America in the 1820s appeared to many a complex and bewildering place. Certain social realities were soon to seem disturbingly at variance with their high expectations and fixed moral codes.

These future abolitionists entered young adulthood at a time when rapid mobility, technological advance, and dizzying geographic expansion were transforming traditional institutions. Those who took up pastorates, seminary study, or positions in benevolent agencies were shocked to discover that the Protestant establishment was hardly free from the acquisitive taint and bureaucratic selfishness that they had been brought up to disdain. Expecting to lead communities of godfearing, Christian families, young ministers like Amos A. Phelps, Elizur Wright, Jr., and Charles T. Torrey confronted instead a fragmented society of entrepreneurs. Theodore Dwight Weld, for example, wrote critically to the great evangelist Charles G. Finney that "*revivals* are fast becoming with you a sort of trade, to be worked at so many hours a day." Promoters of colonization, such as James G. Birney and Joshua Leavitt, became increasingly disturbed that many of their coworkers were far less interested in Christian benevolence than in ridding the nation of inferior blacks. In politics, Lewis Tappan, William Jay, and William Lloyd Garrison searched desperately and without success for a truly Christian leader, an alternative to impious Andrew Jackson and the godless party he led.

Predictably, misgiving became ever more frequent among young evangelicals. They began to question their abilities, to rethink their choices of career, and to doubt the Christianity of the churches, seminaries, and benevolent societies. Just possibly, the nation was far more deeply mired in sin than anyone had imagined. Just possibly, parental formulas for godly reformation were fatally compromised. And, most disturbing of all, just possibly the idealist-reformer himself needed reforming— a new relationship with God, a new vision of his responsibility as a Christian American.

The powerful combination in the 1820s of Yankee conservatism, revivalist benevolence, New England upbringing, and social unrest was leading young evangelicals toward a genuinely radical vision. Given this setting, it hardly seems surprising that a militant abolitionist movement began to take shape. Opposition to slavery certainly constituted a dramatic affirmation of one's Christian identity and commitment to a life of Protestant purity. Economic exploitation, sexual license, gambling, drinking and dueling, disregard for family ties—all traits associated with slaveowning—could easily be set in bold contrast with the pure ideals of Yankee evangelicalism.

There were a few militant antislavery spokesmen in the upper south in the 1820s, but their influence on young New Englanders was negligible. The manumission societies organized largely by evangelical Quakers and Moravian Brethren in Tennessee, Kentucky, and other border areas were already collapsing at the start of New England's crusade for immediate emancipation. The southern antislavery movement's chief spokesman, editor Benjamin Lundy, had retreated northward from Tennessee. By 1829 he was living in Baltimore and had hired a zealous young editorial assistant from Newburyport, Massachusetts: William Lloyd Garrison.

The sudden emergence of immediate abolitionism in New England thus cannot be explained as a predictable offshoot of Yankee revivalism or a legacy from the upper south. Instead, one must emphasize the interaction between the rebellious feelings of these religious men and women and the events of the early 1830s. As the 1830s opened in an atmosphere of crisis, their attentions became intensely fixed on slavery. As in the early 1820s, the nation was again beset by black rebellions and threats of southern secession. Concurrently, events in England and in its sugar islands empire seemed to confirm the necessity of demanding the immediate emancipation of all slaves, everywhere. An unprecedented array of circumstances and jarring events suddenly converged on these anxious young people and launched them upon the lifetime task of abolishing slavery.

By far the most alarming was the ominous note of black militancy on which the new decade opened. In Boston in 1829, an ex-slave from North Carolina, David Walker, published the first edition of his famous *Appeal.* A landmark in black protest literature, Walker's *Appeal* condemned colonization as a white supremacist hoax, excoriated members of his own race for their passivity, and called, as a last resort, for armed resistance. "I do declare," wrote Walker, "that one good black man can put to death six white men." Whites have never hesitated to kill blacks, he advised, so "if you commence . . . do not trifle, for they will not trifle with you." Other events, even more shocking, were to follow. In 1831, William Lloyd Garrison, now living in Boston, issued a call for immediate emancipation in the *Liberator.* Soon after, Southampton County, Virginia, erupted in the bloody Nat Turner insurrection, the largest slave revolt in antebellum America. Still another massive slave rebellion broke out in British Jamaica in 1831. Coinciding with these racial traumas was the Nullification Crisis of 1831–32, a confrontation ignited by South Carolina's opposition to national tariff policy and by the deeper fear that the federal government might someday abolish slavery. Intent on preserving state sovereignty and hence slavery, South Carolina politicians led by John C. Calhoun temporarily defied national authority, threatened secession, and risked occupation of federal troops.

As these frightening events unfolded, young evangelicals cast aside their self-doubt. Unfocused discontent gave way to soul-wrenching commitments to eradicating the sin of slavery. The combined actions of Nat Turner, the South Carolina "Nullifiers," and David Walker suggested with dramatic force that slavery was the fundamental cause of society's degraded state. As Theodore D. Weld observed, the abolitionist cause "not only *overshadows* all others, but . . . absorbs them into itself. Revivals, moral Reform etc. will remain stationary until the temple is cleansed." The step-by-step solutions advocated by their parents suddenly appeared to invite only God's retribution. Like Garrison, Arthur Tappan, and many others, James G. Birney sealed his commitment to immediate abolition by decrying colonization. The Colonization Society, Birney charged, acted as "an opiate to the consciences" of those who would otherwise "feel deeply and keenly the sin of slavery."

In one sense, these sudden espousals of immediate abolition can be understood as a strategic innovation developed because of the manifest failures of gradualism. Slaveholders had certainly shown no sympathy to moderate schemes. In England, too, where immediatism was also gaining followers, the general public had remained unmoved by gradualist proposals. Demands for "immediate, unconditional, uncompensated emancipation" thus appealed to young American idealists—at least the slogan was free of moral qualifications. Indeed, in 1831 the British government, responding to immediatist demands, enacted a massive program of gradual, compensated emancipation in the West Indies. But, even more important, by dedicating themselves to immediatism, the young reformers performed acts of self-liberation akin to the experience of conversion.

By freeing themselves from the shackles of gradualism, American abolitionists had finally triumphed over their feelings of selfishness, unworthiness, and alienation. Now they were morally fit to take God's side in the struggle against all the worldliness, license, cruelty, and selfishness that slaveowning had come to embody. Immediatists sensed themselves involved in a cosmic drama, a righteous war to redeem a fallen nation. They now felt ready to make supreme sacrifices and prove their fitness in their new religion of antislavery. "Never were men called on to die in a holier cause," wrote Amos A. Phelps in 1835 as he began his first tour as an abolitionist lecturer. It was far better, he thought, to die "as the negro's plighted friend" than to "sit in silken security, the consentor to & abettor of the manstealer's sin."

The campaign for Protestant reassertion had thus brought forth a vibrant romantic radicalism. Orthodox evangelicals quite rightly recoiled in fear. Abolitionists now put their faith entirely in the individual's ability to recognize and redeem himself from sin. No stifling traditions, no restrictive loyalties to institutions, no timorous concern for moderation or self-interest should be allowed to inhibit the free reign of Christian conscience. In its fullest sense, the phrase "immediate emancipation" described a transformed state of mind dominated by God and wholly at war with slavery. "The doctrine," wrote Elizur Wright, Jr., in 1833, "may be thus briefly stated":

> It is the duty of the holders of slaves to restore them to their liberty, and to extend to them the full protection of the law . . . to restore to them the profits of their labors, . . . to employ them as voluntary laborers on equitable wages. Also it is the *duty* of all men . . . to proclaim this doctrine, to urge upon slaveholders *immediate emancipation,* so long as there is a slave—to agitate the consciences of tyrants, so long as there is a tyrant on the globe.

Embedded in this statement was a vision of a new America, a daring affirmation that people of both races could re-establish their relationships on the basis of justice and Christian brotherhood. Like many other Americans who took up the burdens of reform, abolitionists envisioned their cause as leading to a society reborn in Christian brotherhood. Emancipation, like temperance, women's rights and communitarianism, became synonymous with the redemption of mankind and the opening of a purer phase of human history.

Abolitionists constantly tried to explain that they were not expecting some sudden Day of Jubilee when, with a shudder of collective remorse, the entire planter class would abruptly strike the shackles from all two million slaves and beg their forgiveness. Emancipation, they expected, would be achieved gradually; still it must be immediately begun. Immediatists were also forced to rebut the recurring charge that their demand promoted emancipation by rebellion on the plantations. "Our objects are to save life, not destroy it," Garrison exclaimed in 1831. "Make the slave free and every inducement to revolt is taken away." Few Americans believed these disclaimers. Instead, most suspected that immediate emancipation would suddenly create a large and mobile free population of inferior blacks. Most in the north were quite content to discriminate harshly against their black neighbors while the slaves remained at a safe distance on faraway plantations. According to Alexis de Tocqueville, the unusually acute foreign observer of ante-bellum society of the early 1830s: "Race prejudice seems stronger in those states that have abolished slavery than in those states where it still exists, and nowhere is it more intolerant than in those states where it has never been known." White supremacy and support for slavery were thus inextricably bound up with all phases of American political, economic, and religious life. Immediatist agitation was bound to provoke hostility from nearly every part of the social order.

As we have seen, by the 1830s the northeast and midwest enjoyed a thriving trade with the south, and the nation's economic well-being had become firmly tied to slave labor. Powerful financial considerations could thus dictate that abolitionism be harshly suppressed. Religious denominations were also deeply enmeshed in slavery, for southerners were influential among the Methodists, Presbyterians, Anglicans, and Baptists. Little wonder that most clergymen vigorously rejected demands that their churches declare slaveholders in shocking violation of God's Law.

But by far the most consistent opponents of the abolitionist crusade were found in politics. Young reformers had long ago come to abhor what they saw as the hollow demagoguery and secularism of Jacksonian mass politics. By 1830 they were fully justified in adding the politician's unstinting support of slavery to their bill of particulars. As Richard H. Brown has shown, Jackson's Democratic Party was deliberately designed to uphold the planters' interests. Jacksonian ideology soon became synonymous with racism and antiabolition. In the north, men who aspired to careers in Democratic Party politics had to solicit the approval of slaveholding party chiefs like Amos Kendall, John C. Calhoun, and Jackson himself. When anti-Jacksonian dissidents finally coalesced into the Whig Party during the 1830s, they, too, relied upon this formula for getting votes and recruiting leaders. Obviously, neither party dared to alienate proslavery interests in the south or racist supporters in the north. Moreover, as the Missouri and Nullification controversies had shown, political debates about slavery caused party allegiances to break ominously along sectional lines. For these reasons, party loyalty meant the suppression of all discussions of slavery.

The challenges that the abolitionists faced as they began their crusade were thus enormous. So was their own capability for disruption, although they were hardly aware of it at first. The ending of slavery whether peacefully or violently would require great changes in American life. Yet, if immediate emancipation provoked fear and violent hostility, it was nevertheless a doctrine appropriate to the age. The evangelical outlook with its rejection of tradition and expedience both embodied and challenged the culture that had created it. In retrospect, moderate approaches to the problem of slavery hardly seemed possible in Jacksonian America.

As a result, immediatist goals were anything but limited. Abolitionists now proposed to transform hundreds of millions of dollars worth of slaves into millions of black citizens by eradicating two centuries of American racism. Nevertheless, they sincerely felt that they promoted a conservative enterprise, and in certain respects this was an understandable (if misleading) self-assessment. Their unqualified attacks on slavery were, as they understood them, simply emulations of well-established evangelical methods. The Temperance Society's assault on liquor and the revivalist's denunciation of unbelief had hardly been characterized by restraint. Besides, immediatists were simply proposing an ideal by which all Christians were to measure themselves. They were not planning bloody revolution. They relied solely on voluntary conversion and rejected violence. As agitators, they defined their task as restoring time-honored American freedoms to an unjustly deprived people. Except for their opposition to racism, they offered no criticism of ordinary Protestant values. Was it anarchy, they wondered, to urge that pure Christian morality replace what they believed was the sexual abandon of the slave quarters? "Are we then fanatics," Garrison asked, "because we cry, *Do not rob! Do not murder!?*"

In their own eyes, then, abolitionists were hardly behaving like incendiaries as they opened their crusade. In slaveholding they discovered the ultimate source of the moral collapse that so deeply disturbed them. The race violence of Nat Turner and the secession threats of the "Nullifiers" constituted evidence that the nation had jettisoned all her moral ballasts. But immediate abolition seemed to hold forth the promise of Christian reconciliation between races, sections, and individuals. All motive for race revolt, all reason for political strife, and all inducement for moral degeneracy would be swept away. Indeed, the alternative of silence only invited the further spread of anarchy in a nation that Garrison described in 1831 as already "full of the blood of innocent men, women and babies—full of adultery and concupiscence—full of blasphemy, darkness and woeful rebellion against God—full of wounds and bruises and putrefying sores." Abolitionists were thus filled "with burning earnestness" when they insisted, as Elizur Wright did, that "the instant abolition of the whole slave system is safe." Most other Americans remained firm in their suspicions to the contrary.

Nevertheless, the abolitionists launched their crusade on a note of glowing optimism. Armed with moral certitude, they were also completely naive politically. "The whole system of slavery will fall to pieces with a rapidity which will astonish," wrote Samuel E. Sewall, one of the first adherents to immediatism. Weld predicted in 1834 that complete equality for all blacks in the upper south was but two years away, and that "scores of clergymen in the slaveholding states . . . *are really with us.*" Anxious for the millennium, abolitionists had wholly misjudged the depth of northern racism, not to mention the extent of southern tolerance.

All the same, there was wisdom in the naïveté. Without this romantic faith that God would put all things right, abolitionists would have lacked the incentive and creative stamina necessary for sustained assaults against slavery. Moreover, by stressing intuition as a sure guide to reality, abolitionists made an unprecedented attempt to establish empathy with the slave. One result, to be sure, was racist sentimentalism, a not surprising outcome considering the gulf that separated a Mississippi field hand from an independently wealthy Boston abolitionist. Yet the abolitionists were trying hard to imagine what it was like to be stripped of one's autonomy, prevented from protecting one's family, and deprived of legal safeguards and the rewards of one's own labor. This view of slavery made piecemeal reform completely unacceptable. To give slaves better food, fewer whippings, and some education was not enough. They deserved immediate justice, not charity. So convinced, and certain of ultimate victory, abolitionists set out to induce each American citizen to repent the sin of slavery.

SOURCES

Commission to Theodore Dwight Weld, 1834

Abolitionists have often been pictured as rampant individualists who wanted to throw off the shackles of the existing social order. But, like other reformers of their day, most of them belonged to organizations that put a premium upon concerted action, the power of numbers, rather than individual initiative. The American Anti-Slavery Society, which was formed in 1833, wanted to build up massive followings, which through pressure-group tactics would force others in line. By 1838 the society had organized 1350 auxiliaries in the north. Here are the society's instructions to its most famous organizer, Theodore Dwight Weld.

AMERICAN ANTI-SLAVERY SOCIETY*

Commission to Theodore D. Weld

Dear Sir,

You are hereby appointed and commissioned, by the Executive Committee of the American Anti-Slavery Society, instituted at Philadelphia in 1833, as their Agent, for the space of one year commencing with the first day of January, 1834, in the State of Ohio and elsewhere as the Committee may direct.

The Society was formed for the purpose of awakening the attention of our whole community to the character of American Slavery, and presenting the claims and urging the rights of the colored people of the United States; so as to promote, in the most efficient manner, the immediate abolition of Slavery, and the restoration of our colored brethren to their equal rights as citizens.

For a more definite statement of the objects of your agency, and the methods of its prosecution, the Committee refer you to their printed "Particular Instructions," communicated to you herewith; a full acquaintance and compliance with which, according to your ability, you will, on accepting this commission, consider as indispensable.

The Committee welcome you as a fellow-laborer in this blessed and responsible work; the success of which will depend, in no small degree, under

*This commission is a printed form, with the name of Theodore Weld, the dates, etc., written in.

From Gilbert H. Barnes and Dwight L. Dumond, eds., *Letters of Theodore Dwight Weld, Angelina Grimké Weld, and Sarah Grimké, 1822–1844*, American Historical Association, Washington, D.C., 1934, pp. 124–128. Reprinted by permission.

God, on the results of your efforts. Their ardent desires for your success will continually attend you; you will have their sympathy in trials; and nothing, they trust, will be wanting, on their part, for your encouragement and aid.

They commend you to the kindness and co-operation of all who love Zion; praying that the presence of God may be with you, cheering your heart, sustaining you in your arduous labors, and making them a means of a speedy liberation of all the oppressed.

Given at the Society's Office, No. 130 Nassau-street, New-York, the twentieth day of February in the year of our Lord eighteen hundred and thirty-four.

Arthur Tappan
Chairman of the Executive Committee

Attest,
  E. Wright Jr.
  Secretary of Domestic Correspondence.

PARTICULAR INSTRUCTIONS

To Mr. T. D. Weld

Dear Sir—You have been appointed an Agent of the American Anti-Slavery Society; and will receive the following instructions from the Executive Committee, as a brief expression of the principles they wish you to inculcate, and the course of conduct they wish you to pursue in this agency.

The general principles of the Society are set forth in the Declaration, signed by the members of the Convention which formed it at Philadelphia, Dec. 7, 1833. Our object is, the overthrow of American slavery, the most atrocious and oppressive system of bondage that has ever existed in any country. We expect to accomplish this, mainly by showing to the public its true character and legitimate fruits, its contrariety to the first principles of religion, morals, and humanity, and its special inconsistency with our pretensions, as a free, humane, and enlightened people. In this way, by the force of truth, we expect to correct the common errors that prevail respecting slavery, and to produce a just public sentiment, which shall appeal both to the conscience and love of character, of our slaveholding fellow-citizens, and convince them that both their duty and their welfare require the immediate abolition of slavery.

You will inculcate every where, the great fundamental principle of IMMEDIATE ABOLITION, as the duty of all masters, on the ground that slavery is both unjust and unprofitable. Insist principally on the SIN OF SLAVERY, because our main hope is in the consciences of men, and it requires little logic to prove that it is always safe to do right. To question this, is to impeach the superintending Providence of God.

We reprobate the idea of compensation to slave holders, because it implies the right of slavery. It is also unnecessary, because the abolition of slavery will be an advantage, as free labor is found to be more profitable than the labor of slaves. We also reprobate all plans of expatriation, by whatever specious pretences covered, as a remedy for slavery, for they all proceed from prejudice against color; and we hold that the duty of the whites in regard to this cruel prejudice is not to indulge it, but to repent and overcome it.

The people of color ought at once to be emancipated and recognized as citizens, and their rights secured as such, equal in all respects to others, according to the cardinal principle laid down in the American Declaration of Independence. Of course we have nothing to do with any *equal* laws which the states may make, to prevent or punish vagrancy, idleness, and crime, either in whites or blacks.

Do not allow yourself to be drawn away from the main object, to exhibit a detailed PLAN of abolition; for men's consciences will be greatly relieved from the feeling of present duty, by any objections or difficulties which they can find or fancy in your plan. Let the *principle* be decided on, of immediate abolition, and the plans will easily present themselves. What ought to be done can be done. If the *great* question were decided, and if half the ingenuity now employed to defend slavery were employed to abolish it, it would impeach the wisdom of American statesmen to say they could not, with the Divine blessing, steer the ship through.

You will make yourself familiar with FACTS, for they chiefly influence reflecting minds. Be careful to use only facts that are well authenticated, and always state them with the precision of a witness under oath. You cannot do our cause a greater injury than by overstating facts. Clarkson's "Thoughts," and Stuart's "West India Question," are Magazines of facts respecting the safety and benefit of immediate emancipation. Mrs. Child's Book, Stroud's Slave Laws, Paxton's and Rankin's Letters, D. L. Child's Address, are good authorities respecting the character of American slavery. The African Repository and Garrison's Thoughts will show the whole subject of expatriation.

The field marked out by the Committee for your agency is the State of Ohio.

The Committee expect you to confine your labors to that field, unless some special circumstances call you elsewhere. And in such case you will confer with the Committee before changing your field, if time will allow. And if not, we wish immediate notice of the fact.

In traversing your field, you will generally find it wise to visit first several prominent places in it, particularly those where it is known our cause has friends. In going to a place, you will naturally call upon those who are friendly to our objects, and take advice from them. Also call on ministers of the gospel and other leading characters, and labor specially to enlighten them and secure their favor and influence. Ministers are the hinges of community, and ought to be moved, if possible. If they can be gained, much is gained. But if not, you will not be discouraged; and if not plainly inexpedient, attempt to obtain a house of worship; or if none can be had, some other convenient place—and hold a public meeting, where you can present our cause, its facts, arguments and appeals, to as many people as you can collect, by notices in pulpits and newspapers, and other proper means.

From Auxiliary Societies, both male and female, in every place where it is practicable. Even if such societies are very small at the outset, they may do much good as centres of light, and means of future access to the people. Encourage them to raise funds and apply them in purchasing and circulating anti-slavery publications gratuitously; particularly the Anti-Slavery Reporter, of which you will keep specimens with you, and which can always be had of the Society at $2.00 per 100. You are at liberty, with due discretion, to recommend other publications, *so far* as they advocate our views of immediate abolition. We hold ourselves responsible only for our own.

You are not to take up collections in your public meetings, as the practice often prevents persons from attending, whom it might be desirable to reach. Let this be stated in the public notice of the meeting. If you find individuals friendly to our views, who are able to give us money, you will make special personal application, and urge upon them the duty of liberally supporting this cause. You can also give notice of some place where those disposed can give you their donations. Generally, it is best to invite them to do this *the next morning.*

We shall expect you to write frequently to the Secretary for Domestic Correspondence, and give minute accounts of your proceedings and success. If you receive money for the Society, you will transmit it *by mail,* WITHOUT DELAY, to the Treasurer.

Always keep us advised, if possible, of the place where letters may reach you.

Believing as we do, that the hearts of all men are in the hand of Almighty God, we wish particularly to engage the prayers of all good men in behalf of our enterprise. Let them pray that *we* and our agents may have Divine guidance and zeal; and slave-holders, penitence; and slaves, patience; and statesmen, wisdom; so that this grand experiment of moral influence may be crowned with glorious and speedy success. Especially stir up ministers and others to the duty of making continual mention of the oppressed slaves in all social and public prayers. And as far as you can, procure the stated observance of the LAST MONDAY EVENING in every month, as a season of special prayer in behalf of the people of color.

We will only remind you, that the Society is but the almoner of the public— that the silver and the gold are the Lord's—that the amount as yet set apart by his people for promoting this particular object is small—our work is great and our resources limited—and we therefore trust that you will not fail to use a faithful economy in regard to the expenses of traveling, and reduce them as low as you can without impairing your usefulness.

The Anti-Slavery Record, 1835–1836

In 1835, thanks to a sudden reduction in the costs of printing, the American Anti-Slavery Society was able to flood the country with propaganda. Able agitators, abolitionists were among the first to use lithographs for political ends. Images of women being whipped or separated from their children and of men being beaten were the bread-and-butter of the antislavery message. Here are some of the pictographs that appeared on the front page of the Anti-Slavery Record, *the pamphlet with by far the greatest circulation.*

Anti-Slavery Record/
New York Public Library.

See p. 27.

A punishment, practised in the United States, for the crime of loving liberty.

Anti-Slavery Record/
New York Public Library.

Anti-Slavery Record/*New York Public Library.*

Anti-Slavery Record/*New York Public Library.*

Anti-Slavery Record/*New York Public Library.*

Anti-Slavery Record/*New York Public Library.*

"Fathers and Rulers" Petition

The abolitionists, like other reformers of the age, relied heavily on church-women. While lacking the right to vote, women were generally regarded to be inherently more moral than men, and hence their opinions on moral questions were highly respected. Capitalizing on this sentiment, women gathered thousands of signatures for massive petitions to Congress calling for the end of slavery in Washington, D.C. To shut off the flood, Congress in 1836 passed a "gag law," which was designed to keep the petitions from being read, printed, or considered by Congress. The law remained in effect until 1844. Here is one of the more famous "female petitions."

[NOVEMBER (?) 1834]

TO THE HON. SENATE AND HOUSE OF REPRESENTATIVES OF THE U. STATES, IN CONGRESS ASSEMBLED

Petition of Ladies resident in _____ County, State of Ohio.*
Fathers and Rulers of our Country,
Suffer us, we pray you, with the sympathies which we are constrained to feel as wives, as mothers, and as daughters, to plead with you in behalf of a long oppressed and deeply injured class of native Americans, residing in that portion of our country which is under your exclusive control. We should poorly estimate the virtues which ought ever to distinguish your honorable body could we anticipate any other than a favorable hearing when our appeal is to men, to philanthropists, to patriots, to the legislators and guardians of a Christian people. We should be less than women, if the nameless and unnumbered wrongs of which the slaves of our sex are made the defenseless victims, did not fill us with horror and constrain us, in earnestness and agony of spirit to pray for their deliverance. By day and night, their woes and wrongs rise up before us, throwing shades of mournful contrast over the joys of domestic life, and filling our hearts with sadness at the recollection of those whose hearths are desolate.

Nor do we forget, in the contemplation of their other sufferings, the intellectual and moral degradation to which they are doomed; how the soul formed

---

*This is a printed form. The signatures of the petitioners were to be secured separately and pasted upon the form, and the whole petition then mailed to a congressman in Washington. This was by far the most popular form for "female petitions" until 1840. Tens of thousands are in the files of the House of Representatives (boxes 85–126) in the Library of Congress. Except for short "sentence forms" distributed by the American Anti-Slavery Society during the period 1837–1840, it was the commonest form in the campaign.

From Gilbert H. Barnes and Dwight L. Dumond, eds., *Letters of Theodore Dwight Weld, Angelina Grimké Weld, and Sarah Grimké, 1822–1844,* American Historical Association, Washington, D.C., 1934, pp. 175–176. Reprinted by permission.

for companionship with angels, is despoiled and brutified, and consigned to ignorance, pollution, and ruin.

Surely then, as the representatives of a people professedly Christian, you will bear with us when we express our solemn apprehensions in the language of the patriotic Jefferson "we tremble for our country when we remember that God is just, and that his justice cannot sleep forever," and when in obedience to a divine command "we remember them who are in bonds as bound with them." Impelled by these sentiments, we solemnly purpose, the grace of God assisting, to importune high Heaven with prayer, and our national Legislature with appeals, until this Christian people abjure forever a traffic in the souls of men, and the groans of the oppressed no longer ascend to God from the dust where they now welter.

We do not ask your honorable body to transcend your constitutional powers, by legislating on the subject of slavery within the boundaries of any slaveholding State; but we do conjure you to abolish slavery in the District of Columbia where you exercise exclusive jurisdiction. In the name of humanity, justice, equal rights and impartial law, our country's weal, her honor and her cherished hopes we earnestly implore for this our humble petition, your favorable regard. If both in Christian and in heathen lands, Kings have revoked their edicts, at the intercession of woman, and tyrants have relented when she appeared a suppliant for mercy, surely we may hope that the Legislators of a free, enlightened and Christian people will lend their ear to our appeals, when the only boon we crave is the restoration of rights unjustly wrested from the innocent and defenseless.—And as in duty bound your petitioners will ever pray.

NAMES	NAMES

Theodore Dwight Weld

Slavery as It Is, 1839

The most impressive antislavery indictment was compiled by Theodore Dwight Weld, his wife, Angelina, and her sister, Sarah Grimké. The two women spent six months going through thousands upon thousands of southern newspapers, looking for items in which slaveholders effectively condemned themselves. Weld then assembled the clippings into a book, Slavery as It Is: The Testimony of a Thousand Witnesses, *which was published in 1839 and quickly sold 22,000 copies. Here is an excerpt from that book.*

The slaves are often branded with hot irons, pursued with firearms and *shot*, hunted with dogs and torn by them, shockingly maimed with knives, dirks, &c.; have their ears cut off, their eyes knocked out, their bones dislocated and bro-

From Theodore Dwight Weld, *American Slavery as It Is*, American Anti-Slavery Society, New York, 1839, pp. 79–81.

ken with bludgeons, their fingers disfigured with scars and gashes, *besides* those made with the lash.

We shall adopt, under this head, the same course as that pursued under previous ones,—first give the testimony of the slaveholders themselves, to the mutilations, &c. by copying their own graphic descriptions of them, in advertisements published under their own names, and in newspapers published in the slave states, and, generally, in their own immediate vicinity. We shall, as heretofore, insert only so much of each advertisement as will be necessary to make the point intelligible.

TESTIMONY

"Ranaway, a Negro woman and two children; a few days before she went off, *I burnt her with a hot iron*, on the left side of her face, *I tried to make the letter M.*"

"Ranaway a Negro man named Henry, *his left eye out*, some scars from a *dirk* on and under his left arm, and *much scarred* from the whip."

"One hundred dollars reward for a Negro fellow Pompey, 40 years old, he is *branded* on the *left jaw.*"

"Ranaway a Negro named Arthur, has a considerable *scar* across his *breast* and *each arm*, made by a knife; loves to talk much of the goodness of God."

"Ranaway a Negro named Mary, has a small scar over her eye, *a good many teeth missing*, the letter A. *is branded on her cheek and forehead.*"

"Ranaway a Negro named Hambleton, *limps* on his left foot where he was *shot* a few weeks ago, while runaway."

"Ranaway a Negro boy name Mose, he has a *wound* in the right shoulder near the backbone, which was occasioned by *a rifle shot.*"

"Was committed to jail a Negro man, says his name is Josiah, his back very much scarred by the whip, and *branded on the thigh and hips, in three or four places,* thus (J.M.) the *rim of his right ear has been bit or cut off.*"

"Ranaway from the plantation of James Surgette, the following Negroes, Randal, *has one ear cropped;* Bob, *has lost one eye;* Kentucky Tom, *has one jaw broken.*"

"Was committed, a Negro man, has a *scar* on his right side by a burn, one on his knee, and one on the calf of his leg *by the bite of a dog.*"

"Fifty dollars reward, for the Negro Jim Blake—has a *piece cut out of each ear*, and the middle finger of the left hand cut off to the second joint."

"Ranaway, the mulatto wench Mary—has a *cut on the left arm, a scar on the shoulder, and two upper teeth missing.*"

"Ranaway, my man Fountain—has *holes in his ears*, a *scar* on the right side of his forehead—has been *shot in the hind parts of his legs*—is marked on the back with the whip."

CHAPTER 12

Western Expansion

Andrew Jackson and his colleagues were anxious to silence the abolitionists and to keep slavery out of politics. But at the same time they were zealous expansionists. Arguing that it was God's will for the United States to expand over North America, Jackson and his followers drove the Indians off their ancestral lands in Georgia, Alabama, Mississippi, and other states in the 1830s, annexed Texas in 1845, secured by treaty much of the vast Oregon country in 1846, and took California and the southwest from Mexico in 1848. Jacksonian expansionism doubled the size of the country, but the process left ugly scars. Force, fraud, and murder were necessary to get choice Indian lands. And war was necessary to get lands from Mexico.

Expansion also brought slavery into the center of American politics. What was to become of the "new country"? Was it to become a covey of slave states—or free states? Texas was admitted to the Union in 1845 as a slave state, with the right to subdivide into as many as four additional states. Having lost Texas to slavery, antislavery forces in Congress were determined to keep slavery out of the territory seized from Mexico during the Mexican War. In 1846 an obscure Pennsylvania congressman named David Wilmot added to a money bill a proviso declaring that none of the territory acquired from Mexico should ever be open to slavery. Although solid opposition from the south, plus crucial votes from some northern Democrats, killed the Wilmot Proviso, it was added to bill after bill. It was never adopted, but it infuriated southern congressmen, who became angrier still when California in 1850 gained admission to the Union as a free state. The issue of slavery in the territories caused trouble time and again, snapping the bonds of union, shattering the national political parties, and by 1861 splitting the country itself into two warring nations.

INTERPRETIVE ESSAY

William L. Barney

The Quest for Room

It was one thing for politicians in Washington to debate the future of the west, and another for New England and New York reformers to see the west as a fateful breeding ground for slavery. But what of the southerners themselves, the men who actually owned the slaves? Many historians have argued that the west was really irrelevant, that no white southerner in his right mind would have thought seriously of taking slaves into Nebraska, let alone California or Arizona. But another argument, represented in the following essay by William L. Barney, holds that the west was *important to the slaveholders as a place where they might transport their "peculiar institution."*

The history of slavery in the south was largely the story of its expansion. This expansion, from the tidewater of Virginia and the Carolinas in the late seventeenth century to the river valleys of eastern Texas by the mid-nineteenth century, enabled successive generations of southerners to carry slavery into new territories. These surges of growth not only were converted into political power in Washington through increased representation but also satisfied two basic internal needs of the south. Additional slave territory sustained the economic viability of slavery by providing fresh land to replace the exhausted soil of the older plantation regions, creating markets for the sale of surplus and agriculturally unprofitable slaves from the upper south, and enlarging opportunities for both the slaveholders and those striving to attain that status. Moreover, the diffusion of slaves through expansion permitted southerners to avoid the fundamental problem of how to maintain control over a growing number of slaves confined to a closed area. The slaves had to be kept ignorant and tied to the land, because urbanization and industrialization entailed too grave a risk of slackened discipline and eventual race warfare. But a given amount of land subjected to an exploitive agriculture could support both whites and blacks for only a limited period before losing its fertility. Meanwhile, the concentration of slaves would grow ever denser until it reached unmanageable proportions. Soon— within a generation, some southerners prophesied—the master would be fleeing his slaves. This was the southern dilemma. The continual maturation of slavery within a fixed geographical area created class and racial stresses that could be relieved only through expansion. The extension of slavery, in turn, generated powerful opposition, capped in 1860 by the triumph of the Republican party, which was pledged to the strict containment of slavery within its existing limits. For the south, the dilemma had become a question of survival.

From William L. Barney, *The Road to Secession: A New Perspective on the Old South,* Praeger, New York, 1972, pp. 6–17. Reprinted by permission of William L. Barney.

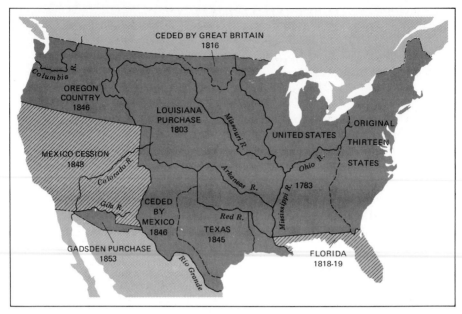

Westward Expansion.

LAND AS THE ECONOMIC ELIXIR

Of the many myths spawned by the plantation legend of the old south, few are as alluring, or as deceptive, as the languorous, timeless image of the white-columned plantation, the homestead of the planter—that polished aristocrat with deep ties to the land, moving with grace and ease in a milieu of wealth, stability, and refinement. In fact, most planters were grasping parvenus, and their homes were simply overgrown log cabins. But what most distorts reality in this image is the absence of a sense of time and movement. It was precisely the restlessness and dynamism of most planters that attracted the attention of contemporaries. Thomas Cobb, a leading jurist of ante-bellum Georgia, described the planters as a class that was "never settled. Such a population is almost nomadic." Cobb explained this mobility by noting that the prime determinant of a planter's wealth and status was not his land but his slaves. As a result, his surplus income was invested in more slaves rather than in improvements to the land.

> The homestead is valued only so long as the adjacent lands are profitable to cultivation. The planter himself having no local attachments, his children inherit none. On the contrary, he encourages in them a disposition to seek new lands. His valuable property (his slaves) are easily removed to fresh lands, much more easily than to bring the fertilizing materials to the old.

Mobility was characteristic of all southerners and appears to have been a function of economic class. In Jefferson County, Mississippi, an alluvial planting area on the banks of the Mississippi, about 87 percent of the nonslaveholders left the county during the 1850s. This percentage dropped among slaveholders in proportion to the number of slaves held, until it reached a low of 17 percent for those owning 100 slaves or more. The main flow of migration was from the worn-out lands of the Southern Atlantic states to the virgin soils of the southwest and across Louisiana into Texas. By 1860, South Carolina, an older state, had lost to emigration nearly half of all white natives born after 1800. (The annual and even seasonal movement was also quite heavy, but, because of gaps in the census returns, it cannot be measured.) Writing from the newly opened Alabama frontier in the mid-1830s, a planter's daughter noted that there were "a great many persons moving away from the place and going to the Choctaw [P]urchase and [a] great many coming in which keeps the number pretty much the same."

Whole counties were virtually depopulated by the Texas land fever, only to be refilled by a new wave of settlers. So prevalent was the wanderlust that many resorted to religious metaphor or cited positive secular values to explain their drive. In explaining his lifestyle, which had seen him constantly on the move, the yeoman farmer Gideon Linecum pointed to his "belief and faith in the pleasure of frequent change of country." Eli Lide, a planter's son who had moved to Alabama from South Carolina in the 1830s, rationalized his move to Texas twenty years later in terms of "something within me [that] whispers onward onward and urges me on like a prisoner who has been 58 years and idles in his Lord['js vineyard and lived on his bounty and made no returns for the favors received."

Southern institutions were transplanted across the Appalachians with but minimal disruptions. Planters frequently sent ahead a younger son or a trusted overseer with a few field hands to stake out the new territory and clear the land. When the planter arrived with his wagons, livestock, family, and slaves, he quickly re-established the community leadership to which he was accustomed. He assumed the responsibility of meeting the frontier's rudimentary cultural needs by hiring private tutors, perhaps setting up one of the few schools, and donating land or funds for the upkeep of an imported minister. In a few years, his slaves would have carved out of the wilderness the plantation on which his economic primacy rested. Finally, as long as he catered to the democratic sensibilities of the yeoman farmers, he could be virtually assured of political influence and, even, office. No concessions of substance were required, only of style. For example, it was always politically wise to express antiaristocratic sentiments and to show an acceptably egalitarian spirit in one's personal dealings, no matter what one's natural inclinations. These were the rules of the game, and to violate them brought opprobrium—as one Virginia planter newly arrived on Mississippi discovered. A local farmer, observing that the good gentleman disdained soiling his hands, did not hesitate to tell him that, if he had "taken hold of a plough" and worked by the farmer's side, his help would have been welcomed, but "to see him sitting up on his horse with his gloves on, directing his Negroes how to work," was not to the farmer's taste. Most planters learned the rules soon enough. Generally speaking, then, there was a remarkably successful transfer of the prior structure of institutions and leadership from the old south of Jefferson to the newer one of Jefferson Davis.

A potential source of conflict in the spread of the plantation was class competition for the better lands. This was usually not a problem, however, because the emigrants, naturally enough, sought out a region similar in soil and climate to what they had left behind. Traditionally, the yeomanry had avoided the heavy, sticky prairie soils and the wet, marshy bottomlands. These areas were thought to be unhealthy and required a much greater initial investment to cultivate than the lighter soils in the uplands or the sandy loam back on the ridges. As a result, when the southwest was opened up, much of the prairie and alluvial soils, the most productive and fertile in the south, were left by default to the planters. Where competition did exist, it was usually short-lived. The average farmer was a speculator. For him, it was good business to enter a new region, put up a log cabin, clear the forest and make other improvements, and then sell out for a profit after a few years. If a wealth planter should want the land, all the better. With plenty of land to the west, one could repeat the process several times in a lifetime.

The expansion of the south meant a continual renewal of slave society. Yet, southerners always had the nagging doubt that the process itself had not solved any problems but only perpetuated them. The doubt, akin to a fear of overdependence, can be understood by looking at the economic forces that fueled the south's search for land.

The nature of plantation agriculture and the consistently low ratio of land to labor costs explain much of the south's outward thrust. Besides initially requiring large units of land, staple-crop production on the plantations exhausted the soil at an alarming rate. Throughout most of the ante-bellum period, good land was so cheap and available in such quantity, especially relative to slave labor, that it was more profitable to ruin a plantation, pick up stakes, and start anew on virgin soil than to practice soil-conserving agriculture through crop rotation, deep plowing, and the use of fertilizers. Soil erosion and sterility became serious problems not only in scattered localities but in entire districts. By the early 1850s, the plantation belt of middle Georgia was described as a region of "red old hills stripped of their native growth and virgin soil, and washed with deep gullies, with here and there patches of Bermuda grass, and stunted pine shrubs, struggling for a scanty subsistence on what was one of the richest soils in America." Before 1860, the supposedly inexhaustible new cotton lands of the southwest had already exhibited the "painful signs of senility and decay" familiar to residents of the seaboard states. The complaint of a Georgia editor in 1858 that from the Chesapeake to the Mississippi there was "something fundamentally wrong in southern agriculture" was little more than a stock refrain.

Within a generation, the planters monopolized the agricultural wealth of any given area with the land and transportation facilities suitable for plantation agriculture. Five percent of the south's farmers owned 36 percent of the region's agricultural wealth; the poorest 50 percent of all farmers owned only 6 percent of the land. Indeed, even in the uplands and pine barrens—regions where the plantation never took root and that were supposedly the haven of the small farmer—a slaveholding elite controlled more land and more valuable land than the majority of the yeomanry. With their large labor force, extensive credit arrangements, and the capital resources to buy and utilize the best lands, the planters enjoyed competitive advantages over their small farmer neighbors and gradually were able to displace them.

This encroachment of the planter was not a matter of economic necessity only. As much as the planter needed fresh land to replace what he had destroyed or as a hedge for the future, he was also concerned about the security problems of having his slaves come into contact with nonslaveholders. The poorer whites were accused of interfering with slave discipline by setting an example of shiftlessness and by encouraging the slaves to steal plantation property to exchange for liquor and cheap trinkets. A Louisiana sugar planter told Frederick Law Olmsted, perhaps the most perceptive of all northern travelers in the south, that he wanted to buy out all the poor whites living around his plantation.

> It was better that negroes never saw anybody off their own plantation; that they had no intercourse with other white men than their owner or overseer; especially, it was best that they should not see white men who did not command their respect, and whom they did not always feel to be superior to themselves, and able to command them.

Wasteful agricultural practices, monopolistic patterns of land ownership, and displacement of the yeomanry combined to create the south's land hunger. Down to the 1850s, there had always been a new cotton frontier—whether in the Georgia-Carolina uplands before the War of 1812, the prairies of Alabama and Mississippi in the Jacksonian period, or the river valleys of Arkansas and Texas just before and after the Mexican War—to satisfy this hunger and prevent social tensions from building up. "The way we have been able to give land to the lacklanders, to extend this great country, and to supply the landless with land, has been by the extension of the empire by arms and by money," boasted Senator Robert Toombs of Georgia, as he argued in 1859 for the acquisition of Cuba. Even the moderate Jefferson Davis claimed an economic right of expansion: "We at the South are an agricultural people, and we require an extended territory. Slave labor is a wasteful labor, and it therefore requires a still more extended territory than would the same pursuits if they could be prosecuted by the more economical labor of white men."

THE FAILURE OF EXPANSIONISM

The 1850s witnessed a widening gap between the south's desire to gain more territory and her ability to do so within the Union. The decade opened with the loss of California to the free-soil north. California was the great prize in the lands recently wrested from Mexico. Already noted for its deep ocean ports and its rich valley agriculture, the area became, with the discovery of gold, a mecca for fortune-seeking Americans.

The antislavery forces, with some backing from southern Whigs, argued that the United States was honor-bound to respect the Mexican decrees that had prohibited slavery in the provinces of California and New Mexico. Southern Democrats reacted scornfully to this position. They stressed that the south had contributed more than her fair share of men and arms to the conquest of these territories and thus had a military, as well as a constitutional, right to carry slaves there. Racial stereotypes were employed. "Do they mean to assert," wondered Senator Albert Gallatin Brown of Mississippi, "that the victorious and proud-hearted American is to go, cap in hand, to the miserable, cringing Mexican peon, and ask his permission to settle on the soil won by the valor of our troops at Buena Vista, or before the walls of Mexico?"

To arguments that the climate and soil of these territories were unsuitable for slavery, that the institution was debarred by a "decree of Nature," southerners responded by citing the great profitability of slavery in mining. "Slave labor is never more profitably employed than in mining," said Brown in a letter to his constituents, "and you may judge whether slaves could be advantageously introduced into that country, when I inform you . . . that an able-bodied negro is worth in California from two to six thousand dollars per annum." The slaves were so valuable in the mines, contended a Virginia senator, that, unless the black race were excluded altogether from California, slaveholders could bring them in by the thousands under contracts calling for their manumission within a few years, work them until then, and still show a large profit. Senator Jefferson Davis of Mississippi was certain that, with irrigation, southern California could support a lucrative commercial agriculture in cotton, grapes, and olives. This agriculture, however, required slave labor. The individual pioneer could not settle upon this dry land and support his family with his own exertions as he had traditionally done in the more humid east. Associated labor was needed to establish and maintain the irrigation system. Because Mexican peonage was clearly inconsistent with American law, Davis concluded that black slavery was the only solution.

The admission of California as a free state was a bitter blow to the south. A small but strategically placed proslavery wing of the California Democracy continued to fight for the introduction of slavery and even succeeded by its control of the judiciary in allowing a limited use of slave labor in the mines until the mid-1850s. But the battle had been lost. Although they alleged improper executive interference by the administration of President Taylor with the statehood movement, southerners generally blamed their defeat on the constant antislavery agitation of northerners and the refusal of slaveholders to risk their property under such unsettling conditions. Had it not been for this agitation, insisted Representative Thomas Clingman of North Carolina, "our southern slaveholders would have carried their negroes into the mines of California in such numbers, that I have no doubt but that the majority there would have made it a slaveholding State."

Clingman, however, underestimated the extent of antislavery feelings. S. R. Thurston, the territorial representative from Oregon, explained that white Californians had excluded slavery not from any hostility to the south, nor even from opposition to slavery in the abstract, but solely out of economic self-interest: They feared that the slaveholders would monopolize the wealth of the mines. "One man might work a thousand [slaves], and consequently, on the ground that a slave will do as much work as a white man, the southerner might make a thousand dollars to the northerner['s] one." The miners would never permit such an aristocracy of wealth to arise. So, it was fortunate, Thurston continued, that slavery had never gained legal protection; for, if any man had taken large numbers of slaves into the mines, "they would have been cut down—yes, sir, cut down—cut down by white men. . . . To have maintained slave labor there, during this last year, would have required a standing army of fifty thousand men; and whenever it is desired to redden those mountain streams with human gore, take your slaves there."

Kansas, although economically less significant than California, represented an even more serious psychological defeat for the south. Badly misjudging the strength and sensitivity of the antislavery movement, many southerners had deluded themselves into believing that the Kansas-Nebraska Act, by expressly revoking the Missouri Compromise line of 36° 30′, would take the issue of territorial slavery out of politics and allow the settlers to decide the question for themselves. Even Alexander Stephens of Georgia, a very cautious and moderate politician and a leading congressional spokesman for the Whigs, interpreted the act as a moral victory for the south by its removal of the stigma of slavery exclusion. Far more perceptive was the comment of a Tennessee congressman who predicted that passage of the act would result in a "most impolitic and mad moment for the South, no practical good can come of it because there is none in it."

Infuriated by the organized efforts of some abolitionists groups to send free-soil settlers into Kansas, the south committed herself to an ideological contest that she could not win. Most slaveholders simply were not interested in the flat, windy prairies of Kansas. Hemp and tobacco could be grown profitably in the eastern river valleys of the region, as they were in neighboring Missouri, but few planters wanted to hazard their slaves for such limited economic returns. Although led by slaveholders, the Southern bands that made the long trek to Kansas were composed mainly of land-hungry adventurers. These men were outnumbered by the free-soil settlers, more mobile than slave labor, who moved rapidly into the territory, and who were determined to keep slavery out.

Southern Democrats fought desperately to gain legal recognition of slavery in Kansas. Entrenched among the territorial office-holders, the proslavery forces pushed through the Kansas Lecompton Constitution in a boycotted election. This document, which could not be amended for several years, protected the slave property already within the territory. In attempting to bring Kansas into the Union under this constitution, the southern Democrats downplayed economic motives. They insisted that the issue was whether slavery would ever again be permitted to expand. John Slidell of Louisiana told the Senate that the south was "struggling for the maintenance of a principle, barren, it is true, of present practical fruits, but indispensable for our future protection." If Kansas was refused admission because slavery "nominally and temporarily exists there, what may we expect," he asked, "when application shall be made by a State of which it will be a real and enduring institution?" Representative William Porcher Miles of South Carolina wanted Kansas as a "wall of defense" for Missouri—and for the two additional proslavery votes she would provide in the Senate. In a racist appeal, Brown of Mississippi accused the free-soilers of wanting to force a government upon the white settlers and thereby create a free Kansas that "makes the negro free by enslaving the white man; but my free Kansas makes the white man free, and leaves the negro where the Constitution left him—subject to the authority of his master." As to charges of corruption and irregularities surrounding the Lecompton Constitution, southern Democrats replied that these were no worse than similar problems that had beset California. "Are we of the South to be made to see California hurried into the Union against all law and all precedent *because she is a free state* and Kansas subjected to the rigors of the inquisition because she *has a chance* of being a slave state?" demanded a Mississippi congressman.

In March 1855, David Atchison, a Missouri senator and leader in the struggle to open up Kansas for slavery, offered an early version of the domino theory: "If we win we carry slavery to the Pacific Ocean; if we fail we lose Missouri, Arkansas, and Texas and all the territories; the game must be played boldly. I know that the Union as it exists is in the other scale, but I am willing to take the holyland." In the view of Python, a pseudonymous contributors to *DeBow's Review* in the late 1850s, all the dominoes would fall if the south lost Kansas; for the entire western flank of slavery would be endangered. The emboldened abolitionists, he warned, would first attack slavery in Missouri, then move south into the Oklahoma Indian territories and Texas, and finally turn west into New Mexico and Arizona. The upper south would be the next target, and soon slavery would end up confined to the gulf states.

Southern Whigs, on the other hand, while conceding that the admission of new slave states was vital to southern interests, refused to believe that Kansas represented slavery's Armageddon. For one thing, the south, they argued, was capable of standing on higher ground than the Lecompton Constitution, which one Whig denounced as the "most barefaced fraud and cheating the world ever saw." For another, few of them expected slavery to take permanent hold in Kansas. Senator John Bell of Tennessee, for example, pointed out, in the spring of 1858, that the number of slaves in Kansas had declined in the previous year from about three hundred to no more than one hundred.

In the end, the south was hoisted with her own petard. If the eventual admission of Kansas as a free state was a humiliating defeat, it was largely because too many southerners had made the issue a test of sectional strength and determination. "It will be useless to attempt explanations and excuses, we are condemned, and I think justly," wrote a Georgia judge to Alexander Stephens in June 1857. "We have made the people believe it will be a slave state and we ought to make it good or not assume to hold the reins of power."

Cuba and Mexico offered unique advantages to southern expansionists. The former was already a slave society, and the latter seemed ripe for the taking. Although the unyielding Republican opposition to the expansion of slavery was sufficient to block most designs on these areas, internal resistance within the south was itself a major deterrent.

The pro-Cuban forces were centered in the Democratic party, and they had some support from the northern wing of the party, as exemplified by James Buchanan's acquiescence in the Ostend Manifesto of 1854. In this declaration, three American foreign ministers crudely served warning on Spain that the United States meant to have Cuba. Many of their arguments would sound familiar a century later. Cuba, lying just ninety miles off Florida, was deemed the key to the commerce and defenses of the Caribbean. But, of course, slavery was the overriding issue. "I want Cuba, and I know that sooner or later we must have it. . . . I want Tamaulipas, Potosi, and one or two other Mexican States; and I want them all for the same reason—for the planting or spreading of slavery," announced Albert Gallatin Brown in a speech at Hazlehurst, Mississippi. Cuba was to be the linchpin in a tropical empire founded on outright annexation or on the creation of satellite states. This empire, by giving the south a virtual monopoly over the production of tropical goods, would ensure the perpetuation of slavery.

The annexationists charged that the British were scheming to effect emancipation in Cuba. Furthermore, they warned that the unstable Spaniards might decree emancipation in order to punish the rebellious Creole planters or to make the island unattractive to Americans. A free black government in Cuba was depicted as a threat to slave security all along the Gulf Coast. "Indeed," in the vivid phrase of John Van Evrie, a proslavery propagandist, "Cuba would be a volcano of 'free negroism,' constantly vomiting fire and blood on the neighboring coast." Annexation not only would eliminate this threat but would also prove a boon to the Cuban slaves. Stephen Mallory of Key West assured his Senate colleagues that, under the paternalism of a southern master, "the plantation negro in Cuba would be what he is in Florida, the freest from disease and care, the happiest and the most enduring of his race on the face of the earth."

The southern opposition, once again led by the Whigs, contended that if Cuban sugar were admitted duty-free, the sugar planters of Louisiana, Texas, and Florida would be ruined. These planters depended on tariff protection for their economic survival. If hurt by Cuban competition, they might shift their resources to cotton production, thus depressing the price of that staple. The Whigs stressed that Cuba, unlike Texas in the 1840s, was a settled, heavily populated country that had no room for southern emigrants. The living conditions of the slaves would improve under American rule, but this would result in an even higher population density, which could not absorb the south's own rapidly increasing slave population. "We want land without people on it, and not land and people together," said a Tennessee representative. The problems of assimilating the Cuban people were seen as insurmountable. Their language, religion, and extraction differed from ours, stressed Senator John Thompson of Kentucky, "and our people have regarded them as aliens and outlaws from the pale of humanity and civilization. . . . Saying nothing about color, I think I have been at more respectable weddings than it would be to bring her into the household." The Republicans agreed. Cuban whites were "ignorant, vicious, and priest-ridden," according to one Republican senator, and another wondered what the United States would do with the 200,000 free blacks on the island.

The Whigs could not see how Cuban annexation would strengthen slavery. The old fear of the future of slavery in the upper south was revived. If, as most people expected, the African slave trade with Cuba were prohibited under the Americans, the planters would turn to the upper south to replenish their labor supply and thereby hasten the abolitionizing of these states. One Whig congressman based his opposition on the ground that he did not want to see the area of slavery contracted. Because Spain hated and feared the United States, he reasoned, she would spitefully free the Cuban slaves if she ever became convinced that the island was about to fall into American hands. On the other hand, if Cuba, by some unexpected stroke of good fortune, were acquired with slavery intact, the Whigs foresaw an explosion of antislavery agitation. England and France, suspecting that the United States coveted, and would therefore try to seize, other West Indian islands, would be poised for war.

Despite considerable influence within the Pierce and Buchanan administrations, the Cuban annexationists got nowhere. Their most flamboyant leader, Governor John Quitman of Mississippi, was in constant difficulty with federal authorities over his open defiance of the neutrality laws through his filibustering activities. Quitman was convinced that the south would be able to expand within the Union only if she forced a drastic revision of these neutrality statutes, which barred Americans from private military enterprises against other sovereign powers. Then, southern armies, privately financed and recruited, would be free, he hoped, to carry slavery into the Caribbean and Central America. Quitman was immensely popular in Mississippi, but most southerners rejected his dramatic program. After all, even in the case of Cuba, the expansionists had not resolved certain paradoxes. On the one hand, they predicted that, as a result of the closing of the African slave trade and of American paternalism, the Cuban slave population would be better treated and would increase rapidly by natural causes. With a longer life expectancy, their value would rise, and this, in turn, would inflate the production costs of Cuban sugar, making it more competitive with American sugar. Yet, if the slave population grew after annexation, the island could hardly serve as the outlet the south demanded for her own increasing numbers of slaves.

For some, Mexico could serve as that outlet. In a speech before Congress, Representative O. R. Singleton of Mississippi reasoned that, because there was no settled government in Mexico, the United States had every right to intervene to promote order and set up a stable government. And, "when we have wound it up, there being no better heirs than ourselves, we will be compelled to hold that territory." Such altruism had its rewards. Much of Mexico, Singleton declared, was suitable for cotton, rice, and sugar cultivation. The south would have her outlet. "In my opinion we must, and we are compelled to, expand in that direction, and thus perpetuate it [slavery]—a hundred or a thousand years it may be."

In 1858, William Burwell of Virginia, in urging Senator R. M. T. Hunter of Virginia to exert pressure for a more aggressive Mexican policy, suggested that the acquisition of all Mexico could serve both as a popular issue for the next presidential election and as a means for the south to re-establish her political equality within the Union.

> . . . you have within your grasp a country accessible, abounding in all the metals and staples which civilised man most values, and a territory so extensive as that you can by only promoting the existing communities of Mexico to an equality with the present members of the Union preserve the balance in the Council of States, and so guarantee the peculiar rights of those States of which you are one of the guardians and representatives.

Burwell was confident that southern whites could easily control the racially mixed population. Movement into Mexico would be relatively easy on the railroads, and, with the telegraph, communications would be no problem. In that sense, Mexico was no farther away from Washington than Alabama or Tennessee had been twenty years earlier. If Mexico were not won for slavery, Burwell contended, it would be abolitionized by the north. "And if the worst should befall us could we not cut loose from the Union, throw an emigrant army into Mexico and make it as safe as Texas?" There was no alternative. "The North has more states and more territory than the South. It has the immigration of Europe to aid it. Your subjugation is as certain as the unrelenting operation of these great causes can render it." Out of self-protection, the South must "seize upon all the territory which produces those great staples of social necessity which the world cannot go without. Do so and you are safe."

Southern Democrats did implement a pale replica of the Singleton-Burwell program. The Buchanan administration tried to purchase the northern Mexican states or at least establish a protectorate over them, to extract commercial concessions, and to win diplomatic recognition of the right of the United States to intervene directly in Mexican affairs. These approaches, which met with some success, were held back by the same racial antipathies that had defeated the All-Mexico movement in the aftermath of the Mexican War. This racism was common to nearly all Americans. To Senator A. H. Sevier of Arkansas, the Mexicans were "a people bigoted, superstitious, cruel and ignorant; crossed, in the first place, in blood with the Moor and Spaniard, and recrossed with the negro and Indian." Representative C. Delano of Ohio believed that this intermixture produced a "slothful, indolent, ignorant race of beings." In his Barnwell, South Carolina, speech of 1858, Senator James Hammond used these racial slurs in denouncing any effort to take slavery into Mexico. Not only were Mexicans incapable of self-government, he asserted, but they could not even sustain slavery. Moreover, any attempt to incorporate them into the Union would result in a loss of racial purity.

> Sweep in Mexico at present, and it is the beginning of amalgamation. That is a people of mixed race and blood. So far from marking a line of discrimination between black and white, it is almost utterly obliterated, and would step over, and gradually spread itself over, and instead of aiding this country, debauch it.

There was no better indication of the difficulties, if not outright futility, plaguing the expansionists than the opposition within the south to the reopening of the African slave trade. There were many factors behind the opposition: the vested interest of the upper south in high slave prices; fear of losing racial control by importing savage, heathen Africans; the wish to avoid agitating such a divisive issue; the threat of lower-class discontent if wages were severely depressed by cheap slave competition; and the conviction that the trade was morally wrong. These factors combined to hamstring the expansionists, for southerners of both parties agreed that, without a surplus of cheap slave labor to throw into the territorial competition with free labor, the south had little chance of adding any more slave states. "This great truth seems to take the people by surprise," wrote the Georgia Whig Alexander Stephens. "Some shrink from it as they would from death. Still it is as true as death." Albert Gallatin Brown realized this truth, but, ever sensitive to the land hunger of his piney-woods constituency and aware that land prices in Mississippi had more than doubled during the 1850s, he demanded more land before the trade was reopened. "If . . . labor is trenching, is close upon the lands—I mean lands worth cultivating—then we ought to get more land before we get more labor, since labor without land will be a burden rather than a profit."

The positions of Stephens and Brown were irreconcilable as long as the south remained in the Union. The south needed the slave trade in order to expand, but, even if the north consented to the reopening of the trade, the south feared that she had insufficient land on which to support the additional slaves. As an independent country, however, she would no longer face the political necessity of matching the northern expansion of free labor with her slaves and, even without reviving the African slave trade, could stake out additional slave territory to be occupied whenever economic pressures dictated. . . .

SOURCES

The Kansas-Nebraska Act, 1854

Was there any way to quiet the slavery controversy? Senator Stephen A. Douglas, the north's leading Democrat, thought he had a way. In his eagerness to organize Kansas and Nebraska country, the Illinois senator gave in to southern demands and in 1854 sponsored a bill that specifically repealed the Missouri Compromise of 1820, which barred slavery north of 36° 30'. Douglas proposed that the fate of the territories be decided by "popular sovereignty." Under this system the actual settlers would have the opportunity to vote on slavery, either approving it or prohibiting it.

Below is a map of the country after the Kansas-Nebraska Act was passed by Congress. Do you think the 36° 30' line was a real barrier to slavery or just of symbolic importance? Do you think its repeal was really a meaningless gesture to calm southern nerves, as Douglas claimed? If you were a northerner in 1854, would you have been concerned?

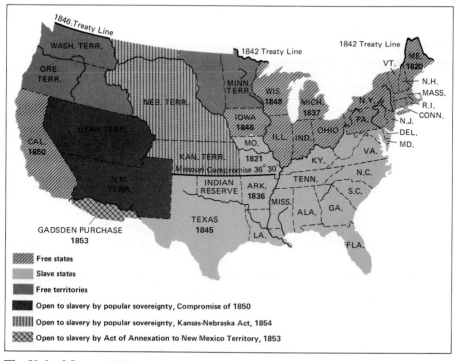

The United States, 1854.

Two Portraits of the West

The Kansas-Nebraska Act raised a storm of protest throughout the north, and almost overnight Anti-Nebraska groups sprang up to fight the extension of slavery. Some called themselves "Republican," which had a nice Jeffersonian ring to it, and the name stuck. Douglas expected the storm to blow itself out once northerners realized that his bill provided millions of acres for land-hungry farmers and a railroad route to the newly discovered gold fields of California. Moreover, argued Douglas, Kansas and Nebraska were obviously unsuited to slavery, and the "principle of dollars and cents" would keep slaveholders out.

But the storm did not blow itself out, and the brand-new Republican party did incredibly well at the polls, routing northern Democrats in one congressional district after another, and carrying eleven of sixteen northern states in the presidential election of 1856. Douglas had clearly misread northern opinion. To many northerners it did not matter that slavery was never likely to take root on the prairies. To them, merely allowing the possibility was an outrage, and even more outrageous was the fact that the federal government had reversed itself and legally opened free territory to slavery.

Here are two documents to help you understand this outrage. The first is a painting by John Gast, "Manifest Destiny," which shows a typical northern view of the American west. Moving westward from eastern port cities is the

"Manifest Destiny." *By John Gast. Library of Congress.*

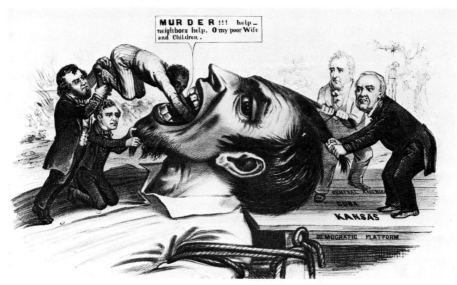

New-York Historical Society.

goddess of Destiny bearing a schoolbook in one hand and a telegraph in the other. Below, white Americans push the Indians and the buffalo ever westward. What is the order of white settlement as envisioned by Gast? What kinds of people are the typical settlers? What do you make of the fact that there are no blacks in the picture? The second illustration is a Republican cartoon showing Douglas, with the help of other leading northern Democrats, trying to force slavery down the throat of a Free-Soiler. What do you make of the Free-Soiler? Is he like the characters in Gast's painting? And why is he so concerned about his wife and children? Is the message of the cartoon racist as well as antislavery? Why do you think that keeping slavery out of the west had broad appeal, while abolishing slavery had very limited appeal?

The Lincoln-Douglas Debates, 1858

While Republicans were blasting the Kansas-Nebraska Act in national politics, Kansas itself became a battleground with northerners and southerners fighting for control. Proslavery forces in Kansas put forward the Lecompton Constitution, which the majority in Kansas clearly opposed. Nevertheless, President James Buchanan, a Pennsylvania Democrat, backed the Lecompton Constitution and tried to bring Kansas into the Union as a slave state. At the same time,

From *Political Debates between Abraham Lincoln and Stephen A. Douglas in the Celebrated Campaign of 1858 in Illinois,* The Arthur H. Clark Company, Cleveland, Ohio, 1902, pp. 1, 14, 18, 33, 101–117 *passim.*

the Supreme Court, in the Dred Scott case, declared that Congress had no right to bar slavery from the territories.

It was against this background that Senator Douglas, who broke with the White House over the Lecompton Constitution, ran for re-election in 1858. His opponent was a cunning Republican lawyer, Abraham Lincoln, who claimed that Douglas's policy of "squatter sovereignty" had become an invitation to chaos. Douglas attacked Lincoln as an abolitionist "Black Republican" whose principles would lead not only to disunion but also to the "amalgamation" of the races and the downfall of white America. Across Illinois the two men battled in debate.

Here are some highlights from these famous debates. Douglas won re-election. Do you think he also won the debates? How did the two men differ on such basic issues as slavery, race, local self-government, the possibility of civil war? Today Lincoln is often referred to as a "racist." If Lincoln was a racist, how would you describe Douglas?

LINCOLN, AT SPRINGFIELD

"A house divided against itself cannot stand." I believe this government cannot endure permanently half slave and half free. . . . I do not expect the house to fall; but I do expect it will cease to be divided. It will become all one thing, or all the other.

DOUGLAS, AT CHICAGO

Mr. Lincoln advocates boldly and clearly a war of sections, a war of the North against the South, of the Free States against the Slave States. . . . He objects to the Dred Scot decision because it does not put the negro in the possession of citizenship on an equality with the white man. I am opposed to negro equality. . . . I am in favor of preserving, not only the purity of the blood, but the purity of the government from any mixture or amalgamation with inferior races.

LINCOLN, AT CHICAGO

I protest, now and forever, against that counterfeit logic which presumes that because I do not want a negro woman for a slave, I do necessarily want her for a wife. My understanding is that I need not have her for either, but, as God made us separate, we can leave one another alone, and do one another much good thereby. . . . The Judge regales us with the terrible enormities that take place by the mixture of races. . . . Why, Judge, if we do not let them get together in the Territories, they won't mix there.

DOUGLAS, AT OTTAWA

Prior to 1854 this country was divided into two great political parties, known as the Whig and Democratic parties. Both were national and patriotic, advocating principles that were universal in their application. An Old Line Whig could proclaim his principles in Louisiana and Massachusetts alike. Whig principles had no boundary section line, they were not limited by the Ohio river, nor by the Potomac, nor by the line of the free and slave states, but applied and were proclaimed wherever the Constitution ruled or the American flag waved over the American soil. So it was, and so it is with the great Democratic party, which, from the days of Jefferson until this period, has proven itself to be the historic party of this nation. While the Whig and Democratic parties differed in regard to a bank, the tariff, distribution, the specie circular and the sub-treasury, they agreed on the great slavery question which now agitates the Union. I say that the Whig party and the Democratic party agreed on this slavery question while they differed on those matters of expediency to which I have referred. The Whig party and the Democratic party jointly adopted the compromise measures of 1850 as the basis of a proper and just solution of this slavery question in all its forms. Clay was the great leader, with Webster on his right and Cass on his left, and sustained by the patriots in the Whig and Democratic ranks, who had devised and enacted the compromise measures of 1850. . . .

Thus you see that up to 1853–'54, the Whig party and the Democratic party both stood on the same platform with regard to the slavery question. That platform was the right of the people of each state and each territory to decide their local and domestic institutions for themselves, subject only to the federal Constitution. . . .

In 1854, Mr. Abraham Lincoln and Mr. Trumbull entered into an arrangement, one with the other, and each with his respective friends, to dissolve the old Whig party on the one hand, and to dissolve the old Democratic party on the other, and to connect the members of both into an Abolition party under the name and disguise of a Republican party. . . . Lincoln went to work to abolitionize the Old Whig party all over the state, pretending that he was then as good a Whig as ever; and Trumbull went to work in his part of the state preaching abolitionism in its milder and lighter form, and trying to abolitionize the Democratic party, and bring old Democrats handcuffed and bound hand and foot into the abolition camp. . . .

Mr. Lincoln, following the example and lead of all the little Abolition orators, who go around and lecture in the basements of schools and churches, reads from the Declaration of Independence, that all men were created equal, and then asks how can you deprive a negro of that equality which God and the Declaration awards to him. . . . I do not question Mr. Lincoln's conscientious belief that the negro was made his equal, and hence is his brother, but for my own part, I do not regard the negro as my equal, and positively deny that he is my brother or any kin to me whatever. . . .

. . . He belongs to an inferior race, and must always occupy an inferior position. I do not hold that because the negro is our inferior that therefore he ought

Illinois Senator Stephen A. Douglas. *The Bettman Archive.*

Abraham Lincoln in 1858. *The Lloyd Ostendorf Collection.*

to be a slave. By no means can such a conclusion be drawn from what I have said. On the contrary, I hold that humanity and Christianity both require that the negro shall have and enjoy every right, every privilege, and even immunity consistent with the safety of the society in which he lives. On that point, I presume, there can be no diversity of opinion. You and I are bound to extend to our inferior and dependent being every right, every privilege, every facility and immunity consistent with the public good. The question then arises what rights and privileges are consistent with the public good. This is a question which each state and each territory must decide for itself. . . .

LINCOLN, AT OTTAWA

Now gentlemen, I hate to waste my time on such things, but in regard to that general abolition tilt that Judge Douglas makes, when he says that I was engaged at that time in selling out and abolitionizing the old Whig party—I hope you will permit me to read a part of a printed speech that I made then at Peoria, which will show altogether a different view of the position I took in that contest of 1854.

VOICE: Put on your specs.
MR LINCOLN: Yes, sir, I am obliged to do so; I am no longer a young man.

> ... we have before us, the chief materials enabling us to correctly judge whether the repeal of the Missouri Compromise is right or wrong.
>
> I think, and shall try to show, that it is wrong; wrong in its direct effect, letting slavery into Kansas and Nebraska—and wrong in its prospective principle, allowing it to spread to every other part of the wide world, where men can be found inclined to take it.
>
> This *declared* indifference, but as I must think, covert *real* zeal for the spread of slavery, I can not but hate. I hate it because of the monstrous injustice of slavery itself. I hate it because it deprives our republican example of its just influence in the world—enables the enemies of free institutions, with plausibility, to taunt us as hypocrites—causes the real friends of freedom to doubt our sincerity, and especially because it forces so many really good men amongst ourselves into an open war with the very fundamental principles of civil liberty—criticising the Declaration of Independence, and insisting that there is no right principle of action but *self-interest.*
>
> Before proceeding, let me say I think I have no prejudice against the Southern people. They are just what we would be in their situation. If slavery did not now exist amongst them, they would not introduce it. If it did now exist amongst us, we should not instantly give it up. This I believe of the masses North and South. Doubtless there are individuals, on both sides, who would not hold slaves under any circumstances; and others who would gladly introduce slavery anew, if it were out of existence. We know that some Southern men do free their slaves, go north, and become tip-top Abolitionists; while some Northern ones go south, and become most cruel slave-masters.
>
> When Southern people tell us they are no more responsible for the origin of slavery, than we; I acknowledge the fact. When it is said that the institution exists, and that it is very difficult to get rid of it, in any satisfactory way, I can understand and appreciate the saying. I surely will not blame them for not doing what I should not know how to do myself. If all earthly power were given me, I should not know what to do, as to the existing institution. My first impulse would be to free all the slaves, and send them to Liberia,—to their own native land. But a moment's reflection would convince me, that whatever of high hope, (as I think there is) there may be in this, in the long run, its sudden execution is impossible. If they were all landed there in a day, they would all perish in the next ten days; and there are not surplus shipping and surplus money enough in the world to carry them there in many times ten days. What then? Free them all, and keep them among us as underlings? Is it quite certain that this betters their condition? I think I would not hold one in slavery, at any rate; yet

the point is not clear enough to me to denounce people upon. What next? Free them, and make them politically and socially, our equals? My own feelings will not admit this; and if mine would, we well know that those of the great mass of white people will not. Whether this feeling accords with justice and sound judgment, is not the sole question, if indeed, it is any part of it. A universal feeling, whether well or ill-founded, can not be safely disregarded. We can not, then, make them equals. It does seem to me that systems of gradual emancipation might be adopted; but for their tardiness in this, I will not undertake to judge our brethren of the South.

When they remind us of their constitutional rights, I acknowledge them not grudgingly, but fully, and fairly; and I would give them any legislation for the reclaiming of their fugitives, which should not in its stringency, be more likely to carry a free man into slavery, than our ordinary criminal laws are to hang an innocent one.

Now gentlemen, I don't want to read at any greater length, but this is the true complexion of all I have ever said in regard to the institution of slavery and the black race. This is the whole of it, and anything that argues me into his idea of perfect social and political equality with the negro, is but a specious and fantastic arrangement of words, by which a man can prove a horse chestnut to be a chestnut horse. I will say here, while upon this subject, that I have no purpose directly or indirectly to interfere with the institution of slavery in the states where it exists. I believe I have no lawful right to do so, and I have no inclination to do so. I have no purpose to introduce political and social equality between the white and the black races. There is a physical difference between the two, which in my judgment will probably forever forbid their living together upon the footing of perfect equality, and inasmuch as it becomes a necessity that there must be a difference, I, as well as Judge Douglas, am in favor of the race to which I belong, having the superior position. I have never said anything to the contrary, but I hold that notwithstanding all this, there is no reason in the world why the negro is not entitled to all the natural rights enumerated in the Declaration of Independence, the right to life, liberty and the pursuit of happiness. I hold that he is as much entitled to these as the white man. I agree with Judge Douglas he is not my equal in many respects—certainly not in color, perhaps not in moral or intellectual endowment. But in the right to eat the bread, without leave of anybody else, which his own hand earns, *he is my equal and the equal of Judge Douglas, and the equal of every living man.* . . .

When he [Douglas] undertakes to say that because I think this nation, so far as the question of slavery is concerned, will all become one thing or all the other, I am in favor of bringing about a dead uniformity in the various states, in all their institutions, he argues erroneously. The great variety of the local institutions in the states, springing from differences in the soil, differences in the face of the country, and in the climate, are bonds of union. They do not make "a house divided against itself," but they make a house united. If they produce in one section of the country what is called for by the wants of another section, and this other section can supply the wants of the first, they are not matters of discord but bonds of union, true bonds of union. But can this question of slavery

be considered as among *these* varieties in the institutions of the country? I leave
it to you so say whether, in the history of our government, this institution of
slavery has not always failed to be a bond of union, and, on the contrary, been
an apple of discord and an element of division in the house. . . . If so, then I have
a right to say that in regard to this question, the Union is a house divided against
itself, and when the Judge reminds me that I have often said to him that the institution of slavery has existed for eighty years in some states, and yet it does
not exist in some others, I agree to the fact, and I account for it by looking at the
position in which our fathers originally placed it—restricting it from the new
territories where it had not gone, and legislating to cut off its source by the ab-
rogation of the slave trade, thus putting the seal of legislation *against its spread*.
The public mind *did* rest in the belief that it was in the course of ultimate extinction. But lately, I think—and in this I charge nothing on the Judge's motives—lately, I think, that he, and those acting with him, have placed that institution on a new basis, which looks to the *perpetuity and nationalization of slavery.*
And while it is placed upon this new basis, I say, and I have said, that I believe
we shall not have peace upon the question until the opponents of slavery arrest
the further spread of it, and place it where the public mind shall rest in the belief that it is in the course of ultimate extinction; or, on the other hand, that its
advocates will push it forward until it shall become alike lawful in all the states,
old as well as new, North as well as South. Now, I believe if we would arrest the
spread, and place it where Washington, and Jefferson, and Madison placed it, it
would be in the course of ultimate extinction, and the public mind *would*, as for
eighty years past, believe that it was in the course of ultimate extinction. The crisis would be past and the institution might be let alone for a hundred years, if it
should live so long, in the states where it exists, yet it would be going out of existence in the way best for both the black and white races. . . .

When I made my speech at Springfield, of which the Judge complains, and
from which he quotes, I really was not thinking of the things which he ascribes
to me at all. I had no thought in the world that I was doing anything to bring
about a war between the free and slave states. I had no thought in the world that
I was doing anything to bring about a political and social equality of the black
and white races. It never occurred to me that I was doing anything or favoring
anything to reduce to a dead uniformity all the local institutions of the various
states. But I must say, in all fairness to him, if he thinks I am doing something
which leads to these bad results, it is none the better that I did not mean it. It is
just as fatal to the country, if I have any influence in producing it, whether I intend it or not. But can it be true, that placing this institution upon the original
basis—the basis upon which our fathers placed it—can have any tendency to set
the Northern and the Southern states at war with one another, or that it can have
any tendency to make the people of Vermont raise sugar cane, because they
raise it in Louisiana, or that it can compel the people of Illinois to cut pine logs
on the Grand Prairie, where they will not grow, because they cut pine logs in
Maine, where they do grow? . . .

CHAPTER 13

The Civil War

Americans have studied the Civil War with almost obsessive fascination. The main reason is that the Civil War was the nation's great trauma. It was the one instance where orderly democratic processes failed miserably. With Lincoln's election in 1860, the lower south refused to abide by the dictates of the electorate, play democratic politics, and try to regain power in the next election. During the first seventy-two years of the American republic, slaveholders had held the presidency for fifty years. Now the nation had a president who was committed to the "ultimate extinction" of slavery. Now the nation was governed by a northern party that owed nothing to the south. Indeed, the Republicans were not even on the ballot in ten southern states, and Lincoln captured only 26,000 votes in the slaveholding states as compared with 1,800,000 in the free states. With Lincoln's victory, the lower south seceded from the Union, and when the first shots were fired four states in the upper south followed suit.

The Civil War was also a brothers' war. If we wish, we can blame the American Revolution on the British, the Mexican War on the Mexicans, World War I on German submarines, World War II on the Japanese and Hitler, Korea and Vietnam on the Communists; but we can blame the Civil War on nobody but Americans. Thus, even though Americans have studied this war with fascination, they have never been able to agree which brother—if either—was to blame.

The Civil War was also a bloodbath. That, in fact, is what distinguished it from earlier American wars. The War of 1812 cost the country only 7000 lives, with fewer than 2000 men dying in action. The Mexican War cost the nation fewer than 2000 lives on the battlefield and some 11,000 from diseases. Most Americans in 1861 expected the Civil War to be much the same. But it was not. By the time it was over, more than 600,000 men were dead, and many of the "lucky" survivors were missing arms and legs.

The war has fascinated Americans, too, because of its totality. Indeed, some historians have argued that it was the first modern war not only because of its scale, but also because of the unprecedented extent to which both sides were mobilized. North and south, the war touched more aspects of more lives than any other had done. Factories and railroads became crucial objects of strategic concern. Women and children were involved as supporters—their traditional roles—but also as victims on a scale that Americans had not known before. Blacks were active participants in a war fought over the issue of slavery and its political consequences. In the end, too, the war sought not only a political statement but a social and economic one that went to the heart of the institutions by which half a nation had ordered its life.

INTERPRETIVE ESSAY

Bruce Catton

Hayfoot, Strawfoot

The way a society goes to war tells much about its economic and social life. In the following essay, one of the most popular historians of the Civil War examines the military life of both sides. From such portraits as this, we can learn much about the skills, the education, and the attitudes of those plain men, Yankee and Confederate, who bore the brunt of some of the most bloody fighting the world had witnessed.

The volunteer soldier in the American Civil War used a clumsy muzzle-loading rifle, lived chiefly on salt pork and hardtack, and retained to the very end a loose-jointed, informal attitude toward the army with which he had cast his lot. But despite all of the surface differences, he was at bottom blood brother to the G.I. Joe of modern days.

Which is to say that he was basically, and incurably, a civilian in arms. A volunteer, he was still a soldier because he had to be one, and he lived for the day when he could leave the army forever. His attitude toward discipline, toward his officers, and toward the whole spit-and-polish concept of military existence was essentially one of careless tolerance. He refused to hate his enemies—indeed, he often got along with them much better than with some of his own comrades—and his indoctrination was often so imperfect that what was sometimes despairingly said of the American soldier in World War II would apply equally to him: he seemed to be fighting chiefly so that he could some day get back to Mom's cooking.

What really set the Civil War soldier apart was the fact that he came from a less sophisticated society. He was no starry-eyed innocent, to be sure—or, if he was, the army quickly took care of that—but the America of the 1860s was less highly developed than modern America. It lacked the ineffable advantages of radio, television, and moving pictures. It was still essentially a rural nation; it had growing cities but they were smaller and somehow less urban than today's cities; a much greater percentage of the population lived on farms or in country towns and villages than is the case now, and there was a more backwoods, hayseed-in-the-hair flavor to the people who came from them.

For example: every war finds some ardent youngsters who want to enlist despite the fact that they are under the military age limit of eighteen. Such a lad today simply goes to the recruiting station, swears that he is eighteen, and signs up. The lad of the 1860s saw it a little differently. He could not swear that he was eighteen when he was only sixteen; in his innocent way, he felt that to lie to his own government was just plain wrong. But he worked out a little dodge that got

From Bruce Catton, "Hayfoot, Strawfoot," *American Heritage,* vol. 3, no. 3, April 1857, pp. 31–37. © 1957 by American Heritage Publishing Co., Inc. Reprinted by permission from *American Heritage.*

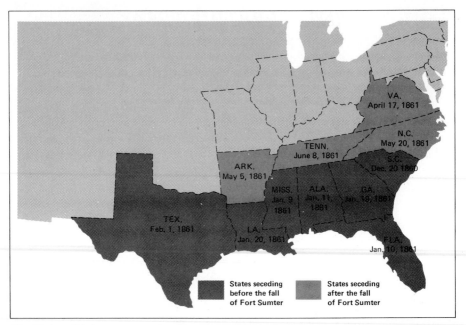

The Union Disintegrates.

him into the army anyway. He would take a bit of paper, scribble the number *18* on it, and put it in the sole of his shoe. Then, when the recruiting officer asked him how old he was, he could truthfully say: "I am over eighteen." That was a common happening, early in the Civil War; one cannot possibly imagine it being tried today.

Similarly, the drill sergeants repeatedly found that among the raw recruits there were men so abysmally untaught that they did not know left from right,

Deaths in the Civil War and Other Wars

	TOTAL DEATHS	*DEATHS PER 100,000 POPULATION*
Civil War	618,000	1967
World War II	318,000	241
Revolutionary War	4000	144
World War I	115,000	109
Mexican War	13,270	57
War of 1812	2200	31
Vietnam War	56,000	28
Korean War	33,000	22
Spanish-American War and Philippine Insurrection	9700	13

and hence could not step off on the left foot as all soldiers should. To teach these lads how to march, the sergeants would tie a wisp of hay to the left foot and a wisp of straw to the right; then, setting the men to march, they would chant, "Hay-foot, straw-foot, hay-foot, straw-foot"—and so on, until everybody had caught on. A common name for a green recruit in those days was "strawfoot."

On the drill field, when a squad was getting basic training, the men were as likely as not to intone a little rhythmic chant as they tramped across the sod—thus:

March! March! March old soldier march!
Hayfoot, strawfoot,
Belly-full of bean soup—
March old soldier march!

Because of his unsophistication, the ordinary soldier in the Civil War, north and south alike, usually joined up with very romantic ideas about soldiering. Army life rubbed the romance off just as rapidly then as it does now, but at the start every volunteer went into the army thinking that he was heading off to high adventure. Under everything else, he enlisted because he thought army life was going to be fun, and usually it took quite a few weeks in camp to disabuse him of this strange notion. Right at the start, soldiering had an almost idyllic quality; if this quality faded rapidly, the memory of it remained through all the rest of life.

Early days in camp simply cemented the idea. An Illinois recruit, writing home from training camp, confessed: "It is fun to lie around, face unwashed, hair uncombed, shirt unbuttoned and everything uneverythinged. It sure beats clerking." Another Illinois boy confessed: "I don't see why people will stay at home when they can get to soldiering. A year of it is worth getting shot for to any man." And a Massachusetts boy, recalling the early days of army life, wrote, "Our drill, as I remember it, consisted largely of running around the Old West-bury town hall, yelling like Devils and firing at an imaginary foe." One of the commonest discoveries that comes from a reading of Civil War diaries is that the chief worry, in training camp, was a fear that the war would be over before the ardent young recruits could get into it. It is only fair to say that most of the di-arists looked back on this innocent worry, a year or so afterward, with rueful amusement.

There was a regiment recruited in northern Pennsylvania in 1861—thir-teenth Pennsylvania Reserves officially, known to the rest of the Union Army as the Bucktails because the rookies decorated their caps with strips of fur from the carcass of a deer that was hanging in front of a butcher shop near their camp—and in mid-spring these youthful soldiers were ordered to rendezvous at Har-risburg. So they marched cross-country (along a road known today as the Buck-tail Trail) to the north branch of the Susquehanna, where they built rafts. One raft, for the colonel, was made oversized with a stable; the colonel's horse had to ride, too. Then the Bucktails floated down the river, singing and firing their muskets and having a gay old time, camping out along the bank at night, and finally they got to Harrisburg; and they served through the worst of the war, getting badly shot up and losing most of their men to Confederate bullets, but they never forgot the picnic air of those first days of army life, when they drifted down a river through the forests, with a song in the air and the bright light of adventure shining just ahead. Men do not go to war that way nowadays.

Discipline in those early regiments was pretty sketchy. The big catch was that most regiments were recruited locally—in one town, or one county, or in one part of a city—and everybody more or less knew everybody else. Particularly, the privates knew their officers—most of whom were elected to their jobs by the enlisted men—and they never saw any sense in being formal with them. Within reasonable limits, the Civil War private was willing to do what his company commander told him to do, but he saw little point in carrying it to extremes.

So an Indiana soldier wrote: "We had enlisted to put down the Rebellion, and had no patience with the red-tape tomfoolery of the regular service. The boys recognized no superiors, except in the line of legitimate duty. Shoulder straps waived, a private was ready at the drop of a hat to thrash his commander—a thing that occurred more than once." A New York regiment, drilling on a hot parade ground, heard a private address his company commander thus: "Say, Tom, let's quit this darn foolin' around and go over to the sutler's and get a drink." There was a very little of the "Captain, sir" business in those armies. If a company or regimental officer got anything especial in the way of obedience, he got it because the enlisted men recognized him as a natural leader and superior and not just because he had a commission signed by Abraham Lincoln.

Odd rivalries developed between regiments. (It should be noted that the Civil War soldier's first loyalty went usually to his regiment, just as a navy man's loyalty goes to his ship; he liked to believe that his regiment was better than all others, and he would fight for it, any time and anywhere.) The army legends of those days tell of a Manhattan regiment, camped near Washington, whose nearest neighbor was a regiment from Brooklyn, with which the Manhattanites nursed a deep rivalry. Neither regiment had a chaplain; and there came to the Mahattan colonel one day a minister, who volunteered to hold religious services for the men in the ranks.

The colonel doubted that this would be a good idea. His men, he said, were rather irreligious, not to say godless, and he feared they would not give the reverend gentleman a respectful hearing. But the minister said he would take his chances; after all, he had just held services with the Brooklyn regiment, and the men there had been very quiet and devout. That was enough for the colonel. What the Brooklyn regiment could do, his regiment could do. He ordered the men paraded for divine worship, announcing that any man who talked, laughed, or even coughed would be summarily court-martialed.

So the clergyman held services, and everyone was attentive. At the end of the sermon, the minister asked if any of his hearers would care to step forward and make public profession of faith; in the Brooklyn regiment, he said, fourteen men had done this. Instantly the New York colonel was on his feet.

"Adjutant!" he bellowed. "We're not going to let that damn Brooklyn regiment beat us at anything. Detail twenty men and have them baptized at once!"

Each regiment seemed to have its own mythology, tales that may have been false but that, by their mere existence, reflected faithfully certain aspects of army life. The forty-eighth New York, for instance, was said to have an unusually large number of ministers in its ranks, serving not as chaplains but as combat soldiers. The forty-eighth, fairly early in the war, found itself posted in a swamp along the South Carolina coast, toiling mightily in semitropical heat, amid clouds of mosquitoes, to build fortifications, and it was noted that all hands became excessively profane, including the one-time clergymen. A visiting general, watching the regiment at work one day, recalled the legend and asked the regiment's lieutenant colonel if he himself was a minister in private life.

"Well, no, General," said the officer apologetically. "I can't say that I was a regularly ordained minister. I was just one of these———local preachers."

Another story was hung on this same forty-eighth New York. A Confederate ironclad gunboat was supposed to be ready to steam through channels in the swamp and attack the forty-eighth's outposts, and elaborate plans were made to trap it with obstructions in the channel, a tangle of ropes to snarl the propellers, and so on. But it occurred to the colonel that even if the gunboat was trapped the soldiers could not get into it; it was sheathed in iron, all its ports would be closed, and men with axes could never chop their way into it. Then the colonel had an inspiration. Remembering that many of his men had been recruited from the less savory districts of New York City, he paraded the regiment and (according to legend) announced:

"Now men, you've been in this cursed swamp for two weeks—up to your ears in mud, no fun, no glory and blessed poor pay. Here's a chance. Let every man who has had experience as a cracksman or a safe-blower step to the front." To the last man, the regiment marched forward four paces and came expectantly to attention.

Not unlike this was the reputation of the sixth New York, which contained so many Bowery toughs that the rest of the army said a man had to be able to show that he had done time in prison in order to get into the regiment. It was about to leave for the south, and the colonel gave his men an inspirational talk. They were going, he said, to a land of wealthy plantation owners, where each southerner had riches of which he could be despoiled; and he took out his own gold watch and held it up for all to see, remarking that any deserving soldier could easily get one like it, once they got down to plantation-land. Half an hour later, wishing to see what time it was, he felt for his watch . . . and it was gone.

If the Civil War army spun queer tales about itself, it had to face a reality that, in all of its aspects, was singularly unpleasant. One of the worst aspects had to do with food.

From first to last, the Civil War armies enlisted no men as cooks, and there were no cooks' and bakers' schools to help matters. Often enough, when in camp, a company would simply be issued a quantity of provisions—flour, pork, beans, potatoes, and so on—and invited to prepare the stuff as best it could. Half a dozen men would form a mess, members would take turns with the cooking, and everybody had to eat what these amateurs prepared or go hungry. Later in the war, each company commander would usually detail two men to act as cooks for the company, and if either of the two happened to know anything about cooking the company was in luck. One army legend held that company officers usually detailed the least valuable soldiers to this job, on the theory that they would do less harm in the cook shack than anywhere else. One soldier, writing after the war, asserted flatly: "A company cook is a most peculiar being; he generally knows less about cooking than any other man in the company. Not being able to learn the drill, and too dirty to appear on inspection, he is sent to the cook house to get him out of the ranks."

When an army was on the march, the ration issue usually consisted of salt pork, hardtack, and coffee. (In the Confederate Army the coffee was often missing, and the hardtack was frequently replaced by corn bread; often enough the meal was not sifted, and stray bits of cob would appear in it.) The hardtack was good enough, if fresh, which was not always the case; with age it usually got infested with weevils, and veterans remarked that it was better to eat it in the dark.

In the Union Army, most of the time, the soldier could supplement his rations (if he had money) by buying extras from the sutler—the latter being a civilian merchant licensed to accompany the army, functioning somewhat as the regular post exchange functions nowadays. The sutler charged high prices and specialized in indigestibles like pies, canned lobster salad, and so on; and it was noted that men who patronized him regularly came down with stomach upsets. The Confederate Army had few sutlers, which helps to explain why the hungry Confederates were so delighted when they could capture a Yankee camp: to seize a sutler's tent meant high living for the captors, and the men in Lee's army were furious when, in the 1864 campaign, they learned that General Grant had offered the Union Army to move without sutlers. Johnny Reb felt that Grant was really taking an unfair advantage by cutting off this possible source of supply.

If Civil War cooking arrangements were impromptu and imperfect, the same applied to its hospital system. The surgeons, usually, were good men by the standards of that day—which were low since no one on earth knew anything about germs or about how wounds became infected, and antisepsis in the operating room was a concept that had not yet come into existence; it is common to read of a surgeon whetting his scalpel on the sole of his shoe just before operating. But the hospital attendants, stretcher-bearers, and the like were chosen just as the company cooks were chosen; that is, they were detailed from the ranks, and the average officer selected the most worthless men he had simply because he wanted to get rid of men who could not be counted on in combat. As a result, sick or wounded men often got atrocious care.

A result of all this—coupled with the fact that many men enlisted without being given any medical examinations—was that every Civil War regiment suffered a constant wastage from sickness. On paper, a regiment was supposed to have a strength ranging between 960 and 1040 men; actually, no regiment ever got to the battlefield with anything like that strength, and since there was no established system for sending in replacements a veteran regiment that could muster 350 enlisted men present for duty was considered pretty solid. From first to late, approximately twice as many Civil War soldiers died of disease—typhoid, dysentery, and pneumonia were the great killers—as died in action; and in addition to those who died, a great many more got medical discharges.

In its wisdom, the northern government set up a number of base hospitals in northern states, far from the battle fronts, on the theory that a man recovering from wounds or sickness would recuperate better back home. Unfortunately, the hospitals thus established were under local control, and the men in them were no longer under the orders of their own regiments or armies. As a result, thousands of men who were sent north for convalescence never returned to the army. Many were detailed for light work at the hospitals, and in these details they stayed because nobody had the authority to extract them and send them back to duty. Others, recovering their health, simply went home and stayed there. They were answerable to the hospital authorities, not to the army command, and the hospital authorities rarely cared very much whether they returned to duty or not. The whole system was ideally designed to make desertion easy.

On top of all of this, many men had very little understanding of the requirements of military discipline. A homesick boy often saw nothing wrong in leaving the army and going home to see the folks for a time. A man from a farm might slip off to go home and put in a crop. In neither case would the man look on himself as a deserter; he meant to return, he figured he would get back in time for any fighting that would take place, and in his own mind he was innocent of any wrongdoing. But in many cases the date of return would be postponed from week to week; the man might end as a deserter, even though he had not intended to be one when he left.

This merely reflected the loose discipline that prevailed in Civil War armies, which in turn reflected the underlying civilian-mindedness that pervaded the rank and file. The behavior of northern armies on the march in southern territory reflected the same thing—and, in the end, had a profound effect on the institution of chattel slavery.

Armies of occupation always tend to bear down hard on civilian property in enemy territory. Union armies in the Civil War, being imperfectly disciplined to begin with—and suffering, furthermore, from a highly defective rationing system—bore down with especial fervor. Chickens, hams, cornfields, anything edible that might be found on a southern plantation, looked like fair game, and the loose fringe of stragglers that always trailed around the edges of a moving Union army looted with a fine disregard for civilian property rights.

This was made all the more pointed by the fact that the average northern soldier, poorly indoctrinated though he was, had strong feelings about the evils of secession. To his mind, the southerners who sought to set up a nation of their own were in rebellion against the best government mankind had ever known. Being rebels, they had forfeited their rights; if evil things happened to them that (as the average northern soldier saw it) was no more than just retribution. This meant that even when the army command tried earnestly to prevent looting and individual foraging, the officers at company and regimental levels seldom tried very hard to carry out the high command's orders.

William Tecumseh Sherman has come down in history as the very archetype of the northern soldier who believed in pillage and looting; yet during the first years of the war Sherman resorted to all manner of ferocious punishments to keep his men from despoiling southern property. He had looters tied up by the thumbs, ordered courts-martial, issued any number of stern orders—and all to very little effect. Long before he adopted the practice of commandeering or destroying southern property as a war measure, his soldiers were practicing it against his will, partly because discipline was poor and partly because they saw nothing wrong with it.

It was common for a Union colonel, as his regiment made camp in a southern state, to address his men, pointing to a nearby farm, and say: "Now, boys, that barn is full of nice fat pigs and chickens. I don't want to see any of you take any of them"—whereupon he would fold his arms and look sternly in the opposite direction. It was also common for a regimental commander to read, on parade, some ukase from higher authority forbidding foraging, and then to wink solemnly—a clear hint that he did not expect anyone to take the order seriously. One colonel, punishing some men who had robbed a chicken house, said angrily: "Boys, I want you to understand that I am not punishing you for stealing but for getting caught at it."

It is more than a century since that war was fought, and things look a little different now than they looked at the time. At this distance, it may be possible to look indulgently on the wholesale foraging in which Union armies indulged; to the southern farmers who bore the brunt of it, the business looked very ugly indeed. Many a southern family saw the foodstuffs needed for the winter swept away in an hour by grinning hoodlums who did not need and could not use a quarter of what they took. Among the foragers there were many lawless characters who took watches, jewels, and any other valuables they could find; it is recorded that a squad would now and then carry a piano out to the lawn, take it apart, and use the wires to hang pots and pans over the campfire. . . . The Civil War was really romantic only at a considerable distance.

Underneath his feeling that it was good to add chickens and hams to the army ration, and his belief civilians in a state of secession could expect no better fate, the Union soldier also came to believe that to destroy southern property was to help win the war. Under orders, he tore up railroads and burned warehouses; it was not long before he realized that anything that damaged the Confederate economy weakened the Confederate war effort, so he rationalized his looting and foraging by arguing that it was a step in breaking the southern will to resist. It is at this point that the institution of human slavery enters the picture.

Most northern soldiers had very little feeling against slavery as such, and very little sympathy for the Negro himself. They thought they were fighting to save the Union, not to end slavery, and except for New England troops most Union regiments contained very little abolition sentiment. Nevertheless, the soldiers moved energetically and effectively to destroy slavery, not because they especially intended to but simply because they were out to do all the damage they could do. They were operating against southern property—and the most obvious, important, and easily removable property of all was the slave. To help the slaves get away from the plantation was, clearly, to weaken southern productive capacity, which in turn weakened Confederate armies. Hence the Union soldier, wherever he went, took the peculiar institution apart, chattel by chattel.

As a result, slavery had been fatally weakened long before the war itself came to an end. The mere act of fighting the war killed it. Of all institutions on earth, the institution of human slavery was the one least adapted to survive a war. It could not survive the presence of loose-jointed, heavy-handed armies of occupation. It may hardly be too much to say that the mere act of taking up arms in slavery's defense doomed slavery.

Above and beyond everything else, of course, the business of the Civil War soldier was to fight. He fought with weapons that look very crude to modern eyes, and he moved by an outmoded system of tactics, but the price he paid when he got into action was just as high as the price modern soldiers pay despite the almost infinite development of firepower since the 1860s.

Standard infantry weapon in the Civil War was the rifled Springfield—a muzzle-loader firing a conical lead bullet, usually of .54 caliber.

To load was rather laborious, and it took a good man to get off more than two shots a minute. The weapon had a range of nearly a mile, and its "effective range"—that is, the range at which it would hit often enough to make infantry fire truly effective—was figured at about 250 yards. Compared to a modern Garand, the old muzzle-loader is no better than a museum piece; but compared to all previous weapons—the weapons on which infantry tactics in the 1860s were still based—it was a fearfully destructive and efficient piece.

For the infantry of that day still moved and fought in formations dictated in the old days of smoothbore muskets, whose effective range was no more than 100 yards and which were wildly inaccurate at any distance. Armies using those weapons attacked in solid mass formations, the men standing, literally, elbow to elbow. They could get from effective range to hand-to-hand fighting in a very short time, and if they had a proper numerical advantage over the defensive line they could come to grips without losing too many men along the way. But in the Civil War the conditions had changed radically; men would be hit while the rival lines were still half a mile apart, and to advance in mass was simply to invite wholesale destruction. Tactics had not yet been adjusted to the new rifles; as a result, Civil War attacks could be fearfully costly, and when the defenders dug entrenchments and got some protection—as the men learned to do, very quickly—a direct frontal assault could be little better than a form of mass suicide.

It took the high command a long time to revise tactics to meet this changed situation, and Civil War battles ran up dreadful casualty lists. For an army to lose 25 percent of its numbers in a major battle was by no means uncommon, and in some fights—the Confederate army at Gettysburg is an outstanding example—the percentage of loss ran close to one-third of the total number engaged. Individual units were sometimes nearly wiped out. Some of the Union and Confederate regiments that fought at Gettysburg lost up to 80 percent of their numbers; a regiment with such losses was usually wrecked, as an effective fighting force, for the rest of the war.

The point of all of which is that the discipline that took the Civil War soldier into action, while it may have been very sketchy by modern standards, was nevertheless highly effective on the field of battle. Any armies that could go through such battles as Antietam, Stone's River, Franklin, or Chickamauga and come back for more had very little to learn about the business of fighting.

Perhaps the Confederate General D. H. Hill said it, once and for all. The battle of Malvern Hill, fought on the Virginia peninsula early in the summer of 1862, finished the famous Seven Days campaign, in which George B. McClellan's Army of the Potomac was driven back from in front of Richmond by Robert E. Lee's Army of Northern Virginia. At Malvern Hill, McClellan's men fought a rear-guard action—a bitter, confused fight that came at the end of a solid week of wearing, costly battles and forced marches. Federal artillery wrecked the Confederate assault columns, and at the end of the day Hill looked out over the battlefield, strewn with dead and wounded boys. Shaking his head, and reflecting on the valor in attack and in defense that the two armies had displayed, Hill never forgot about this. Looking back on it, long after the war was over, he declared, in substance:

"Give me Confederate military and Yankee artillery and I'll whip the world!"

SOURCES

The Photographers' War

The Civil War was the first war in history to be photographed on a large scale. Matthew Brady, Alexander Gardner, T. H. O'Sullivan, and others used large box cameras on tripods and collodion-coated glass plates that had to be sensitized in one chemical bath before exposure and developed immediately after in another chemical bath. The process was incredibly awkward, and it was impossible to take action shots. But the photographers produced a magnificent record of the war.

Here are two memorable photographs that show the strain of war. Below, Abraham Lincoln in Springfield, Illinois, on June 3, 1860.

Chicago Historical Society.

Library of Congress.

Above, after four years of war, Lincoln in Washington, April 10, 1865.

And in the photograph at the top of page 309 one gets some idea why Lincoln aged so quickly. It shows the dead of both sides lying together after the battle of Gettysburg, where 150,000 men fired their muskets for several days, hour after hour, and left the ground littered with over 7000 corpses.

Following is a series of pictures that more or less speak for themselves. Most are the work of Matthew Brady, who followed the Union army, and especially the wagons that collected the dead after battle.

Library of Congress.

**Private Edwin Francis Jennison,
Georgia Infantry.**
Killed at Malvern Hill.
Library of Congress.

The 107th U.S. Colored Infantry.
Library of Congress.

**Powder Monkey,
USS *New Hampshire*.**
Off Charleston, South
Carolina, 1865.
*The Brady Collection/
Library of Congress.*

**Ruins of Charleston,
South Carolina, 1865.**
Library of Congress.

Union Dead. Trapped in the Sunken Road, Battle of Chancellorsville, May 3–5, 1863.
The Brady Collection/Library of Congress.

Union Wouded. Battle of Chancellorsville, May 3–5, 1863.
Library of Congress.

The Richmond and Petersburg Railroad Depot, 1865.
Library of Congress.

Richmond, Virginia, at War's End.
Library of Congress.

Freedmen in Richmond, Virginia.
Library of Congress.

John Wilkes Booth's accomplices (Mary Surratt, David Herold, Lewis Paine, George Atserodt) in a Washington jailyard, July 7, 1865, three months after Lincoln's assassination. Booth himself had been shot and killed earlier, two weeks after he killed Lincoln.
Library of Congress.

David P. Conyngham

Sherman's March Through Georgia, 1865

The South had lost the war by 1865, and southerners knew it. One reason was General William Tecumseh Sherman's army, which in 1864 marched through Georgia and destroyed a civilization. Along with Sherman's army went a young newspaperman, David P. Conyngham, who was hired by the New York Herald to write on-the-spot reports. Here are some of his observations. What effect do you think they had on the people back home?

THE RED BADGE OF COURAGE

Night had set in. The ground was strewn with the dead and wounded. Our men slept beside their arms, for the rebel lines were quite close to them. The living, the dying, and the dead slept beside one another. Rebel and Union officers and men lay piled together; some transfixed with bayonet wounds, their faces wearing that fierce, contorted look that marks those who have suffered agony. Others, who were shot dead, lay with their calm faces and glassy eyes turned to heaven. One might think they were but sleeping.

Others had their skulls crashed in by the end of a musket, while the owner of the musket lay stiff beside them, with the death grip tightened on the piece.

Clinging to one of the guns, with his hand on the spoke, and his body bent as if drawing it, lay a youth with the top of his head shot off. Another near him, with his body cut in two, still clung to the ropes.

Men writhing in pain, men stark and cold; broken caissons, rifles, and bayonets; bloody clothes and torn haversacks with all the other debris of war's havoc, were the price we paid for two old cannon.

A battle-field, when the carnage of the day is over, when the angry passions of men have subsided; when the death silence follows the din and roar of battle; when the victors have returned triumphant to their camps to celebrate their victory, regardless of the many comrades they have left behind; when the conquered sullenly fall back to a new position, awaiting to renew the struggle,—is a sad sight. It is hard to listen to the hushed groans and cries of the dying, and to witness the lacerated bodies of your fellow-soldiers strewn around, some with broken limbs, torn and mangled bodies, writhing in agony. How often has some poor fellow besought me to shoot him, and put him out of pain! It would be a mercy to do so, yet I dared not.

Piled up together in a ditch, near a battery which they supported with their lines, I found several rebel dead and wounded. I dragged some of the wounded out under the shelter of the trees.

From David P. Conyngham, *Sherman's March Through Georgia*, Sheldon and Company, New York, 1865, *passim*.

The ghouls of the army were there before me; they had rifled the pockets of the dead and wounded indiscriminately.

I gave many a poor fellow a reviving drink, amidst silent prayers.

In one place I found a mere boy of about fifteen. His leg was shattered with a piece of shell. I placed his knapsack under his head. Poor child! what stories he told me about his mother, away down in Carolina; and his little sisters, how glad they would be, now that he was wounded, to see him home.

They never saw him home, for he went to the home where the weary are at rest.

I came up to the corpse of a rebel soldier, over whom a huge Kentuckian federal soldier was weeping.

"My man," I exclaimed, "why do you weep over him? Look at your comrades around you."

"True, sir," he replied, wiping his eyes; and pointing to a federal soldier near, he said, "There is my brother; this man shot him: I killed him in return. He was my bosom friend. I loved him as a father loves his child."

Next morning, as we were removing our wounded to hospital, I saw a group collected. I rode up, and found that they were some raw troops jeering and insulting rebel wounded. Veteran troops will never do this, but share their last drink and bite with them. I rated them pretty roundly, and ordered the cowardly sneaks to their regiments. After another battle or two, these very boys would feel indignant at such conduct.

It is an affecting sight to witness the removal of the dead and wounded from a battle-field, and the manner in which the former are interred. In some case, deep pits are sunk, and, perhaps, a hundred or more bodies are flung promiscuously into it, as if no one owned them, or cared for them.

In other cases, where the bodies had been recognized, they were buried with some semblance of decency. I was once riding with a column over a battle-field, in which the skeletons of the hastily buried were partly exposed. . . .

Women and children were dreadfully frightened at the approach of our army. It was almost painful to witness the horror and fear depicted on their features. They were schooled up to this by lying statements of what atrocious murders we were committing.

The country people trembled at our approach, and hid themselves away in woods and caves. I rode out one evening alone to pay a visit to another camp which lay some six miles beyond us. In trying to make a short way through the woods, I lost the road, and rambled on through the forest, trying to recover it. This is no easy matter, as I soon discovered; for I only got deeper and deeper into the forest. I then turned my horse's head down a valley that I knew would lead me out on a camp somewhere.

In riding along this, I thought I saw a woman among the trees. I rode in the direction, and saw her darting like a frightened deer towards a thick copse of tangled briers, wild vines, and underbrush.

Fearing some snare, I followed, with pistol in hand; and heavens, what a sight met my view! In the midst of the thicket, sheltered by a bold bluff, were about a dozen women, as many children, and three old men, almost crazy with fear and excitement.

Some of them screamed when they saw me, and all huddled closer, as if re-solved to die together. I tied my horse, and assured them that they had no cause for fear; that I was not going to harm them, but would protect them, if needed. Thus assured, they became somewhat communicative.

They told me that they thought the soldiers would kill them, and that they hid here on our approach. Thinking that we were only passing through, they had brought nothing to eat or to cover them. They were here now near three days, and had nothing but the berries they picked up in the woods. They looked wretched, their features wan and thin, their eyes wild and haggard; and their lips stained from the unripe wild fruit. Some of them were lying down, huddled together to keep themselves warm; their clothes were all saturated from the dew and a heavy shower of rain which fell during the day.

I do not think one could realize so much wretchedness and suffering as that group presented. Some of the women were evidently planters' wives and daughters; their appearance and worn dresses betokened it; others were their servants, or the wives of the farm-laborers.

There were two black women, and some three picaninnies. Under the shel-ter of a tree, I saw a woman sitting down, rocking her baby to and fro, as she wept bitterly.

I went over to her. Beside her was a girl of some fourteen years, lying at full length. As I approached, she looked so pale and statuelike, I exclaimed,—

"What's the matter. Is she in a faint?"

"Yes; in one that she won't waken from," said an old crone near.

"Dead!" I exclaimed.

"Well, stranger, I reckon so; better for her to go, poor darling, than have the Yankees cotch her."

It was so. She was dead. I understood she was delicate; and the hunger and cold had killed her. So much were they afraid of being discovered that they had not even a fire lighted.

I inquired my way to the camp, and soon returned with some provisions. The dead body was removed, and the sorrowing group returned to their homes; but some of them had no homes, for the soldiers, on the principle that all aban-doned houses belong to rebels, had laid them in ashes. . . .

On one occasion General Johnston sent a flag of truce to Sherman, in order to give time to carry off the wounded and bury the dead, who were festering in front of their lines.

A truce followed, and Rebels and Federals freely participated in the work of charity. It was a strange sight to see friends, to see old acquaintances, and in some instances brothers, who had been separated for years, and now pitted in deadly hostility, meet and have a good talk over old times, and home scenes, and connections. They drank together, smoked together, appeared on the best possible terms, though the next day they were sure to meet in deadly conflict again.

Even some of the generals freely mixed with the men, and seemed to view the painful sight with melancholy interest.

An officer, speaking of this sad burial, said, "I witnessed a strange scene yesterday in front of Davis's division. During the burial of the dead, grouped together in seemingly fraternal unity, were officers and men of both contending armies, who, but five minutes before, were engaged in the work of slaughter and death."

Under the shelter of a pine, I noticed a huge gray Kentuckian rebel, with his arm affectionately placed around the neck of a Federal soldier, a mere boy. The bronzed warrior cried and laughed by turns, and then kissed the young Federal.

Attracted by such a strange proceeding, I went over to them, and said to the veteran, "Why, you seem very much taken by that boy; I suppose he is some old friend of yours."

"Old friend, sir! Why, he is my son!"

I have often seen a rebel and a Federal soldier making right for the same rifle-pit, their friends on both sides loudly cheering them on. As they would not have time to fight, they reserved their fire until they got into the pit, then woe betide the laggard, for the other was sure to pop him as soon as he got into cover. Sometimes they got in together, and then came the tug of war; for they fought for possession with their bayonets and closed fists. In some cases however, they made a truce, and took joint possession of it.

It was no unusual thing to see our pickets and skirmishers enjoying themselves very comfortably with the rebels, drinking bad whiskey, smoking and chewing worse tobacco, and trading coffee and other little articles. The rebels had no coffee, and our men plenty, while the rebels had plenty of whiskey; so they very soon came to an understanding. It was strange to see these men, who had been just pitted in deadly conflict, trading, and bantering, and chatting, as if they were the best friends in the world. They discussed a battle with the same gusto they would a cock-fight, or horse-race, and made inquiries about their friends, as to who was killed, and who not, in the respective armies. Friends that have been separated for years have met in this way. Brothers who parted to try their fortune have often met on the picket line, or on the battlefield. I once met a German soldier with the head of a dying rebel on his lap. The stern veteran was weeping, whilst the boy on his knee looked pityingly into his face. They were speaking in German, and from my poor knowledge of the language, all I could make out was, they were brothers; that the elder had come out here several years before; the younger followed him, and being informed that he was in Macon, he went in search of him, and got conscripted; while the elder brother, who was in the north all the time, joined our army. The young boy was scarcely twenty, with light hair, and a soft, fair complexion. The pallor of death on his brow, and the blood was flowing from his breast, and gurgled in his throat and mouth, which the other wiped away with his handkerchief. When he could speak, the dying youth's conversation was of the old home in Germany, of his brothers and sisters, and dear father and mother, who were never to see him again.

In those improvised truces, the best possible faith was observed by the men. These truces were brought about chiefly in the following manner. A rebel, who was heartily tired of his crippled position in his pit, would call out, "I say, Yank!"

"Well, Johnny Reb," would echo from another hole or tree.

"I'm going to put out my head; don't shoot."

"Well, I won't."

The reb would pop up his head; the Yank would do the same.

"Hain't you got any coffee, Johnny?"

"Na'r a bit, but plenty of rot-gut."

"All right; we'll have a trade."

They would meet, while several others would follow the example, until there would be a regular bartering mart established. In some cases the men would come to know each other so well, that they would often call out,—"Look out, reb; we're going to shoot," or, "Look out, Yank, we're going to shoot," as the case may be. . . .

THE SIEGE OF ATLANTA

From several points along the lines we could plainly see the doomed city, with the smoke of burning houses and bursting shells enveloping it in one black canopy, hanging over it like a funeral pall.

The scene at night was sublimely grand and terrific! The din of artillery rang on the night air. In front of General Geary's headquarters was a prominent hill, from which we had a splendid view of the tragedy enacting before us. One night I sat there with the general and staff, and several other officers, while a group of men sat near us enjoying the scene, and speculating on the effects of the shells. It was a lovely, still night, with the stars twinkling in the sky. The lights from the campfires along the hills and valleys, and from amidst the trees, glimmered like the gas-lights of a city in the distance. We could see the dark forms reclining around them, and mark the solemn tread of the sentinel on his beat. A rattle of musketry rang from some point along the line. It was a false alarm. The men for a moment listened, and then renewed their song and revelry, which was for a while interrupted. The song, and music, and laughter floated to our ears from the city of camps, that dotted the country all round.

Sherman had lately ordered from Chattanooga a battery of four and a half inch rifles, and these were trying their metal on the city.

Several batteries, forts, and bastions joined in the fierce chorus. Shells flew from the batteries, up through the air, whizzing and shrieking, until they reached a point over the devoted city, when down they went, hurling the fragments, and leaving in their train a balloon-shaped cloud of smoke. From right, and left, and centre flew these dread missiles, all converging towards the city. From our commanding position we could see the flash from the guns, then the shells, with their burning fuses, hurtling through the air like flying meteors.

"War is a cruelty," said the general beside me; "we know not how many innocents are now suffering in this miserable city."

"I'm dog gone if I like it," said a soldier, slapping his brawny hand upon his thigh; "I can fight my weight of rattlesnakes; but this thing of smoking out women and children, darn me if it's fair."

On the night of September 1, Hood blew up all the magazines and ammunition, destroyed all the supplies he could not move, comprising eight locomotives, and near one hundred cars laden with ammunition, small arms, and

stores, and then retreated. Our troops, advancing near the city, met with no resistance. Observing that it was evacuated, they entered it about 11 o'clock on the
morning of September 2, 1864.

Atlanta was now in our hands, the crowning point of Sherman's great campaign. Hood had been outgeneraled, outmanoeuvred, and outflanked, and was
now trying to concentrate his scattered army. On the night of the 1st, when the
rebel army was vacating, the stampede was frightful to those engaged, but
grandly ludicrous to casual spectators. . . .

The city had suffered much from our projectiles. Several houses had been
burned, and several fallen down. In some places the streets were blocked up
with the rubbish. The suburbs were in ruins, and few houses escaped without
being perforated. Many of the citizens were killed, and many more had hair-
breadth escapes. Some shells had passed through the Trout House Hotel, kick-
ing up a regular muss among beds and tables.

One woman pointed out to me where a shell dashed through her house as
she was sitting down to dinner. It upset the table and things, passed through the
house, and killed her neighbor in the next house.

Several had been killed; some in their houss, others in the streets.

When the rebels were evacuating, in the confusion several of our sick and
wounded escaped from the hospitals, and were sheltered by the citizens.

Almost every garden and yard around the city had its cave. These were
sunk down with a winding entrance to them, so that pieces of shells could not
go in. When dug deep enough, boards were placed on the top, and the earth
piled upon them in a conical shape, and deep enough to withstand even a shell.
Some of these caves, or bomb-proofs, were fifteen feet deep, and well covered.
All along the railroad, around the intrenchments and the bluff near the city,
were gopher holes, where soldiers and citizens concealed themselves.

In some cases it happened that our shells burst so as to close up the mouths
of the caves, thus burying the inmates in a living tomb.

. . . The first fire burst out on the night of Friday, the 11th of November, in a
block of wooden tenements on Decatur Street, where eight buildings were destroyed.

Soon after, fires burst out in other parts of the city. These certainly were the
works of some of the soldiers, who expected to get some booty under cover of
the fires. . . .

It was hard to restrain the soldiers from burning it down. With that licentiousness that characterizes an army they wanted a bonfire.

On Sunday night a kind of long streak of light, like an aurora, marked the
line of march, and the burning stores, depots, and bridges, in the train of the
army.

The Michigan engineers had been detailed to destroy the depots and public
buildings in Atlanta. Everything in the way of destruction was now considered
legalized. The workmen tore up the rails and piled them on the smoking fires.
Winship's iron foundery and machine shops were early set on fire. This valuable
property was calculated to be worth about half a million dollars.

An oil refinery near by next got on fire, and was soon in a fierce blaze. Next followed a freight warehouse, in which were stored several bales of cotton. The depot, turning-tables, freight sheds, and stores around, were soon a fiery mass. The heart was burning out of beautiful Atlanta. . . .

ATLANTA TO THE SEA

It was pretty well known that Sherman was going to cut loose from all communications, and to destroy all the factories, founderies, railroads, mills, and all government property, thus preventing the rebels from using them in his rear. After the troops destroyed Rome, Kingston, and Marietta, tore up the track, and set fire to sleepers, railroad depots, and stores, Sherman issued a special field order:

"The army will forage liberally on the country during the march. To this end each brigade commander will organize a good and efficient foraging party, under command of one or more discreet officers. To regular foraging parties must be instructed the gathering of provisions and forage at any distance from the roads travelled.

"As for horses, mules, wagons, &c., the cavalry and artillery may appropriate freely and without limit. Foraging parties may also take mules or horses to replace the jaded animals of their trains, or to serve as pack-mules for the regiments or brigades."

These orders were all right, if literally carried out; but they were soon converted into licenses for indiscriminate plunder. The followers of an army, in the shape of servants, hangers-on, and bummers, are generally as numerous as the effective force. Every brigade and regiment had its organized, foraging party, which were joined by every officer's servant and idler about the camps. . . .

"Living off the country" was fast becoming the order. The men knew that Sherman had started with some sixteen days' supplies, and they wished to preserve them if possible; besides, they thought that a change of diet would be good for their health. There was nothing to be got the first two days' march, as the country all around Atlanta had been foraged by Slocum's corps while hemmed in there. Now we were opening on a country where pits of sweet potatoes, yards of poultry and hogs, and cellars of bacon and flour, were making their appearance. A new spirit began to animate the men; they were as busy as so many bees about a honey-pot, and commenced important voyages of discovery, and returned well laden with spoils. Foragers, bummers, and camp followers scattered over the country for miles, and black clouds of smoke showed where they had been. Small lots of cotton were found near most of the plantation houses. These, with the gins and presses, were burned, oftentimes firing the houses and offices. Near Madison we passed some wealthy plantations; one, the property of a Mr. Lane, who was courteous enough to wait to receive us, was full of decrepit, dilapidated negroes, presided over by a few brimstone-looking white ladies. They were viciously rabid, and only wished they could eat us with the same facility that the troops consumed all the edibles on the place, and eloped with plump grunters and indignant roosters, and their families. . . .

CHAPTER 14

Reconstruction

When it was first coined in the crisis months between the election of Lincoln and the beginnings of the Civil War, the term "Reconstruction" meant simply the re-unification of the nation. By the time the war ended in 1865, the idea of Reconstruction was more complicated: it now meant more than simple political re-establishment of the Union; it meant reconstructing the south, refashioning its social and economic life to some degree or other. For the freedmen—many only days removed from slavery—Reconstruction would soon come to represent freedom itself. Even in 1865, most southern blacks realized that without thoroughgoing Reconstruction, in which freedmen obtained land as well as the right to vote, freedom would mean only a new kind of economic oppression.

Twelve years later, in 1877, many people, north and south, realized that Reconstruction had ended. But by then the term had taken on intense moral meanings. To most white southerners, it was a term of resentment, the name of a bleak period during which vindictive Yankee politicians had tried to force "black rule" on a "prostate south." Tried and finally failed, for the south had in the end been "redeemed" by its own leaders. Slavery had ended, but white supremacy had been firmly re-established. To perhaps a majority of whites in the north, Reconstruction had over the years become a nuisance, and they were glad to let go of it, to reaffirm the value of the Union, and to let the bitter past die. There were other northerners, however, who looked back from 1877 to twelve years of moral failure, of lost opportunities to force freedom and equality on an unrepentant south.

There were hundreds of thousands of freedmen who experienced this "moral failure" in very real ways. Instead of farming their own land, they farmed the lands of whites as tenants and sharecroppers. Far from benefiting from meaningful voting rights, most blacks were denied the franchise, and those who continued to exercise it did so in a climate of hostility hardly conducive to political freedom. Nonetheless, it was possible for blacks to look back positively at the Reconstruction experience. The 1866 Civil Rights Act granted blacks both citizenship and all the civil rights possessed by whites. When the constitutionality of that statute seemed in doubt, Congress made ratification of the Fourteenth Amendment (accomplished in 1868) a precondition for southern restoration to the Union. In theory, that amendment made the federal government the protector of rights that might be invaded by the states. Under "Radical" reconstruction, carried out by Congress after 1867, hundreds of thousands of southern blacks voted, and many held high elective office. And in 1875, when whites had re-established their authority throughout most of the region, a new civil rights act "guaranteed" blacks equal rights in theaters, inns, and other public places. If in the end it proved impossible to maintain these gains, Reconstruction still remained the bright spot in the lives of many former slaves.

INTERPRETIVE ESSAY

Elizabeth Rauh Bethel

Promised Land

Most accounts of the Reconstruction period have been written largely from the perspective of powerful white men such as presidents, northern congressmen, or southern "redeemers." As a result, students often get the impression that all decisions were made by whites, and blacks were idly sitting on their hands, just the beneficiaries or victims of white actions. That was not the case. Throughout the south black men and women, even though they were just months away from slavery, actively shaped their own futures and challenged the power and prejudices of their white neighbors. Most wanted to own land and become family farmers. The odds against them were immense, and many struggled valiantly only to see their hopes dashed by their lack of money, or by political decisions made in distant Washington, or by white terrorists such as the Ku Klux Klan. But some, as Elizabeth Rauh Bethel documents in the following selection, overcame great obstacles and established tightly knit communities. What do you think accounts for the courage and determination of the families Bethel describes? Do you think the course of American history would have been changed if most black families during Reconstruction had obtained a forty-acre farm? In what respect?

The opportunity to acquire land was a potent attraction for a people just emerging from bondage, and one commonly pursued by freedmen throughout the south. Cooperative agrarian communities, instigated in some cases by the invading Union Army and in other cases by the freedmen themselves, were scattered across the plantation lands of the south as early as 1863. Collective land purchases and cooperative farming ventures developed in the Tidewater area of Virginia, the Sea Islands of South Carolina and Georgia, and along the Mississippi River as refugees at the earliest contraband camps struggled to establish economic and social stability.

These initial land tenure arrangements, always temporary, stimulated high levels of industrious labor among both those fortunate enough to obtain land and those whose expectations were raised by their neighbors' good fortunes. Although for most freedmen the initial promise of landownership was never realized, heightened expectations resulted in "entire families laboring together, improving their material conditions, laying aside money that might hopefully be used to purchase a farm or a few acres for a homestead of their own" during the final years of the war.

The desire for a plot of land dominated public expressions among the freedmen as well as their day-to-day activities and behaviors. In 1864 Secretary of War Stanton met with Negro leaders in Savannah to discuss the problems of re-settlement. During that meeting sixty-seven-year-old freedman Garrison Fra-zier responded to an inquiry regarding living arrangements by telling Stanton that "we would prefer to 'live by ourselves' rather than 'scattered among the whites.'" These arrangements, he added, should include self-sufficiency estab-lished on Negro-owned lands. The sentiments Frazier expressed were not un-usual. They were repeated by other freedmen across the south. Tunis Campbell, also recently emancipated, testified before the congressional committee investi-gating the Ku Klux Klan that "the great cry of our people is to have land." A del-egate to the Tennessee Colored Citizens' Convention of 1866 stated that "what is needed for the colored people is land which they own." A recently emanci-pated Negro representative to the 1868 South Carolina Constitutional Conven-tion, speaking in support of that state's land redistribution program, which eventually gave birth to the Promised Land community, said of the relationship between landownership and the state's Negro population: "Night and day they dream" of owning their own land. "It is their all in all."

At Davis Bend, Mississippi, and Port Royal, South Carolina, as well as sim-ilar settlements in Louisiana, North Carolina, and Virginia, this dream was in fact realized for a time. Freedmen worked "with commendable zeal . . . out in the morning before it is light and at work 'til darkness drives them to their homes" whenever they farmed land that was their own. John Eaton, who su-pervised the Davis Bend project, observed that the most successful land exper-iments among the freedmen were those in which plantations were subdivided into individually owned and farmed tracts. These small farms, rather than the larger cooperative ventures, "appeared to hold the greatest chance for success." The contraband camps and federally directed farm projects afforded newly emancipated freedmen an opportunity to "rediscover and redefine themselves, and to establish communities." Within the various settlements a stability and so-cial order developed that combined economic self-sufficiency with locally di-rected and controlled schools, churches, and mutual aid societies. In the years before the Freedmen's Bureau or the northern missionary societies penetrated the interior of the south, the freedmen, through their own resourcefulness, erected and supported such community institutions at every opportunity. In ob-scure settlements with names like Slabtown and Acreville, Hampton, Alexan-dria, Saxtonville, and Mitchelville, "status, experience, history, and ideology were potent forces operating toward cohesiveness and community." . . .

. . . In South Carolina, perhaps more intensely than any of the other south-ern states, the thirst for land was acute. It was a possibility sparked first by Gen-eral William T. Sherman's military actions along the Sea Islands, then dashed as quickly as it was born in the distant arena of Washington politics. Still, the de-sire for land remained a goal not readily abandoned by the state's freedpeople, and they implemented a plan to achieve that goal at the first opportunity. Their chance came at the 1868 South Carolina Constitutional Convention.

South Carolina was among the southern states that refused to ratify the

Fourteenth Amendment to the Constitution, the amendment that established the citizenship of the freedmen. Like her recalcitrant neighbors, the state was then placed under military government, as outlined by the Military Reconstruction Act of 1867. Among the mandates of that federal legislation was a requirement that each of the states in question draft a new state constitution incorporating the principles of the Fourteenth Amendment. Only after such new constitutions were completed and implemented were the separate states of the defeated Confederacy eligible for readmission to the Union.

The representatives to these constitutional conventions were selected by a revolutionary electorate, one that included all adult male Negroes. Registration for the elections was handled by the army with some informal assistance by "that God-forsaken institution, the Freedman's Bureau." Only South Carolina among the ten states of the former Confederacy elected a Negro majority to its convention. The instrument those representatives drafted called for four major social and political reforms in state government: a statewide system of free common schools; universal manhood suffrage; a jury law that included the Negro electorate in county pools of qualified jurors; and a land redistribution system designed to benefit the state's landless population, primarily the freedmen.

White response to the new constitution and the social reforms that it outlined was predictably vitriolic. It was condemned by one white newspaper as "the work of sixty-odd Negroes, many of them ignorant and depraved." The authors were publicly ridiculed as representing "the maddest, most unscrupulous, and infamous revolution in history." Despite this and similar vilification, the constitution was ratified in the 1868 referendum, an election boycotted by many white voters and dominated by South Carolina's 81,000 newly enfranchised Negroes, who cast their votes overwhelmingly with the Republicans and for the new constitution.

That same election selected representatives to the state legislature charged with implementing the constitutional reforms. That body, like the constitutional convention, was constituted with a Negro majority; and it moved immediately to establish a common school system and land redistribution program. The freedmen were already registered, and the new jury pools remained the prerogative of the individual counties. The 1868 election also was notable for the numerous attacks and "outrages" that occurred against the more politically active freedmen. Among those Negroes assaulted, beaten, shot, and lynched during the pre-election campaign months were four men who subsequently bought small farms from the Land Commission and settled at Promised Land. Like other freedmen in South Carolina, their open involvement in the state's Republican political machinery led to personal violence.

Wilson Nash was the first of the future Promised Land residents to encounter white brutality and retaliation for his political activities. Nash was nominated by the Republicans as their candidate for Abbeville County's seat in the state legislature at the August 1868 county convention. In October of that year, less than two weeks before the general election, Nash was attacked and shot in the leg by two unidentified white assailants. The "outrage" took place in the barn on his rented farm, not far from Dr. Marshall's farm on Curltail Creek. Wilson Nash was thirty-three years old in 1868, married, and the father of three small children. He had moved from "up around Cokesbury" within Abbeville County, shortly after emancipation to the rented land further west. Within months after the Nash family was settled on their farm, Wilson Nash joined the many Negroes who affiliated with the Republicans, an alliance probably instigated and encouraged by Republican promises of land to the freedmen. The extent of Nash's involvement with local politics was apparent in his nomination for public office; and this same nomination brought him to the forefront of county Negro leadership and to the attention of local whites.

After the attack Nash sent his wife and young children to a neighbor's home, where he probably believed they would be safe. He then mounted his mule and fled his farm, leaving behind thirty bushels of recently harvested corn. Whether Nash also left behind a cotton crop is unknown. It was the unprotected corn crop that worried him as much as his concern for his own safety. He rode his mule into Abbeville and there sought refuge at the local Freedman's Bureau office where he reported the attack to the local bureau agent and requested military protection for his family and his corn crop. Captain W. F. DeKnight was sympathetic to Nash's plight but was powerless to assist or protect him. DeKnight had no authority in civil matters such as this, and the men who held that power generally ignored such assaults on Negroes. The Nash incident was typical and followed a familiar pattern. The assailants remained unidentified, unapprehended, and unpunished. The attack achieved the desired end, however, for Nash withdrew his name from the slate of legislative candidates. For him there were other considerations that took priority over politics.

Violence against the freedmen of Abbeville County, as elsewhere in the state, continued that fall and escalated as the 1868 election day neared. The victims had in common an involvement with the Republicans, and there was little distinction made between direct and indirect partisan activity. Politically visible Negroes were open targets. Shortly after the Nash shooting young Willis Smith was assaulted, yet another victim of Reconstruction violence. Smith was still a teenager and too young to vote in the elections, but his age afforded him no immunity. He was a known member of the Union League, the most radical and secret of the political organizations that attracted freedmen. While attending a dance one evening, Smith and four other League members were dragged outside the dance hall and brutally beaten by four white men whose identities were hidden by hoods. This attack, too, was an act of political vengeance. It was, as well, one of the earliest Ku Klux Klan appearances in Abbeville. Like other crimes committed against politically active Negroes, this one remained unsolved.

On election day freedmen Washington Green and Allen Goode were precinct managers at the White Hall polling place, near the southern edge of the Marshall land. Their position was a political appointment of some prestige, their reward for affiliation with and loyalty to the Republican cause. The appointment brought them, like Wilson Nash and Willis Smith, to the attention of local whites. On election day the voting proceeded without incident until midday, when two white men attempted to block Negroes from entering the polling site. A scuffle ensued as Green and Goode, acting in their capacity as voting officials, tried to bring the matter to a halt and were shot by the white men. One freedman was killed, two others injured, in the incident that also went unsolved. In none of the attacks were the assailants ever apprehended. Within twenty-four months all four men—Wilson Nash, Willis Smith, Washington Green, and Allen Goode—bought farms at Promised Land.

Despite the violence surrounding the 1868 elections, the Republicans carried the whole of the state. White Democrats refused to support an election they deemed illegal, and they intimidated the newly enfranchised Negro electorate at every opportunity. The freedmen, nevertheless, flocked to the polls in an unprecedented exercise of their new franchise and sent a body of legislative representatives to the state capitol of Columbia who were wholly committed to the mandates and reforms of the new constitution. Among the first legislative acts was one that formalized the land redistribution program through the creation of the South Carolina Land Commission.

The Land Commission program, as designed by the legislature, was financed through the public sale of state bonds. The capital generated from the bond sales was used to purchase privately owned plantation tracts that were then subdivided and resold to freedmen through long-term (ten years), low-interest (7 percent per annum) loans. The bulk of the commission's transactions occurred along the coastal areas of the state where land was readily available. The labor and financial problems of the rice planters of the low-country were generally more acute than those of the up-country cotton planters. As a result, they were more eager to dispose of a portion of the landholdings at a reasonable price, and their motives for their dealings with the Land Commission were primarily pecuniary.

Piedmont planters were not so motivated. Many were able to salvage their production by negotiating sharecropping and tenant arrangements. Most operated on a smaller scale than the low-country planters and were less dependent on gang labor arrangements. As a consequence, few were as financially pressed as their low-country counterparts, and land was less available for purchase by the Land Commission in the Piedmont region. With only 9 percent of the commission purchases lying in the up-country, the Marshall lands were the exception rather than the rule.

The Marshall sons first advertised the land for sale in 1865. These lands, like others at the eastern edge of the Cotton Belt, were exhausted from generations of cultivation and attendant soil erosion; and for such worn-out land the price was greatly inflated. Additionally, two successive years of crop failures, low cotton prices, and a general lack of capital discouraged serious planters from purchasing the lands. The sons then advertised the tract for rent, but the land stood idle. The family wanted to dispose of the land in a single transaction rather than subdivide it, and Dr. Marshall's farm was no competition for the less expensive and more fertile land to the west that was opened for settlement after the war. In 1869 the two sons once again advertised the land for sale, but conditions in Abbeville County were not improved for farmers, and no private buyer came forth.

Having exhausted the possibilities for negotiating a private sale, the family considered alternative prospects for the disposition of a farm that was of little use to them. James L. Orr, a moderate Democrat, former governor (1865 to 1868), and family son-in-law, served as negotiator when the tract was offered to the Land Commission at the grossly inflated price of ten dollars an acre. Equivalent land in Abbeville County was selling for as little as two dollars an acre, and the commission rejected the offer. Political promises took precedence over financial considerations when the commission's regional agent wrote the Land Commission's Advisory Board that "if the land is not bought the (Republican) party is lost in this district." Upon receipt of his advice the commission immediately met the Marshall family's ten dollar an acre price. By January 1870 the land had been subdivided into fifty small farms, averaging slightly less than fifty acres each, which were publicly offered for sale to Negro as well as white buyers.

The Marshall Tract was located in the central sector of old Abbeville County and was easily accessible to most of the freedmen who were to make the lands their home. . . .

The farms on the Marshall Tract were no bargain for the Negroes who bought them. The land was only partially cleared and ready for cultivation, and that which was free of pine trees and underbrush was badly eroded. There was little to recommend the land to cotton farming. Crop failures in 1868 and 1869 severely limited the local economy, which further reduced the possibilities for small farmers working on badly depleted soil. There was little credit available to Abbeville farmers, white or black; and farming lacked not only an unqualified promise of financial gain but even the possibility of breaking even at harvest. Still, it was not the fertility of the soil or the possibility of economic profit that attracted the freedmen to those farms. The single opportunity for landownership, a status that for most Negroes in 1870 symbolized the essence of their freedom, was the prime attraction for the freedmen who bought farms from the subdivided Marshall Tract.

Most of the Negroes who settled the farms knew the area and local conditions well. Many were native to Abbeville County. In addition to Wilson Nash, the Moragne family and their in-laws, the Turners, the Pinckneys, the Letmans, and the Williamses were also natives of Abbeville, from "down over by Bordeaux" in the southwestern rim of the county that borders Georgia. Others came to their new farms from "Dark Corner, over by McCormick," and another nearby Negro settlement, Pettigrew Station—both in Abbeville County. The Redd family lived in Newberry, South Carolina before they bought their farm; and James and Hannah Fields came to Promised Land from the state capital, Columbia, eighty miles to the east.

Many of the settlers from Abbeville County shared their names with prominent white families—Moragne, Burt, Marshall, Pressley, Frazier, and Pinckney. Their claims to heritage were diverse. One recalled "my grandaddy was a white man from England," and others remembered slavery times to their children in terms of white fathers who "didn't allow nobody to mess with the colored boys of his." Others dismissed the past and told their grandchildren that "some things is best forget." A few were so fair skinned that "they could have passed for white if they wanted to," while others who bought farms from the Land Commission "was so black there wasn't no doubt about who their daddy was."

After emancipation many of these former bondsmen stayed in their old neighborhoods, farming in much the same way as they had during slavery times. Some "worked for the marsters at daytime and for theyselves at night" in an early Piedmont version of sharecropping. Old Samuel Marshall was one former slaveowner who retained many of his bondsmen as laborers by assuring them that they would receive some land of their own—promising them that "if you clean two acres you get two acres; if you clean ten acres you get ten acres" of farmland. It was this promise that kept some freedmen on the Marshall land until it was sold to the Land Commission. They cut and cleared part of the tract of the native pines and readied it for planting in anticipation of ownership. But the promise proved empty, and Marshall's death and the subsequent sale of his lands to the state deprived many of those who labored day and night on the land of the free farms they hoped would be theirs. "After they had cleaned it up they still had to pay for it." Other freedmen in the county "moved off after slavery ended but couldn't get no place" of their own to farm. Unable to negotiate labor or lease arrangements, they faced a time of homelessness with few resources and limited options until the farms became available to them. A few entered into labor contracts supervised by the Freedman's Bureau or settled on rented farms in the county for a time.

The details of the various postemancipation economic arrangements made by the freedmen who settled on the small tracts at Dr. Marshall's farm, whatever the form they assumed, were dominated by three conscious choices all had in common. The first was their decision to stay in Abbeville County following emancipation. For most of the people who eventually settled in Promised Land, Abbeville was their home as well as the site of their enslavement. There they were surrounded by friends, family, and a familiar environment. The second choice this group of freedmen shared was occupational. They had been Piedmont farmers throughout their enslavement, and they chose to remain farmers in their freedom.

Local Negroes made a third conscious decision that for many had long-range importance in their lives and those of their descendents. Through the influence of the Union League, the Freedman's Bureau, the African Methodist Church, and each other, many of the Negroes in Abbeville aligned politically with the Republicans between 1865 and 1870. In Abbeville as elsewhere in the state, the alliance was established enthusiastically. The Republicans promised land as well as suffrage to those who supported them. If their political activities became public knowledge, the freedmen "were safe nowhere"; and men like Wilson Nash, Willis Smith, Washington Green, and Allen Goode who were highly visible Negro politicians took great risks in this exercise of freedom. Those risks were not without justification. It was probably not a coincidence that loyalty to the Republican cause was followed by a chance to own land.

. . . The Land Commission first advertised the farms on the Marshall Tract in January and February 1870. Eleven freedmen and their families established conditional ownership of their farms before spring planting that year. They were among a vanguard of some 14,000 Negro families who acquired small farms in South Carolina through the Land Commission program between 1868 and 1879. With a ten-dollar down payment they acquired the right to settle on and till the thin soil. They were also obliged to place at least half their land under cultivation within three years and to pay all taxes due annually in order to retain their ownership rights.

Among the earliest settlers to the newly created farms was Allen Goode, the precinct manager at White Hall, who bought land in January 1870, almost immediately after it was put on the market. Two brothers-in-law, J. H. Turner and Primus Letman, also bought farms in the early spring that year. Turner was married to LeAnna Moragne and Letman to LeAnna's sister Francis. Elias Harris, a widower with six young children to raise, also came to his lands that spring, as did George Hearst, his son Robert, and their families. Another father-son partnership, Carson and Will Donnelly, settled on adjacent tracts. Willis Smith's father, Daniel, also bought a farm in 1870.

Allen Goode was the wealthiest of these early settlers. He owned a horse, two oxen, four milk cows, and six hogs. For the other families, both material resources and farm production were modest. Few of the homesteaders produced more than a single bale of cotton on their new farms that first year; but all, like Wilson Nash two years earlier, had respectable corn harvests, a crop essential to "both us and the animals." Most households also had sizable pea, bean, and sweet potato crops and produced their own butter. All but the cotton crops were destined for household consumption, as these earliest settlers established a pattern of subsistence farming that would prevail as a community economic strategy in the coming decades.

This decision by the Promised Land farmers to intensify food production and minimize cotton cultivation, whether intentional or the result of other conditions, was an important initial step toward their attainment of economic self-sufficiency. Small-scale cotton farmers in the Black Belt were rarely free agents. Most were quickly trapped in a web of chronic indebtedness and marketing restrictions. Diversification of cash crops was inhibited during the 1870s and 1880s not only by custom and these economic entanglements but also by an absence of local markets, adequate roads, and methods of transportation to move crops other than cotton to larger markets. The Promised Land farmers, generally unwilling to incur debts with the local lien men if they could avoid it, turned to a modified form of subsistence farming as their only realistic land-use option. Through this strategy many of them avoided the "economic nightmare" that fixed the status of other small-scale cotton growers at a level of permanent peonage well into the twentieth century.

The following year, 1871, twenty-five more families scratched up their ten-dollar down payment; and upon presenting it to Hollinshead obtained conditional titles to farms on the Marshall Tract. The Williams family, Amanda and her four adult sons—William, Henry, James, and Moses—purchased farms together that year, probably withdrawing their money from their accounts at the Freedman's Savings and Trust Company Augusta Branch for their separate down payments. Three of the Moragne brothers—Eli, Calvin, and Moses—joined the Turners and the Letmans, their sisters and brothers-in-law, making five households in that corner of the tract soon designated "Moragne Town." John Valentine, whose family was involved in A.M.E. organizational work in Abbeville County, also obtained a conditional title to a farm, although he did not settle there permanently. Henry Redd, like the Williamses, withdrew his savings from the Freedman's Bank and moved to his farm from Newberry, a small town about thirty miles to the east. Moses Wideman, Wells Gray, Frank Hutchison, Samuel Bulow, and Samuel Burt also settled on their farms before spring planting.

As the cluster of Negro-owned farms grew more densely populated, it gradually assumed a unique identity; and this identity, in turn, gave rise to a name, Promised Land. Some remember their grandparents telling them that "the Governor in Columbia [South Carolina] named this place when he sold it to the Negroes." Others contend that the governor had no part in the naming. They argue that these earliest settlers derived the name Promised Land from the conditions of their purchase. "They only promised to pay for it, but they never did!" Indeed, there is some truth in that statement. For although the initial buyers agreed to pay between nine and ten dollars per acre for their land in the original promissory notes, few fulfilled the conditions of those contracts. Final purchase prices were greatly reduced, from ten dollars to $3.25 per acre, a price more in line with prevailing land prices in the Piedmont.

By the end of 1873 forty-four of the fifty farms on the Marshall Tract had been sold. The remaining land, less than seven hundred acres, was the poorest in the tract, badly eroded and at the perimeter of the community. Some of those farms remained unsold until the early 1880s, but even so the land did not go unused. Families too poor to consider buying the farms lived on the state-owned property throughout the 1870s. They were squatters, living there illegally and rent-free, perhaps working a small cotton patch, always a garden. Their condition contrasted sharply with that of the landowners who, like other Negroes who purchased farmland during the 1870s, were considered the most prosperous of the rural freedmen. The freeholders in the community were among the pioneers in a movement to acquire land, a movement that stretched across geographical and temporal limits. Even in the absence of state or federal assistance in other regions, and despite the difficulties Negroes faced in negotiating land purchases directly from white landowners during Reconstruction, by 1875 Negroes across the south owned five million acres of farmland. The promises of emancipation were fulfilled for a few, among them the families at Promised Land.

Settlement of the community coincided with the establishment of a public school, another of the revolutionary social reforms mandated by the 1868 constitution. It was the first of several public facilities to serve community residents and was built on land still described officially as "Dr. Marshall's farm." J. H. Turner, Larkin Reynolds, Iverson Reynolds, and Hutson Lomax, all Negroes, were the first school trustees. The families established on their new farms sent more than ninety children to the one-room school. Everyone who could be spared from the fields was in the classroom for the short 1870 school term. Although few of the children in the landless families attended school regularly, the landowning families early established a tradition of school attendance for their children consonant with their new status. With limited resources the school began the task of educating local children.

The violence and terror experienced by some of the men of Promised Land during 1868 recurred three years later when Eli and Wade Moragne were attacked and viciously beaten with a wagon whip by a band of Klansmen. Wade was twenty-three that year, Eli two years older. Both were married and had small children. It was rumored that the Moragne brothers were among the most prominent and influential of the Negro Republicans in Abbeville County. Their political activity, compounded by an unusual degree of self-assurance, pride, and dignity, infuriated local whites. Like Wilson Nash, Willis Smith, Washington Green, and Allen Goode, the Moragne brothers were victims of insidious political reprisals. Involvement in Reconstruction politics for Negroes was a dangerous enterprise and one that addressed the past as well as the future. It was an activity suited to young men and those who faced the future bravely. It was not for the timid.

The Republican influence on the freedmen at Promised Land was unmistakable, and there was no evidence that the "outrages" and terrorizations against them slowed their participation in local partisan activities. In addition to the risks, there were benefits to be accrued from their alliance with the Republicans. They enjoyed appointments as precinct managers and school trustees. As candidates for various public offices, they experienced a degree of prestige and public recognition that offset the element of danger they faced. These men, born slaves, rose to positions of prominence as landowners, as political figures, and as makers of a community. Few probably had dared to dream of such possibilities a decade earlier.

During the violent years of Reconstruction there was at least one official attempt to end the anarchy in Abbeville County. The representative to the state legislature, J. Hollinshead—the former regional agent for the Land Commission—stated publicly what many local Negroes already knew privately, that "numerous outrages occur in the county and the laws cannot be enforced by civil authorities." From the floor of the General Assembly of South Carolina Hollinshead called for martial law in Abbeville, a request that did not pass unnoticed locally. The editor of the *Press* commented on Hollinshead's request for martial law by declaring that such outrages against the freedmen "exist only in the imagination of the legislator." His response was probably typical of the cavalier attitude of southern whites toward the problems of their former bondsmen. Indeed, there were no further reports of violence and attacks against freedmen carried by the *Press*, which failed to note the murder of County Commissioner Henry Nash in February 1871. Like other victims of white terrorists, Nash was a Negro.

While settlement of Dr. Marshall's farm by the freedmen proceeded, three community residents were arrested for the theft of "some oxen from Dr. H. Drennan who lives near the 'Promiseland.'" Authorities found the heads, tails, and feet of the slaughtered animals near the homes of Ezekiel and Moses Williams and Colbert Jordan. The circumstantial evidence against them seemed convincing; and the three were arrested and then released without bond, pending trial. Colonel Cothran, a former Confederate officer and respected barrister in Abbeville, represented the trio at their trial. Although freedmen in Abbeville courts were generally convicted of whatever crime they were charged with, the Williamses and Jordan were acquitted. Justice for Negroes was always a tenuous affair; but it was especially so before black, as well as white, qualified electors were included in the jury pool. The trial of the Williams brothers and Jordan signaled a temporary truce in the racial war, a truce that at least applied to those Negroes settling the farms at Promised Land.

In 1872, the third year of settlement, Promised Land gained nine more households as families moved to land that they "bought for a dollar an acre." There they "plow old oxen, build log cabin houses" as they settled the land they bought "from the Governor in Columbia." Colbert Jordan and Ezekiel Williams, cleared of the oxen stealing charges, both purchased farms that year. Family and kinship ties drew some of the new migrants to the community. Joshuway Wilson, married to Moses Wideman's sister Delphia, bought a farm near his brother-in-law. Two more Moragne brothers, William and Wade, settled near the other family members in "Moragne Town." Whitfield Hutchison, a jack-leg preacher, bought the farm adjacent to his brother Frank. "Old Whit Hutchison could sing about let's go down to the water and be baptized. He didn't have no education, and he didn't know exactly how to put his words, but when he got to singing he could make your hair rise up. He was a number one preacher." Hutchison was not the only preacher among those first settlers. Isaac Y. Moragne, who moved to Promised Land the following year, and several men in the Turner family all combined preaching and farming.

Not all the settlers came to their new farms as members of such extensive kinship networks as the Moragnes, who counted nine brothers, four sisters, and an assortment of spouses and children among the first Promised Land residents. Even those who joined the community in relative isolation, however, were seldom long in establishing kinship alliances with their neighbors. One such couple was James and Hannah Fields, who lived in Columbia before emancipation. While still a slave, James Fields owned property in the state capital, which was held in trust for him by his master. After emancipation Fields worked for a time as a porter on the Columbia and Greenville Railroad and heard about the upcountry land for sale to Negroes as he carried carpet bags and listened to political gossip on the train. Fields went to Abbeville County to inspect the land before he purchased a farm there. While he was visiting, he "run up on Mr. Nathan Redd," old Henry Redd's son. The Fieldses' granddaughter Emily and Nathan were about the same age, and Fields proposed a match to young Redd. "You marry my granddaughter, and I'll will all this land to you and her." The marriage was arranged before the farm was purchased, and eventually the land was transferred to the young couple.

By the conclusion of 1872 forty-eight families were settled on farms in Promised Land. Most of the land was under cultivation, as required by law; but the farmers were also busy with other activities. In addition to the houses and barns that had to be raised as each new family arrived with their few possessions, the men continued their political activities. Iverson Reynolds, J. H. Turner, John and Elias Tolbert, Judson Reynolds, Oscar Pressley, and Washington Green, all community residents, were delegates to the county Republican convention in August 1872. Three of the group were landowners. Their political activities were still not received with much enthusiasm by local whites, but reaction to Negro involvement in politics was lessening in hostility. The *Press* mildly observed that the fall cotton crop was being gathered with good speed and "the farmers have generally been making good use of their time." Cotton picking and politics were both seasonal, and the newspaper chided local Negroes for their priorities. "The blacks have been indulging a little too much in politics but are getting right again." Iverson Reynolds and Washington Green, always among the community's Republican leadership during the 1870s, served as local election managers again for the 1872 fall elections. The men from Promised Land voted without incident that year.

Civic participation among the Promised Land residents extended beyond partisan politics when the county implemented the new jury law in 1872. There had been no Negro jurors for the trial of the Williams brothers and Colbert Jordan the previous year. Although the inclusion of Negroes in the jury pools was a reform mandated in 1868, four years passed before Abbeville authorities drew up new jury lists from the revised voter registration rolls. The jury law was as repugnant to the whites as Negro suffrage, termed "a wretched attempt at legislation, which surpasses anything which has yet been achieved by the Salons in Columbia." When the new lists were finally completed in 1872 the *Press*, ever the reflection of local white public opinion, predicted that "many of [the freedmen] probably have moved away; and the chances are that not many of them will be forthcoming" in the call to jury duty. Neither the initial condemnation of the law nor the optimistic undertones of the *Press* prediction stopped Pope Moragne and Iverson Reynolds from responding to their notices from the Abbeville Courthouse. Both landowners rode their mules up Five Notch Road from Promised Land to Abbeville and served on the county's first integrated jury in the fall of 1872. Moragne and Reynolds were soon followed by others from the community—Allen Goode, Robert Wideman, William Moragne, James Richie, and Luther (Shack) Moragne. By 1874, less than five years after settlement of Dr. Marshall's farm by the new Negro landowners began, the residents of Promised Land remained actively involved in Abbeville County politics. They were undaunted by the *Press* warning that "just so soon as the colored people lose the confidence and support of the North their doom is fixed. The fate of the red man will be theirs." They were voters, jurors, taxpayers, and trustees of the school their children attended. Their collective identity as an exclusively Negro community was well established. . . .

The representatives to the 1868 South Carolina Constitutional Convention who formulated the state's land redistribution hoped to establish an economically independent Negro yeomanry in South Carolina. The Land Commission intended the purchase and resale of Dr. Marshall's farm to solidify the interests of radical Republicanism in Abbeville County, at least for a time. Both of these designs were realized. A third and unintended consequence also resulted. The land fostered a socially autonomous, identifiable community. Drawing on resources and social structures well established within an extant Negro culture, the men and women who settled Promised Land established churches and schools and a viable economic system based on landownership. They maintained that economic autonomy by subsistence farming and supported many of their routine needs by patronizing the locally owned and operated grist mills and general store. The men were actively involved in Reconstruction politics as well as other aspects of civil life, serving regularly on county juries and paying their taxes. Attracted by the security and prestige Promised Land afforded and the possible hope of eventual landownership, fifty additional landless households moved into the community during the 1870s, expanding the 1880 population to almost twice its original size. Together the eighty-nine households laid claim to slightly more than four square miles of land, and within that small territory they "carved out their own little piece of the world."

SOURCES

The Meaning of Freedom

What did it mean to be free? As Bethel's account of the settlers of Promised Land indicates, there were many obstacles in the path of every freedman and only a few succeeded in becoming independent small farmers. Some twentieth-century writers have argued that the gains for most blacks were minuscule, that being a poor tenant farmer or share-cropper was often even worse than being a slave. But these writers, of course, never experienced the change from slavery to freedom. Here is a man who did.

Dayton, Ohio, August 7, 1865

To My Old Master, Colonel P. H. Anderson,
Big Spring, Tennessee

Sir: I got your letter and was glad to find you had not forgotten Jourdon, and that you wanted me to come back and live with you again, promising to do better for me than anybody else can. I have often felt uneasy about you. I thought the Yankees would have hung you long before this for harboring Rebs they found at your house. I suppose they never heard about your going to Col. Martin's to kill the Union soldier that was left by his company in their stable. Although you shot at me twice before I left you, I did not want to hear of your being hurt, and am glad you are still living. It would do me good to go back to the dear old home and see Miss Mary and Miss Martha and Allen, Esther, Green, and Lee. Give my love to them all, and tell them I hope we will meet in the better world, if not in this. I would have gone back to see you all when I was working in the Nashville hospital, but one of the neighbors told me Henry intended to shoot me if he ever got a chance.

I want to know particularly what the good chance is you propose to give me. I am doing tolerably well here; I get $25 a month, with victuals and clothing; have a comfortable home for Mandy (the folks here call her Mrs. Anderson), and the children, Milly, Jane and Grundy, go to school and are learning well; the teacher says Grundy has a head for a preacher. They go to Sunday-School, and Mandy and me attend church regularly. We are kindly treated; sometimes we overhear others saying, "Them colored people were slaves" down in Tennessee. The children feel hurt when they hear such remarks, but I tell them it was no disgrace in Tennessee to belong to Col. Anderson. Many darkies would have been proud, as I used to was, to call you master. Now, if you will write and say what wages you will give me, I will be better able to decide whether it would be to my advantage to move back again.

As to my freedom, which you say I can have, there is nothing to be gained

From Lydia Maria Child, ed., *The Freedmen's Book*, Boston, 1865, pp. 265–267.

on that score, as I got my free-papers in 1864 from the Provist-Marshal-General of the Department at Nashville. Mandy says she would be afraid to go back without some proof that you are sincerely disposed to treat us justly and kindly—and we have concluded to test your sincerity by asking you to send us our wages for the time we served you. This will make us forget and forgive old scores, and rely on your justice and friendship in the future. I served you faithfully for thirty-two years and Mandy twenty years. At $25 a month for me, and $2 a week for Mandy, our earnings would amount to $11,680. Add to this the interest for the time our wages has been kept back and deduct what you paid for our clothing and three doctor's visits to me, and pulling a tooth for Mandy, and the balance will show what we are in justice entitled to. Please send the money by Adams Express, in care of V. Winters, esq., Dayton, Ohio. If you fail to pay us for faithful labors in the past we can have little faith in your promises in the future. We trust the good Maker has opened your eyes to the wrongs which you and your fathers have done to me and my fathers, in making us toil for you for generations without recompense. Here I draw my wages every Saturday night, but in Tennessee there was never any pay day for the negroes any more than for the horses and cows. Surely there will be a day of reckoning for those who defraud the laborer of his hire.

In answering this letter please state if there would be any safety for my Milly and Jane, who are now grown up and both good-looking girls. You know how it was with poor Matilda and Catherine. I would rather stay here and starve and die if it comes to that than have my girls brought to shame by the violence and wickedness of their young masters. You will also please state if there has been any schools opened for the colored children in your neighborhood, the great desire of my life now is to give my children an education, and have them form virtuous habits.

P.S.—Say howdy to George Carter, and thank him for taking the pistol from you when you were shooting at me.

From your old servant,
Jourdon Anderson

The Cartoonist's View of Reconstruction

Thomas Nast was America's foremost political cartoonist. He also was a Radical Republican who had no love for the white south or the Democratic party. The touchstone cause of Radical Republicans was black civil rights—particularly the right to vote—and conflict with the Democrats and the white south often focused on this issue. Nast's drawings in Harper's Weekly, *as you will notice, illustrated vividly this ongoing battle. The high point for Nast came when Hiram Revels, a black, occupied the Senate seat from Mississippi once held by Jefferson Davis. The low point came shortly afterward. What effect do you think each cartoon had on the electorate? Were any more compelling than the others?*

PARDON.

Columbia–"Shall I Trust These Men,

FRANCHISE.

And Not This Man?"

Thomas Nast, *Harpers Weekly, August 5, 1865. Courtesy of The Research Libraries, The New York Public Library, Astor, Linox, and Tilden Foundations.*

"This Is a White Man's Government."
"We regard the Reconstruction Acts (so called) of Congress as usurpations, and unconstitutional, revolutionary, and void."—*Democratic Platform. Thomas Nast, Harper's Weekly, September 5, 1868, Courtesy of The Research Libraries, The New York Public Library, Astor, Lenox and Tilden Foundations.*

"TIME WORKS WONDERS."

IAGO.(JEFF DAVIS.) "FOR THAT I DO SUSPECT THE LUSTY MOOR
HATH LEAP'D INTO MY SEAT : THE THOUGHT WHEREOF
DOTH LIKE A POISONOUS MINERAL GNAW MY INWARDS." — OTHELLO.

Thomas Nast, Harper's Weekly, April 9, 1870. Courtesy of The Research Libraries, The New York Public Library, Astor, Lenox and Tilden Foundations.

The Commandments in South Carolina.
"We've pretty well smashed that; but I suppose, Massa Moses, you can get another one." *Thomas Nast, Harper's Weekly, September 26, 1874. Courtesy of The Research Libraries, The New York Public Library, Astor, Lenox and Tilden Foundations.*

Thomas Nast, Harper's Weekly, October 24, 1874. Courtesy of The Research Libraries, The New York Public Library, Astor, Lenox and Tilden Foundations.

The Target
" * * They (Messrs. Phleps & Potter) seem to regard the White League as innocent as a Target Company."—Special Dispatch to the N.Y. Times, from Washington, Jan. 17, 1875. Thomas Nast, Harper's Weekly, February 6, 1875. Courtesy of The Research Libraries, The New York Public Library, Astor, Lenox and Tilden Foundations.*

"To Thine Own Self Be True."
Thomas Nast, Harper's Weekly, April 24, 1875. Courtesy of The Research Libraries, The New York Public Library, Astor, Lenox and Tilden Foundations.

"These Few Precepts in Thy Memory"
Beware of entrance to a quarrel; but, being in,
Bear it that the opposer may beware of thee.
Give every man thine ear, but few thy voice:
Take each man's censure, but reserve thy judgment.
Costly thy habit as thy purse can but,
But not express'd in fancy; rich, not gaudy:
For the apparel oft proclaims the man.

This above all,—To thine own self be true;
And it must follow, as the night the day,
Thou canst not then be false to any man.
Shakespeare

The "Civil Rights" Scare Is Nearly Over.
The game of (Colored) fox and (White) goose. Thomas Nast, Harper's Weekly, May 22, 1875. Courtesy of The Research Libraries, The New York Public Library, Astor, Lenox and Tilden Foundations.

"Is *This* a Republican Form of Government? Is *This* Protecting Life, Liberty, or Property? Is *This* the Equal Protection of the Laws?"
Mr. Lamar (Democrat, Mississippi). "In the words of the inspired poet, 'Thy gentleness has made thee great.'" [Did Mr. Lamar mean the colored race?] *Thomas Nast, Harper's Weekly, September 2, 1876. Courtesy of The Research Libraries, The New York Public Library, Astor, Lenox and Tilden Foundations.*

The South Redeemed

As Nast's cartoons indicate, the crusade for black voting rights and other civil rights ran into stiff opposition and eventually failed. By 1877, white supremacy was firmly re-established throughout the south, and black political voices were almost completely stilled. The south, according to many white southerners, had been "redeemed" by its white leaders. But the white south did not get back everything it wanted. Black men had refused to work as gang laborers, and black families had refused to let women and children work long hours in the field. Grudgingly, while land owners had let blacks work the land in family plots, usually as either tenant farmers or share-croppers. Thus, despite "redemption," the southern landscape would look startlingly different from Reconstruction. Here are maps of the same Georgia plantation in 1860 and in 1880. What, in your judgment, were the important features in the new and the old landscape? Do the changes match up with the kinds of attitudes discussed in Bethel's essay? How many of the 1880 families, would you guess, once lived in the old slave quarters?

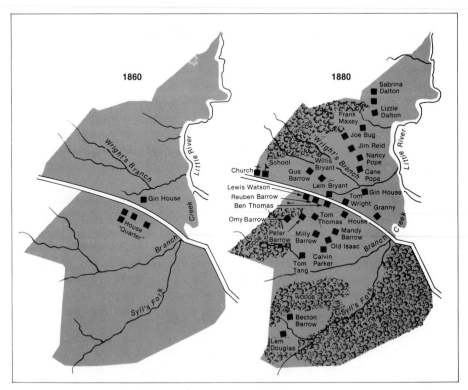

Adapted from Scribner's Monthly, vol. 21, April 1881, 832–833.